The Indo-European

Facts and Fallacies in Histo~~~~ ~~~~~~~~~

Asya Pereltsvaig and Martin W. Lewis

CAMBRIDGE
UNIVERSITY PRESS

University Printing House, Cambridge CB2 8BS, United Kingdom

One Liberty Plaza, 20th Floor, New York, NY 10006, USA

477 Williamstown Road, Port Melbourne, VIC 3207, Australia

4843/24, 2nd Floor, Ansari Road, Daryaganj, Delhi - 110002, India

79 Anson Road, #06-04/06, Singapore 079906

Cambridge University Press is part of the University of Cambridge.

It furthers the University's mission by disseminating knowledge in the pursuit of education, learning and research at the highest international levels of excellence.

www.cambridge.org
Information on this title: www.cambridge.org/9781107665385

© Asya Pereltsvaig and Martin W. Lewis 2015

This publication is in copyright. Subject to statutory exception and to the provisions of relevant collective licensing agreements, no reproduction of any part may take place without the written permission of Cambridge University Press.

First published 2015
First paperback edition 2017

A catalogue record for this publication is available from the British Library

Library of Congress Cataloging in Publication data
Pereltsvaig, Asya, 1972–
The Indo-European controversy : facts and fallacies in historical linguistics /
by Asya Pereltsvaig and Martin W. Lewis.
      pages   cm
ISBN 978-1-107-05453-0 (Hardback)
1. Indo-European languages–Study and teaching.   2. Indo-European languages–
Research.   3. Historical linguistics.   4. Linguistic analysis (Linguistics)
5. Indo-Europeans–Origin.   6. Indo-Europeans–Migrations.   7. Evolution
(Biology)   8. Phylogeny.   9. Phylogeography.   10. Bayesian statistical decision
theory.   I. Lewis, Martin W.   II. Title.
P569.P37 2015
410–dc23   2014040462

ISBN 978-1-107-05453-0 Hardback
ISBN 978-1-107-66538-5 Paperback

Cambridge University Press has no responsibility for the persistence or accuracy of URLs for external or third-party internet websites referred to in this publication, and does not guarantee that any content on such websites is, or will remain, accurate or appropriate.

Contents

Figures

Maps

Tables

Acknowledgments

This book would not have been possible without the support of numerous friends, colleagues, and family members. Helen Barton of Cambridge University Press has been extremely helpful in ushering the project through its various phases, and the three anonymous reviewers that she selected have also earned our gratitude by providing constructive criticism and helpful suggestions. We are particularly grateful to James Clackson, who has offered a wealth of thorough and thoughtful comments on the pre-publication version of the manuscript. A number of other linguists have provided insightful comments and general assistance as well. We would particularly like to thank Michael Weiss for his extensive help with the reconstructions of PIE forms and Stephane Goyette for his perennial willingness to lend assistance. Don Ringe has earned our deep appreciation, and we are most thankful to Wayles Browne for his consultation on the matters pertaining to Slavic linguistics. We would also like to acknowledge the helpful discussions, comments, and criticisms of Alan Bomhard, John Colarusso, Ricardo Duchesne, Andrew Garrett, Jaakko Häkkinen, Hans J. J. Holm, Alexei Kassian, Paul Kiparsky, Giuseppe Longobardi, Yaron Matras, and Rory van Tuyl. Special thanks are due to David Pesetsky for helping to make possible a trip to Rome where we were able to present some of our findings, and to Claudia Ribet and Jacobo Romoli for running a superb Science Festival and facilitating our presentation. Mark Baker provided much needed encouragement as well. Profound thanks are also due to archeologists James P. Mallory and David Anthony, both for their helpful comments and for their indefatigable devotion to Indo-European studies. John Simeone graciously consulted us on the distribution of tree species in Eurasia, and Douglas L. Brutlag, Daniel B. Davison, and Dan Lassiter provided invaluable help in leading us through the details of the Bayesian computational methods. We would also like to thank Masha Yelagin for her general research assistance, and to tip our hats to GeoCurrents discussants Dale H. (Day) Brown, Evan Centanni, Osten Dahl, Trond Engen, Alfia Wallace, and James T. Wilson for their insightful comments.

Many thanks are due to family members who have not only offered assistance and inspiration, but who have also put up with our sometimes obsessive attention to this project over the past year and a half. Karen Wigen, Evan Lewis, and Eleanor Lewis deserve special mention here, as does Vitaliy Rayz, whose help on issues of diffusion and advection has been vital to this project.

Introduction: the Indo-European debate and why it matters

On August 23, 2012, leading media outlets across much of the world announced that one of the major puzzles of human history had at long last been resolved: the origin of the Indo-European language family. "Family Tree of Languages Has Roots in Anatolia", proclaimed the *New York Times*'s sprawling front-section article.[1] The *Times* stressed the role of biologists in determining Indo-European origins, highlighting their use of "tools for drawing evolutionary family trees". On the same day, *Scientific American* showcased the same study, emphasizing instead its novel use of cartography: "Disease Maps Pinpoint Origin of Indo-European Languages".[2] Two days later, the BBC went so far as to announce that the "English Language 'Originated in Turkey'", illustrated with an image of the great lexicographer Samuel Johnson looking especially grumpy.[3] Similarly, Spanish, French, Italian, and Polish media outlets all saw the origins of their respective languages placed in Turkey as well.[4] One Russian blog went as far as to ask: "Are we all a little bit Turks?"[5] As the extra set of quotation marks in the BBC headline shows, such headlines were not meant to be taken literally, as English undoubtedly originated in England, just as Italian originated in Italy. The point was rather that the most

---

[1] nytimes.com/2012/08/24/science/indo-european-languages-originated-in-anatolia-analysis-suggests.html?_r=0

[2] scientificamerican.com/article/disease-maps-pinpoint-origin-of-indo-european-languages/

[3] bbc.co.uk/news/science-environment-19368988

[4] "El idioma español podría tener su origen en Turquía" [The Spanish language might have been originated in Turkey]: aprendemas.com/Noticias/html/N10747_F27082012.html

   "Finalement, la langue française serait née en Turquie" [Finally, the French language was born in Turkey]: http://rue89.nouvelobs.com/2012/08/24/finalement-le-francais-serait-plutot-ne-en-turquie-234823

   "L'origine turca dell'Italiano" [The Turkish origin of the Italian language]: http://oggiscienza.wordpress.com/2012/08/27/lorigine-turca-dellitaliano/

   "Nasza mowa narodziła się w Turcji, nie w Rosji" [Our language was born in Turkey, not in Russia]: polskieradio.pl/23/3/Artykul/670988,Nasza-mowa-narodzila-sie-w-Turcji-nie-w-Rosji

[5] "Все мы немножко турки?" [Are we all a little bit Turks?]: http://echo.msk.ru/blog/ramera1/922907-echo/

1

distant ancestor of English, as well as of Spanish, French, Italian, Polish, Russian, and so on, supposedly emerged in what is now Turkey.

The study on which these articles were based – "Mapping the Origins and Expansion of the Indo-European Language Family" – appeared at the same time in *Science*, arguably the world's premier scientific journal. As is typical of a paper in the natural sciences, it was written by a team of scholars; although Remco Bouckaert is listed first, the actual leaders were Russell Gray and Quentin Atkinson, both at the School of Psychology at the University of Auckland. These scholars claim to have found "decisive support" for Indo-European origins among Neolithic farmers in central Anatolia some 8,000 to 9,500 years ago by using techniques of phylogenetic and phylogeographical analysis designed, respectively, to construct evolutionary family trees and trace the spread of viruses. Such methods, they claimed, allowed them to overturn the reigning hypothesis, which holds instead that the language family emerged among pastoral peoples living in the grasslands, or steppes, north of the Black Sea some 4,000 to 6,000 years ago. According to the *Science* study, an Indo-European homeland in Anatolia must now be regarded as orders of magnitude more likely than one in the steppe zone.

It might seem odd that this seemingly obscure topic would have attracted such intense media attention. But the Indo-European question, with its long, complex, and vexed heritage, is more intellectually significant than it might appear at first glance. No other language family comes close to the global significance of Indo-European, which encompasses the mother tongues spoken by almost half of humankind (Maps 1 and 2). Almost all languages found from central India through Iran and across Europe, and by extension through most of the Americas, descended from a single ancestral tongue spoken in some limited part of Eurasia thousands of years ago. That the daughter languages of this one variety of speech spread so widely has long intrigued scholars and has periodically engaged the public imagination as well. Indo-European studies, moreover, have often been ideologically misused by those seeking to establish their own pet theories of human history and cultural diversity. As a result, the announcement of a solution of the puzzle of Indo-European origins is indeed a newsworthy event.

Mere claims to scientific progress, however, do not guarantee the discovery of truth; nor do advanced mathematical approaches always generate accurate or even serviceable results. If such promises are to be realized, the data must be solid and the assumptions must accord with reality. Yet in regard to "Mapping the Origins" – and more generally the research program that generated it – neither stipulation holds true. Here, incorrect and in some cases incoherent linguistic information is fed into complex equations, systematically corrupting the results; as the common adage puts it, "garbage in/garbage out". The cartography underlying the phylogeographic component of "Mapping the

Origins" is no better than its linguistics. When it comes to issues of historical geography, the model produces incorrect results at virtually every turn, consistently contradicting the empirical record. It is thus not merely that the approach fails, but rather that it fails spectacularly. But the problems go deeper, as even ideal data would have yielded untenable conclusions in this case. Key here are the authors' erroneous and unexamined suppositions about language differentiation, distribution, and expansion. In actuality, linguistic evolution is only vaguely analogous to organic evolution, and hence cannot be analyzed with the same techniques, whereas language-group expansion has virtually nothing in common with the spread of viruses. The distribution of human languages, it turns out, has been heavily molded by historical contingencies, events that have not, and probably cannot, be factored into the biological model employed by the authors. Given both the faulty data and the demonstrably incorrect assumptions, the model used in "Mapping the Origins" can never deliver what it promises.

Although our opposition to a single *Science* article might strike some readers as excessive, much larger issues are at stake. Significantly, the vast majority of Indo-European specialists, whether linguists or archeologists, reject the Anatolian theory of Indo-European origins and remain skeptical of the phylogenetic and phylogeographical methods employed by the Gray–Atkinson approach. This near unanimity of opinion brings up a crucial yet largely unexamined issue. Most of the publications that acclaimed this study also maintain that it is essential to recognize the consensus of the scientific community on the fundamental issues of the day, such as climate change. It would be unthinkable, for example, for the *New York Times, Scientific American*, or the BBC to showcase in such a manner a single study purporting to debunk global warming based on techniques rejected by the vast majority of climatologists. Yet when it comes to matters of historical linguistics, scientific consensus appears to count for little, if anything. Why this should be the case is itself an interesting and important topic that demands investigation.

Unfortunately, such lack of respect for the scientific consensus in linguistics appears to be relatively widespread. As David Pesetsky emphasized in his plenary address at the 2013 annual meeting of the Linguistics Society of America, the "absence of [...] responsible publications [...] in high profile journals" is not limited to historical linguistics, as it extends as well to generative syntax and other linguistic subfields (Pesetsky 2013). Articles seeking to discredit generative grammar, arguably the theoretical heart of modern linguistics, that have appeared recently in major scientific journals often misconstrue the key concepts of the generative approach, such as hierarchical structure and linguistic universals. (Notably, several of these papers were co-authored by scholars who contributed to "Mapping the Origins"). This is not, however, to argue that works seeking to discredit such fields as generative grammar are somehow inadmissible, much less to insist that scholars from other disciplines should avoid treading in this domain. To the contrary, all key scientific concepts must remain perennially open to challenge and dissent. Such challenges, however, have the responsibility of fairly and adequately grappling with the ideas that they are trying to dismantle. Unfortunately, in the field of linguistics this is often not the case. As Pesetsky further argues, the lack of publications in the broader scientific field "that *do* engage the field of generative syntax and accurately represent its results [...] probably reflects nothing more than the complete ignorance on the part of editors and reviewers that there even *is* a field and a set of results that should be engaged". If true, such ignorance needs to be remedied, and we hope that this book is a contribution in that direction.

The problems, however, go deeper still, as the Gray–Atkinson research program has gained traction not only with editors of high-profile scientific journals and the popular media, but they are beginning to make inroads into scholarship in neighboring disciplines as well. This broader appeal of the Gray–Atkinson approach is partly based on the fact that it claims to do much more than merely solve linguistic puzzles of the distant past. If confirmed, this research program would substantially discredit conventional research in historical linguistics, replacing its language-focused methods with those of evolutionary biology and epidemiology. Since languages differentiate, spread, and evolve just as species do, or so these authors contend, the same tools should be able to determine lines of descent and areas of origin for both. At the same time, they dismiss two key geo-historical methods of linguistic scholarship – comparative reconstruction and linguistic paleontology – as inadequately rigorous. Frustrated that historical linguists have been unable to definitely resolve some of their own central problems, the Gray–Atkinson team would reformulate the field on a supposedly more thoroughly scientific basis, employing cutting-edge bioinformatic methods and promising a computational revolution in knowledge. As a result, some scholars and journalists are now assuming the conclusions reached in "Mapping the Origins" as given and are basing further speculations upon them. For example, recent genetic research showing that the ancient Minoans were likely descended from Anatolian farmers has been extended by claims that "the Minoans may have spoken a proto-Indo-European language".[6] The only way to deduce this claim is by *assuming* that Neolithic Anatolian farmers spoke an Indo-European language, turning a highly questionable hypothesis into a foregone conclusion. (The claim is, moreover, linguistically nonsensical, as *Proto*-Indo-European was by definition a single language.)

[6] Tia Ghose, "Mysterious Minoans Were European, DNA Finds", *LiveScience*, May 14, 2013.

The broader drive to refashion the field of linguistics on a supposedly more scientific basis extends to the study of phonology and morphology. A number of scholars have recently sought to explain such purely linguistic attributes on the basis of adaptive pressures rooted in the physical environment. Such hypotheses include putative correlations between rich systems of case marking expressing fine spatial distinctions and the complex topography of the mountainous landscapes (languages of the Caucasus fit this correlation particularly well), and the supposed connection between the presence of nasal vowels and cold and damp climates (showcasing the fact that Modern French, based on the dialect of allegedly cold and damp Paris, has nasal vowels, whereas Spanish and Italian, mostly spoken in warmer and drier climes, do not). Such theories, while perhaps plausible for a small set of languages, fail to apply if a global language sample is used. A more recent article by anthropologist Caleb Everett, "Evidence for Direct Geographic Influences on Linguistic Sounds: The Case of Ejectives", purports to solve this problem by engaging in a large-scope typological study considering 567 languages. Here the author argues that the relatively rare type of sound called ejectives (discussed in more detail in Chapter 9), which involve the closure of the glottis to generate a dramatic burst of air when the oral closure is released, is linked to geographical elevation. Everett claims that such sounds are easier to make under conditions of low air pressure found at high elevations, and he further speculates that "ejective sounds may help to mitigate rates of water vapor loss through exhaled air". Unfortunately for Everett, these supposed causal mechanisms actually make no sense, and a careful examination of the distribution of languages with ejective sounds fails to reveal any actual correlation with altitude.[7] As Johanna Nichols puts it, "ejectives [. . .] can be found in mountain areas – not because harsh mountain geography deterministically causes languages to add harsh consonant series (!), but because isolation favors complexity" (2013: 38). In the end, supposedly scientific accounts of phonological and morphological properties such as Everett's tend to have the characteristics of just-so stories, providing superficially appealing explanations that fail to withstand scrutiny.

Other attempts to generate a supposedly scientific approach to the study of languages come from social scientists claiming to find correlations between linguistic features and various non-linguistic social or cultural traits. For example, a recent paper by three economists (Gay *et al.* 2013) links linguistic gender systems with female economic and political empowerment: women in countries with languages that make gender distinctions are supposedly less likely to participate in the labor market or in politics and have a reduced ability to obtain credit or own land. A somewhat similar paper by Boroditsky *et al.*

---

[7] See our discussion found at http://languagesoftheworld.info/geolinguistics/ejectives-high-altitudes-grandiose-linguistic-hypotheses.html

(2003) reported a connection between linguistic gender and attributes ascribed to various inanimate objects. A study by behavioral economist Keith Chen from Yale University highlights a supposed correlation between tense marking and financial behavior: people whose native language makes few distinctions between the future and the present purportedly think differently about the future and therefore make different financial decisions than those whose language makes systematic temporal distinctions (Chen 2013).[8]

These and similar studies are reminiscent of the strong version of the Whorf–Sapir hypothesis, which claims that one's language determines how one thinks. Professional linguists and psychologists, however, long ago under-mined such claims of linguistic determinism. As Steven Pinker puts it, "The cognitive revolution in psychology, which made the study of pure thought possible, and a number of studies showing the meager effects of language on concepts, appeared to kill the hypothesis by the 1990s, and I gave it an obituary in my book *The Language Instinct*" (2007: 124). In the end, Pinker justly observes that, "The Whorfian interpretation is a classic example of the fallacy of confusing correlation with causation" (2007: 127). John McWhorter echoes Pinker's sentiment in his recent book *The Language Hoax: Why the World Looks the Same in Any Language*: "Yet most would consider it a fair assessment that the work of [the "Neo-Whorfians"] has shown that language's effect on thought is distinctly subtle and, overall, minor. Not uninteresting – but nevertheless, minor" (2014: xiv).

Many of these problematic linguistic studies are also reminiscent of geo-graphical determinism, a hoary idea abandoned by professional geographers generations ago that holds that the physical environment determines how people think and behave. In the early twentieth century, ambitious geographers argued that stark desert vistas automatically lead the human mind to mono-theism (Semple 1911: 512); now their epigones are telling us that climate and altitude determine the sounds that we make. Not much has changed.

Yet, despite all the evidence to the contrary, such theorizing refuses to die, in large part because it has the semblance, although not the substance, of scientific reasoning. And as the digitization of linguistic information advances, the ability, and temptation, to advance such specious claims grows apace. As Mark Liberman perceptively noted in a *LanguageLog* blog post:[9]

[M]any relevant linguistic and non-linguistic datasets are now pre-compiled and avail-able for easy download, and the software needed for fitting various sorts of statistical models can easily be run on your laptop. So if you have a bright idea – maybe alcohol consumption correlates with phonotactic complexity? – really, it could – the chances are

[8] For our critique of this study, see languagesoftheworld.info/language-and-mind/you-save-what-you-speak.html
[9] http://languagelog.ldc.upenn.edu/nll/?p=4685

that you can test a model within a few hours. If it doesn't work out, there are plenty more to try – maybe coffee consumption helps to preserve morphological inflection?

Efforts to reformulate the study of language thus extend deep into the core practices of linguistic scholarship. But as Pesetsky put it in reference to recent articles on linguistic issues in high-profile scientific journals, "none of these papers [. . .] contain any linguistic theory, any linguistic analysis or any significant set of linguistic facts" (2013: 107).

The current push to reinvent linguistics on a supposedly more scientific basis is not the first. In the 1950s, the renowned psychologist B. F. Skinner (1957) argued that speech should be analyzed like any other behavior, in terms of stimuli and responses. Skinner's linguistics, like his psychology more generally, has not fared well in the intervening decades, and his key language concepts, such as that of the "mand", have all but vanished. Even at the time of publication, the Skinnerian approach never made much headway in linguistics, owing in part to Noam Chomsky's (1959) devastating critique. Chomsky's contrasting approach of generative grammar, which postulates an innate human proclivity for language acquisition based on universal principles and parameters, has instead emerged as the theoretical core of modern linguistics. It has done so for good reason, as it can account for the variety and complexity of language much better than any competing framework.

On the surface, the Gray–Atkinson approach to historical linguistics has little in common with B. F. Skinner's attempt to understand language acquisition on the basis of operant conditioning, or with studies that link specific sounds to specific features of the physical environment, or with works that purport to show how the grammar of a particular language determines the thought and behavior of the people who speak it. These various approaches, however, are similar insofar as they attempt to explain or at least comprehend crucial features of language on non-linguistic grounds or by applying non-linguistic methods. As a result, we contend, none of these approaches has much explanatory power, as language must be understood in its own terms. It is difficult to avoid the pitfalls of pseudo-scientific research, in short, when one engages in the non-linguistic study of language.

The seductive attractions of linguistic scientism

Owing to this broader intellectual environment, the present book should not be construed as a long-winded response to one rather short paper, even though most of it does focus on "Mapping the Origins" (also referred to here more formally as Bouckaert *et al.* 2012). Instead, we use this single article as a springboard for discussing far more fundamental issues than those pertaining to the origin of a particular language family. By scrutinizing the methods used, the assumptions made, and the errors produced in this article and related works, we can gain insight into the actual nature of linguistic origination and change, allowing us to specify more precisely how languages diversify from each other and spread across landscapes. Doing so, in turn, can help clarify crucial processes in human history, as well as shed light on the nature of interdisciplinary research.

Ultimately, we seek to defend the established disciplinary methods used to investigate language change and other linguistic phenomena. Linguistics itself has long been a highly rigorous endeavor based on rational inquiry and empirical justification. Already a science in the broad sense of the term, it does not need to be reformulated to *look* more scientific. This is not to say that linguists should ignore new techniques pioneered in other disciplines or shun collaboration with scientists schooled in other disciplines. We do contend, however, that any such work should seek to complement rather than supplant the time-tested methods of linguistic research. These difficult and demanding linguistic techniques continue to produce new and important findings on human communication and indeed on the human condition itself. As such, they deserve to be cherished, not tossed away on the rubbish bin of intellectual history by overly eager, would-be paradigm shifters.

One of our key questions in regard to "Mapping the Origins" is why such deep and pervasive errors in research design and execution went unnoticed, whether by the authors themselves, brilliant and accomplished scientists as they are, by the peer reviewers at *Science*, or by the funding agencies that lavishly supported the research. Why were top science journalists, such as Nicholas Wade at the *New York Times*, so eager to trumpet such a deeply flawed study, giving only lip service to its critics? Although such questions elude simple answers, surely overweening faith in the methods of scientific research plays a central role. We are not concerned here with genuine science, an endeavor that we treasure and defend, but rather with *scientism*, or the uncritical belief in the universal applicability of specific scientific methods. In biological taxonomy, the new bioinformatic methods have indeed constituted a revolution in knowledge, but that is hardly a guarantee that they would do the same in linguistics. Insisting that they must, regardless of all evidence to the contrary, is not the reasoning of science, but rather that of scientism.

The appeal of linguistic scientism is easy to understand. The research techniques employed are themselves brilliant, requiring vast computational resources and mind-boggling mathematics. As Simon Greenhill and Russell Gray have noted, the number of possible family trees computed and weighed in "Mapping the Origins" exceeds the number of atoms in the universe (2012: 529). Bouckaert *et al.* (2012) assess probabilities through the ingenious techniques of Bayesian analysis, recently brought to wide public attention by statistician Nate Silver (2012). These authors produce impressive and sometimes stunning visualizations of the branching and spreading patterns of language families. Their techniques, moreover, are fully generalizable, able to handle – or mishandle – any language grouping with equal facility. The new approach thus promises a great shortcut to knowledge, allowing one to dispense with the welter of empirical detail that traditional Indo-Europeanists, like students of other language families, must master. By the same token, most of the painstaking work of linguistic reconstruction is avoided. Once the model has been established and the inputs entered, the grinding toil of analysis is automated, carried out by extraordinarily capable computers.

But untempered enthusiasm for conceptually elegant procedures can easily lead one astray. At the extreme, a project so conceptualized can become unmoored from the empirical world, and hence impervious to criticism. Unfortunately, "Mapping the Origins" – and the wider research program in which it belongs – seems to fall into this category. As our correspondences with the authors, as well as their responses to other critics, have revealed, they dismiss any error as a mere triviality, and wave away mistakes by the hundreds as temporary imperfections that will eventually be overcome as their model is fine-tuned. Sloppy and indeed unjustifiable language selection and language mapping are not regarded as significant, nor is faulty data tabulation. As a December 20, 2013 communication to the editors of *Science* reveals, the authors forgot to fix their data matrix after they removed thirteen languages from their original sample, resulting in "283 'empty' columns of zeros".[10] After repairing this flaw, the authors substituted a new version of the Supplementary Materials with a revised phylogenetic tree, although the publication date indicated by the *Science* website is still "24 August 2012".[11] Thus, the sheer fact of the substitution is concealed from the public, as if the original "results" never existed in the first place. Many of our criticisms are based on the originally published Supplementary Materials, but most hold for the revised version as well. We also indicate at several points in this book how the simple "tweaking" by the authors of the *Science* article changed their claims about the Indo-European (pre-)history. The biggest change is that the new tree places the divergence of the main Indo-European branches 500 years closer to the present. Yet, this new divergence date still deviates from the established consensus by some 2,500 years – not much of an improvement. As we show in the following pages, some of the results produced by this modification are not improvements at all, as they take the Gray–Atkinson model even further away from the established consensus in historical linguistics while making it even more vulnerable to counterevidence from the archeological record.

[10] *Science* 342: 1446 (sciencemag.org)
[11] http://www.sciencemag.org/content/suppl/2012/08/22/337.6097.957.DC1

But an even deeper problem stems from the authors excusing what turn out to be demonstrably false assumptions about language diversification and spread with the trivially true but misleading observation that science always demands simplification. In short, their approach seems to be unfalsifiable, and hence unscientific. When it comes to matters as complex and multifaceted as the origin and dispersion of language families, it turns out, massive shortcuts to knowledge necessarily fail, as the details matter. If one ignores or dismisses them, one cannot help but reproduce ignorance.

Unfortunately, such misleading scientific research is not limited to biologically inspired efforts to reinvent linguistics. In late 2013, the global scientific establishment was shocked when Nobel laureate Randy Schekman announced that he would no longer publish in the highly prestigious journals *Nature, Cell*, and *Science* in order to protest their tendency to showcase flashy but shoddy studies designed to attract the attention of journalists.[12] As Walter Russell Mead and his colleagues insightfully summarized the situation:

The race for immediately exciting or actionable science has led to lots of "bunk science" that other scientists are often unable to later verify. The costs of this are enormous. It sends us down a lot of false alleys, fueling flashy but superficial headlines in the popular press and giving cover to bad politics. But most importantly it means resources and energies are [being] subtly but surely directed away from research that makes for less click-bait headlines but is nevertheless vitally important to innovation and scientific progress.[13]

In our view, the research program that produced "Mapping the Origins" exemplifies this problem, indicating a fundamental failure both in the vetting of articles at *Science* and in the reporting of such "scientific breakthroughs" by leading newspapers including the *New York Times*.

Such harsh charges, it is essential to note, are specific to the research methods used in "Mapping the Origins", not applying to computational linguistics more generally. When combined with rigorous linguistic analysis, computational linguistics shows great promise. Nor do we even seek to entirely discredit the bioinformatic approach; we may disagree with the manner in which it has been carried out, but we acknowledge its impressive computations, respect its audacity, and value its prompting of productive debate. Had the authors of the *Science* article in question framed their findings as suggestive rather than decisive, we would have shrugged it off as an intriguing if misguided effort. But by claiming to have resolved a crucial debate, they have crossed a line, veering from inadequately conceptualized science into a pernicious form of scientism that demands firm rebuttal.

[12] "Nobel winner declares boycott of top science journals". *The Guardian*, December 9, 2013: theguardian.com/science/2013/dec/09/nobel-winner-boycott-science-journals
[13] the-american-interest.com/blog/2013/12/14/nobel-prize-winner-criticizes-leading-science-journals/

The abiding significance of Indo-European studies

This ill-conceived challenge to traditional historical linguists is ironically emerging just as the new interdisciplinary project of "deep history" is strengthening our grasp of the distant past. Linking the techniques of archeologists, geneticists, linguists, and other scholars, deep-historians such as Andrew Shryock and Daniel Smail (2012) are pushing back the frontiers of historical research, which traditionally date only to the invention of writing some 5,000 years ago. In Indo-European studies itself, linguistically informed deep historical investigations by archeologists such as J. P. Mallory and David Anthony have generated a vastly more complex and nuanced understanding of Indo-European origins and dispersion than was previously possible. But if this multidisciplinary project is to continue to bear fruit, solid linguistic contributions will be necessary. To the extent that the Gray–Atkinson approach triumphs and the Anatolian hypothesis is unquestioningly accepted by the educated public, our understanding of the further reaches of the human past will be compromised.

Regardless of any such overarching theoretical issues, surely the origin and spread of the Indo-European languages is a significant and fascinating topic in its own right. The history of Indo-European studies, however, has also long been intellectually charged – and highly problematic. Indo-European languages have been at the forefront of historical linguistics and philology ever since Sir William Jones and others pointed out the relationships among Sanskrit, Latin, Ancient Greek, and other tongues in the late 1700s. Since then, far more research has been devoted to determining the origin of this family than that of any other language group. In earlier generations, such work was often ideologically misused, sometimes horrifically so. Nazi ideologues and their ilk regarded the speakers of the original tongue – Proto-Indo-European – as constituting the Aryan race, supposedly superior specimens of humankind. In the 1970s and 1980s, a certain school of feminist scholarship turned the Aryan thesis on its head, portraying the speakers of Proto-Indo-European as history's archvillains, horse-riding marauders who destroyed the peaceful and gender-egalitarian societies of "Old Europe", instituting in their place a regime of bloody male domination that has persisted to this day. Little light, needless to say, was shed in the process.

Given this troublesome intellectual history, the announcement that scientists had traced the ancestry of the Indo-European languages to simple Neolithic farmers proved satisfying to many. Some scholars were impatient with Indo-European studies, frustrated that hundreds of linguists laboring for centuries had failed to reach certainty about the language family's origin. Others viewed the entire field with misgivings, suspicious of its vulnerability to ideological manipulation. The Gray–Atkinson *Science* study seemed to many to have overcome such objections. It claims to have located the Indo-European home-land with an extremely high degree of confidence based on disinterested technical analysis, linking the expansion of the family to the non-dramatic diffusion of Neolithic farmers pushing out of the margins of the Fertile Crescent. Without the need to imagine warrior tribes spreading Indo-European languages as they carved a path of bloodshed across western Eurasia, the late Neolithic and early Bronze Age suddenly becomes a more comfortable period of human history.

Not everyone, of course, was pleased with the new study. As the more incisive media reports allowed, most linguists and archeologists working on Indo-European origins reacted with skepticism. And well they should have, as "Mapping the Origins" presents a challenge not just to their ideas, but to their fields of study if not their very careers. The article, after all, purports to overturn the reigning hypothesis not by refuting any of the arguments made on its behalf or by challenging any of the evidence used to support it, but rather by wholesale methodological transformation. A vast scholarly literature is thus essentially bypassed, either ignored or waved aside as if it were of no account. The implicit argument is that the many lines of meticulous research that have led most experts to endorse the Steppe hypothesis were mere dead-ends, seemingly persuasive but ultimately failing to withstand the test of scientific scrutiny. It is thus no surprise that most Indo-Europeanists, linguists and archeologists alike, failed to embrace this new contribution to their field.

The question of credentials

Despite their expertise in the pertinent issues, Indo-Europeanists are hampered in responding to the challenge of computational phylogeny, as they have deep personal interests in the established forms of inquiry. It is always disconcerting for insiders to see scholars from other disciplines impinging on their own specializations and attempting to overturn accepted paradigms, and here we find a team of scientists with little linguistic training and no archeological proficiency informing practitioners of those disciplines that they have had it all wrong all along.[14] Maintaining impartiality in such circumstances can be difficult. Indo-European linguists, moreover, are hindered by their discipline, which does not generally encourage works on broad themes for general

---

[14] The only people with any linguistic credentials among the authors of "Mapping the Origins" are Michael Dunn, evolutionary linguist at Max Planck Institute for Psycholinguistics (Nijmegen), and Simon J. Greenhill, whose doctoral thesis "applies computational Bayesian phylogenetic methods to language data to test hypotheses about the human settlement of the Pacific" (Ph.D. thesis summary). The other authors' areas of expertise include psychology; cognitive and evolutionary anthropology; evolutionary and computational virology; computer science; bioinformatics; computational biology; biomathematics; and the like.

audiences, demanding instead rigorous analysis for fellow specialists. It is no coincidence that most of the key books on Indo-European origins have been written by archeologists, not historical linguists.

A sustained critique of the Gray–Atkinson research program is thus perhaps best left to other outsiders. In this regard, our own qualifications are solid. Neither one of us is an Indo-Europeanist, a historical linguist, or an archeologist by training, and we have never published in any of these fields. We are, moreover, only vaguely acquainted with a few of the individuals engaged in these contretemps, and we are thus not motivated by friendship, professional networking, or score-settling. We have, in short, no personal or career stakes in any of the issues under consideration, and are motivated instead merely by the desire to set the record straight on a momentous and contentious intellectual matter.

But if we lack such professional qualifications, are we even eligible to assess the controversy? Or are we "would-be savants who can take pen to hand" (Mallory 1989: 143), attracted to "the quest for the origins of the Indo-Europeans" like "moths to the flame" (Atkinson and Gray 2006)? The same charge could of course be leveled against Gray, Atkinson, and most of their colleagues, who also approach Indo-European origins from outside the field, drawing on expertise in other disciplines. Like them, we reject the notion that professional training and standing are prerequisites for entering the fray. What counts is one's understanding of the issues and one's familiarity with the relevant literature. Here we are ready to stand.

But we also think that our own academic training lends us certain advantages in wading into these muddy waters. One of us (Asya Pereltsvaig) is a professional linguist, an expert in the synchronic study of syntax rather than in historical development, who has written broadly on the global distribution of languages, language families, and linguistic patterns. The other (Martin Lewis) is a historical geographer, professionally trained to evaluate the geographical claims and cartographic techniques employed by Gray, Atkinson, and their colleagues, who has also published on the philosophy of science (Gross *et al.* 1997). Together, we have been developing a new pedagogical approach that combines our respective skill-sets, one that might best be termed "geo-linguistic history". We have jointly taught courses such as "The History and Geography of the World's Major Language Families", and we have written extensively about these and similar issues on our blogs, *Languages of the World* and *GeoCurrents*. Now we turn our attention in a more scholarly direction, bringing our joint expertise to bear on the freighted matter of Indo-European origins and expansion.

Overview of the book

The first part of this book considers the intellectually charged history of Indo-European studies. Chapter 1 begins with the eighteenth-century philologers who adopted literal interpretations of the Biblical stories of Noah's flood and the tower of Babel as their starting point, yet made astute observations about the affinity of distant and distinctive languages such as Latin and Hindi. We briefly trace the development of comparative philology through the works of Franz Bopp, Rasmus Rask, and especially Max Müller; examine the pernicious confusion of language and race that emerged around the term "Aryan"; and discuss a number of ideologically charged perspectives that affected the understanding of the Indo-European question throughout the nineteenth and twentieth centuries. In Chapter 2, we examine the development of the Anatolian hypothesis, first proposed by the renowned British archeologist Colin Renfrew, and outline as well the emergence of a competing "Revised Steppe hypothesis" in the late twentieth century. In scrutinizing the Anatolian hypothesis, we also explore some of the ideological and intra-disciplinary considerations that appear to have contributed to its widespread acceptance by journalists and scholars outside of the Indo-European field.

In Part II, we mount our main critique of "Mapping the Origins". Chapter 3 shows that it belongs to a wider and more ambitious research program that applies similar phylogenetic methods to a wide array of language families and subfamilies. This chapter also lays out three criteria for evaluating scientific theories in general and theories of Indo-European origins specifically. Chapters 4 through 7 might be said to constitute the heart of the book, as here we show in detail how the Gray–Atkinson theory violates those criteria. Chapter 4 is dedicated to the linguistic fallacies of the Gray–Atkinson method, the main one being their reliance on vocabulary at the expense of other components of language, such as sound system (phonology) and grammar (morphology and syntax). Chapter 5 discusses the problems surrounding Gray–Atkinson's methods of dating the emergence of Proto-Indo-European and its subsequent diversification into its various branches. Chapter 6 is concerned with the historical and geographical failures of the model, while Chapter 7 addresses three key but fundamentally flawed assumptions of the Gray–Atkinson approach to historical linguistics: that languages spread via demic diffusion; that the geographical distribution of language groups can be modeled and mapped as spatially discrete, non-overlapping polygons; and that linguistic evolution is so similar to biological evolution that it can be analyzed in the same terms, using the same tools.

In Part III, we turn to the evidence brought to bear on the Indo-European question by linguists using justifiable techniques, both those of traditional historical linguistics and those that use more innovative approaches. In Chapter 8, we claim that – contrary to assertions from the Gray–Atkinson camp – methods employed in traditional historical linguistics can date phylogenetic trees, usually in relative terms but occasionally in absolute terms as well. Here we show that the most reliable dates for Proto-Indo-European contradict Gray and

Atkinson's neo-Anatolian hypothesis. In Chapter 9, we reassess the evidence used to locate the Indo-European homeland from three approaches: linguistic paleontology, linguistic contact, and aligning the phylogenetic language tree with the archeological evidence of migrations. In Chapter 10, we return to the question posed throughout our examination of Indo-European historiography: is the sustained expansion of the Indo-European language family in any way exceptional and extraordinary, or can it be explained by ordinary processes? Finally, in Chapter 11, we provide a brief overview of promising recent work that aims to answer some of the same questions as the Gray–Atkinson research program and applies some of the same computational techniques, yet does so without committing the many errors that mar "Mapping the Origins".

Part I

The vexatious history of Indo-European studies

Debates about Indo-European origins and dispersion have played a surprisingly central role in modern intellectual history. At first glance, the ancient source of a group of languages whose very relatedness is invisible to non-specialists would seem to be an obscure issue, of interest only to a few academics. Yet it is difficult to locate a topic of historical debate over the past two centuries that has been more intellectually provocative, ideologically fraught, and politically laden than that of Indo-European origins and expansion. Although the controversies have diminished in the Western public imagination since the middle of the twentieth century, they still rage in India, and elsewhere their reverberations persist. As a result, the Indo-European question is anything but trivial or recondite. To understand the significance of the current controversy, it is therefore necessary to examine the historical development of Indo-European studies in detail, paying particular attention to the potential ideological ramifications of the theories advanced to account for the success of this particular language family.

The following pages do not, however, provide a comprehensive overview of the development of either Indo-European studies in general or even of its misuse by specific schools of thought, which have been amply provided elsewhere (Lehmann 1993; Campbell and Poser 2008; *inter alia*). Rather we stress the most problematic and contentious aspects of the field as it has developed from the late 1700s to the present day. We do so in order to shed light on our key questions regarding the reception of both the Anatolian theory and of phylogenetic and phylogeographical analysis by the broader scientific and journalistic communities. As noted in the introduction, we were taken aback by the alacrity with which leading news organizations announced that the puzzle of Indo-European origins had been solved based on a single article that defied the scientific consensus and produced incoherent results. Provided that one has basic knowledge of world history and of the distribution of languages and language families, all one has to do is glance at the maps generated by the authors' model to see that they fail to accord with historical reality. Nor does one need to possess a great deal of knowledge about either viruses or languages to realize that it is unreasonable to assume that they would necessarily spread in the same manner. As a result, the public reception of "Mapping the Origins and Expansion of the Indo-European Language Family" presents as much of a mystery as does the origin of the Indo-European language family itself.

To a large extent, the immediate celebration of "Mapping the Origins" by journalists probably stems from the respect they accord to the journal *Science* coupled with their failure to understand the methods used, which are presented in a user-hostile manner that demands prior knowledge of Bayesian methods and terminology. But for journalists knowledgeable about historical linguistics and scientific methodology, we suspect that the problematic history of Indo-European studies played a significant role as well. If the expansion of this language family could be linked to the gradual and essentially peaceful spread of Neolithic farmers out of Anatolia, a series of historically troublesome interpretations would be immediately undermined. But if, as we contend, neither the Anatolian thesis nor the techniques now being used to support it have any merit, the result is merely the generation of yet another ideologically loaded interpretation that can only obscure the deeper reaches of the human past.

1 Ideology and interpretation from the 1700s to the 1970s

Before the mid-1800s, most European scholars conceptualized human diversity primarily through the story of the sons of Noah – Ham, Shem, and Japheth – whose descendants supposedly gave rise to the various "nations", "stocks", or "races", of humankind, terms that were usually applied interchangeably. Although the geological and biological theories of Charles Lyell and Charles Darwin are rightly viewed as having effectively undermined the religious understanding of prehistory – thus ushering in the secular intellectual age – historical linguistics, or philology as it was then called, played a key role as well. The discovery of deep linguistic connections that cut across the conventional geography of Noah's descendants unsettled the religious view of the past, encouraging the emergence of a secular conception of human development. As historical linguistics developed over the first half of the nineteenth century, Bible-based ethnography grew ever less tenable. (Although the noted linguist Mark Baker [1996: 514] currently argues that the Tower of Babel story, which recounts the diversification of languages among Noah's descendants, might convey a non-literal truth, insofar as the macroparameters built into the deep structures of human language necessarily generate "serious linguistic diversity" – which he claims indicate an origin "distinctly spiritual in nature").[1]

Although the account of Noah's progeny in Genesis 10 is geographically spare and ambiguous, traditional Jewish accounts usually identified the descendants of Japheth with the north, those of Ham with the south, and those of Shem – the ancient Hebrews and relatives – with the middle zone. In medieval and early modern Christendom, however, the tripartite continental division of

---

[1] Genesis 10 explicitly states that the various Noahic descent groups developed their own languages, while the next chapter, Genesis 11, which recounts the story of the Tower of Babel, tells us that all people at the time spoke the same language. Current-day Biblical literalists deal with this seeming contradiction by arguing that the sequencing of the Bible does not necessarily reflect chronological order, and that as a result many of the passages in Genesis 10 recount episodes that occurred after the events outlined in Genesis 11. In Christian literalist circles today, the origin of human diversity is largely explained on the basis of the "confounding of languages" that followed the construction of the Tower of Babel, although the story of the sons of Noah still figures prominently as well.

the world led most scholars to identify Ham's descendants with Africa, those of Shem with Asia (or at least western Asia), and those of Japheth with Europe. Early attempts at serious linguistic classification remained within this general framework. The precursor of formal historical linguistics in England, the physician and antiquarian James Parsons (1705–1770), viewed the deep similarities across many European languages as evidence of descent from a common ancestral tongue, which he linked to Japheth. Although the use of the term "Japhethic" to denote the Indo-European language family was abandoned long ago, Noahic terminology lingers on: "Semitic", a subfamily of the Afroasiatic languages, derives its name from Shem, while "Cushitic", another subfamily in the same group, stems from Cush, the eldest son of Ham. (The term "Hamitic", long used to cover all of the non-Semitic Afroasiatic languages of Africa, was abandoned only in the 1960s after Joseph Greenberg showed that these languages did not descend from a single common ancestor.)

Although the similarities of Sanskrit and Latin had long been noted, Indo-European studies as a concerted endeavor is usually traced back to Sir William Jones (1746–1794), a well-trained philologist working as a civil servant with the British East India Company in Calcutta. Jones understood that Sanskrit was related to Greek and Latin, and probably to Gothic, Celtic, and Persian as well. As he put it, the resemblances between Sanskrit, Latin, and Classical Greek are so profound that "no philologer could examine them all three, without believing them to have sprung from some common source, which, perhaps, no longer exists" (Jones 1824: 28). Thus was born the idea of an Indo-European linguistic family, along with that of a long-lost proto-Indo-European ancestral tongue (although these terms were coined much later). The significance of Jones's work stemmed not so much from his recognition of Indo-European linguistic affinity, which had long been noted, but rather from his conviction that these languages had sprung from a common but long extinct ancestral tongue.

But as Thomas Trautmann (1997) explains in *Aryans and British India*, Jones's comparative linguistics was compromised by his pre-modern ethnographic convictions and designs, as he remained wedded to a Biblical vision of the past. Jones's ultimate project apparently aimed at "recovering the lost language of Noah and of Adam through the comparison of vocabularies" (1997: 52). To square the kinship of Sanskrit with the languages of Europe within the Biblical narrative, Jones had to reorient the territories of Noah's three lines of descent. In his retelling, the children of Ham settled in India and Egypt, where they "invented letters, observed and named the stars and planets", and otherwise created civilization; later movements brought these same people to Greece, India, northern Europe, and perhaps even Mexico and Peru (1997: 52). In Jones's idiosyncratic view, the descendants of Japheth were not the Europeans, but rather the pastoral peoples of Central Asia and perhaps even the stateless tribes of the Americas – groups that he claimed "cultivat[ed] no liberal arts" and had "no use for letters" (1997: 52). Such a view represented an inversion of mainstream European accounts, which celebrated the Japhethic line of Europe while denigrating the progeny of Ham in Africa and, in some accounts, southern and eastern Asia as well.

Jones's eccentric revision of the story of Noah's sons had little influence on other scholars, as it rested on fanciful migration scenarios that challenged mainstream Biblical understanding. In the long run, however, his linguistic research led to work that undermined religiously inspired ethnography. To be sure, the Noahic thesis continued to have its adherents throughout the 1800s. In the 1850s, the forerunner of "scientific racism", Arthur de Gobineau (1855), accepted the narrative of Noah's sons, although he regarded all three as progenitors of the White race, as he did not think that non-Whites descended from Adam. By the late 1800s, however, academic scholars could no longer invoke the Bible to sketch the contours of prehistory.

The emergence of Indo-European philology

The work of Jones and his successors forced European scholars to grapple with the deep connections between the peoples of Europe and those of South Asia. Traditional "universal" histories produced in Christendom had limited their attention to western Asia, Europe, and North Africa, areas known from the Bible and classical literature. Such works typically dispensed with India and areas further east with a few dismissive paragraphs. Such a blinkered view had been challenged by Voltaire and other *philosophes* of the French Enlightenment, but their assessments were dismissed by both religious stalwarts and European chauvinists (Lewis and Wigen 1997). With the rise of comparative philology, however, the Enlightenment's ecumenical perspective received a temporary boost. Jones's successors in Britain and India in the early 1800s continued to delve into Sanskrit linguistics and literature, examining as well the relationship between Sanskrit and other South Asian languages. In doing so, these Orientalist scholars emphasized the antiquity and the sophistication of the Indian tradition. At the same time, continental European researchers such as Franz Bopp, Rasmus Rask, Jacob and Wilhelm Grimm, and others put the study of historical linguistics on a sound scientific basis, with Rask especially outlining systematic laws of sound change and grammatical transformation. Such work solidified the historical linkages among the languages, and hence the cultures and peoples, of northern India, Persia, and Europe.

Of signal importance to this endeavor was the German scholar of Sanskrit, Max Müller, who long taught at Oxford. Müller coined the term "Aryan", derived from Sanskrit texts, to denote the original group of people whose language spread so broadly and diversified so extensively. The Aryan homeland, he suspected, lay in Central Asia, probably in Bactria (northern Afghanistan), a theory supported more recently by the noted linguist Johanna Nichols (1997, 1999). To Müller and many of his fellow Orientalists, the differences in physical appearance between Europeans and their Indian relatives were superficial; the latter had darker skin merely because of their ancestors' prolonged exposure to the sun. The revealed kinship of what later became known as the Indo-European peoples fostered deep interest in India and, to a lesser extent, Persia. As knowledge accumulated, a veritable "Indomania" grabbed hold in a few corners of European intellectual life.

The resulting respect accorded to India, however, generated a strong reaction, a movement propelled as well by the intensifying economic and technological divergence of Europe and Asia and by the steady advance of Western imperialism. In philosophy, Hegel and most of his heirs disdained all things Indian in withering terms (see Lewis and Wigen 1997), while in Britain utilitarian thinkers such as James Mill disparaged Indian civilization and attacked its Orientalist defenders, contending that progress in South Asia could only be realized by wholesale Westernization. But at least Mill and his fellow British liberals believed that progress in India was possible; as the nineteenth century wore on, the rise of so-called racial science led to a ratcheting up of anti-Asian antipathy and other forms of bigotry, a movement that would culminate in the horrors of the Holocaust.

"Race science" and the challenge of philology

As "race science" gained strength in late nineteenth-century Europe, it faced a major obstacle in Indo-European philology. European racial theorists maintained a stark separation between the so-called Caucasian peoples of Europe and environs and the darker-skinned inhabitants of South Asia, yet the philologists argued that Europeans and northern Indians stemmed from the same stock.[2] Some of the early efforts to mesh the new racial ideas with linguistic findings were rather strained. The popular American writer Charles Morris, for example, argued in 1888 that races are divided on the basis of both language and physical type, which generally but not always coincide; he further contended that "the Aryan is one of these linguistic races" (1888: 5) that had lost its original physical essence. The general tendency, however, was to emphasize ever more strongly this supposed loss of "purity", and thus for physical

---

[2] The racial term "Caucasian", proposed by the German proto-racist scholar Christoph Meiners and popularized by the anatomist and physical anthropologist Johann Friedrich Blumenbach, was based on the idea that certain peoples from the Caucasus Mountains, particularly Circassians and to a lesser extent Georgians, formed the ideal specimens of humankind. This idea, in turn, may have been rooted in part in the trade of "Circassian beauties" to the Ottoman Imperial harem. The idea that Noah's ark came to rest in the Caucasus region may have played a minor role as well.

type to trump linguistic commonality. As Isaac Taylor, the Anglican Canon of York, noted a few years later, "The old assumption of the philologists, that the relationship of language implies a relationship of race, has been decisively disproved and rejected by the anthropologists" (1898: 5). By the end of the century, the increasingly victorious racialists regarded the philologists as their main opponents. Taylor concluded his influential *The Origin of the Aryans* by noting that "the whilom tyranny of the Sanskritists is happily overpast"; he also charged philology with having "retarded [. . .] the progress of science" (1898: 332, 6).

Paradoxically, race scientists relied on the findings of the Indo-European philologists while denouncing them and turning their key discovery on its head. Writers propounding the racialized Aryan thesis emphasized the massive expansion of the Indo-European people in ancient times – a fact demonstrated by historical linguistics – seeing in it prime evidence of Aryan superiority. The preeminence of the ancient Aryans, such writers believed, was evident in the intrinsic restlessness that led them to explore strange new lands and subdue their indigenous inhabitants. As early as the 1850s, Arthur de Gobineau (1855) argued that the civilizations not only of India but also of Egypt and China – and perhaps even Mexico and Peru – had been founded by Aryans, whom he extolled as the world's natural aristocrats. Gobineau and his successors claimed that the original Aryans lost their racial essence as they spread from their homeland and interbred with lesser peoples. The resulting mixture supposedly led to degeneration and loss of vigor. As the century progressed, more extreme racists argued that "mixed races" cannot maintain themselves, as one of the genetic stocks that went into their creation would necessarily prevail. Isaac Taylor went so far as to argue that the children of parents from "diverse" races are usually infertile, much like the offspring of horses and donkeys (1898: 198). As a result, most race scientists concluded that Aryan blood had been swamped out long ago in India, although the more moderate ones allowed that a measure of Aryan nobility could still be found among the Brahmins, owing to their steadfast rejection of cross-caste marriage.

As the Indo-European commonalties discovered by the philologists were reduced to a distant episode of heroic conquest followed by miscegenation, degeneration, and the local extinction of the racial line, race theorists sought to relocate the original Aryan homeland. This search for a European *Urheimat* became intertwined with a simultaneous development in racial thinking: an emerging fixation on head shape as the key to racial identity and origins. Armed with the seemingly scientific tools of head calipers and cranial indices, anthropologists divided Europeans into several distinct physical types, viewed either as sub-races of the Caucasian stock or as discrete races in their own right. Although disagreements persisted, most racial scientists came to identify the Aryans with the narrow-headed (dolichocephalic), fair-skinned, light-haired people of the north, rather than the broader-headed (brachycephalic) "Alpines" of central Europe or the darker-complexioned, shorter "Mediterranean" peoples of the south. (German theorists of the Nazi era added yet more European races, such as the stocky blond "Falisch" race supposedly found in parts of western Germany; see Ehrenreich 2007: 2–3.) In this reading, the original Celts, Slavs, Greeks, and Italics had been Aryans, but by intermarrying with others they had lost their racial essence, retaining only the linguistic marker. Only the Nordic peoples – often identified with current and past speakers of the Germanic languages[3] – could count as true Aryans, a notion closely identified with the German[4] linguist and archeologist Gustaf Kossinna. If northern Europeans represented the genuine Aryan line, uncontaminated with the blood of the subjugated peoples, then it stood to reason that the Aryans had been the indigenous inhabitants of northern Europe. Various theories were consequently advanced to locate the Indo-European cradle somewhere near the shores of the Baltic Sea. The linguistic evidence remained ambiguous, however, leading to prolonged debates about the precise location of the homeland, as we discuss in more detail in Chapter 9.

The many inconsistencies and contradictions that riddled this emerging synthesis were either bypassed or accommodated through special pleading. Western European writers who denigrated the Slavs while celebrating the Germans overlooked the fact that northern Poles and northern Russians tend to have narrower heads and fairer complexions than southern Germans. The non-Indo-European Finnic peoples with their Uralic languages presented a greater problem; Estonians in particular tend to be rather narrow-headed and extremely fair. One expedient was to classify the Uralic language family as a distant cousin of the Indo-European family,[5] assuming that the speakers of the two original proto-languages sprang from the same racial stock. The widespread notion that the Uralic tongues belonged to a Ural-Altaic family that also included Mongolian, however, challenged this idea, leading to profound discomfiture. One result was awkward descriptions of the Finns, with one writer describing them as "linguistic Mongolians" who are nonetheless "intermediate between the blond and the Mongolian [physical] types, although much nearer the former" (Morris 1888: 22).

As the racial interpretation of prehistory gained predominance in the late nineteenth century, Max Müller attempted to stem the tide, objecting strenuously to the misappropriation of his work. In his *Biographies of Words and the Home of the Aryas* (1887), published when he was sixty-four, Müller forwarded a surprisingly modern conception of linguistic history. Although he

---

[3] Baltic speakers were sometimes put into this same category.
[4] Kossinna was actually of Masurian (Slavic) heritage.
[5] This might actually be the case; see Chapter 9.

had long stressed the kinship of northern Indians and Europeans, he now denied that he had ever conceptualized it in terms of race. Instead he denounced *any* identification of language groups with racial stocks, contending that "an ethnologist who speaks of Aryan race, Aryan blood, Aryan eyes and hair, is as great a sinner as a linguist who speaks of a dolichocephalic dictionary or a brachycephalic grammar" (Müller 1887: 120). Müller further sought to discredit the romantic celebration of the proto-Indo-Europeans, mocking the "taken for granted idea" that "in the beginning [. . .] there was an immense Aryan population somewhere, and that large swarms issued from a central bee-hive which contained untold millions of human beings" (1887: 88). Müller went so far as to cast doubt on the core notion of an undifferentiated Proto-Indo-European language, arguing instead that the language family could have emerged out of a welter of related dialects. He further contended that speakers of these dialects might have spread their tongues not by way of massive invasions but rather through the gradual infiltration of relatively small numbers of people out of their Asian homeland. But Müller (1887: 121) reserved his most profound contempt for those who associated an Aryan race with northern Europeans:

But where is there an atom of evidence for saying that the nearer to Scandinavia a people lived, the purer would be its Aryan race and speech, while in Greece and Armenia, Persia and India, we should find mixture and decay? Is not this not only different from the truth, but the very opposite of it?

It is thus for good reason that Trautmann (1997: 172) contends that Müller was the "Public Enemy Number One" of the racial scientists.

The triumph and decline of "racial science" and the Aryan ideal

After the turn of the century, racialist writers tended to distance themselves ever further from the Indo-European idea. The influential polemicist Houston Stewart Chamberlain (1912) – one of Hitler's favorites – hesitated to use the term "Aryan" for his favored race due to its association with the Indo-European language family, preferring instead "Teutonic". Chamberlain granted that "there was once a common ancestral Indo-European race", but assumed that its essential traits had long ago vanished everywhere except among the Teutonic folk of northern Europe. Oddly, he wanted to restrict the term "Aryan" in the modern world to *individuals* who embodied the supposed traits of their distant forebears (1912: 264). Chamberlain's 1899 *The Foundations of the Nineteenth Century* went through twenty-four editions and sold more than 250,000 copies by the late 1930s.[6] But despite its public

[6] As noted by the Wikipedia article on the book, citing William L. Shire's *The Rise and Fall of the Third Reich*.

success, its flaws were so overwhelming that it failed to impress even some of the world's most ardent imperialists. In this regard, Theodore Roosevelt's trenchant review is worth quoting at some length:

[*The Foundations of the Nineteenth Century*] ranks with Buckle's "History of Civiliza-tion," and still more with Gobineau's "*Inégalité des Races Humaines*," for its brilliancy and suggestiveness and also for its startling inaccuracies and lack of judgment [...] Mr. Chamberlain's hatreds cover a wide gamut. They include Jews, Darwinists, the Roman Catholic Church, the people of southern Europe, Peruvians, Semites, and an odd variety of literary men and historians. But in his anxiety to claim everything good for Aryans and Teutons he finally reduces himself to the position of insisting that wherever he sees a man whom he admires he must postulate for him Aryan, and, better still, Teutonic blood. He likes David, so he promptly makes him an Aryan Amorite.[7]

Despite Roosevelt's skepticism, "Aryanism" in its various guises emerged as a potent force in the United States, where it often took on a particularly American cast. An important text here is Joseph Pomeroy Widney's 1907 *Race Life of the Aryan Peoples*. Widney was an influential thinker, founder of the Los Angeles Medical Society, and the second president of the University of Southern California. A man of his times, he disparaged philology while arguing that "the history of the world is largely only the history of the Aryan man" (Widney 1907: 26). Widney often compared the original Indo-European expansion to the settlement of the United States by Europeans. Like many of his predecessors, he found their racial essence in pioneering restlessness: "For there is unrest in the Aryan blood, an unrest which is ever urging it out and on" (1907: 48). Widney's signal contribution, if one could call it that, was synthesizing racism with environmental determinism. At the time, geographers stressed the contrast between the salubrious temperate climates and the deleterious tropics, and here Widney eagerly followed suit. The Aryans of India, he argued, succumbed not only to race mixing but also to the enervating heat, whereas those of Russia were undone by frost along with Mongolian admixture. As he unambiguously put it, "Aryans retain racial vitality only in temperate climates" (1907: 11–12).

Another well-known American racial theorist, Madison Grant, also pictured the prehistoric Aryan adventure through the lens of the westward expansion of the United States. Even more than Chamberlain, Grant rejected the terms "Aryan" and "Indo-European", contending that the race so denoted had long since vanished almost everywhere. But among the "Nordics", who alone preserved the racial essence, he found the same spirit of adventure that produced all the world's great sailors, explorers, and pioneers. "Practically every 49er" in the California Gold Rush, he told his readers, "was a Nordic"

---

[7] The review is found online at bartleby.com/56/8.html. Note also that the Amorites were actually a Semitic-speaking people.

(Grant 1916: 75). Grant's 1916 book *The Passing of the Great Race* was deeply felt in US intellectual circles. The extent of Grant's racism is evident in the fact that as secretary of the New York Zoological Society he helped arrange to have a Congolese Pygmy exhibited in a cage in the Monkey House of the Bronx Zoo (Bradford and Blume 1992).

It is difficult to exaggerate the sway of racial science in North America and northern Europe in the early twentieth century. This was not merely the favored theory of bigots and chauvinists, but a widely accepted doctrine that cut across political lines. It was embraced by some of the most knowledgeable, sophisticated, and progressive thinkers of the time. Even the socialist playwright George Bernard Shaw found much to admire in Chamberlain's hymns of racial hatred, arguing that his book "should be read by all good Fabians as a 'masterpiece of really scientific history'" (Griffith 1993: 265). Of particular significance was V. Gordon Childe, perhaps the foremost pre-historian of the era. An Australian by birth who was long affiliated with the University of Edinburgh, Childe was an accomplished philologist as well as a preeminent archeologist. He was also a lifelong Marxist, committed to a variety of leftist causes. To be sure, Childe was wary of the extremism of "Houston Stewart Chamberlain and his ilk", warning that "the word 'Aryan' has become the watchword of dangerous factions and especially the more brutal and blatant forms of anti-Semitism" (1926: 164). But despite these cautionary remarks, Childe embraced the core of the Aryan thesis. As he concluded in his hallmark 1926 book, *The Aryans: A Study of Indo-European Origins*: "Thus the Aryans do appear everywhere as promoters of true progress and in Europe their expansion marks the moment when the prehistory of our continent begins to diverge from that of Africa and the Pacific" (1926: 211).

Childe was too knowledgeable and intellectually honest to impute all human progress to the Aryans. Indeed, he emphasized the fact that the early Indo-Europeans had repeatedly "annexed areas previously occupied by higher types of culture" (1926: 200). How to explain such annexations was an intellectual challenge. In one passage, Childe opined that it was "only explicable in racial terms", which he later specified to be largely a matter of brawn: "the physical qualities of that stock did enable them by the bare fact of superior strength to conquer even more advanced people" (1926: 200, 212). But in the end, Childe claimed that it was neither bodily strength nor a more generalized racial superiority that allowed the Aryans to triumph, but their language itself, a view originally put forward by the German philosopher and bureaucrat Wilhelm von Humboldt (1767–1835).[8] The final lines of Childe's text attribute Aryan domination to the "more excellent language and mentality that [they]

---

[8] See, for example, Humboldt (1988).

generated" (1926: 212). This supposed excellence is also spelled out in the first few pages of the book (1926: 4):

[T]he Indo-European languages and their assumed parent-speech have been throughout exceptionally delicate and flexible instruments of thought. They were almost unique, for instance, in possessing a substantive verb and at least a rudimentary machinery for building subordinate clauses that might express conceptual relations in a chain of ratiocination.

Childe, the "great synthesizer" of European prehistory, thus returned to the philological roots of inquiry to explain the ancient mushrooming of the Indo-European language family.

Childe's theories of Aryan linguistic supremacy, however, had little impact, and he later came to regret having written the book. Over the next decade, a new generation of social and cultural anthropologists transformed the field. Scholars were now committing themselves to learning the languages of the peoples they studied, and in so doing they undermined the idea that primitive peoples have primitive languages, incapable of expressing abstract concepts. Philologists who examined non-Indo-European languages, moreover, knew full well that there was nothing uniquely Aryan about subordinate clauses.[9] Childe's linguistic understanding had become antiquated, invalidating the key component of his Aryan theory.

Meanwhile, the emerging school of sociocultural anthropology discredited scientific racism on other fronts (Barkan 1992). Franz Boas, the German founder of the discipline in the United States, showed that head shape is determined in part by parenting practices, as the cranial indices of American-born children of immigrants deviated from those of their mothers and fathers (Gravlee *et al.* 2003). The behavioral disparities found in different human groups, Boas argued, stemmed from cultural difference rather than innate temperaments. As the students of Boas gained positions of leadership in anthropology departments across the country, racialists such as Madison Grant despaired.

But it is important to recognize that the revisionism of Boas had its limits. Despite his staunch opposition to scientific racism, Boas, like Childe, remained wedded to the idea that language embodies the worldview of the group that speaks it, revealing its *volksgeist*, or ethnic essence. This idea would be further elaborated by his student Edward Sapir and Sapir's student Benjamin Whorf into the eponymous Sapir–Whorf hypothesis of linguistic relativism, which claims that language determines thought.[10] Although a "soft" version of this

---

[9] The idea that "primitive languages" of "primitive peoples" lack subordinate clauses has resurfaced more recently in the works of Dan Everett on the Pirahã language (see Everett 2005).

[10] The term "Sapir–Whorf hypothesis" was introduced by Harry Hoijer, another student of Sapir, even though the two scholars never actually advanced any such hypothesis; nor did they ever co-author anything (see Hoijer 1954: 92–105).

hypothesis has many defenders, almost all linguists and psychologists reject outright the stronger version of the original formulation, which denies the universality of basic human cognition.

Regardless of developments in linguistic theory, by the 1930s, scientific racism was in rapid retreat in the United States and Britain, and by the late 1940s it was discredited even in Germany. With the postwar revelations of Nazi atrocities, the thesis of Aryan superiority was thoroughly ejected from mainstream intellectual life. To be sure, it continued – and continues – to fester in odd corners. These days, it is easy to be reminded of its existence by doing ethnographic map and image searches, in which content from the neo-Nazi website *Stormfront* appears distressingly often.

Renewed confusion of race and language

While early twentieth-century racial scholars were reducing the scope of the White (or "Caucasian") race in Europe, stressing the separation of its so-called Nordic, Alpine, and Mediterranean stocks, a countervailing tendency operated in Africa. Although this movement was not directly linked to debates about Indo-European origins, it did feed into a renewed conflation of race and language in the postwar period that influenced popular conceptions of the so-called Indo-European-speaking peoples. It also provoked a sequence of scholarly reactions that would eventually begin to sever the race–language connection.

The main tendency in early twentieth-century African physical anthropology was to inflate the geographical bounds of the Caucasians at the expense of Black Africans. Some writers have traced this maneuver to the defeat of the Italian Army by the Kingdom of Abyssinia at the Battle of Adwa in 1896; since Blacks were widely thought to be incapable of defeating a modern European military force, the conclusion followed that the victorious Ethiopians must actually be sun-darkened Whites (Jonas 2011). As the facial features of Ethiopians tend to be more like those of North Africans than those of sub-Saharan Africans, this idea received some support from physical anthropology. But by the mid-twentieth century, cartographers were expanding the Caucasian label deep into the heart of the continent, encompassing peoples of wholly African appearance. A map in the 1946 *Atlas of World Affairs* (McFadden *et al.* 1946), produced with support from the US military, treated not just Ethiopia and Somalia as demographically dominated by "Caucasian (or white)" people, but also northern Kenya, South Sudan, Uganda, and the northeastern corner of D. R. Congo.

As the peoples of Uganda and South Sudan are hardly "White" by any physical indicators, one must ask how they could have been so classified. The answer, in essence, is language. The scholars responsible for this maneuver knew that it was problematic. Yet as C. G. Seligman explained in his influential book *The Races of Africa* (1930: 9–10):

Language – helpful as it may be – is no safe guide to race. Yet the study of the races of Africa has been so largely determined by the interest in speech [. . .] that names based on linguistic criteria are constantly applied to large groups of mankind and, indeed, if intelligently used, often fit quite well [. . .] [I]n this volume linguistic criteria will play a considerable part in the somewhat mixed classification adopted.

The key construct employed by Seligman and his peers was the "Hamitic Hypothesis", which takes us back to Noah's son Ham. As Hebrew, Arabic, and other closely related languages were defined as Semitic (i.e., linked to the progeny of Shem), more distantly related languages in the same family, such as Ancient Egyptian, Somali, and Galla (Oromo), were linked to Ham and hence deemed Hamitic. As Europeans gained knowledge of interior Africa, scholars increasingly linked all advances in African culture to conquests or incursions by the generally dark-skinned yet putatively Caucasian Hamites; as Seligman put it, "the civilizations of Africa are the civilizations of the Hamites" (1930: 96). European writers often seized on dubious physical or linguistic markers among elite African populations as a sign of Hamitic descent. Thus the generally taller and more sharply featured Tutsi aristocrats of Rwanda/Burundi were viewed as largely Caucasian Hamites, unlike the Hutu commoners. In this case, the two communities spoke the same Bantu language, but it was reasoned that the Tutsis must have spoken a Hamitic language before they overcame the more numerous Hutus. As linguistic information was gathered from eastern Africa, Nilotic-speaking peoples – including many of the pastoralists of the region – were often subsumed into the same putative Hamitic family (although Seligman classified the southern Nilotes such as the Masai as "half-Hamites" while regarding those of what is now South Sudan as "hamiticized Negroes" [1930: 157, 169]). At the extreme, as in the portrayal in the 1946 *Atlas of World Affairs*, it would seem that all eastern Africans speaking non-Bantu languages, such as the Zande of northern D. R. Congo, were assigned to a Caucasian or at least a half-Caucasian racial position, regardless of their physical attributes. Yet Seligman himself thought that even the Bantus have some "Hamitic blood" (1930: 178), and he thus limited the "True Negroes" to the coastal zone of West Africa.

Africa was not the only part of the world in which race was widely confused with language. In the post-WWII intellectual environment, the extreme claims of prewar racial scientists were no longer admissible, but race remained a key concept for understanding human diversity. For general pedagogical purposes, the most expedient solution was simply to map races along language lines. As a result, peoples speaking Indo-European languages in Europe and India were often racially separated from peoples speaking Uralic, Turkic, and Dravidian languages. In the 1946 *Atlas of World Affairs* mentioned above, Turks, Hungarians, and (most) Finns were mapped as "Mongolian (or yellow)" (McFadden *et al.* 1946). In the popular *World Book Atlas* (1966), Hungarians, Finns, and Estonians are classified as mixed Caucasian and Mongolian, whereas most Turks were depicted as purely Mongolian, as were the Hungarians living in the Carpathian Mountains of Romania. A more extreme conflation of race and language was found in a map edited by the noted Welsh geographer and anthropologist H. J. Fleure, published in *Bartholomew's Advanced Atlas of Modern Geography* of 1962. Here Finns and Estonians were mapped as "Asiatic or Mongolian" because of their "yellow skin colour". On the same map, "Dravidian" was also advanced as a skin-color group (as part of an "Australo-Dravidian" race of "Melanodermic" people).

This chaotic conception of racial diversity in the postwar period provoked a minor reaction. One scholar in particular, the American physical anthropologist Carleton Coon, sought to place racial understanding on a more scientific basis by stripping out involuted taxonomies and firmly rejecting the mixing of racial and linguistic categories. Coon (1963) noted the absurdity of classifying the Finns as "yellow" – albeit while failing to see that there is nothing "yellow" about the skin of East Asians – and scoffed at the idea that Europeans are divided into discrete races. Relying on a variety of physical indicators and guided by evolutionary theory, Coon divided humankind into Caucasoid, Mongoloid, Congoid (sub-Saharan African), Australoid, and Capeoid (far southwestern African) stocks, which he regarded as distinctive enough to constitute separate subspecies. Coon's conception remained racially hierarchical, but he no longer placed Caucasians – let alone Aryans – at the apogee. In an illustration tellingly captioned "The Alpha and Omega of *Homo sapiens*", Coon contrasted an Australian Aborigine, supposedly possessing a cranial capacity of a mere 1,000 cubic centimeters, with a Chinese scholar enjoying "a brain nearly twice that size" (1963: XXXII).

Just as Coon was developing his evolutionary approach to racial taxonomy, the entire concept of physical race came under devastating attack. The key figure here was the anthropologist Ashley Montagu (1964), who cartographically demonstrated that the main diagnostic traits for race – including skin color, cranial index, nose shape, stature, and so on – have their own distributional patterns, failing to exhibit the spatial co-variation that would be required to support the notion of distinct races. By the late 1970s, few scholars considered race as anything but a social construct, and a pernicious one at that. The pendulum swing was so extreme that any talk of physically based divisions among humankind came to be seen as unacceptable, leading some scholars of genetic diversity to despair. As modern analysis shows, numerous genetic markers do indicate significant physical differentiation among such groups as western Eurasians and eastern Eurasians. Partly as a result of such findings, racial thinking is making a comeback in some corners of intellectual life. Unfortunately, some writers are seemingly trying to push the pendulum back to where it had been in the days of so-called racial science. Such a problem is most glaringly apparent in Nicholas Wade's *A Troublesome Inheritance: Genes, Race and Human History* (2014). Wade, arguably the world's foremost science journalist, is also one of the main champions of the Gray–Atkinson approach to historical linguistics. But recent research also indicates that some supposedly diagnostic racial traits can change rapidly under the force of natural selection, undermining many of the older racial constructs. Indeed, according to Wilde *et al.* (2014), the early Bronze-Age denizens of the Pontic Steppes – the original "Aryans", perhaps – had much darker skin coloration than most present-day Europeans.

Yet despite such scholarly developments, the conflation of race with wholly non-racial attributes persists in the public imagination. In the United States, Hispanics, defined broadly as people with historical connections to Iberian culture, are often regarded as automatically non-White, even though the US census explicitly states that Hispanics can be of any race. Muslims are often put in the same category, regardless of skin color or any other physical attributes. It sometimes seems that racial discourse has historically been so invidious as to generate its own form of color blindness.

Marija Gimbutas and the feminist revision of Indo-European studies

As racial anthropology was being reformulated and then abandoned, Indo-European archeological and religious studies were undergoing their own transformation. The key figure here was the Lithuanian-American archeologist Marija Gimbutas, who turned the Aryan hypothesis on its head, portraying the original Indo-Europeans not as history's heroes but rather as its villains (see Gimbutas *et al.* 1997). In 1956, Gimbutas linked the *kurgan* burial mounds in the Pontic Steppes north of the Black Sea to speakers of the proto-Indo-European language. She associated this so-called Kurgan culture with pastoral, patriarchal warrior bands. In later excavations of Neolithic villages in southeastern Europe, she described a culture that seemed to be the opposite on all scores: sedentary, peaceful, and gender egalitarian. Gimbutas (1974; Gimbutas and Marler 1991) later elaborated this thesis in a series of books on the deities of what she called Old Europe, essentially the Balkan Peninsula before the coming of the Kurgans. These female-centered, goddess-worshiping societies, Gimbutas claimed, were highly cultured, almost fully egalitarian, and peaceful, lacking fortifications and offensive weapons. Their irenic civilization, she further argued, was demolished by the Kurgan invasions, which spread not just the Indo-European language family but also warfare, hierarchy, and male domination.

Gimbutas's basic archeological work was solid, and most archeologists working on Indo-European origins have accepted some version of her Kurgan hypothesis that places the origin of the language family among the pastoral (or semi-pastoral) peoples of the Pontic Steppes. But her characterizations of both the "Kurgans" and the "Old Europeans" went too far for most specialists, who saw vast leaps from scanty remains to huge generalizations. And some of her lay followers went farther still. In Riane Eisler's 1987 treatise, *The Chalice and the Blade*, the Kurgan conquests are seen as ushering in a *global* age of male domination, social hierarchy, and mass violence. The implication was that a gentle, egalitarian social order is the human birthright, and could yet be reclaimed if only we had the will to undo the social damage imparted by the early Indo-Europeans. The *Chalice and the Blade* was a bestseller, helping propel the wave of goddess worship that swept certain feminist circles in the late twentieth century. It was lauded by prominent intellectuals, including Joseph Campbell, the doyen of mythology study. The famed anthropologist Ashley Montagu, noted above for his dismantling of the biological concept of race, hailed *The Chalice and the Blade* as the "most important book since Darwin's *Origin of Species*".[11] And in odd corners of current popular culture, "Kurgans" still play the role of malevolent sub-humans; in the popular *Highlander* film series, for example, a character named "the Kurgan" comes from a tribe of the same name, people who are "infamous for their cruelty, and [...] known to 'toss children into pits full of starved dogs, and watch them fight for [the] meat' for amusement".[12] The same idea reappears in the video game Blackmoor Archives.

Still, Eisler's comprehensive vision failed from the onset. As male domination characterized almost all historically known human societies, it can hardly be attributed to a single ancient people located in one particular part of the Earth. In today's world, rates of male-on-female violence may reach their height in Melanesia (see Jolly *et al.* 2012), a realm of small-scale societies about as far removed from the "Kurgans" as could be imagined. And despite its appeal to the left, Eisler's (1987) thesis was overwhelmingly Eurocentric, substituting Europe (actually, a corner of Europe) for the world as a whole. But even many of the less extreme assertions of Gimbutas herself have been undermined by scholarly analysis. The peoples of Old Europe were not altogether peaceful and female-centered, just as the speakers of Proto-Indo-European and

[11] See the book itself for Montagu's blurb.
[12] We are indebted to *GeoCurrents* reader William Barnard for bringing this character to my attention. The quotation is from the Wikipedia article on the character: http://en.wikipedia.org/wiki/Kurgan_(Highlander)

their immediate descendants were almost certainly not overwhelmingly andro-
centric and violent.

Work in world history also casts doubt on the Gimbutas vision. It is easy to
imagine militaristic nomads from the Eurasian steppes as much more male-
dominated than their sedentary neighbors, but comparative analysis suggests
otherwise. Through the early modern and modern periods, women among the
traditionally pastoral Kazakhs and Kirghiz of Central Asia have generally
enjoyed much more autonomy and power than those living in the village and
urban societies of the (Sart) Uzbeks[13] and Tajiks. In medieval Mongolia,
female empowerment was pronounced (Weatherford 2011); as Mongol men
were often absent at war, it is hardly surprising that women took on major
managerial and political roles in the homeland. It is also noteworthy that the
Scythians, ancient Indo-European-speaking pastoralists of the Pontic Steppes,
not uncommonly buried their females in military gear. Perhaps Herodotus was
on to something when he wrote of Amazon warrior women among the tribes
of the area (Guliaev 2003; Wilde 2000). Whether such conditions of relative
female empowerment existed among the Proto-Indo-European speakers is
anyone's guess, but it is clear that we cannot simply assume overwhelming
male domination based on pastoralism and military prowess.

Orientalism, Black Athena, and the renewed assault on Indo-European philology

In the works of the pre-WWII Aryan school and those of the late twentieth-
century feminist revisionists alike, the deep Indo-European past primarily
served ideological ends. Certainly the goals of the two camps were opposed;
where the former romanticized violence and domination, the latter sought to
bolster peace and equality. But whatever their motivations, writers in both
groups allowed their desires and prejudgments to guide their conclusions.
In this regard, the early Orientalist philologists stood on much more solid
ground. Max Müller and his fellows certainly had their biases and blind spots –
as we all do – but their commitment to empirical scholarship allowed them to
partially transcend their prejudices.

Yet at the same time that the early Indo-European past was being reimagined
by Gimbutas and her followers, the reputation of the early Indo-European

---

[13] The term "Uzbek" has been used to refer to two separate groups. Originally it referred to a
largely pastoral group speaking a Turkic language closely related to Kazakh, a group that
created the Uzbek Khanate of the Early Modern Period. In the early twentieth century, Soviet
ethnographers reassigned the term to the sedentary peoples of the region who speak a heavily
Persian-influenced Turkic language. Previously, these people, along with their Tajik neighbors,
had generally been called "Sarts".

philologists was again being savaged, just as the field itself was again brought to the forefront of scholarly debates. The key text here was Edward Said's 1978 book *Orientalism*, which condemned the entire project of philological scholarship for serving European imperialism by facilitating intellectual domination over the non-Western world. To be sure, Said subjected Jones to relatively light criticism and mostly ignored Müller, but both were ultimately damned. Said accused Jones of trying to "subdue the infinite variety of the Orient" by attempting to codify the main texts of the region (1978: 78). For Said, there was no escaping the taint; even "great Orientalist works of genuine scholarship", he argued, "came out of the same impulse" as "Gobineau's racial ideas" (1978: 8).

From a historical point of view, there was something deeply ironic about this broad-brush attack on the Indo-European philologists. For the early Orientalists who wrote on India were demonized by the arch-racialists of their own day precisely because they sought to *erase* rather than inscribe the "ontological and epistemological distinction between 'the Orient' and [...] 'the Occident'" – the very distinction in which Said located the essence of Orientalism (1978: 2). To be sure, one can find passages in Jones, Müller, and their peers that strike the modern reader as inadequately sensitive or even bigoted, but so too one can find such sentiments in all writers of the period. In the end, to tar all Orientalists as complicit in the imperial project is to descend into a form of anti-intellectualism, rejecting out-of-hand an invaluable legacy of thought. As Robert Irwin (2006: 124) cogently notes, "The establishment of an [Indo-European] family of languages by European philologists is something that has been resented by Edward Said and he appears to doubt the validity of their findings, though he does not explain why".

Edward Said was not the only leftist scholar of the late twentieth century to disparage the legacy of Indo-European philology. Martin Bernal, a student of China who later turned his attention to the origins of Classical Greek civilization, played a similar role. In his mammoth three-volume work *Black Athena: The Afroasiatic Roots of Classical Civilization* (1987, 1991, 2006), Bernal dismissed the so-called Aryan Model of Greek Indo-European origins in favor of what he called the Ancient Model, which attributed the most important aspects of classical Greek civilization to the Phoenicians and especially the Egyptians. Although he did not deny that ancient Greek had Indo-European (or Indo-Hittite, as he preferred) affinities, he regarded it as a mixed language with a heavily Afroasiatic vocabulary; he also viewed the Indo-European and Afroasiatic languages as having sprung from a common ancestral tongue (Bernal 1987: 11). Not surprisingly, Bernal followed Colin Renfrew in locating the origin of the Indo-European branch of this macro-family in Neolithic Anatolia (1987: 13). Bernal further suspected that Bronze-Age Crete and the Cyclades had been Semitic-speaking (1987:17).

The first volume of *Black Athena* had a major intellectual impact, but by the publication of the third volume (2006), which focuses on linguistic issues, interest had subsided. The waning influence of Bernal's work can be largely attributed to a series of devastating critiques of his evidence and argumentation, particularly those of Mary Lefkowitz (1996), a classicist who convincingly argued that *Black Athena* was little more than "an excuse to teach myth as history", as the subtitle of her 1996 book *Not Out of Africa* puts it. In a more recent and restrained but nonetheless shattering review of Bernal's third volume, J.-F. Nardelli contends that, "[Bernal's] faith in his ability to pinpoint sound shifts in (P)IE matching, or stemming from, Afroasiatic [...] looks misplaced; for he has not checked his facts and stands at the mercy of sources notorious for their quirks and errors [...] His own proneness to blunders further complicates his construct" (2013: 142). In short, Bernal's dismissal of traditional Indo-European philology rests on little more than a combination of shoddy scholarship and wishful thinking.

Indo-European revisionism in South Asia

Meanwhile, the legacy of Müller and his peers came under increasing attack from another quarter altogether, that of Indian nationalism. This school is epitomized in D. N. Tripathi's edited collection of 2005 entitled *A Discourse on Indo European Languages and Cultures*. The various contributors to this volume understandably object to the old narrative of the Aryan invasion of the subcontinent, a story that emerged in the nineteenth century from a combination of philological inquiry and racial science. According to this account, superior Aryans invaded South Asia in the Bronze Age, conquering and ruling over the indigenous dark-skinned people and then creating the caste system to ensure that the two groups remained distinct and unequal. Support for this theory was supposedly found in the Rigveda, one of humankind's oldest texts. Yet as Trautmann (1997) shows, this neat and simplistic narrative of Aryan invasion had actually been opposed by most of the leading European Sanskritologists of the nineteenth century. It has also been rejected by modern mainstream scholars, who deny stark racial divisions and tend to posit plodding infiltrations of Indo-European speakers into the Indian subcontinent, along with a gradual and complex development of caste ideology. And regardless of the seemingly clear division of South Asia into an Indo-European north and Dravidian south, it has long been recognized that the entire region shares numerous linguistic features, making it a *Sprachbund* or linguistic convergence zone (Masica 1976).

The current school of Indo-European revisionism in India, however, goes much further in denouncing the old Aryan hypothesis. Some of these writers deny any foreign impact on ancient South Asian civilization, as if in fear that acknowledgment would sunder the unity of India and compromise the nationalist agenda. As Tripathi (2005) specifies in his introduction, the main point of the volume is to show that the Indo-European language family originated in South Asia with the Indus Valley civilization and subsequently spread westward. Sanskrit, he contends, "is the most suited choice as the proto-Indo-European language", adding that the "antiquity of the Vedas is far more than what Max Müller and others have tried to fix" (2005: 13). Other chapters redeploy from Europe to India the exhausted trope of the intrinsic Aryan inclination to migrate. Ajay Mitra Shastri, for example, argues that, "the frequent migrations of enterprising peoples from India westward are responsible for the commonness and great similarity in the vocabulary of the speakers of Indian, West Asia, and European languages" (2005: 106). Yet Shastri is moderate compared to T. P. Verma, who claims not only that Sanskrit was the original language of all humankind, but that it was a direct gift from above. As he boldly argues, "Vedas are verbal transformations of God" (Verma 2005: 116), essentially taking us back to an early nineteenth-century conception of human prehistory.

This Indocentric school of Indo-European studies has generated significant opposition among more traditional scholars, both in the West and in India. According to Edwin Bryant, tensions grew so pronounced that it became "increasingly difficult for scholars of South Asia to have a cordial exchange on the matter without being branded a 'Hindu nationalist,' 'western neo-colonialist,' 'Marxist secularist,' or some other simplistic and derogatory stereotype" (2005: 470). In an attempt to break down such barriers, a joint volume entitled *The Indo-Aryan Controversy* was published in 2005 – in which Bryant's essay appears – containing insightful arguments from both camps, with several authors emphasizing the influence of the non-Indo-European languages of South Asia on the region's Indo-European tongues. A 2013 volume edited by Angela Marcantonio and Girish Nath Jha also sought common ground and more generally emphasized uncertainty; as James Clackson's essay (2013: 286) concludes, "From the linguistic data alone [...] it is not possible to draw definite conclusions about the homeland of the speakers if PIE, or even the age of the language family". Although this is a useful reminder, it remains true that, the "out of India" theory favored by Tripathi and his colleagues cannot withstand the linguistic scrutiny that it has recently received. As Michael Witzel (2005: 375) argues, no linguistic evidence supports an Indian origin of the Indo-European languages, whereas a vast amount of evidence can be found against it. Or as Romila Tharpar (2002: 109) framed the thesis that Vedic Sanskrit originated with the Indus Valley Civilization, "This view overlooks the data from linguistics, and does not present an analytic understanding of the archaeological evidence".

Although many Indian scholars have been trying to put the Aryan invasion myth to rest once and for all, the idea nonetheless retains potency elsewhere in South Asia. In the far south of India, many so-called Dravidianists have accepted the Aryan invasion thesis, but have given it a negative spin to oppose Brahmin interests, favor Tamil over Sanskrit and Hindi, and more generally advocate Tamil nationalism (Ramaswamy 1997). In northern India, Pakistan, Afghanistan, and especially Iran, a pro-Aryanist movement still attracts widespread support, as evidenced by a minor YouTube video genre that celebrates the racial nature of the local population. More than 300,000 views, for example, have been garnered by a video entitled "Aryan Race in Iran, Afghanistan, Tajikistan, Pakistan, India"; its creator (Persian Cyrus) claims that:

The real Aryans live in Iran, Afghanistan Tajikistan, Pakistan and India. With the attack of the mongols and turks [*sic*] most of the people there got "turkified" or "mongolized". However some of those survived![14]

In such a manner, anti-Arab and anti-Turkish prejudice in Iran is given a pseudo-scholarly gloss.

[14] Found online at youtube.com/watch?v=o0TQ1gj8GQo

2   Anatolia vs. the Steppes

As we saw in the preceding chapter, Indo-European inquiry has been an ideologically charged field from the beginning. Although a tremendous amount of solid research has been continually forthcoming, a number of scholars and popularizers of diverse perspectives have made great speculative jumps from meager bits of information, twisting the evidence to serve their own ends, often to inflate pride in their own nation, language group, or supposed race. The Indo-European past is hardly unique in this regard, as history is always vulnerable to self-interested manipulations. But it does seem that partisan inquiry has been especially pronounced in this domain. Why this should have been the case is an interesting and important topic in its own right.

Indo-European expansion has been such a fraught subject in large part because it has seemed to be tremendously important yet all but inexplicable. How could one small prehistoric language have spread so extensively, covering most of western and southern Eurasia by the dawn of recorded history and eventually encompassing more than half of the terrestrial world and almost half of humankind? Surely, many have concluded, there must have been something exceptional about the early Indo-European speakers that allowed such success. The extraordinary nature of these people could be framed positively or negatively, but most popular writers of earlier generations agreed that there was something awe-inspiring about them, something that demanded an overarching explanation, something that just might provide a key to understanding the larger course of human history.

By the late twentieth century, however, the search for a master narrative of world history had become an antiquated quest, as scholars increasingly stressed contingency, diversity, and multiple paths of historical development. By the same token, the idea that a single population of the deep past could have played a central world-historical role, whether for good or ill, now seemed impossible, reflecting a biased and blinkered view of human development. The time was thus ripe for a wholesale reappraisal, one that could knock the Proto-Indo-Europeans off their pedestal of distinction, reframing them as a normal people whose descendants were able to spread their languages through ordinary means.

Colin Renfrew and Anatolian alternative

Such a thorough reassessment did appear, initiated in 1987 with the publication of *Archaeology and Language* by the renowned archeologist Colin
Renfrew. Here Renfrew rejected all theories of Indo-European expansion predicated on migration, more specifically dismissing the idea that pastoralists from
the steppes could have spread their languages among the farming peoples of
Europe. The archeological evidence of such movements, Renfrew argued, was
not adequate to make the case. Instead, he linked the expansion of the Indo-
European family into Europe with the initial Neolithic spread of agriculture,
a process well demonstrated by the archeological record. This movement
began in Anatolia, located on the fringe of the original agricultural hearth in
the Fertile Crescent, and then spread westward into the Mediterranean Basin
and up the Danube Valley into central Europe. Such a population expansion,
Renfrew emphasized, did not entail rapid mass movement, but was rather
based on the forward creep of a settlement frontier, advancing on average
something on the order of one kilometer a year (Renfrew 1987: 129). Such
gradual movement, he contended, was best conceptualized through the model
of demic diffusion, initially advanced by the geneticist Luigi Luca Cavalli-
Sforza.

Renfrew's Anatolian hypothesis seemed to many non-specialists to have
solved the most confounding problems of Indo-European history. The extraordinary nature of the Proto-Indo-Europeans vanishes if they were mere farmers
gradually expanding into the lands of hunter–gatherers. Farmers almost always
occupy the landscape at much higher population densities than hunter–
gatherers, as they produce a much larger and more dependable supply of food
from the same area of land. They also tend to have higher birthrates, as
children in farming societies can be weaned earlier and as women can more
easily accumulate the body fat necessary for sustained fertility. Agricultural
societies are thus expected to demographically dominate non-agricultural ones,
and in so doing spread both their genes and their languages. Although the
native hunter–gatherers in such a scenario will tend to give way as farmers
gradually encroach, their genetic stock is not expected to disappear, as some
individuals will intermarry or otherwise interbreed with the newcomers.
Some foraging groups, moreover, will likely adopt the technologies of the
farmers, allowing them to hold their place against the incoming demographic
tide. Such a process would, in the Anatolian model, explain the survival of
non-Indo-European Basques.

In Renfrew's scheme, Indo-European expansion thus becomes an unexcep-
tional process, one replicated across the world whenever agriculture made its
first appearance. In an important 1994 article, Renfrew argued that almost all
instances of language family expansion that did not entail either initial human

settlement or reoccupation of formerly uninhabitable lands after post-glacial climatic change stemmed from the gradual spread of farming populations into the lands of hunter–gatherers (the only other possibility that he allowed is the imposition of languages by conquering elites, a mechanism supposedly limited to complex societies of the relatively recent past). In Renfrew's theory, all of the heroic (or dastardly) aspects of Aryan adventure dissolve into the monotonous lives of sedentary cultivators, none of whom would have been expected to have traversed more than a dozen or so kilometers over the course of a lifetime. Thus the migratory impetus of the early Indo-Europeans so celebrated by earlier generations is abandoned, as is any intrinsic aptitude for warfare or domination, much less any racial – or linguistic – superiority.

Considering the troublesome history of Indo-European inquiry, the appeal of Renfrew's theory is easy to understand. But in taking on the steppe model, Renfrew attacks an outmoded version, one based on the wholesale migrations of entire peoples. Even when he admits that the views that he is rejecting are associated with an earlier time, Renfrew fails to convey the fact that they have been antiquated for many decades. For example, after correctly pointing out that overwhelming Indo-European migrations would have run against the demographic gradient, pushing people from lightly populated pasturelands into more densely settled agricultural landscapes, Renfrew (1987: 94) further claims that "This view was adopted rather unthinkingly by earlier writers, who liked to use a metaphor of a swarm of bees; the Indo-European *swarmed* from their northern *hive*. But it is not at all clear why the population density should be greater in the 'homeland' than in neighboring areas." Yet as we have seen, the idea of an "Indo-European swarm" had been rejected and even mocked by Max Müller in the nineteenth century. Although the idea of Indo-European "swarming" continued to be advanced through the mid-twentieth century, it had been rejected by the field by the time that Renfrew's book was published.

The denial of migration

Renfrew's dismissal of migration stems largely from mid- and late twentieth-century developments in archeological theory. In the prewar period, archeologists tended to exaggerate the role of mass movement, often attributing any changes in artifacts to the entry of a new "culture", discounting the possibilities of innovation from within a society or of borrowing from neighboring peoples. Prewar scholars, moreover, tended to view migrating populations as forming cleanly bounded ethnic groups if not proto-nations. The new postwar school of "processual archaeology" rightly concluded that automatic explanation by migration was unwarranted, noting as well that ethnicity is often a fluid construct, as individuals can sometimes move from one ethnic group to another depending on the situation. But as is often the case, in rejecting one extreme position the new school tended to embrace an opposite and equally untenable alternative; over-correcting, many archeologists came to reject the mere possibility of significant migration. Such a swing of the pendulum is evident in *Archaeology and Language*. Although Renfrew states early on that "no one is asserting that migrations do not occur" (1987: 5), the possibility that Indo-European languages spread in such a manner is essentially rejected. Instead, Renfrew tells us that migration is a "hazardous business" that has "little chance of success" (1987: 133).

The postwar shift in archeological reasoning from an overweeningly migrational to a dogmatically anti-migrational perspective is not surprising. The tendency for corrections to overshoot their mark is a common feature of inquiry into the human condition. In geography, scholars in the 1920s commonly attributed almost everything in human culture to the influences of climate and the physical landscape; even something as abstract as monotheism was linked to the stark and sweeping vistas of desert landscapes, which supposedly led minds in southwestern Asia inexorably to the idea of a single God. Similar theories were popular at the same time in linguistics as well, as mentioned in the introduction of this book. By the postwar period, however, such environmental determinism had been rejected so vehemently that most geographers came to deny that the physical environment could play any role in human development, a position that deflated the whole point of geographical analysis. In the end, both extremes proved damaging to the discipline – one of the reasons why geography is such an underrepresented field of study in the United States. In recent years, scholars from other disciplines – most notably Jared Diamond (1997) – who have demonstrated the historical significance of physical geography have had to face an uphill battle in geographical circles, widely tarred as deterministic throwbacks to an earlier epoch (e.g. Blaut 1999). A similar story can be told in regard to studies of human physical diversity. Here a pseudo-scientific obsession with racial differences provoked an equally pseudo-scientific denial that any significant genetic differences could possibly distinguish major human populations.

We have emphasized Renfrew's rejection of migration because it lies at the heart of the Anatolian thesis of Indo-European origins. Renfrew makes this point clear roughly a third of the way through *Archeology and Language*, where he tells his reader why he rejects a "south Russian homeland for the Proto-Indo-Europeans". As Renfrew (1987: 98) puts it:

> The main reason for the failure to locate such a homeland arises, I think, first from an unwise reliance on linguistic paleontology in a rather uncritical way. Secondly it is a migrationist view. And thirdly it springs from a tendency not to consider with sufficient care the processes at work.

Taken together, these objections make a poor case for abandoning the Steppe hypothesis. As we shall see in Chapter 9, "linguistic paleontology" is merely one of many strands of evidence used to locate the Indo-European homeland in the steppe zone. And despite Renfrew's assertion, the techniques of linguistic paleontology have been critically cross-examined by linguists for decades. Renfrew's third charge, that proponents of the Steppe thesis have not considered "the processes at work", is not credible. Such an accusation could have been fairly leveled against many individual researchers of earlier generations, but it was untenable to apply it in blanket terms to the entire Steppe school in the 1980s. We are therefore left with the underlying reason for the rejection of "a south Russian homeland": "it is a migrationist view" (Renfrew 1987: 97, 98). Such a position may indicate the donning of ideological blinders as much as the impartial weighing of evidence. As J. P. Mallory (1989: 242) suggests, Renfrew casts aside migration because it is "heretical to the 'immobilist' dogma" that had come to characterize mainstream archeology. Yet as we shall see in the following chapter, a wide array of migrational *processes* have been omnipresent in the human past, most likely from the very beginning. Or as Peter Heather (2010: 2) more bluntly puts it in the introduction to his magisterial book *Empires and Barbarians*, "The history of humankind is the history of migration".

The Revised Steppe hypothesis

If many earlier Indo-Europeanists had not, in the words of Renfrew, "adequately explained why all of these languages, or the speakers of all of these languages, should be wandering around Europe and western Asia so tirelessly, in series of migrations" (1987: 75), the same charge cannot be applied to scholars writing at the time of the publication of *Archeology and Language*. The new view, perhaps best labeled the "Revised Steppe hypothesis", is most closely identified with J. P. Mallory (1989) and David Anthony (2007), archeologists who, like V. Gordon Childe before them, also mastered the relevant literature in historical linguistics. Their revivified Steppe thesis focuses precisely on the *processes* of language spread that Renfrew found so wanting in earlier attempts, conceptualizing migration as a complex and fluid process that can be propelled by a variety of causes.

J. P. Mallory's *In Search of the Indo-Europeans*, published two years after Renfrew's *Archeology and Language*, advanced this revivified Steppe hypothesis. Mallory's comprehensive yet cautious work sought more to weigh the evidence than to advance a specific theory, much less to "solve" the problem of Indo-European origins. But the cumulative evidence leads Mallory to favor a steppe homeland and to reject the Anatolian hypothesis. The pastoral progenitors that he envisions, however, bear little resemblance to the fierce Aryan conquerors of early depictions. Mallory notes, for example, that we have no reason to assume that the speakers of Proto-Indo-European had a particularly warlike orientation.

Mallory's (1989) synthesis does not posit mass migrations of Indo-European societies conquering indigenous nations and imposing their language on them. Instead, the stress is placed on more gradual processes of intrusion by pastorialist clans into agricultural landscapes followed by periods of intensive cross-cultural interaction that could eventually lead to the adoption of Indo-European tongues by the agricultural indigenes (1989: 258–259). Yet as he alludes, the distinction between "migration" and "intrusion" can be vague, as such terms signify different portions of a continuum of group movement. Mallory also shows that mainstream Indo-Europeanists had long since moved on from the stock mass-movement scenario. As he put it:

> Logically, it is easier to move small numbers of people around rather than large numbers, but the traditional tendency to assure one's audience that you intend only small intrusions probably has more to do with the embarrassment one associates with long-ridiculed invasion hypotheses. We are always wary of suggesting models of expansion that will be characterized as hordes of frenzied Aryans bursting out of the Russian steppes and slashing their way into the comparative grammars of historical linguists. (1989: 258)

David Anthony's award-winning book *The Horse, the Wheel, and Language*, published in 2007, is in many ways more ambitious than Mallory's *Archeology and Language*, as it seeks above all to determine the most likely homeland of Proto-Indo-European. Through a series of complex arguments based on a huge trove of information, Anthony locates this *Urheimat* in the Pontic Steppes to the north of the Black Sea, and associates it with the domestication of the horse and the development of horse-related technologies. He finds abundant evidence that the early Indo-European speakers were separated from their more sedentary, agricultural neighbors to the west by a persistent cultural frontier, one marked by numerous differences in artifacts that coincided with an ecotone, or environmental transition zone. As Anthony shows, such "robust" cultural/ecological frontiers are historically common across much of the world, although they have often been denied by archeologists on theoretical grounds, as "pre-state tribal borders" are supposed to be "ephemeral and unstable" (2007: 104).

Indo-European languages most likely breached this frontier, Anthony argues, not through wholesale invasions, but rather by mobile clans pushing into the lands of agricultural peoples and then establishing patronage networks among them. Expertise in trade as well as a pre-established ideological system could have enhanced the power of the newcomers, who likely remained well outnumbered in most areas. Anthony justifies both the migratory process and the establishment of the inter-cultural relations that would lead to language change on the basis of theoretically informed, comparative work from similar historically attested situations. As a possible close parallel, he cites the spread of the Nilotic Luo language, and in particular its Acholi dialect, in East Africa, which was carried by relatively small groups of people into more densely populated environments. His discussion is worth quoting at some length:

Indo-European languages probably spread out in a similar way among the tribal societies of prehistoric Europe. Out-migrating Indo-European chiefs probably carried with them an ideology of political clientage like that of the Acholi chiefs, becoming patrons of their new clients among the local population; and they introduced a new ritual system in which they [. . .] provided the animals for public sacrifices and feasts, and were in turn rewarded with the recitation of praise poetry – all solidly reconstructed for proto-Indo-European culture, and all effective recruiting activities. Later Proto-Indo-European migrations also introduced a new, mobile kind of pastoral economy made possible by the combination of ox-drawn wagons and horseback riding. Expansion beyond a few islands of authority might have waited until the new chiefdoms successfully responded to external stresses, climatic or political. Then the original chiefly core became the foundation for the development of a new regional ethnic identity. (2007: 118)

Recent works by J. P. Mallory, David Anthony, and numerous other Indo-Europeanists have thus thoroughly undermined one of Colin Renfrew's three main reasons for rejecting the Steppe hypothesis – namely, its "tendency not to consider with sufficient care the processes at work". One is thus left with Renfrew's objection to linguistic paleontology along with his thoroughgoing dismissal of migration in favor of demic diffusion. Both Mallory and Anthony ably defend the judicious use of linguistic paleontology, but such techniques are by no means central to their arguments. All that remains is therefore the refusal to accept prehistoric language spread by any process that smacks of migration.

The Anatolian hypothesis redux: linguistic phylogeny and the Gray–Atkinson approach

Around the turn of the millennium, a team of scholars led by Russell Gray and Quentin Atkinson initiated a long-term project to solve the problems of Indo-European origins and expansion by using computational techniques borrowed from the biological sciences. In framing the debate, they strip down the complex array of origination theories to a mere two: the Neolithic Anatolian thesis of Renfrew and the Bronze-Age Steppe theory held by most researchers in the field. Competing ideas, such as the Armenian theory of Gamkrelidze and Ivanov (1984, 1995) and the Balkan theory of Diakonoff (1985), considered in this book in Chapter 9, are ignored. Gray and Atkinson frame the Anatolian and Steppe theories as having equivalent standing, although the former is closely identified with a single scholar and has little credibility in the field, whereas the latter verges on being the consensus view. And although they claim to be neutral in testing these two hypotheses, in actuality they structure their methodology to favor the Anatolian hypothesis, as we shall see in Chapters 6 and 7. Like Renfrew, Gray and Atkinson reject the field of linguistic paleontology outright, although in their case they do so without justification. More importantly, they also disallow the possibility of migration – a key component of the Mallory–Anthony approach – and instead model the expansion of the Indo-European languages solely on the basis of demic diffusion, again as postulated by Renfrew.

Gray and Atkinson thus follow lockstep with Renfrew in denying migration and rejecting linguistic paleontology. But how do they stand in regard to his third major objection to the Steppe school, its supposed overlooking of the "processes at work"? As it turns out, their approach marks a major retrenchment on this score, as they barely consider processes at all. Instead, they merely assume a stripped-down version of Renfrew's account, that of population diffusion along settlement frontiers. Despite its flaws, Renfrew's *Archeology and Language* is a deeply learned book rooted in an impressive synthesis of traditional archeological, historical, and linguistic methods that grapples thoughtfully with complexities and potential contradictions. Unfortunately, one cannot say the same in regard to the works of his epigones in modeling the origin and spread of the Indo-European languages.

The lack of attention to processes in the demic diffusion model is evident in the fact that it ignores all possible interactions between populations that are expanding and those whose lands are being encroached upon. In the Gray–Atkinson schema, populations diffuse into new landscapes in exactly the same manner in all social circumstances and in all historical periods, regardless of whether the lands in question are unoccupied, lightly settled by hunter–gatherers, moderately populated by tribal cultivators, or heavily peopled by members of state-level societies. In actuality, the rate of advance – and indeed, the ability to advance – into new lands varies massively in these different scenarios. Diffusion from a less densely populated to a more densely populated environment is highly unlikely unless the incoming group has some significant military, technological, or organizational advantages over the native inhabitants, factors ignored in the Gray–Atkinson model.

The lack of attention to process, however, is not the most disturbing aspect of the demic diffusion model. More problematic is the fact that it risks reinscribing the identity between language groups and biologically defined human populations that so bedeviled the early history of Indo-European studies. It does so, however, in a covert manner; nowhere do the authors specifically link any language group to a race or race-like aggregation. But the linkage is implicit in the model, as a "demic" group is by definition a biologically conceptualized population, one characterized by descent from common ancestors. In this model, each demic group is associated with its own language. No room is allowed in the model for complex social inter-actions characterized by cross-cultural marriages, inter-cultural patronage networks, pervasive multilingualism, and wholesale language adoption and abandonment, yet we know that such features characterized linguistic history during the period of historical documentation. Instead, languages are straight-forwardly modeled as coincident with biologically conceptualized populations.

The question of violence

The conflation of language and race, as we have seen, was responsible for untold intellectual mischief through the mid-twentieth century. To be sure, the demic diffusion model does not risk descending back into the swamps of racist ethnography, as in this instance all language-carrying biological populations are regarded as essentially the same, differentiated only by their tongues. But the result is still a fundamental misapprehension not merely of human history but of human nature. Instead of imagining heroic and adventuresome Aryans lording it over the more sedentary lesser breeds, the demic model portrays all peoples of the past as timid stay-at-homes who move into new lands only when compelled by demographic pressure, and then only to the minimal extent possible. More importantly, they are modeled as pushing into new territories in a mindless manner, diffusing across an undifferentiated landscape in exactly the same manner as viruses spreading in an epidemic. Such senseless automatons do not make suitable specimens for recruitment into ideologically laden narratives, unlike the noble Aryans or the bloodthirsty Kurgans, but they are every bit as much a mental projection that can only obscure the already dim reaches of the human past.

Considering the misuses of earlier theories of Indo-European origins and expansion, it is understandable that many journalists and other non-experts would embrace the Anatolian theory and demic diffusion model. All such troublesome interpretations would vanish if Indo-European expansion could be linked not to galloping horse-riders from some remote homeland but rather to the gradual movement of simple farmers into the sparsely settled lands of Mesolithic Europe. Such a scenario appeals in part because it can easily be framed as essentially peaceful, with no war or conflict of any kind imagined – or at least incorporated into the model – between the newcomers and the indigen-ous peoples. Although we have no way of knowing whether such motivations have influenced the authors' theory and methods, it does seem from comments posted on *Geocurrents* that they view the possibility of violent incursions with marked distaste. Quentin Atkinson quotes Larry Trask to make this point:

Nevertheless, the vision of fierce IE warriors, riding horses and driving chariots, sweeping down on their neighbours brandishing bloody swords, has proven to be an enduring one, and scholars have found it difficult to dislodge from the popular consciousness the idea of the PIE-speakers as warlike conquerors in chariots.[1]

Although the desire to wish away the "bloody swords" of the past is understandable, it is also naïve, as violence unfortunately pervades human history. One does not have to embrace the vision of Thomas Hobbes, recently updated and re-theorized by Steven Pinker (2011) in his *The Better Angels of Our Nature: Why Violence Has Declined*, to accept that this is indeed the case. We suspect that Pinker exaggerates the bloodiness of hunting–gathering societies, a charge made most forcefully by Christopher Ryan,[2] co-author of the intriguing and controversial *Sex at Dawn* (2010), yet we also suspect that Ryan and his co-author, Cacilda Jethá, descend into hyperbole of their own in emphasizing the peacefulness and sexual license of our Paleolithic ancestors. But when it comes to pre-modern agricultural and pastoral societies, the evidence is overwhelming: enveloping violence was the norm. If one wants to rule out the possibility of bloody swords, one would be advised to examine something other than the human past.

But even if armed struggle has been pervasive for most of the past 10,000 years, it does not follow that all non-foraging societies have been equally bloody. As is always the case, different groups vary considerably on this score. If one searches the ethnographic literature, one can find a few documented tribal farming societies, such as the Hanunó'o and other Mangyan tribes of the island of Mindoro in the Philippines, that shunned warfare and all of its trappings (Lopez 1976). Yet the unfortunate truth is that such groups were usually victimized by their more aggressive neighbors, and hence were seldom successful in maintaining their numbers and territories. The Mangyans, for example, were able to maintain their gentle way of life only by retreating to rugged and inaccessible areas, and even so they were still targeted for centuries by slave raiders from the Sulu Archipelago (Helbling and Schult 2004). Intriguingly, the Hanunó'o seem to be a remnant of what was once a much larger and more sophisticated society, evident by the fact that they have long enjoyed widespread literacy in their own script (Conklin 1949), an unprecedented phenomenon in a small-scale, tribal society. That society, however, was destroyed long ago by a combination of Spanish imperialism and Moro raiding.

An alternative scenario?

The "Revised Steppe hypothesis" and the "Anatolian demic diffusion model" are surely not the ultimate stances in the prodigious Indo-European debate.

---

[1] See his comments on our website, *GeoCurrents*: geocurrents.info/cultural-geography/linguistic-geography/why-the-indo-european-debate-matters-and-matters-deeply

[2] See Ryan's post, "Pinker's Dirty War on Prehistoric Peace", at Huffington Post, January 9, 2012: huffingtonpost.com/christopher-ryan/pinkers-dirty-war-on-preh_b_1187329.html

As the topic is both compelling and mysterious, we think that it will continue to generate new interpretations – and new controversies – for some time. In all likelihood, we will never reach airtight conclusions about the origins of the Indo-European languages, as too much time has passed and the surviving evidence is too scanty. Although we tentatively endorse the Revised Steppe thesis, we nonetheless retain a degree of skepticism about all such theorizing. At the same time, we try to keep an open mind in regard to alternative hypotheses, even seemingly outrageous ones. To conclude this chapter, let us therefore briefly explore a novel construal of Indo-European expansion proposed by the anthropological blogger Al West. West's ideas are forwarded tentatively, perhaps in a tongue-in-check manner. Yet even if we do not take them too seriously, they might still be able to shed some light on the issue.

West begins by surmising that the early Indo-European speakers could have gained influence by trading horses and animal products, generated in excess by their pastoral economy, to nearby sedentary farmers, an idea that meshes well with the Revised Steppe hypothesis. He goes on, however, to turn the Kurgan thesis of Gimbutas on its head, portraying the early Indo-Europeans not as marauding warriors but rather as the original hippies. Building on the works of Andrew Sherratt and David Anthony, he argues that, "it's possible that proto-Indo-European speakers became rich and powerful through selling [. . .] intoxicants" – in particular, marijuana. In fleshing out the argument, he continues:

Indo-European-speaking people traded THC-laden hemp from the steppes all the way down into the Near Eastern cities, which were naturally a major centre for trade from all over Eurasia [. . .] If this scenario is right, then to the people of Babylon the arrival of Indo-European speakers must have seemed like one crazy dream.[3]

Although West is probably off-track in suggesting that *Proto*-Indo-European speakers were responsible for the spread of cannabis as a recreational or spiritual drug, such an association is more reasonably made for the progenitors of one of the main branches of the family, the Proto-Indo-Iranians. Evidence here comes from both Herodotus, who famously wrote of cannabis ingestion among the Scythians, and from archeological digs. The noted archeologist Andrew Sherratt (1995: 27) argued that cannabis ingestion in the steppe zone dates back thousands of years, and "was the focus of the social and religious rituals of the pastoral peoples of central Eurasia in prehistoric and early historic times" (see also the discussion in Clarke and Merlin 2013: 80 ff). Linguistic evidence is also intriguing. The hemp plant, which produces valuable fibers and seeds in addition to its mind-altering resin, has been known across much of Eurasia for millennia, and was thus undoubtedly referred to by a welter of local names. Cognate terms linked to the word "cannabis", however, evidently spread widely in the third

---

[3] See his blog, *West's Meditations*, "Proto-Sticky-Icky: Ancient Cannabis", July 18, 2012: http://alwestmeditates.blogspot.com/2012/07/proto-sticky-icky-archaeology-of.html

millennium BCE, borrowed into Latin and other Indo-European languages, which is believed by some to indicate that a new pharmaceutical use for the plant had been discovered and was itself expanding (Barber 1992: 36).

Cannabis was not the only mind-altering substance used by early speakers of Indo-Iranian languages. Perhaps the largest mystery in the history of pharmacology is the identification of *soma*, the ritual intoxicant of the Rigveda, known as *haoma* in the Avesta (the sacred text of Zoroastrianism). More than a hundred Vedic hymns extol this unknown substance. Numerous plants and fungi have been proposed as soma candidates, but linguistic evidence indicates that *soma/haoma* was almost certainly not cannabis. In 1968, the noted ethnomycologist (student of the cultural uses of fungi) and J. P. Morgan vice president R. Gordon Wasson (1968) identified *soma* with the hallucinogenic mushroom *Amanita muscaria*, also known as fly agaric. As a vigorous debate subsequently unfolded, other researchers came to favor the view that the sacred substance was a mere stimulant, most likely ephedra (also known as máhuáng or "Mormon tea") (Falk 1989).

Recent research on the identity of *soma* has tended away from mushrooms and toward ephedra, due largely to archeological discoveries. Sherratt (1995: 29) linked the substance to early fire worship in Central Asia, noting that "ash repositories from sacred fires, and preparation rooms" contain pollen from *Ephedra* as well as from *Cannabis* and *Papaver* (the genus containing the opium poppy). But it is questionable whether ephedra is a potent enough psychoactive substance to have received the attention that it did in the Rigveda and the Avesta. Sherratt (1995: 30) thus went on to speculate that *soma* could have been harmel, or Syrian rue (*Peganun harmela*), a plant containing a powerful hallucinatory substance called harmine, which was "used as a 'truth drug' by the Nazis". Syrian rue also produces a widely employed red dye, leading Sherratt to wonder whether "the entoptic images produced by harmine [are] reflected [. . .] in the geometric designs of traditional Persian and Central Asian carpets; and [if] the hallucinogenic properties of this drug, and the flying sensation that it produces, give rise to the motif of the 'flying carpet'" (1995: 30). Regardless of its true identity, "soma" was ensconced in the Western public imagination by the publication of Aldous Huxley's *Brave New World* in 1932, in which a drug of the same name is used as a mechanism of social control. More recently, the word has been embraced by the cannabis-growing community of northern California. Wikipedia includes a "soma" article dedicated to a marijuana breeder who goes by that name; the article notes that this particular Soma is "internationally known as a 'Ganja Guru' after developing award-winning cannabis strains".[4]

We very much doubt that any ancient Indo-Iranian folk pharmacologists would have recognized the pot-breeder named Soma as a kindred spirit. But

[4] http://en.wikipedia.org/wiki/Soma_(cannabis_grower)

returning to West's thesis, it is not entirely out-of-bounds to highlight modern parallels to his hypothesized drug-assisted spread of Indo-European languages. As recently as the 1970s, the Pashtun areas of northern Pakistan and southern and eastern Afghanistan were noted for their cannabis-intoxicated Sufi holy men who were able to pass with impunity between feuding clans and tribes, seeking to make peace and calm tensions (see Lindholm 1982). As Sidky (1990) argues, Pashtun mystics called "malangs", widely thought to have great supernatural powers, were noted for the use of cannabis, as well as that of *Datura*, a plant with extraordinarily powerful – and often terrifying – psycho-active properties. Sidky also contends that such practices represented a survival of ancient Central Asian shamanism. The Sufi mendicant system of the Pashtun people, however, has been undermined by the intensification of puritanical, anti-mystical Deobandi-oriented interpretations of Islam, and perhaps by UN-inspired anti-drug campaigns as well. Difficult though it may be for us to now imagine, the Pashto-speaking realm that is today so beset with violence and intolerance was recently a major destination for Western hippie travelers on the storied "hashish trail".

All told, we find it highly unlikely that the early spread of Indo-European languages (or, more narrowly, Indo-Iranian languages) had anything to do with drug-ingesting mediators. The point of this excursion is not to argue that such an anachronistic "proto-hippie thesis" has any merit, but rather merely to show that making the argument is possible. Our knowledge of the prehistoric past in general, and of the distribution of language groups in particular, remains quite spotty, behooving us to retain an open mind, even when it comes to seemingly outrageous ideas.

Our central thesis concerns methods of inquiry, not conclusions, and as a result we do not deny the possibility that the Indo-European languages originated in Anatolia, or elsewhere for that matter. We thus take seriously Gordon Whittaker's (2008) thesis that the first town-dwellers of southern Mesopotamia spoke an Indo-European language rather than Sumerian, a notion that, if true, would require a substantial reassessment of all major theories of Indo-European origins and expansion. We are certainly not convinced by Whittaker, but we are intrigued, and we do hope to see more research on the topic.

It is equally important that we continue to remind ourselves that all human cultures are complex assemblages of ideas and practices, any number of which can be selected for emphasis. Especially when it comes to poorly understood cultures of the ancient past, we should be wary of any thesis that is based on any kinds of *essential* traits. Although portraying the Proto-Indo-Europeans as proto-hippies strays into the realm of fantasy, it is no less reasonable than picturing them as intrepid members of the *Herrenvolk* ("master race"), as demonic Kurgans, or as timorous cultivators mindlessly advancing across the landscape like diffusing viruses.

Part II

The failings of the Bayesian phylogenetic research program

Although it may be comforting to some to imagine that Indo-European languages spread across Europe and much of southern Asia through the essentially peaceful diffusion of Neolithic farmers, scholarly responsibility requires us to subject this notion to rigorous assessment. If the evidence strongly indicates that such a process did not occur, then we must reject it, at least provisionally, regardless of our hopes and desires. In this section of the book, we scrutinize both the model used in "Mapping the Origins and Expansion of the Indo-European Language Family" and the results that it produces, both of which turn out to be seriously deficient. Wherever we look, we find that the model produces multiple chains of errors, consistently failing to accord with known facts about the diversification and spread of the Indo-European languages.

Chapter 3 is devoted to the theoretical basis of the Gray–Atkinson approach to historical linguistics. It begins by outlining the scope of the larger research program, showing the range of languages and linguistic issues that have been analyzed through the techniques of Bayesian phylogenetics. Our attention then turns to the more general issue of the use of theory in historical linguistics, specifying what a useful theory should be able to accomplish. We then show, through several short examples, how the Gray–Atkinson approach fails to fulfill this basic mandate.

The remainder of Part II goes into much greater detail, showing how the model used in "Mapping the Origins" produces inaccurate results. Chapters 4 and 5 take on the phylogenetic component of analysis, first by examining the language trees that it generates and testing them against the empirical record (Chapter 4) and then by scrutinizing in the same manner the dates that it gives to linguistic diversification "events" (Chapter 5). Chapter 6 turns to the phylogeographical aspects of the research program in question, weighing the cartographic results of the model against what we know to be true from the historical record. Finally, Chapter 7 examines three of the key assumptions that inform the authors' geographical approach to language diversification and expansion. As we show, although such assumptions are necessary for the model to operate they are neither justified nor warranted. In the end, such faulty assumptions do not merely simplify complex patterns and processes to the point of caricature, but actually distort reality into unrecognizable forms.

3   What theory we want and what theory we get

"Mapping the Origins and Expansion of the Indo-European Language Family" is not a singular work on one particular language family, as some journalists have portrayed it to be. It is rather merely one product of an ambitious research program whose adherents have been employing the same computational methods – that is, Bayesian phylogeny – to infer the internal classifications of multiple language families. Over the past decade, this program has consumed massive amounts of research funds, produced a large volume of publications, and gained the attention of many linguists and scholars from other disciplines.

The main purpose of this chapter is to spell out our metrics for evaluating scientific theories and to ask whether the phylogenetic approach to historical linguistics satisfies such requirements. Before doing so, however, it is necessary to demonstrate the breadth and depth of the new biologically oriented approach to determining the origin, diversification, and expansion of language families.

The broader challenge to conventional historical linguistic scholarship

Russell D. Gray and Quentin D. Atkinson themselves have been working on the origin and diversification of the Indo-European family for more than a decade, publishing their initial results in *Nature* in 2003 (Gray and Atkinson 2003) and their subsequent work in a series of later articles (Atkinson and Gray 2006; Gray *et al.* 2011; *inter alia*). A larger project of Gray and his colleagues concerns the classification, origins, and spread of the Austronesian language family (cf. Gray and Jordan 2000; Greenhill *et al.* 2008; Gray *et al.* 2009; Greenhill and Gray 2009; Greenhill *et al.* 2009; Greenhill, Drummond, and Gray 2010; Gray *et al.* 2011). Michael Dunn, a co-author of the *Science* article in question, has applied computational phylogenetics to Papuan languages (Dunn *et al.* 2005) and to Aslian languages, a branch of the Austroasiatic family spoken by aboriginal inhabitants of Malaya and peninsular Thailand (Dunn, Burenhult, *et al.* 2011). Additional articles co-authored by Dunn employed the same methodology in regard to the languages of Melanesia (Dunn *et al.* 2007; Dunn *et al.* 2008), while Gray and Dunn collaborated on a similar analysis of the Uto-Aztecan languages (Dunn, Greenhill, *et al.* 2011). Gray collaborated with Claire Holden on an analysis of Bantu languages (Holden and Gray 2006), while Atkinson collaborated with Claire Bowern on an analysis of Pama-Nyungan languages in Australia (Atkinson and Bowern 2012).

Other scholars have also used various computational phylogenetic methods for language families around the world. Studies of Indo-European languages are especially numerous (Dunn *et al.* 2005; Forster and Toth 2003; Nakhleh *et al.* 2005; Rexová *et al.* 2003; Ringe *et al.* 2002; *inter alia*). A somewhat different approach is taken by Alexandre Bouchard-Côté and his colleagues in their work on the phylogenetic tree of Austronesian languages (Bouchard-Côté *et al.* 2013): they attempt to develop an algorithm for automatically reconstructing words of a proto-language based on the modern languages. The accuracy of such reconstruction, however, is questionable. Other language groups studied through an application of computational phylogenetic methods, with varying degrees of success, include such well-established families as Bantu (Holden 2002; Rexová *et al.* 2006; Grollemund 2012; Currie *et al.* 2013), Japonic (Lee and Hasegawa 2011), and Semitic (Kitchen *et al.* 2009). Other scholars have applied similar methods to lesser-studied groupings. Laura Robinson and Gary Holton used computational phylogenetic tools to reassess the genealogical affiliation of the Alor-Pantar languages, non-Austronesian languages spoken in eastern Indonesia (Robinson and Holton 2012). Robert S. Walker and Lincoln A. Ribeiro used methods similar to those developed by Gray and Atkinson to investigate the expansion of Arawak, one of the most widely dispersed language families in the Americas, scattered from the Antilles to Argentina, concluding that the Arawak homeland is in Western Amazonia rather than Northwest Amazonia, as determined by earlier studies (Walker and Ribeiro 2011). Aymeric Daval-Markussen and Peter Bakker have used similar phylogenetic tools in investigating and visualizing the relationships of creole languages to other languages, both creoles and non-creoles (Daval-Markussen and Bakker 2011, 2012). In addition, similar computational techniques are found in another recent article that received wide acclaim in the popular media: "Ultraconserved Words Point to Deep Language Ancestry across Eurasia", by Mark Pagel, Quentin Atkinson, and their colleagues (Pagel *et al.* 2013). Yet most of these works are deeply problematic and some of them, such as "Ultraconserved Words", are almost incoherent.[1]

---

[1] A few recent articles have tested and compared the different computational phylogenetic methods; see Barbançon *et al.* (2013) and Kassian (2014).

In addition to published articles, several conferences have convened over the last four years to discuss the application of computational phylogenetic methods to various language groupings, including the First Conference on ASJP (Automated Similarity Judgment Program) and Language Prehistory at the Max Planck Institute for Evolutionary Anthropology (Leipzig) in September 2010; "Bridging Disciplines: Evolution and Classification in Biology, Linguistics and the History of Science", which took place at Ulm University, Germany in June 2011; a workshop titled "Beyond Phylogeny: Quantitative Diachronic Explanations of Language Diversity", which took place in conjunction with the 45th Annual Meeting of the Societas Linguistica Europaea in Stockholm, Sweden in August–September 2012; a tutorial and workshop on "Phylometric and Phylogenetic Methods in the Humanities" at Bern University, Switzerland in November 2012; a parasession on "Human Prehistory through Linguistics" at the 39th Annual Meeting of the Berkeley Linguistics Society in February 2013 (which one of the present authors, Asya Pereltsvaig, has attended); a workshop on "Advances in Phylogenetic Linguistics" in Ragusa Ibla, Italy in July 2013; a workshop on "Time and Space in Linguistics: Interdisciplinary Computational Approaches" (TaSiL 2014) at Aarhus University in January 2014; a "Workshop on Historical and Empirical Evolutionary Linguistics" (WheeL) in Tübingen, Germany in February 2014; and a conference on "Language Diversity and History" in Poznań, Poland in September 2014.

As this quick exploration shows, the recent article in *Science* on the origin and expansion of the Indo-European language family is merely the tip of an iceberg. Many of our criticisms of the phylogenetic approach apply to all or most of the papers mentioned above, although some are specific to the single article that commands our attention. In general terms, our critique focuses on "Mapping the Origins" for three reasons: it represents the pinnacle of the research program in question, it has received the most attention in the public media, and the Indo-European language family is particularly important and has an especially problematic intellectual history, as discussed in previous chapters.

What theory do we want?

Not every causal assertion qualifies as a scientific hypothesis.[2] To take an extreme example, a conjecture that herds of mammoths grazing in New York's Central Park are attracted to this urban oasis by the abundance of wild cactuses cannot pass for a scientific hypothesis. Neither mammoths nor wild cactuses can be found in Central Park. Thus, the abovementioned speculation does not

---

[2] This paragraph is inspired by historiographic writings of Mark Solonin: solonin.org/articles

pass the first test of scientific theory: it does not rely on solid data. As the common adage puts it, "garbage in/garbage out". But even if we suppose for the sake of the argument that both mammoths and wild cactuses live in the center of New York City, our conjecture still fails the second test, as it does not accord with what we know about mammoths and cactuses in other environments. Simply put, mammoths do not eat cactuses. Yet even if we assume that the mammoths of Central Park can eat cactuses, can this hypothesis be extended to other pachyderms in other locales? Does it make interesting – and testable – predictions? As Mark Baker once wrote: "The best theory is not the one that brings everything into line with its one favorite fact, but the one that finds the greatest degree of harmony and convergence among all the facts" (2001a: 31).

As we move from the fanciful realm of mammoths and cactuses to the more grounded but still elusive terrain of Indo-European origins and dispersion, an "ideal theory" must fulfill the three general "verification and validation" conditions. It must:

a. rely on solid linguistic, historical, geographical data,
b. be consistent with what we know of languages in general, and
c. account for as many facts as possible, with a minimal theoretical apparatus.

As we show throughout this book, the Gray–Atkinson theory of Indo-European origins and spread fails on all three counts. The data fed into its Bayesian phylogenetic and phylogeographical computational algorithms, whether in the form of linguistic characters, historical dates, or geographical patterns (more on which in Chapters 4, 5, and 6 below, respectively), are severely flawed. Moreover, as discussed in detail in Chapter 7, their assumptions about language diversification, spread, and intergenerational transmission are not consistent with what we know "about languages whose native speakers we can still observe" (Ringe et al. 2002: 60). The Gray–Atkinson model contradicts recent findings in a number of linguistic subfields, including sociolinguistics, language acquisition by children and adults, bilingualism and language attrition, and even findings involving linguistic change in the documented past. Furthermore, the model fails to account for a myriad of facts pertaining to the Indo-European language family that are known from linguistics, history, archeology, geography, and even genetics (although, admittedly, the genetic trace of the speakers of Proto-Indo-European is muddled). In Mark Baker's words, the Gray–Atkinson approach apparently "brings everything into line with its one favorite fact" rather than seeking a systematic convergence of multiple known facts. A number of these blunders will be discussed in later chapters; here we merely give the reader a taste of the most egregious mistakes.

Let us begin with one seemingly minor but deeply revealing error in the Gray–Atkinson "consensus tree" of the Indo-European languages: its placement of Romani, the language (or languages) of the Roma, or "Gypsies", of Europe. Although it positions Romani in the Indo-Aryan subfamily of Indo-European, as has been understood since Johann Rüdiger's pioneering work first published in 1782, the "consensus tree" shows this language as having branched off from the other languages in this subfamily some 3,500 years ago, a date that is almost certainly a whopping 2,500 years too early.[3] Research in historical linguists, genetics, and other fields shows that the ancestors of the Roma departed South Asia around 1000 CE, gradually making their way westward before arriving in Europe circa 1300 CE. Prior to their departure, their language was not sharply differentiated from other tongues of northern India, and hence its separation from the main branch of the Indo-Aryan languages could not have occurred much earlier than a thousand years ago.

Although numerous lines of linguistic evidence, to which we return in more detail in Chapter 5, indicate a relatively recent separation of Romani from the languages of northern India, for the time being we will only mention one: the reassignment of nouns to gender categories, one of the changes characterizing the transition from Middle Indo-Aryan (MIA) to New Indo-Aryan (NIA) languages that happened circa 1000 CE, as evidenced from written records. The MIA languages used a three-gender system – masculine, feminine, and neuter – while most NIA languages feature a two-way distinction between masculine and feminine. In languages in which the neuter category disappeared, formerly neuter nouns were reassigned to either the masculine or feminine gender. Crucially, this transformation occurred in an identical manner in Romani and in Hindi: in both cases, exactly the same neuter nouns became either masculine or feminine (cf. Matras 2002). If Romani had diverged from the language ancestral to Hindi some 3,500 years ago, as the Gray–Atkinson model has it, such independent but identical reassignment would have been, statistically speaking, essentially impossible. But had the ancestral forms of the two languages been part of the same dialect cluster at the time, as standard linguistic theory has it, one would have expected such parallel developments.

What theory we get: "beautiful trees on unstable ground"

The woeful misclassification of Romani in the Gray–Atkinson approach is not a mere aberration, but rather follows systematically from a central flaw of their approach. Their model draws linguistic trees merely on the basis of vocabulary elements derived from common ancestral terms (cognates). Its scope is further narrowed by the choice of a small subset of vocabulary elements – the so-called

---

[3] The revised tree, substituted in December 2013, places the split of the Romani and Kashmiri branch from the rest of the Indo-Aryan languages at 2,600 years before present and the split between Romani and Kashmiri shortly thereafter, at 2,500 years before present.

"basic vocabulary" – chosen on a semi-arbitrary basis, as we discuss in more detail in Chapter 4. Crucially, the Gray–Atkinson research program ignores grammatical and sound changes. The result is "beautiful trees on unstable ground", as Geisler and List (in press) put it; minor changes in the input data result in major changes in the resulting diagrams of linguistic relationship, as evidenced from a comparison of the "consensus trees" in Bouckaert *et al.* (2012) and Gray and Atkinson (2003); see Figures 1 and 2 in the Appendix.

The Gray–Atkinson model essentially treats cognates the same way that genes (or, more specifically, proteins encoded by genes) are treated in biological phylogenies. Cognates are not, however, the linguistic equivalents of genes. To begin with, words are shared among unrelated languages vastly more often than genes are shared among unrelated biological lineages. Although Gray and colleagues claim to have "spent considerable time identifying loanwords and [...] remov[ing] identified loans" (Greenhill and Gray 2012: 528), we show in Chapters 4 and 5 below that unidentified loanwords creep into their data, systematically biasing their findings. The end result is a misshaped family tree with skewed dates for the various splits along its branches. Such problems extend all the way to the Proto-Indo-European (PIE) root of the entire family.

Such failings can again be illustrated with the Romani example. If its vocabulary only is considered, Romani does indeed appear highly distinctive from other Indo-Aryan languages, which would seemingly justify the early date of separation posited by the Gray–Atkinson model. But, as is well documented, Romani borrowed words massively from Greek, Persian, Armenian, and other languages as its speakers migrated from India to Europe (see Matras 2002). Such borrowing masks the language's actual relationships, which become visible only when one examines other aspects of Romani, such as phonology and syntax. Tracing out linguistic family relationships through the analysis of sounds and grammatical forms, as well as that of cognates, is a demanding and often tedious exercise that cannot (yet) be automated, as it requires detailed knowledge of the languages whose mutual relations are being assessed. But as numerous lines of evidence are compared against each other, the results can be robust, at least for those language branches that are relatively well known and historically attested. Replacing these meticulously constructed family trees with diagrams produced on the basis of incomplete and often faulty lists of cognates does not represent a methodological advance.

The Romani fiasco highlights not only the shaky nature of the lexical data that constitutes the foundation of the Gray–Atkinson model, but also its departure from what we "know about languages whose native speakers we can still observe" (Ringe *et al.* 2002: 60). Mainstream historical linguists typically presuppose consistency between contemporary languages and those of the documented past, though they rarely discuss this stipulation explicitly.

Ringe *et al.* (2002: 60), however, elevate this assumption to the level of the Uniformitarian Principle, which holds that:

> we can constrain our hypotheses about the structure and history of languages of the past only by reference to what we know of contemporary language structures, linguistic behavior and changes in progress, since the recoverable information about any language or speech community of the past is always far more limited than what we can know about languages whose native speakers we can still observe [...] Positing for any time in the past any structure or development inconsistent with what is known from modern work on living languages is unacceptable, and positing for prehistory any type of long-term development that we do not observe in documented history is likewise unacceptable.

Recent linguistic research has buttressed the traditional view that most aspects of grammar are more resistant to change than the lexicon. Although all types of linguistic elements – words, sounds, grammatical patterns – can be borrowed, lexical loans are far more common and less restricted than those of grammar and sound. Phonological and morphological borrowing is limited in the sense of what can be transferred under what specific conditions. As Ringe *et al.* (2002: 61) cogently observe, "natively acquired sound systems [...] are resistant to change later in life": anyone who has tried to learn a foreign language as an adult can attest to just how difficult it is to acquire an unfamiliar sound.[4]

At the morphological level, borrowing also tends to be highly constrained, though some elements lend themselves to transfer more easily than others (Winford 2010: 175–181). Matras (2000: 567) summarizes the relevant research (especially Moravcsik 1978 and Thomason and Kaufman 1988; see also Curnow 2001; Aikhenvald 2006; Matras 2009; Haspelmath and Tadmor 2009) by stating that "elements which show structural autonomy and referential stability are more likely to be affected by contact than those which display stronger structural dependency and referential vagueness or abstractness". The borrowing of morphological elements, moreover, is "mediated by lexical borrowing" (Winford 2010: 175; cf. also King 2000). More specifically, free functional elements such as prepositions, conjunctions, pronouns, and complementizers are more likely to be borrowed than bound morphemes (Johanson and Robbeets 2012). Derivational morphemes are borrowed more easily than

---

[4] The only exception to this generalization appears to be phonological – and to a lesser extent, morphosyntactic – borrowing into a speaker's native language in the context of *language attrition*: that is, when the speaker's first language loses the status of his/her dominant tongue. Such cases are often referred to in the literature as "heritage" or "home" languages (see Seliger and Vago 1991; Kaufman 1998; Schmid *et al.* 2004; Pereltsvaig 2004, 2008; and the references cited therein for a more detailed discussion). However, the phenomenon of language attrition is not particularly relevant to the issues at hand, as speakers undergoing attrition rarely if ever transmit their first yet non-dominant language to the next generation. In addition to instances of language attrition, cases where a new, mixed language is created (such as Angloromani and Asia Minor Greek; cf. Thomason and Kaufman 1988) need to be set aside.

inflectional ones, especially if enough loanwords containing them enter the target language.

Such technical consideration can be more easily understood through the use of concrete examples. Borrowed derivational morphemes in English include *-ess*, *-ee*, *-esque*, *-ette*, *-oid*, and *-nik* (Kiparsky 2014: 69). The latter suffix is notable for entering English via Yiddish into which it had been borrowed from Slavic languages. In Yiddish, the agentive *-nik* attaches to roots from a variety of sources: Slavic roots with which it does not appear in donor Slavic languages (e.g. *nudnik* 'a bore, a nuisance'; cf. Russian *zanuda* 'a bore'); Hebrew-derived roots (e.g. *lamed-vovnik* 'one of the 36 Good Men mentioned in the Kabbalah', from Hebrew *lamed-vav* '36'); and English roots (e.g. *alrightnik* 'a successful person, a *nouveau riche*', *refusenik* 'an individual refused permission to emigrate from the Soviet Union', cf. Russian *otkaznik*) (Blech 2000: 230; Jakobs 2005: 157). Thus, at least in Yiddish, *-nik* has a life of its own, independent of the lexical items through which it originally entered the language.

The borrowing of inflectional morphemes appears to be even more limited than that of derivation morphemes; it too typically results from lexical borrowing (Gardani 2008). One example of such a process is the introduction of the plural inflection *-im* into Yiddish from Hebrew via borrowed pairs such as *min/minim* 'kind/kinds'. Borrowing of (morpho-)syntactic patterns is even more restricted and also typically happens as a side-effect of lexical borrowing. As an example, consider the form of the noun used with numerals in the Jerusalem dialect of Domari, an Indo-Aryan language spoken by certain "traditionally nomadic and socially segregated communities throughout the Middle East" (Matras 2012: 1), sometimes likened to the Roma in Europe. Jerusalem Domari uses three sets of numerals: numerals 'two' and 'three' appear with nouns in the singular; numerals from 'four' to 'ten' appear with nouns in the plural; and numerals above 'ten' appear with singular nouns (Matras 2012: 187–201). This complexity derives from the fact that 'two' and 'three' are "inherited numerals" (i.e. they are of the Indo-Aryan origin), whereas all numerals above 'three' are borrowed from Arabic and thus replicate the morphosyntactic pattern found in that language. Likewise, Moravcsik (1978) showed that the rules of linear ordering that apply in the donor language will accompany grammatical elements borrowed from that language.

In contrast to phonological and grammatical borrowing, lexical borrowing is much more widespread. The transfer of vocabulary elements is generally determined – either promoted or hindered – by such considerations as the need to keep abreast of technological developments, considerations of prestige, patterns of social interaction between groups, and language ideology. But even minimal contact between languages is often sufficient to allow the transfer of mere words. Few young people in the Soviet Union in the 1970s and 1980s ever encountered a native speaker of English, yet loanwords such as *šuzy* 'shoes' (typically, 'Western sports shoes'), *truzera* 'trousers' (typically, 'jeans'), *lejbla* 'label', *girla* 'girlfriend', and numerous others penetrated Russian youth slang in that period. Both socially dominant and subordinate languages often borrow terms from one another. For example, English has acquired a great deal of its lexical items from other tongues, some from languages of learning, culture, and prestige such as Latin, Greek, and French, and others from the languages of colonized peoples (e.g. *skunk* and *moccasin* from Algonquian languages, *kangaroo* and *boomerang* from Australian Aboriginal languages, *curry* and *mulligatawny* from Tamil).

The upshot of this discussion is that "morphology and phonology provide better information about linguistic descent [. . .] than lexical evidence" (Ringe *et al.* 2002: 65). This generalization has been understood in historical linguistics at least since Meillet (1925), yet the work within the Gray–Atkinson approach consistently ignores this key principle, focusing instead exclusively on the lexicon. This focus on the vocabulary results in the model's failure to account for the facts beyond those that serve as input into the complex computational tools employed, thus failing the third validation-and-verification criterion listed above. In the following chapter, we turn our attention to the further problems that arise from the exclusive focus on lexical material, which in sum effectively derail the Gray–Atkinson model.

4   Linguistic fallacies of the Bayesian phylogenetic model

The Gray–Atkinson phylogenetic model of Indo-European origins and spread demands a close analysis from a linguistic perspective. Since the publication of the initial articles from the Gray–Atkinson school, reactions from most historical linguists have ranged from scepticism to outright hostility. Some historical linguists have even suggested, explicitly or implicitly, that these scholars, few of whom are linguists, fail to grasp the most basic truths about language. Although some of these charges have no doubt been exaggerated, deep problems with linguistic analysis do undermine the Gray–Atkinson approach, as we shall demonstrate in the following pages.

This chapter lays out four specific fallacies found across the works within the Gray–Atkinson approach. As we show, the authors: (1) ignore the differences between similarities that reflect shared retentions and those that reflect shared innovations; (2) examine only lexical material, which is intrinsically unreliable; (3) inadequately identify borrowings, especially those occurring between closely related languages; and (4) ignore the misplacement of individual languages on the family tree, claiming such errors do not affect the overall shape of the tree or the dating of Proto-Indo-European (PIE) itself. Many of these criticisms have been brought up before (in particular, by Donohue *et al.* 2012a, 2012b) and have been addressed – in our opinion, unsatisfactorily – by Gray and his colleagues (most directly in Greenhill and Gray 2012). As a result, in the critique below we will respond not only to the Gray–Atkinson model itself, especially as laid out in "Mapping the Origins and Expansion of the Indo-European Language Family" (Bouckaert *et al.* 2012), but to their response to earlier criticisms as well.

Fallacy 1. Failure to distinguish innovations from retentions

Historical linguists at least since Brugmann (1884) have understood that only shared innovations – that is, linguistic changes that cannot be reduced to chance parallel developments – provide reliable evidence of common descent. Shared retentions – that is, features inherited from an ancestral language – cannot be taken as solid evidence of common descent along any specific branch of any given language tree. Such common retentions are often found in outlying branches of a language family, often located in peripheral areas that did not experience a particular innovation that spread in the core zone. A good example of such a retention in the peripheral areas of the Indo-European family is the preservation of a primary middle ending with -r (e.g. Latin -tur), which occurred in Latin, Celtic, Tocharian, and Hittite, but not in Germanic or Slavic languages.[1]

A somewhat more complicated example of the contrast between shared retentions and shared innovations is the distinction between *centum* and *satem* Indo-European languages, named after the word for 'hundred' in two representative languages: Latin and Avestan. In *centum* languages, which include those in the Germanic, Romance, and Celtic branches, the palatalized $*\hat{k}$ of PIE became a k.[2] In contrast, in *satem* languages, which include those in the Indo-Iranian, Balto-Slavic, Armenian, and Albanian branches, $*\hat{k}$ became s.[3] It was originally thought that this distinction offered evidence that PIE initially split into two languages, each of which underwent its own set of changes. The *centum–satem* division was thus thought of as "a division between eastern and western cultural provinces (*Kulturkreise*)" (von Bradke 1890: 108). This picture was called into question by the discovery of Tocharian, a now-extinct group of closely related languages once spoken in what is now Xinjiang, China: despite their location at the eastern extremity of the Indo-European range, Tocharian languages nevertheless exhibited signs of *centumization*. If the *centum* development is taken to be evidence of common descent – either because it is analyzed as an innovation or because shared retentions in general are considered to be evidence of common descent on a par with shared innovations – we must hypothesize that Tocharian languages belonged to the same major Indo-European branch as Germanic, Romance, and Celtic languages. But in such a scenario the geographic location of Tocharian is exceedingly difficult to explain: a long-distance migration from the *centum* zone eastwards needs to be postulated. A more recent view is that *centum* languages are simply those that did not undergo the phonological innovation that led to

---

[1] We are grateful to James Clackson (personal communication) for drawing this example to our attention.

[2] Many *centum* languages subsequently underwent other phonological changes that conceal the k derived by *centumization*. For example, most Romance languages (descended from Latin) later underwent a similar palatalization change that resulted in [tʃ], [s], or [θ] sounds in the corresponding words; cf. Italian *cento*, French *cent*, and Spanish *cien* (pronounced with [θ] in European Spanish and with [s] in Latin American Spanish). In Germanic languages, the inherited /k/ became an [h] as a result of the sound change described by Grimm's Law.

[3] A more precise definition of *centumization* is a merger of PIE palatovelars $*\hat{k}$, $*\hat{g}$, $*\hat{g}^h$ and plain velars $*k$, $*g$, $*gh$, yielding plain velars only, but retaining the labiovelars $*k^w$, $*g^w$, and $*g^{wh}$ as a distinct set; *satemization* involved a merger of the PIE labiovelars with the plain velars, while the palatovelars remained distinct.

the emergence of *satem* languages (Fortson 2010: 178).[4] This innovation affected only the geographically central branches of the family, not spreading to those at either the western or the eastern peripheries of the Indo-European realm.[5]

As the Gray–Atkinson approach focuses solely on cognates – words that have been, by definition, inherited from a common proto-language – it has been widely accused of failing to discriminate between shared retentions and shared innovations. For instance, Donohue *et al.* (2012a: 516) point out that the classification of Tongan and Samoan in the same Austronesian subfamily in Gray *et al.* (2009) is erroneously based on shared retentions. Gray's team has countered such charges by claiming that "far from ignoring the distinction between innovations and retentions, our methodology is based on inferring them" (Greenhill and Gray 2012: 526). They further contend that "modern Bayesian phylogenetic methods do not require an a priori distinction between retentions and innovations. Rather innovations are inferred probabilistically in the analysis. They are an outcome rather than an input into the analysis" (Greenhill and Gray 2012: 525). But such inference is exactly the problem! As discussed above, including not only shared innovations but also shared retentions in the input muddles the signal.

Greenhill and Gray defend their approach by arguing that the traditional comparative method suffers from the same flaw: "the distinction between innovations and retentions is not a given in the comparative method, but rather an *outcome* of subgrouping hypotheses, as different subgroupings make different claims about innovations" (Greenhill and Gray 2012: 525). This argument, however, is based on a misunderstanding of the comparative method, which in many cases does not require prior subgroupings in order to distinguish innovations from retentions. Such judgments can often (though not always) be made solely on the types of proposed changes themselves. As an illustration, consider how the two methods would reconstruct the morpheme for 'nose' in Proto-Polynesian, based on cognates in five descendant languages, listed in Table 4.1 (based on Donohue *et al.* 2012b: 542, Table 1). As noted by Donohue *et al.* (2012b: 542), "a stochastic method would, with high probability, assume **ihu*, since the **s* is preserved as such only in Nuclear Polynesian, whereas **h* is found at all levels of the Polynesian tree". The comparative method, however, would reconstruct the form as **isu*, since the

---

[4] More precisely, *centumization* can be thought of as bleeding the environment for *satemization* by removing the palatovelars from the language, leaving none to *satemize*. It should be pointed out, however, that not all of the *satem* languages seem to have undergone the innovation in the same way: for example, some evidence exists in Armenian and Albanian, as well as possibly in Sanskrit, for the non-merger of velars and labiovelars. We thank James Clackson (personal communication) for his comments on this topic.

[5] The position of Hittite, and of the Anatolian languages more generally, on the *centum–satem* divide is a more complicated matter still, which we will leave aside.

Table 4.1 *The word 'nose' in Polynesian languages*

Polynesian	Tongic	Tongan	ihu
		Niuean	ihu
	Nuclear Polynesian	Anuta	iu
		Emae	isu
		Hawaiian	ihu

change from /s/ to /h/, known as debuccalization, is widely attested across all language groupings, especially in intervocalic position, while the reverse change is virtually unknown.

Having assembled deep troves of information about language changes, historical linguists realized long ago that many phonological and grammatical changes are unidirectional. One notable grammatical change that applies in only one direction is the development of articles from demonstratives. Such a development is attested in various language groups, including Germanic and Romance, where the change happened independently. Although articles can emerge in other ways, the reverse transformation from articles to demonstratives is unknown. Likewise, case markers often arise from postpositions, but postpositions are never created out of case markers. Similarly, tense affixes may arise from auxiliary verbs, but the opposite does not occur. Numerous other examples of grammaticalization of free morphemes into bound morphemes can be brought to illustrate this point.

Many sound changes likewise are unidirectional. Debuccalization, mentioned above, is an instance of a more general phonological process known as lenition (weakening). Lenition may also involve (some combination of) voicing, spirantization (i.e. a stop sound becoming a fricative or an affricate), or the deletion of consonants. Lenition in an intervocalic position (i.e. between vowels) is extremely common cross-linguistically, both as a historical change and as a synchronic process.[6] Consider the development of the intervocalic consonant of the Latin *vita* 'life' in its Romance descendants: Italian retained the voiceless stop (*vita*), Portuguese voiced the stop (*vida*), (European) Spanish both voiced the consonant and turned into a fricative (pronounced [viða]), and French deleted the consonant altogether (*vie*). The reverse change in which the consonant is strengthened (fortition), particularly in the intervocalic position, is much less common: although a development of fricatives into stops intervocalically is well documented in Germanic and Romance (e.g. Latin

---

[6] Examples of synchronic lenition include the so-called *rendaku* in Japanese and the so-called *beged-kefet* rule in Hebrew.

medius from the earlier **međyo-*), devoicing of voiced consonants in the intervocalic position is virtually unknown.[7]

Another example of a "one-way" phonological change involves the palatalization of velars, such as turning /k/ into /s/, /ʃ/, /ts/, or /tʃ/.[8] This change is very common cross-linguistically. The second members of English doublets such as *kirk* vs. *church*, *dike* vs. *ditch*, and *skirt* vs. *shirt* reveal signs of palatalization from the earlier Germanic /k/ into /tʃ/ or /ʃ/. In the Romance grouping, palatalization turned the /k/ of Latin into /ʃ/ in French: the Latin *causam* 'thing' and *cattum* 'cat' became the French *chose* and *chat*. This change, however, happened only before /a/, so that the /k/ in Latin *corem* 'heart' was retained in the French *coeur*. A set of similar palatalization changes marks the history of Slavic languages (see Schenker 1995: 83–84, 89–92). For example, the Proto-Slavic /k/ in *kendŏ* 'child' (cognate with the Proto-Germanic **kinda* 'child, infant') and *vŭlkījĭ* 'pertaining to a wolf' turned into /tʃ/ in the Russian words *čado* and *volčij* (this change too applied only in front of certain vowels, which may have changed or dropped out completely in a later period). A later palatalization process in some Slavic languages turned other instances of /k/ into /ts/, as in Proto-Slavic **kwajtu* 'flower' developing into Russian *cvet* (pronounced [tsvet]). Palatalization of velars is also well documented in languages outside the Indo-European family. For example, a **k > č* change must have occurred in Mayan languages such as Cholan sometime before 250 CE (Campbell 2000: 5). The reverse change, however, which would involve /s/, /ʃ/, /ts/, or /tʃ/ turning into a /k/, has not been attested. Thus, we can safely assume that languages with a velar sound in a given linguistic branch are conservative, whereas those with a corresponding palatal or alveolar sound are innovative. Crucially, we need not have a family tree to make that judgment.

As another example, consider the correspondence between /k/ and /ts/ in Slavic languages, illustrated in Table 4.2 with the word 'whole' in a few representative languages from the three Slavic subgroupings: West, South, and East Slavic. As can be seen from Table 4.2, all Slavic languages have a root for this meaning beginning with /ts/, except one: the Novgorod dialect of Old Russian.[9] Several birch bark documents written in the Novgorod dialect contain forms with a velar sound rather than a palatal or alveolar sound expected on the basis of Modern Russian, other modern Slavic languages, and Old Russian forms from southern Russian manuscripts. For example, birch bark letter #247 dating from the eleventh century contains two instances of

---

[7] We thank James Clackson and Stephane Goyette (personal communication) for helpful discussions of this point.

[8] For the definitions of "velars" and "palatalization", see the Glossary.

[9] The Novgorod dialect of Old Russian is known from more than a thousand birch bark documents found in the last sixty years near the city of Novgorod in northwestern Russia.

Table 4.2 *The root 'whole' in Slavic languages*[10]

West Slavic	Polish	cał-
	Czech, Slovak	cel-
South Slavic	Bulgarian	tsjal-
	Serbian	tsel-
East Slavic	Russian	tsel-
	Belarusian	tsèl-
	Ukrainian	tsil-
	Old Novgorod	kěl-

kěl- 'whole', while birch bark letter #130 exhibits several instances of *xěr-* 'gray cloth', cognate with Modern Russian *seryj* [serɪj] 'gray' and Polish *szary* [šary] 'gray'.

As in the Polynesian example discussed above, a stochastic method applied to the data in Table 4.2 would almost certainly reconstruct the Proto-Slavic form for 'whole' as beginning with /ts/, as the initial /k/ appears only in one language of one branch, East Slavic, whereas /ts/ is found at all levels of the Slavic tree. Based on this analysis, the Novgorod dialect of Old Russian would be regarded as the innovative member of the family. In contrast, the comparative method reconstructs the Proto-Slavic form with the initial **k*, which later turned into /ts/ as part of a more general phonological process known as the Second Slavic Palatalization.[11] As mentioned above, this change is an example of a more general historical phonological process, lenition. Thus, contrary to the Bayesian phylogenetic method developed by the Gray–Atkinson school, which groups languages first and then seeks to identify innovations based on those groupings, the classical comparative method identifies innovations first, then bases the grouping decisions on shared patterns of innovations rather than retentions.

Fallacy 2. Exclusive dependence on the lexical level, which is intrinsically unreliable

A second common criticism against the Gray–Atkinson model concerns their exclusive reliance on *vocabulary* in constructing language trees, ignoring

---

[10] Languages using Roman script are given in traditional orthography, while languages using Cyrillic are given in transliteration. The symbol *c* is pronounced as [ts].

[11] The consensus among Slavicists is that there were three waves of palatalization in Slavic languages, though there is uncertainty as to whether the innovation commonly called the "Third Slavic Palatalization" indeed happened *after* the Second Slavic Palatalization or *before* it.

phonological and grammatical systems, from which they draw grandiose conclusions about *languages* as a whole. Such erroneous equation of "language" with "lexicon" is common enough in lay discourse about language: for example, in a recent *New York Times* article entitled "What Our Words Tell Us", David Brooks equated the changing frequencies of certain words, as seen in Google Ngram Viewer, as "gradual shifts in language" mirroring cultural change.[12] In another *New York Times* piece, titled "Labels of Married Life, in a New Light", Margot Page reflected on her feelings about the traditional "language", as she called it (not "lexicon" or "vocabulary"!), associated with the institution of marriage.[13] One would hope that this confusion of "words" and "language" would not creep into ostensibly professional linguistic articles, yet it sometimes does. For example, it is evident in the first sentence of the abstract in Pagel *et al.* (2013: 8471):

> The search for ever deeper relationships among the World's **languages** is bedeviled by the fact that most **words** evolve too rapidly to reserve evidence of their ancestry beyond 5,000 to 9,000 years. (boldface ours)

The focus on vocabulary, at the exclusion of grammar, is particularly dangerous in historical linguistics. As Jaakko Häkkinen has noted, "a word appears, disappears or gets replaced independently from all the other words, but sound change affects the whole vocabulary" (2012: 2). Grammatical changes are likewise systematic and holistic. The same point is echoed in Nakhleh *et al.* (2005: 172): "analyses based upon datasets that use only lexical characters [are] probably less accurate than analyses based upon datasets that include morphological and phonological characters". The problems associated with an exclusive reliance on vocabulary have been understood since Meillet (1908: 126), who noted that "Les coincidences de vocabulaire n'ont en general qu'une très petite valeur probante" ["Coincidences of vocabulary are in general of very little probative value"].

Gray and his colleagues counter these criticisms by claiming that their methods are robust enough to avoid the problems faced by older lexicostatistical methods that similarly prioritized the lexicon. But before we address those problems in detail, we need to specify the procedures involved in the Gray–Atkinson method of family tree construction. Following Geisler and List (in press), the procedure used to generate their phylogenetic trees can be broken down into five steps.[14] The first step is to compile a list of meanings

---

[12] Published May 20, 2013 and available online at www.nytimes.com/2013/05/21/opinion/brooks-what-our-words-tell-us.html?_r=2&

[13] Published January 18, 2013 and available online at www.nytimes.com/2013/01/20/fashion/labels-of-married-life-in-a-new-light-modern-love.html?pagewanted=all

[14] The procedures involved in dating the splits on the phylogenetic tree and mapping the tree are discussed in Chapters 5 and 8 of this book.

to be compared (such as a Swadesh list, as discussed below). The second step is to find an appropriate word that expresses each meaning in the list compiled in step 1. The third step involves deciding which words across languages constitute cognate sets. In step 4, the cognacy judgments are converted to a numerical format. Finally, the numerical data are analyzed computationally in order to draw conclusions regarding the phylogeny of the languages under investigation. Steps 4 and 5, which involve the computational procedures, have been discussed in more detail in Nakhleh *et al.* (2005), Atkinson *et al.* (2005), McMahon and McMahon (2008), Nichols and Warnow (2008), among others; here we shall focus on steps 1–3 and the problems associated with them. As we shall see below, inconsistency and subjectivity are built into each of these first three procedures, thus violating a crucial scientific criterion, that of objectivity (Heggarty 2000: 534).

Given the vast size of the lexicon of all human languages, step 1 involves selecting a limited set of vocabulary items to be considered. It is often thought that analyzing only a small selection of words, the so-called "basic vocabulary" (identified in the work of Morris Swadesh; cf. Swadesh 1950, 1952, 1955), allows researchers to avoid most instances of borrowing across languages. Hence, basic vocabulary lists, which include kinship terms such as 'mother' and 'father', body parts like 'belly' and 'breast', adjectives like 'bad' and 'small', and verbs such as 'die', 'vomit', and 'sleep', have become the staple of both the older forms of lexicostatistical analysis and the newer quantificational methods used in historical linguistics. Unfortunately, no single Swadesh list has been generally accepted (see McMahon and McMahon 2005: Chapter 2). Instead, one finds 100-meaning and 200-meaning Swadesh lists (henceforth, Swadesh-100 and Swadesh-200), as well as variant lists proposed specifically for languages found in Australia (Alpher and Nash 1999), Southeast Asia (Matisoff 2000), and the Andes (McMahon *et al.* 2005). These modified versions of the Swadesh list contain items deemed "culturally appropriate" for the language family under investigation, as well as multiple equivalents of certain meanings for which it is impossible to find single equivalents.

Although Gray, Atkinson, and colleagues maintain that the words in Swadesh lists are generally stable across time, unlikely to change, and resistant to borrowing, a quick examination of results based on the Swadesh-100 and Swadesh-200 lists shows how problematic these assumptions can be. As pointed out by Häkkinen (2012: 2–3), studies using Swadesh-200 tend to incorrectly group Germanic and Italic together after the split from Celtic, while those using Swadesh-100 (e.g. Atkinson and Gray 2006) correctly group Italic and Celtic together after Germanic splits off. However, with the Swadesh-200 list, Greek and Armenian correctly form a common branch, but with the Swadesh-100 list they do not. In their 2006 article, Atkinson and Gray contended that Swadesh-100 is more reliable than Swadesh-200, as the shorter list is limited to words that are least prone to borrowing, a proposition confirmed by the calculations of McMahon and McMahon (2006: 157). Note, furthermore, that studies based on Swadesh-100 identify the Italo-Celtic branch but not the Greco-Armenian branch; although historical linguists disagree about the validity of these two groupings, evidence from shared phonological and morphological changes supports the Italo-Celtic branch but not the Greco-Armenian branch, which is supported solely by lexical evidence (see Clackson 1994; Ringe *et al*. 2002: 103). Curiously, "Mapping the Origins" uses the Swadesh-200 list, which two of the article's lead authors disparaged as less reliable than the Swadesh-100 list six years earlier.

But the problems of the Gray–Atkinson method run much deeper than the selection of Swadesh lists. Step 2, which involves finding appropriate words to express the given meanings, is even more fraught. As pointed out by Slaska (2005: 221), "the issue of how exactly these [predefined meaning] slots should be filled in the first instance has been curiously ignored" by the practitioners of lexicostatistic and Bayesian phylogenetic methods alike. Seminal articles, such as Gudschinsky (1956) and Hymes (1960), remain silent on this issue. Morris Swadesh's own criteria for selecting an appropriate word that expresses each meaning are quite vague: he instructs to list "the common, everyday equivalent" (1955: 122). But what constitutes "the common, everyday equivalent" is not always clear in practice, as shown conclusively in Slaska's work: linguists and native speakers may have different opinions on the matter, and even native speakers who are members of the same linguistic community may disagree, as they indeed have in Slaska's experimental work.

Consider, for example, "the common, everyday equivalent" of the meaning 'guts' in French. Different linguists have proposed varying answers: Rea (1973) proposes *entreilles* (*sic*), while Wittman (1973) lists both *tripes* and *intestines*. The latter word is also listed in Kessler (2001), whereas the best-known and most widely used Indo-European database (Dyen *et al*. 1992) fills this meaning slot in French with *boyau*. Similarly, what English word should be selected as the equivalent of the Latin *homō*? Swadesh (1971) proposed *person*, Ringe (1992: 13) has *human (being)*, but one could also argue for the choice of *man*, which at least in its early history meant 'person of either gender', although now it generally refers only to males. But as it turns out, the gender-specific meaning of *man* is relatively new and the gender-neutral meaning is still evident in such terms as *mankind*, *manslaughter*, and *no man's land*. In Old English, *man* (or *mann*) also had additional meanings, including 'servant, vassal', apparent today in the expression *all the king's horses and all the king's men*. The sense of 'adult male' was acquired by *man* only in the Middle English period. In Old English, the meaning 'adult male' was expressed by the word *wer*, which began to disappear in the late thirteenth century and was eventually replaced by *man*, which retained its old, gender-neutral meaning as it acquired its new, gender-specific one. The root *wer* did survive, however, in such words as *werewolf*. Changes in meaning, as in the case of *man*, conceal the preservation of cognates in the language, another issue that tends to be ignored by proponents of lexicostatistics and of the newer quantificational methods alike.

Another often-cited example from English concerns the equivalent for the German *Hund*. The "common, everyday equivalent" in present-day English is unequivocally *dog*; thus the creators of the BBC series *Sherlock*, which takes place in twenty-first-century England, had to be creative in order to explain why a contemporary speaker of English referred to the ghastly apparition as a *hound* of Baskerville, rather than merely a *dog*.[15] However, selecting the word *dog* as "the common, everyday equivalent" of *Hund* conceals the existence of the English cognate *hound*, which in the Old English period meant 'dog' in general but subsequently narrowed its meaning to 'dog used for hunting'. Many additional examples of meaning changes resulting in biased analysis could easily be cited.

While armchair linguists and lexicographers may argue over such examples, data elicited from native speakers is no less ambiguous. According to Slaska's (2005) elicitation study of seventy-two monolingual English-speaking 15-year-old students in Sheffield, every one of forty examined meanings produced more than one lexeme; for three-quarters of the meanings, five or more lexemes were given by the pupils. The meanings 'hit', 'fight', 'vomit', 'child', and 'fear' produced ten or more each. Only a small minority of students, for example, gave the word *vomit* for the meaning 'to vomit'; other lexemes, such as *throw up* and *be sick* were more frequently provided. Even such seemingly trivial choices as the lexeme *child* for the meaning 'child' are not as obvious as they may seem: only twenty-six speakers in Slaska's study selected this term, while nineteen chose *kid* and thirteen picked *toddler*. Other items, such as *chabby*, *baby*, *brat*, *nipper*, and *youngster* were proposed as well. As shown by Slaska, factors such as dialect, register, and even in-group vocabulary affect what is perceived as "the common, everyday equivalent" for a given meaning. Curiously, Slaska found that the lexemes provided by monolingual speakers were more variable than those obtained from bilingual speakers. Still, her overarching conclusion is that "the overall degree of variation uncovered contradicts entirely the one-word-per-meaning assumption prevalent in the lexicostatistical literature" (Slaska 2005: 239).

Depending on the language, particular meanings may present specific problems. As mentioned above, dialect and sociolect variation produce discrepancies in the translation of basic vocabulary meanings. For instance, German has two

---

[15] Screenwriter Mark Gatiss transformed Conan Doyle's monstrous creature from a dog into a man wearing a gas mask and a sweater with the acronym H.O.U.N.D.

Table 4.3 *Meanings with multiple lexemes in Russian*

Meaning	Lexeme in the IELEX database[16]	Alternative lexeme
'moon'	luna	mesjac
'eye'	glaz	oko
'earth'	zemlja	počva
'road'	doroga	put'
'cloud'	oblako	tuča
'child'	rebënok	ditja, čado
'animal'	životnoe	zver'
'dog'	sobaka	pës
'guts'	kiški	vnutrennosti
'ashes'	zola	pepel
'other'	drugoj	inoj
'big'	bol'šoj	velikij
'long'	dlinnyj	dolgij
'small'	malen'kij	malyj
'short'	korotkij	kratkij
'good'	xorošij	dobryj
'bad'	ploxoj	zloj
'smooth'	gladkij	rovnyj
'say'	govorit'	skazat'
'push'	tolkat'	pixat'
'dig'	ryt'	kopat'
'throw'	brosat'	kidat'
'eat'	est'	kušat'
'walk'	xodit'	idti
'come'	prixodit'	priezžat'
'vomit'	rvat'	blevat', vytošnit'
'know'	znat'	vedat'
'cut'	rezat'	rubit'
'here'	zdes'	tut

"common, everyday equivalents" of 'to kill': *umbringen* is a colloquial term, while *töten* is a formal variant. For other meanings, the target language may offer more than one translation because the language makes a specific differentiation not accounted for by the compilers of the Swadesh lists. For example, the basic concept 'bird' can be translated into Spanish or Portuguese in two ways: Spanish *pájaro* and Portuguese *pássaro* refer to small birds and *ave* in both languages refers to large birds. Similarly, 'to know' can be translated into German as either *wissen* or *kennen* and into French as either *savoir* or *connaître* (the former French word is used for 'knowing facts', while the latter

---

[16] See http://ielex.mpi.nl./language/Russian/

is for 'knowing people'). The choice between *little* and *small* in English, with their various cognates in other Germanic languages, is another vexing case, much discussed in the literature.

Our study of the Russian Swadesh list provides further illustration of these problems. In Russian, a large number of the meanings from the Swadesh-200 list can be expressed in multiple ways, without a single obvious, unambiguous "common, everyday equivalent". Table 4.3 lists twenty-nine such meanings, nearly 15 percent of the Swadesh list.

As can be seen from this table, such problematic meanings are found in all lexical categories: nouns, adjectives, verbs, and even adverbs. For example, the meaning 'eye' can be expressed as either *glaz* or *oko* and that of 'child' as *rebënok* or *ditja*: the latter word in each pair belongs to a higher register and is somewhat archaic but still used.[17] Likewise, the meaning 'earth' can be rendered as either *zemlja* or *počva*; the latter is specific to the meaning indicated in the Swadesh list ('earth' = 'soil', not the planet), whereas *zemlja* can be used for both 'soil' and the Earth. Similarly, *mesjac* means both 'moon' and 'month', but *luna* means only the former. Another problematic pair is the words for 'ash(es)', *zola* and *pepel*. The former is listed in the IELEX database, yet the latter is about five times more frequent in a corpus (cf. Sharoff 2002). The differences in meaning are very subtle indeed: our informal survey of fifteen native speakers reveals that in many contexts the two words are interchangeable, yet in other cases, speakers have a very strong preference for one or the other word. For example, ash in a fireplace is *zola*, ash in an ashtray is *pepel*, and ash in a campfire is *zola* to some speakers and *pepel* to others. A volcanic eruption produces *pepel*, as does cremation of human remains, but *zola* is used as a fertilizer. *Zola* may be darker and may contain bits of the burned substance, while *pepel* is more light-colored and dust-like. The two words also differ in their collocational uses: one sprinkles *pepel* over one's head (as a sign of mourning; cf. Book of Esther, 4:1), but Cinderella is *Zoluška*, not *Pepeluška*.

Adjectives too are not always indisputably translatable, nor are verbs.[18] For instance, the basic verb meaning 'to eat' can be translatable as either *est'*

[17] To further complicate matters, the plural of *rebënok* is *deti*, formed by suppletion from the root of *ditja*. Another alternative lexeme for 'child' is *čado* (mentioned in the main text above). Unlike *rebënok* and *ditja*, *čado* is a cognate of English *child*.

[18] Another example is the meaning 'hot', which appeared in some earlier versions of the Swadesh list, but not in the version used in the IELEX database, which the Gray–Atkinson team relies on. This meaning can be rendered in Russian as either *gorjačij* or *žarkij*. Generally speaking, the former word has a wider range of applications and is more frequent, but in some cases the choice is collocational: for example, a Google search reveals that *gorjačie ob"jatija* 'hot embraces' is nearly five times more common than *žarkije ob"jatija*, yet *žarkij poceluj* 'hot kiss' is nearly three hundred (!) times more frequent than *gorjačij poceluj*. In other collocations, the two adjectives have subtle differences in meaning: for instance, *žarkij sviter* 'hot sweater'

or *kušat'*, depending on the register and who is engaged in eating, and 'to cut' can be either *rezat'* or *rubit'*, depending on how the cut is made: *rezat'* means cutting with a horizontal motion and *rubit'* means cutting with a vertical motion. The aspectual contrast between perfective and imperfective forms (which, simplifying greatly, refer to completed vs. ongoing events) further complicates matters with Russian verbs, though in many cases perfective and imperfective verbs share the same root. However, verbs of motion in Russian come in two versions, depending on whether the motion is unidirectional or not; in some cases, such as 'walk', two different roots may be involved, as in *idti* (unidirectional) vs. *xodit'* (non-unidirectional). The way that one expresses the meaning 'come' in Russian depends not only on aspect and unidirectionality, as mentioned above, but also on whether one arrives by foot (*pridti/prixodit'*) or by some transport vehicle (*priexat'/ priezžat'*). In some cases, the choice of the lexeme selected in the IELEX database, which the Gray–Atkinson team relies on, appears to depend on lexical frequency (as determined in accordance with Sharoff 2002). For example, *brosat'* 'to throw' is almost four times more commonly used than *kidat'*, *est'* 'to eat' is almost seven times more frequent than *kušat'*, and *drugoj* 'other' is nearly ten times more frequent than *inoj*. But frequency does not always coincide with the choices made in the IELEX database: for instance, *put'* 'road' and *doroga* are equally frequent in Sharoff's corpus, *tut* 'here' is about one and a half times more common than *zdes'*,[19] *rovnyj* 'smooth' appears twice as often as *gladkij*, and *idti* 'walk' is almost three times more frequent than *xodit'*.[20]

Kassian *et al.* (2010) attempt to explain and justify the choice of particular items for the English and Russian Swadesh lists (working with a modified version of the 100-word list). Yet these authors readily admit that they "do not pretend to completeness of the offered solutions", conceding that their justifications are "entry-specific" (and therefore necessarily language-specific) (2010: 47). In particular, they provide justifications for fifteen of the lexeme choices in the IELEX database (listed in the middle column in Table 4.3), but they also justify the choice of two alternative lexemes not selected in the

---

means a sweater that makes the wearer feel hot, while *gorjačij sviter* refers to a garment that is hot to touch (e.g. just pulled out of a dryer). Crucially, for our present purposes, only *žarkij* can be used for weather, the meaning specified in Swadesh (1952).

[19] Note the Russian idiom *Zdes' vam ne tut* (variant *Tut vam ne zdes'*; literally, 'Here for you isn't here'), said to underscore the addressee's lack of knowledge about the subject being discussed. It is ascribed alternatively to army folklore or to Viktor Černomyrdin (former prime minister of Russia, known for his personal idioms bordering on absurd and ungrammatical).

[20] It is also worth noting that the frequency of some of the most and least frequent of the words in the Swadesh list differs by two orders of magnitude.

IELEX database (listed in the right column in Table 4.3): *idti* 'to walk, go' and *skazat'* 'to say' (Kassian *et al.* 2010: 62, 75). They explain their departure from the IELEX lexeme choices in the latter two cases by analyzing *xodit'* 'to walk, go' and *govorit'* 'to say' as denoting a "durative action" (translating *govorit'* as 'to talk'). While we agree with their explanation for 'to say', an alternative analysis of 'to walk, go', with *xodit'* rather than *idti* as the unmarked lexeme is readily available (for detailed discussions of this issue, see the various contributions in Hasko and Perelmutter 2010, especially Kagan 2010). We also do not subscribe to Kassian *et al.*'s (2010: 51) choice of *zola* rather than *pepel* for the meaning 'ashes' (see our discussion above).

The issues identified above in compiling Swadesh lists for extant, well-documented languages are greatly compounded when such lists are created for extinct languages or earlier stages of modern ones. Based on what we know of languages spoken today, we must assume that speakers of Hittite, Latin, or Ancient Greek would have provided word lists as varied as those produced by Slaska's subjects from Sheffield. Copious written records from these languages contain extensive lexical information that indicates that the same factors of dialect, register, and the like were always at play. Hence, the choices of lexemes for Swadesh list meanings made by lexical database compilers for these languages are just as fraught with problems as the French or Russian lists are. Even more problematic are Swadesh lists for languages such as Luwian (see Yakubovitch 2010, 2011), which is known from a relatively small corpus of surviving texts, or Illyrian, which left nothing but a few names and glosses. Because of the paucity of lexical material from such little-known languages, studies based on Swadesh lists often exclude them from consideration entirely, which introduces preservation bias that can further compromise the project.

But even for languages that are well documented in both modern and earlier stages, an over-reliance on the lexical level can distort the analysis. A good example of such difficulties involves the Germanic languages. It has long been noted that the Germanic grouping poses problems in terms of both its position in the overall Indo-European tree (cf. Ringe *et al.* 2002) and of its internal classification (cf. Nielsen 1981; Forster *et al.* 2006). The accepted consensus is to divide Germanic languages into three branches. East Germanic (represented by extinct Gothic), North Germanic (or Scandinavian, including Icelandic, Faroese, Danish, Norwegian, and Swedish), and West Germanic (including German, Yiddish, Dutch, Frisian, and Afrikaans). The position of English within that classification scheme is most troublesome. Studies relying exclusively on lexical material either classify English as an aberrant branch of West Germanic (Gray and Atkinson 2003; Bouckaert *et al.* 2012) or place it in its own, distinct branch, closer to North Germanic than to West Germanic (cf. Forster *et al.* 2006). In contrast, an examination of phonological and grammatical

Table 4.4 *Vowels ē, ǣ, and ā in older Germanic languages*

	Old English	Old Frisian	Old Saxon	Old High German	Old Norse	Gothic
'deed'	dǣd	dēd	dād	tāt	dáð	gadēþs
'were' (pl.)	wǣron	wēron	wārun	wārun	váru	wēsun

innovations within Germanic reveals English to be within the West Germanic branch, most closely related to Frisian (Nielsen 1981; Robinson 1992; Mugglestone 2006). Historical information seals the case. English clearly traces back to the tongues of the Angles and Saxons, which were both closely related to and in extensive contact with the language of the ancient Frisians.[21]

One shared phonological innovation, which supports the grouping of Old English and Old Frisian (as well as Old Saxon, but not Old High German, or North and East Germanic languages) is the loss of an original *n* or *m* between a vowel and *f*, *þ*, or *s*, as illustrated by Old English *fīf*, Old Frisian *fīf*, in contrast with Gothic *fimf* 'five' (Robinson 1992: 159, 192; Hoad 2006: 26). Another phonological feature that separates Old English and Old Frisian from other Germanic languages concerns pronunciation of certain vowels (Robinson 1992: 157, 191; Hoad 2006: 27–28). Specifically, Old English and Old Frisian both have *ē* or *ǣ*, where other West Germanic languages (Old Saxon, Old High German) and North Germanic languages (Old Norse) have *ā*, and East Germanic (Gothic) has *ē*. This pattern is illustrated in Table 4.4 with the words 'deed' and 'were'.

However, it is not clear whether such vowel patterns are a case of shared innovation or shared retention. Under the former scenario, all Germanic languages except Gothic originally changed the vowel *ǣ* to *ā* and then Old English and Old Frisian later changed the *ā* back to *ǣ*. While this possibility may seem unlikely, evidence does exist for the intermediate stage when Old English had *ā*: this vowel appears written as *ā* in some texts under certain circumstances, especially before *w* (Robinson 1992: 157). An alternative analysis, however, treats this similarity as a shared retention: under this scenario, Old Frisian and Old English have merely preserved the inherited Proto-Germanic vowel unchanged, along with Gothic, while the other languages innovated with *ā*. Under this analysis, the shared retention provides no information on the grouping of the three languages: Old English, Old Frisian, and Gothic.

---

[21] Unfortunately, the oldest surviving texts in Old Frisian date from the second half of the thirteenth century, though some of them are copies of eleventh-century manuscripts. Older texts in Old Frisian must have existed but were lost during the Viking incursions.

Fortunately, Old English and Old Frisian share an important grammatical innovation (Old Saxon has it too): they use the same form of the first- and second-person pronouns for the accusative case ('Please help *me*') and the dative case ('Give the book to *me*'). In Old Frisian *mī* 'me' and *thī* 'you' (singular) served as both accusative and dative forms, whereas in Old English *mē* and *þē* did. In contrast, Gothic, Old Norse, and Old High German have distinct accusative and dative forms: Gothic *mik* and *mis* for 'me', *þuk* and *þus* for 'you'; Old Norse *mik* and *mér* for 'me', *þik* and *þér* for 'you'; and Old High German *mih* and *mir* for 'me', *dih* and *dir* for 'you' (see Nielsen 1981: 113; Robinson 1992: 160–161; Hoad 2006).

Due to such shared innovations, most scholars of Germanic languages believe that English and Frisian stemmed from a common ancestral tongue, while accounting for whatever similarities are found between English and the Scandinavian languages in some alternative way. Many grammatical similarities found here are explained as parallel developments. For instance, parallelism seems most appropriate for the Subject–Verb–Object (SVO) order in both English and the Scandinavian languages, as opposed to the Subject–Object–Verb (SOV) found in German and Dutch. Old English shared with other West Germanic languages the possibility of the SOV order, although it also allowed alternative word orders including SVO, as illustrated in the examples below from *The Homilies of the Anglo-Saxon Church, containing Sermones Catholici or Homilies of Ælfric*, composed in the late tenth or early eleventh century.[22]

SOV in Old English:

On	twam	þingum	hæfde	God	þæs	mannes	sawle	**gegodod**
in	two	things	had	God	the	man's	soul	endowed

'With two things God had endowed man's soul.'

SVO in Old English:

þæt	he	nolde	**niman**	mancyn	neadunga	of	ðam	deofle
that	he	not-would	take	mankind	forcibly	from	the	devil

'That he would not have taken mankind forcibly from the devil.'

The emergence of SVO as the basic/default order in English was neither inherited from a common ancestor with the North Germanic languages, nor was it a grammatical borrowing from Old Norse. In all likelihood, this feature resulted from the changing frequency of the two pre-existing patterns, which happened gradually during the Middle English period (i.e. eleventh to fifteenth centuries). Another construction shared by English and the Scandinavian languages that is best explained by way of parallel developments is the phrasal genitive in which *'s* attaches to the whole phrase rather than its head, as in *the Queen of England's hat* or *Mom and Dad's only child*.

---

[22] Available online at gutenberg.org/files/38334/38334-h/38334-h.htm

In contrast, lexical items shared between English and Scandinavian languages – other than inherited cognates – are typically borrowings from Old
Norse into Old English, including basic kinship terms (*sister, husband*), body
parts (*leg, neck, skin*), other common nouns (*dirt, sky, window*), adjectives
(*flat, loose, ugly*), and verbs (*drag, get, smile*).[23] Norse borrowings are so
common in English that one can produce whole sentences, such as *The guests
cut the rotten cake with a knife*, where all words except the articles *the* and
a are traceable to Scandinavian sources.[24] As we shall see in the following
section, borrowing is a fundamental problem for Bayesian phylogenetic
analyses, precisely because they rely exclusively on lexical material.

Fallacy 3. Inadequate identification of borrowings

Step 3 in the Gray–Atkinson method, which involves making cognacy judgments, is also highly problematic. By definition, cognates are words that can be
traced back to a common ancestral form. For example, English *night*, French
nuit, and Lithuanian *naktis* can be traced back to a common PIE root *$nók^w t$-.[25]
Cognates are rarely identical in form, as each language undergoes its own set
of sound changes. For example, the Spanish word for 'leaf', *hoja* (pronounced
/oxa/) is cognate with the French *feuille* (pronounced /føj/), even though they
do not share a single sound.[26] Yet both words can be traced to the Latin *folia*
(pronounced /folja/), and the widely different pronunciations in Spanish and
French arose from distinct sound changes in the two languages: in Spanish the
initial /f/ was lost and /lj/ became a /x/, while in French the final /a/ was
deleted, /lj/ became /j/ and stressed /o/ became /ø/, while the initial /f/ remained

[23] Northern English dialects, spoken in areas that once constituted the Viking-dominated Danelaw, contain additional words from Old Norse, such as *fell* 'hill, mountain' (compare with Norwegian *fjell*) and *kenning* 'knowledge' (compare with Swedish *kännedom* 'understanding, cognizance'). In northern English cities such as Leeds and York, toponyms with *-gate* like Briggate and Kirkgate translate as 'Bridge Street' and 'Church Street' because in Scandinavian *gate* means 'street'; in contrast, in London places such as Aldgate and Newgate actually refer to former gates in the city wall.

[24] In addition to numerous complete Norse loanwords that entered English during the Viking period, in some cases the influence of Old Norse on the English lexicon was more subtle. For example, the word *with* existed in Old English in the form of *wið* meaning 'against, opposite, toward'; this older meaning is preserved in compounds such as *withhold*, *withdraw*, and *withstand*. The influence of the Old Norse *vidh* is responsible for the meaning shift in Middle English to denote association, combination, and union. In this meaning, *with* replaced the Old English *mid* 'with', which survives only as a prefix, as in *midwife*, literally 'woman who is "with"' (the mother at birth). The original sense of *wife* 'woman' (regardless of marital status) is also preserved in the expression *old wives' tale*.

[25] Here and below, reconstructed PIE forms have been standardized, unless noted otherwise. We are very grateful to Michael Weiss for his extensive help with PIE notation and consistency issues. For other PIE reconstructions, see Wodtko *et al.* (2008), Beekes (1995), Ringe (2006), and Pokorny database (available online at utexas.edu/cola/centers/lrc/ielex/PokornyMaster-X.html).

[26] The sound /x/ is a velar fricative; see the Glossary.

unscathed. Note that such cognacy judgments like those that serve as input for the Gray–Atkinson model are all-or-nothing statements. Once the Spanish *hoja* and French *feuille* are judged as cognate, it is irrelevant how different each of them is from the ancestral form (or from each other, or from cognates in other languages, such as the Italian *foglia*), or which particular changes occurred in each language. All this information is simply ignored. To use an example from Heggarty (2000: 532–533), the Gray–Atkinson model cannot capture the observation that although Italian *castello* /kas'tɛllo/ is "different from Spanish *castillo* /kas'tiʎo/, it is far less different from it than is French *château* /ʃa'to/".

If one examines cognates from different branches of a language family, sound correspondences become even harder to detect. For example, Russian *derevo* and English *tree* are cognates as they trace back to the PIE root **doru-*. Similarly, English *eye* and Russian *oko* are cognates (although, as discussed in the previous section, the latter is an archaic word and thus not a "common, everyday equivalent" for the meaning 'eye'). Cognacy, however, is not the only reason for word resemblance in different languages. Besides purely accidental similarities in both meaning and form (e.g. Russian *strannyj* and Italian *strano*, both of which mean 'strange, odd'), the most common reason for look-alikes – apart from cognacy – is borrowing from one language into another.

Gray and his colleagues have been widely faulted for failing to distinguish cognates from borrowings. These accusations are largely due to the fact that they consider solely lexical items, which are widely recognized as "the elements of a language most prone to diffusion, and the least reliable (in the absence of regular sound correspondences) to determine phylogenetic relationships" (Donohue *et al.* 2012a: 508). McMahon *et al.* (2005: 148) and Wang and Minett (2005: 122), among numerous others, warn that undetected loanwords can obscure the genetic signal, leading to erroneous classifications.

Greenhill and Gray (2012: 527) have countered such accusations with four points, all of which are either wrong or misleading.[27] First, they contend that they "did not analyze 'the lexicon' as a whole, but rather carefully selected basic vocabulary items [. . .] relatively resistant to borrowing" (2012: 527). But as April McMahon explains, "it is certainly no longer possible to maintain that the impact of borrowing *on basic vocabulary* will always be negligible" (2005: 114, italics ours). In fact, Embleton (1986) has amply demonstrated massive borrowing of basic vocabulary. For the Swadesh-200 list, she reported twelve borrowings from French into English, sixteen from Scandinavian languages into English, and fifteen from Dutch to Frisian. Kessler (2001), cited in McMahon (2010: 131–132), states that English has borrowed thirty-one items

---

[27] Though Gray and his colleagues claim to recognize the distinction between cognates, which are by definition derived by common descent, and borrowings, nonetheless occasionally an oxymoronic expression like "borrowed cognates" slips in, as in Gray *et al.* (2011: 1095).

in the Swadesh-200 list, Turkish has borrowed twenty-two items, French twenty-seven, and Albanian a whopping forty-one. McMahon *et al.* (2005) further argue that standard meaning lists should be subdivided into more conservative and less conservative sublists, which they call "the hihi list" and "the lolo list", respectively. In their Andean case study, the hihi list contains meanings such as numerals from one to five, 'I', 'thou', 'ear', 'tongue', 'foot', 'day', 'night', 'eat', 'sleep', and so on, while the lolo list contains meanings such as 'year', 'mouth', 'neck', 'bird', 'river', 'walk', 'think', and 'push'. After running these two sublists through computer programs that draw and select trees, McMahon *et al.* (2005: 149) found

identical outputs in terms of branching order for the hihi and lolo sublists in cases where there have been no borrowings [...] When contact has taken place, on the other hand, we observe different trees for the different sublists: for the less conservative meanings, the borrowing language tends to move towards the language or group which is the source of the loans.

As a result of such analysis, the authors concluded that Quechua and Aymara are not related languages, but rather share much of their basic vocabulary due to contact. The crucial conclusion of McMahon *et al.*'s study is that restricting the analysis to the most basic vocabulary does not solve the borrowing problem.[28]

In their second line of defense, Gray and his colleagues repeatedly emphasize that they have "spent considerable time identifying loanwords and [... have] removed identified loans" (Greenhill and Gray 2012: 528). Although they have no doubt removed some loanwords, their efforts in this regard have been far from complete. When their failings are pointed out, they generally place the blame on the historical linguists and etymologists whose cognacy judgments they use (Gray *et al.* 2011: 1094; Greenhill and Gray 2012: 527; and elsewhere). But surely scholarly responsibility lies with the researchers who use incomplete or misleading data as much as with those who produced such data in the first place, especially if the original datasets were produced for a different purpose. A key problem with the Gray–Atkinson method is that it *requires* the use of data that is inevitably incomplete and inconsistent.

A third tactic, seen in Greenhill and Gray (2012: 528), is to claim that they "did not include languages that were known to have high levels of borrowing". It is no simple matter, however, to sort languages according to their degree of borrowing. Doing so requires one "to assume, quite counterfactually, that we always know when languages have had a particularly contact-prone history, and also that most languages are 'non-contact languages'" (McMahon and McMahon

---

[28] For a further discussion of the "index of stability" see Sergei Starostin (2007) and George Starostin (2010).

2006: 155). Donohue *et al.* (2012a, 2012b) question whether Gray and his colleagues indeed removed the most contact-prone languages in their study of the Austronesian family. When it comes to their examination of Indo-European, moreover, many languages known for their extremely high levels of borrowings, including Romani, Albanian, Russian, and English, remained in the sample.

Greenhill and Gray's fourth and final line of defense is asserting that they "used methods that are robust to the effects of borrowing" (2012: 528). In a series of simulation studies, Greenhill *et al.* (2009) showed that the recovery of tree topology remains robust despite levels of borrowing between languages of around 20 percent of basic vocabulary every 1,000 years. Such simulation studies notwithstanding, the *results of their actual studies* strongly suggest that a significant number of *unidentified* loanwords crept into the Swadesh lists for the various languages that they use. In other words, we do not believe that Gray and Atkinson *knowingly* included "identified loanwords" in their dataset, but rather that they *unwittingly* allowed in such loanwords.

A specific example of unidentified loanwords in the Bouckaert *et al.* (2012) "Mapping the Origins" article shows how such problems corrupt the analysis. Their "consensus tree" shows Polish as grouped with Belarusian and Ukrainian, with Russian forming a more distant member of the larger grouping. In their earlier *Nature* article, Gray and Atkinson (2003) had also grouped Polish with Belarusian, Ukrainian, and Russian, although on this tree, it forms the outlier of the group. But scholars of the Slavic languages invariably classify Belarusian, Ukrainian, and Russian in the East Slavic branch, and Polish in the West Slavic group, together with Czech, Slovak, Kashubian, and Upper and Lower Sorbian. This established classification scheme is based not merely on cognates, but also – and more importantly – on sound systems and grammatical features. For example, one of the sound patterns that characterizes the East Slavic languages – but not Polish or other West Slavic languages – is so-called pleophony. Russian, Belarusian, and Ukrainian all have an extra vowel/syllable in words like *moloko* (Belarusian *malako*) for 'milk' or *korova* (Belarusian *karova*) for 'cow', that Polish, like other West Slavic languages, lacks; hence, the Polish *mleko*, the Czech *mleko*, the Slovak *mlieko*.[29] Additional arguments – which are numerous – for classifying Polish as a West Slavic language, closely related to Czech and Slovak, are discussed in detail in Sussex and Cubberley (2006).[30]

---

[29] South Slavic languages, similarly, do not exhibit pleophony; hence, the Slovenian, Serbo-Croatian, and Macedonian *mleko*, and the Bulgarian *mljako*.

[30] Interestingly, earlier glottometric studies, which share with the Gray–Atkinson method their reliance on the lexicon, did not group Polish with Belarusian. Both Polish and Belarusian were indicated by these earlier studies as having close ties to Ukrainian, but weaker connection to each other (Sussex and Cubberley 2006: 474).

How can one account for Gray and Atkinson's unusual classification of Polish as an East Slavic language? One obvious possibility is the high level of mutual lexical borrowing that characterized Polish, Belarusian, and Ukrainian for centuries. From the fourteenth century to the late eighteenth century, the Belarusian and Ukrainian lands were politically tied to Poland, first as part of the Grand Duchy of Lithuania, in personal union with Poland, and later as part of the Polish–Lithuanian Commonwealth. Significant ethnic and linguistic mixing characterized these lands as recently as 100 years ago. Russian, on the other hand, has also borrowed extensively, but from languages that are either less closely related or not related at all. Whole layers of Russian vocabulary were acquired from Old Church Slavonic (a medieval language from the South Slavic group with no direct surviving continuation), Byzantine Greek, Tatar and other Turkic languages, and several Western European languages (particularly, Dutch, German, French, and most recently English). The fact that Russian borrowed lexical items from these other languages much more extensively than Ukrainian, Belarusian, or Polish makes the latter three languages appear more similar – and consequently, more closely related – than they actually are. To cite just one example (which does not pertain to basic vocabulary), Russian has borrowed the names of calendar months from Byzantine Greek via Old Church Slavonic, while Ukrainian, Belarusian, and Polish all retained the old Slavic designations, which refer to climatic patterns and seasonal activities (e.g. February is the "freezing" month, July is the "linden tree" month, November is the "leaf-falling" month, etc.). If only these lexical items are considered, one is inevitably led to conclude – incorrectly! – that Polish is closely related to Belarusian and Ukrainian, and that Russian is a distant cousin.

Ironically, the same phonological patterns that underlie the conventional classification of Slavic languages, such as pleophony, can be used to identify borrowings across the East/West Slavic divide, especially East Slavic loan-words in Polish, such as *koromyslo* 'shoulder-yoke'. Unlike native Polish words such as *groszek* 'peas', *krowa* 'cow', and *zdrowy* 'healthy', which have the non-pleophony sequence *-ro-*, *koromyslo* 'shoulder-yoke' has the extra vowel in *-oro-*, a typical East Slavic "sound signature".

The misclassification of Polish as an East Slavic language is not the only significant error produced by the Gray–Atkinson model as a result of unidenti-fied loanwords. Extensive lexical contact between Frisian and Dutch, as well as between English and languages outside the West Germanic grouping, results in misclassifying Frisian as more closely related to Dutch (and Flemish) than to English, which is treated instead as the West Germanic outlier.

In the Romance branch, Romanian has borrowed massively from its Slavic neighbors, including numerous words in the Swadesh 200-word list, such as *trăi* 'to live' (from the Slavic *trajati* 'to last, continue'), *lovi* 'to hunt' (from the

Slavic *loviti* 'to hunt, chase'), and *zăpadă* 'snow' (from the Slavic *zapadati* 'to fall'). As a result, the Gray–Atkinson model incorrectly places Romanian as the Romance outlier. If sound changes (and grammatical changes) are considered, it becomes clear that Sardinian, rather than Romanian, stands out as the most distinctive member of the Romance grouping, in the sense that the other languages, including Romanian, share common innovations not found in Sardinian. For example, in Sardinian the short *i* inherited from Latin merged with the long *i*, whereas in all other Romance languages, including Romanian, it merged with the long *e*, as evidenced from the reflexes of the Latin *siccus* 'dry': compare Italian *secco*, Spanish *seco*, French *sec*, and Romanian *sec*, but Sardinian has retained the *i*, as in *sicu*. Another change that affected the non-Sardinian branch of Romance languages is the palatalization (lenition) of the inherited Latin /k/ into /tʃ/, /s/, or /θ/, mentioned above. While all non-Sardinian languages palatalized the initial /k/ in Latin *centum* (cf. Italian *cento*, Spanish *cien*, French *cent*, Romanian *sută*), Sardinian retained the /k/ in *kentu*. Moreover, Sardinian preserved both the voiceless intervocalic stops (which were voiced in Western Continental Romance; cf. Spanish *amigos*) and the plural ending *-s* on nouns (which was lost in Eastern Continental Romance; cf. Italian *amici*). The early split of Sardinian and the later split of Romanian is obfuscated, however, if one only considers cognates, without paying attention to sound changes.

Albanian is also misconstrued in the Gray–Atkinson model on the same basis. Indeed, Albanian presents a well-known classification problem due in part to its many early loans from Greek and Latin (cf. Holm 2011: 93), as well as its later loans from Turkish and the Slavic languages (Beekes 1995: 25). In Bouckaert *et al.* (2012), Albanian is, unsurprisingly, grouped with Greek, at the exclusion of Armenian, but in Gray and Atkinson's earlier article (Gray and Atkinson 2003), Albanian is grouped with the Indo-Iranian languages (!), while Greek and Armenian are placed together on a completely different branch.[31] This controversy about the classification of Albanian derives in part from the lack of consensus among scholars as to the etymology of individual Albanian words: Holm (2011) proposed seventeen new etymologies for Albanian but they are not necessarily convincing to other scholars. Given such dubious input data, it comes as no surprise that computational phylogenetic studies produce several alternative placements of Albanian on the family tree.

But perhaps the most glaring misclassification by the Gray–Atkinson model, already mentioned in Chapter 3, involves Romani, which is depicted in their model as the first Indo-Aryan language to split off from the rest of the tree,

---

[31] In the newly substituted Supplementary Materials, Albanian is shown to form a grouping with a Greco-Armenian branch. However, the splits between Albanian and Greco-Armenian and between Greek and Armenian are so close in time, and the "margins of error" so great, that the probability of this tree configuration is very low, as the authors themselves admit.

around 1500 BCE (3,500 years ago).[32] In contrast, the accepted consensus (cf. Turner 1926; Masica 1991; Matras 2010: 31–34) is that Romani belongs to the Central grouping within the Indo-Aryan branch of Indo-European, along-side Hindi, Urdu, Gujarati, and Marwari. As a result, its split from its sibling languages almost certainly took place many centuries later than the date proposed by the Gray–Atkinson team. An early migration must have taken the Roma to Northwestern India, as their language exhibits some features characteristic of Dardic languages found in the region, such as Kashmiri. But according to the Gray–Atkinson model, all of these other languages are merely distant cousins of Romani, equally removed from it as the languages of the Eastern Indo-Aryan grouping (Bengali, Assamese, Oriya), with which Romani shares no innovations.

One of the reasons for such jumbled classification is the high level of borrowing in Romani. The language's core lexicon that can be traced back to the period before the arrival of the Roma to Europe consists of some 650–700 inherited Indo-Aryan lexical roots, supplemented by 200–250 lexical roots of Greek origin, around 70 Iranian and perhaps 40 Armenian lexical roots, as well as additional items of various etymologies, some of which are unclear or controversial (Matras 2002: 21). Extensive borrowing characterizes all aspects of the Romani language, including its basic vocabulary. Fraser (1992) showed that the Romani Swadesh-100 list contains between fifteen and twenty loanwords, depending on the dialect; Boretzky (1992) demon-strated the same level of borrowing for the Swadesh-200 list, between thirty-three and thirty-seven items, again depending on the dialect. This higher-than-expected percentage of loanwords in a Swadesh list make Romani appear less closely related to its sibling- and cousin-languages than it actually is; it also makes it appear unduly "old" – an issue to which we return in Chapter 5.

While careful etymologizing of all the words in the Swadesh lists for 103 languages examined by Gray, Atkinson, and colleagues is beyond the scope of this book, such work has been done by other scholars for a number of individual languages. For example, Holm (2011) considered the etymologies and cognacy judgments given for words in the Albanian Swadesh-100 list in three often-used lexical databases: the Comparative Indoeuropean Database by Isidore Dyen (Dyen et al. 1997), the database employed by Ringe et al. (2002), and the database compiled by the late Russian linguist Sergej Starostin. Holm

---

[32] Gray and Atkinson (2003) classify Romani as most closely related to Singhalese, both of which are outliers within the Indo-Aryan branch, but are not closely related to each other. In the December 2013 version of the tree substituted into the Bouckaert et al. (2012) Supplementary Materials, Romani is most closely related to Kashmiri, with Singhalese as the next outlier within the Indo-Aryan grouping. The Romani-Kashmiri grouping splits off from the rest of the Indo-Aryan family around 500 BCE (2,500 years ago), according to this tree.

(2011: 90) found a "relatively high amount of errors [which] makes the data a bad source for the purpose for which they were designed, and still are (mis) used". In the Dyen database, for example, Holm found a 14 percent error rate; Bouckaert *et al.* (2012, Supplementary Materials: 2) admit that this database "required considerable correction, and changes were made to approximately 26% of coding decisions on individual lexemes". However, the Gray–Atkinson team found little fault with the Ringe database, stating that it "required corrections to only 0.5% of lexemes". Holm (2011: 92), on the other hand, found an approximately 16 percent error rate in Ringe's list for Albanian. He found Starostin's list and cognacy judgments for Albanian wanting as well.[33]

While it is widely understood that borrowings can warp a language tree and as such must be identified and excluded before the comparative method can be applied, historical linguists have also been well aware that such an exercise is often easier said than done. To remedy the situation, some studies (e.g. Warnow *et al.* 2006) explicitly incorporate borrowing, as well as homoplasy (i.e. parallel evolution and/or back-mutation). Other scholars have worked on developing methods for the automated identification of borrowings. One such method was first suggested by Cavalli-Sforza *et al.* (1994) for detecting genetic admixture among human populations and later applied by Wang and Minett (2005) to lexical borrowing, used in conjunction with an arbitrary tree-building algorithm. In this technique, multiple trees are generated, with one or more randomly selected languages removed from the analysis for each iteration. Clusters of languages that are grouped together consistently from tree to tree are considered to be representative of valid relationships of descent. In contrast, languages that are unstable and shift from one subgrouping to another are likely to have borrowed extensively from other tongues. Recall from the discussion above that English is one such language whose classification appears unstable, changing position depending on the lexical items and computational methods used. Indeed, English is known as a particularly "borrowing-prone" language.

Another illustration of how the Wang and Minett's (2005) method works comes from a comparison of two of the "consensus trees" produced within the Gray–Atkinson framework: one in Gray and Atkinson (2003) and that in Bouckaert *et al.* (2012). Languages that shift their position between those two trees have borrowed extensively: Polish (an outlier of the East Slavic grouping in Gray and Atkinson 2003 but deeply embedded inside the East

---

[33] Donohue *et al.* (2012a: 516) point out that "lexical borrowing between geographically and socially proximal languages" may also be responsible for the grouping together of Niuean and East Uvean languages in Gray *et al.* (2009), which applies the same phylogenetic methods to Austronesian languages.

Slavic grouping in Bouckaert *et al.* 2012); Romani (a sister-language to Singhalese with Kashmiri as an Indo-Aryan outlier in Gray and Atkinson 2003, an Indo-Aryan outlier with Kashmiri and Singhalese forming another branch in Bouckaert *et al.* 2012, and a sister to Kashmiri but not to Singhalese in the December 2013 version of their tree); and Albanian (grouped with Indo-Iranian languages in Gray and Atkinson 2003 but with Greek in Bouckaert *et al.* 2012 and with Greco-Armenian in the substituted version of the tree).

The same method has been applied with some success to Indo-European by Ogura and Wang (1996), correctly detecting the heavy lexical borrowing by English from both French and Old Norse. Other methods for detecting borrowings have been developed in Warnow *et al.* (1995), Ringe *et al.* (2002), Minett and Wang (2003), McMahon *et al.* (2005), among others. The Gray–Atkinson model, however, does not incorporate any of these methods.

Fallacy 4. Do procedural issues have a significant impact on the resulting classification?

So far we have argued that the purely lexical input used in the Gray–Atkinson model is bound to generate problems because the data selection is highly subjective and inconsistent (see the discussion of Slaska's work above), and because unidentified borrowings cloud the results. Gray and Atkinson's response has been to simply proclaim that their methods are "robust to errors in cognacy judgments" (Atkinson and Gray 2006: 100; Greenhill and Gray 2012: 528). They also claim to have shown that "the amount of undetected borrowing needs to be very substantial ($>20\%$) to substantially bias either the tree topology or the date estimates" (Gray *et al.* 2009: 479), referring to Atkinson *et al.* 2005). In more general terms, they argue that errors in the input result only in "minor misplacements of individual languages" (Greenhill and Gray 2012: 529), rather than deforming the overall shape of the tree. "Cherry picking languages one thinks are misplaced," they further contend, "is not an appropriate way to compare trees" (Greenhill and Gray 2012: 532). But is it warranted to assume that such errors in translation and coding will not be statistically significant? As McMahon (2005: 114) argues, "this hope may be utopian". McMahon and McMahon (2006: 157) convincingly show that erroneously coding a loanword within a grouping as a cognate results in the misplacement of the recipient language in the same branch as the source language(s). For example, if 'wing' is mistakenly coded as a cognate between English and North Germanic, the resulting tree places English in the North Germanic branch; if 'wing' is correctly recoded as a loanword, English appears as a West Germanic rather than North Germanic language.

Geisler and List (in press) examine the issue of lexical borrowing and the generation of language trees even more thoroughly. After investigating the differences between two large lexical datasets and testing their influence on the shapes of computed trees using Gray–Atkinson's Bayesian model of tree construction (among others), they convincingly demonstrate that such quantitative methods that rely exclusively on the lexicon have inherited the flaws found in older methodologies that relied on the lexicon as well, such as lexicostatistics and glottochronology. One can only conclude that the problems associated with the translation of basic concepts into individual languages and with cognacy judgments have a grave effect on the construction of language trees, and as a result cannot be ignored.

The two databases compared by Geisler and List are the abovementioned Dyen database (Dyen *et al.* 1997) and the Tower of Babel database developed by Sergej Starostin's son, George Starostin (cf. Starostin 2008). In order to have two maximally comparable lists, Geisler and List extracted a set of 46 languages and 103 basic vocabulary items that occur in both datasets. After rectifying the coding systems used in the two datasets, they computed the differences between them, finding that it amounted to about 10 percent in regard to the Romance languages alone. They further estimated that differences in the rest of the datasets are substantially greater. Next, they applied the Gray–Atkinson Bayesian phylogenetic method and produced new trees based on each of the two datasets. The splits in these two trees turned out to vary by about 30 percent.

Since the Gray–Atkinson team has relied in part on the Dyen database and not Starostin's Tower of Babel database, it is expected that the Geisler–List tree based on the Dyen database (see Figure 1 in the Appendix) will replicate the overall shape of the trees presented in Gray and Atkinson's work (e.g. Gray and Atkinson 2003, schematized in Figure 2, and Bouckaert *et al.* 2012, schematized in Figure 3). This is indeed the case although the differences between the trees are instructive as well. For example, Geisler and List's Dyen-based tree groups the Greco-Armenian branch with the Indo-Iranian languages, as does Bouckaert *et al.* (2012). However, in Gray and Atkinson's (2003) paper, Albanian is grouped with Indo-Iranian, whereas Greco-Armenian constitutes a separate branch. According to the tree produced by Ringe *et al.* (2002), in Figure 4, Greco-Armenian is indeed a valid grouping, but the Indo-Iranian languages are classified as more closely related to the Balto-Slavic group than they are to the Greco-Armenian branch. The Dyen-based tree produced by Geisler and List also groups the Germanic and Romance languages together, as do Gray and Atkinson (2003). In Bouckaert *et al.* (2012), Italic and Celtic form an Italo-Celtic grouping, justified also by Ringe *et al.* (2002), whereas Germanic constitutes a separate branch. However, the Dyen-based tree produced by Geisler and List (see Figure 1) includes groupings that have not appeared on any other trees as far as we know, such as a combined Balto-Slavic and Celtic branch. When it comes to the more fine-grained divisions, Geisler and List's Dyen-based tree has a few surprises too. It treats Slovenian as a Slavic outlier (whereas it is a South Slavic language in the conventional scheme), along with Polish (a West Slavic language) and Russian (an East Slavic language). The other Slavic languages are placed on two branches: one corresponding to the (remaining) West Slavic languages, and the other combining what is left of the South Slavic and East Slavic groups. Note that both trees generated by the Gray–Atkinson team group East Slavic languages with West rather than South Slavic.

The tree produced by Geisler and List from the Tower of Babel database (see Figure 5) accords somewhat better with conventional classification schemes, but it also contains a few surprises, as compared to those conventional schemes, such as the lack of an Italo-Celtic branch (which also failed to appear in Gray and Atkinson's 2003 phylogeny). It also postulates a major split between the Indo-Iranian languages and a branch that includes Celtic, Romance, Balto-Slavic, and Germanic languages (marked "Western" in Figure 5), a feature also replicated in both Gray and Atkinson (2003) and Bouckaert *et al.* (2012), shown in Figures 2 and 3 respectively. Conventional classification schemes group Indo-Iranian languages with the Balto-Slavic branch on the basis of such features as the *satem* innovation, discussed above, that occurred in both groupings. As for finer-grained divisions, the Geisler and List's Tower-of-Babel-based tree reproduces the conventional classification of Slavic languages into West, East, and South Slavic; however, it places the West and South Slavic branches together, whereas most analyses combine the West and East Slavic languages.

To sum up, differences between the classifications derived from the two datasets in Geisler and List's study occur in all parts of the trees, both at the higher levels of analysis and in the subgroupings of closely related languages. Crucially, these differences are due solely to discrepancies between lexical choices and cognacy judgments made in each dataset, as the exact same method has been applied to datasets containing the same basic meanings and the same languages.

Take-home message

As Donohue *et al.* (2012b: 544) put it, the Gray–Atkinson method "uses the results of the comparative method to weakly emulate comparative method results". The chief problem with the model is that it remains entirely confined to the lexical level, limiting itself even further to the so-called "basic vocabulary". Ignoring phonological and grammatical changes and focusing exclusively on the retention vs. the replacement of cognates means that it is impossible to identify innovations from retentions *prior to* formulating grouping hypotheses. Moreover, many procedural problems result in the misclassification of both individual languages and larger branches. The failure to detect a significant number of borrowings is particularly distorting. As we shall see in the following chapter, the consistent under-detection of borrowings also skews the dating of splits on the tree, making the root of the Indo-European tree appear much older than it actually is.

5 Dating problems of the Bayesian phylogenetic model

In the previous chapter, we argued that procedural problems inherent in the Gray–Atkinson approach, such as subjective and inconsistent selection of words for Swadesh lists and undiagnosed borrowings, have a significant warping effect on the resulting shapes of its linguistic family trees. In this chapter, we show that such errors also have a major effect on dating the origin and differentiation of the Indo-European family tree. More generally, we address the question of whether the branching patterns – and especially the Proto-Indo-European (PIE) root – can be dated by linguistic means. But before we proceed, we need to clarify what we mean by the timing of PIE or of any node on a family tree: it is the time *just before* the diversification of the ancestral language began. The ancestors of those Indo-Europeans that we seek to locate in time (and place, as discussed in subsequent chapters) might have spoken (an earlier form of) PIE and might have lived in some other location, but the history and geography of such ancestral groups is irrelevant for resolving the Indo-European debate. Ultimately, the most distant ancestral language of PIE speakers traces back to the cradle of humanity somewhere in Africa, but that too is beside the point.

Contrary to Gray–Atkinson's claim that (traditional) historical linguists "don't do dates", the issue of dating lies at the core of historical linguistics as the very fact of language change implies "before" and "after", "earlier" and "later" phases. However, most historical linguists remain highly skeptical about the possibility of attaching absolute and precise dates to language divergence events, as indicated by such article titles as "Why Lexicostatistics Doesn't Work: The 'Universal Constant' Hypothesis and the Austronesian Languages" (Blust 2000), "On the Uselessness of Glottochronology for the Subgrouping of Tibeto-Burman" (Matisoff 2000), and "Why Linguists Don't Do Dates: Evidence from Indo-European and Australian Languages" (McMahon and McMahon 2006). As Dolgopolsky (2000: 404) summarizes the skeptic's view:

we cannot help concluding that the *lapis philosophorum* of glottochronology is unable to transmute the baser metals of lexicostatistical numbers into pure gold of reliable dating. The radiocarbon method of dating is good for atoms, but is not good for culture-bound human languages.

Although scholars working within the Gray–Atkinson approach deem this view "pessimistic" (Gray *et al.* 2011: 1090), we think a certain degree of skepticism about precise dates is the more realistic position. Advocates of Bayesian dating methods' contrasting claim is that their approach is more scientific, as science involves getting things partly wrong and then refining the methods until they get things right. We, however, concur with McMahon and McMahon (2006: 159–160) that it is "quite unscientific to persist in attempting to date language splits when we do not have enough information to know whether and how far we are wrong. Any attempts to refine our methods and measurements in those circumstances can be no more than stabs in the dark." In the following pages, we examine the development of linguistic methods of dating nodes on a family tree, ranging from lexicostatistics and glottochronology to the cutting-edge Bayesian phylogenetic dating methods employed by the Gray–Atkinson approach, highlighting the shortcomings of various techniques. In subsequent chapters (particularly Chapter 8), we turn our attention to the ways in which historical linguists working within the comparative method have been able to establish relative chronologies and, in some cases, absolute dates as well.

The rise and demise of glottochronology

The first attempts to "do dates" (in the Gray–Atkinson sense) in historical linguistics go back to the 1950s when Morris Swadesh developed an approach known as lexicostatistics that in turn gave rise to "glottochronology" (Swadesh 1952, 1955).[1] Lexicostatistical methods infer language trees on the basis of the percentage of shared cognates between languages – the more cognates the languages share, the more closely related they are thought to be. But when it comes to dating the tree, lexicostatistical approaches can only provide relative chronologies, determining which splits happened before or after other splits. Glottochronology extends lexicostatistics by estimating language divergence dates under the assumption of a "glottoclock", or constant rate of language change (for a more detailed introduction to glottochronology, see Lees 1953). Swadesh examined changes in languages for which we have historical documentation covering more than a thousand years: from Latin to the Romance languages, from Ancient Greek to Modern Greek, and from Sanskrit to the modern Indo-Aryan languages. For the Swadesh-200 list, the 1,000-year

---

[1] Although often referred to as the linguistic analog of the "molecular clock" idea in biology, glottochronology was actually developed a full decade before Zuckerkandl and Pauling (1962) introduced the idea of using the divergence of molecular sequences to date biological lineages. Instead, the idea of a constant rate of lexical change must have been inspired by earlier work on radioactive decay.

retention rate (i.e. the expected proportion of cognates remaining after a millennium of separation) was found to be 86 percent; in other words, only 14 words out of 100 would be replaced over such a span of time. This method supposedly allowed Swadesh and his followers not only to measure the degree of relatedness between languages, but also to estimate the *absolute* date when their common ancestor split into daughter branches. For example, English and Russian share 34 percent of lexemes in the Swadesh-100, which would imply that their common ancestor split into the Germanic and Slavic branches approximately 4,000 years ago.

This apparently simple and elegant method was challenged as early as the 1960s and by now has been all but discredited; Dixon (1997: 49) thus referred to it as "the chimera of glottochronology". The chief objection, raised first by Bergsland and Vogt (1962), is that languages do not actually evolve at a constant pace. Unlike sub-atomic changes or mutations in genes, which happen at random, changes in language are often precipitated by extra-linguistic, social factors. As a result, lexical replacements in the core vocabulary often happen in waves, and as a result the rate of replacement may differ radically from one language to another and from one period of time to another. Comparing extant languages with their archaic forms, Bergsland and Vogt found considerable evidence of rate variation between languages. Their classical example involves two modern Scandinavian languages: Icelandic and Norwegian, both descendants of Old Norse, spoken roughly a thousand years ago. Norwegian retained 80 percent of the vocabulary of Old Norse, correctly suggesting an age of approximately 1,000 years. Icelandic, however, has retained over 96 percent of the Old Norse vocabulary, falsely suggesting that it split from Old Norse just over 200 years ago.[2] Other similar examples abound. For instance, Blust (2000) documented variation in the rate of basic vocabulary retention ranging from 5 to 50 percent in the approximately 4,000-year period from the emergence of Proto-Malayo-Polynesian to the present. He concludes that these huge differences in retention rates inevitably distort both the trees obtained by lexicostatistics and the dates given to the nodes on the tree by glottochronological analysis. For the Austronesian languages considered by Blust, population size is one of the key factors behind such variation in retention rates. But while population size has been frequently argued to affect rates of change, no agreement has been reached as to whether the pace of

---

[2] The Russian linguist Sergei Starostin proposed distinguishing between "internal replacements" (i.e. when a word is replaced by another word which already existed in the language but had a different meaning; e.g. in Russian the word *brjuxo* 'belly' was replaced by *život*, which originally meant 'life') and "external replacements" (i.e. borrowings). Furthermore, he showed that if loanwords are eliminated from the calculations, the rate of change becomes more constant, approximately 5 percent per millennium. The problem, however, is that loanwords can never be perfectly diagnosed and eliminated, as discussed in the previous chapter.

linguistic change in smaller linguistic groups is faster (Nettle 1999, 2000a, 2000b) or slower (Milroy and Milroy 1985, 1992; see also Bowern 2010). Although population size is less relevant to the Indo-European family, another overarching factor comes into play: language contact. Thus, a more isolated Icelandic retained more of the Old Norse vocabulary than Norwegian did. And as we shall see below, different rates of borrowing, which result in different cognate retention rates, plague the modern Bayesian methods used to date phylogenetic trees as well.

Bayesian phylogenetic methods for dating linguistic trees

Since traditional glottochronology, based on the idea of "glottoclock", has been rejected, new approaches to dating linguistic trees have been developed, based largely on Bayesian methods. One approach, pioneered by Sanderson (2002), is based on the idea of "calibration points" – that is, nodes on the trees that can be constrained to a known date range: relative branch lengths, which are proportional to the number of changes, are converted into time intervals based on the timing of these calibration points. Without relying on a strict clock, this method allows date estimation based on a combination of calibrations, branch-length estimates, and the rate-smoothing algorithm that penalizes trees in which the rates vary too much from branch to branch. An alternative approach, the so-called "relaxed phylogenetics" method, developed by Drummond et al. (2006), estimates the tree and the dates simultaneously. Bouckaert et al. (2012) use a modified version of this latter method.

The proponents of the Bayesian phylogenetic dating methods recognized the dangers of distortion due to both misshapen trees (e.g. because of high levels of borrowing) and mistaken calibration points. Their main response has been to argue that their methods produce tree topologies that are "robust to realistic levels of borrowing in basic vocabulary (0–15%)", while allowing that their inferences about divergence dates are "slightly less robust and showed a tendency to *underestimate* dates" (Gray *et al.* 2011: 1095). Elsewhere Atkinson and Gray reiterate their contention that "widespread borrowing can bias divergence time estimates by making languages seem more similar (and hence *younger*) than they really are" (Atkinson and Gray 2006: 92, italics ours). In other words, while conceding that their dating of PIE may be biased by undetected borrowings, they maintain that if it is, PIE must be even older than their model indicates, not younger, as maintained by adherents of the more generally accepted Steppe theory.

However, other studies suggest that dates produced by the Bayesian phylogenetic dating methods are over- rather than underestimated. Three factors can contribute to making the root of the Indo-European tree look older than it actually is. The first factor, undetected borrowing, along with related procedural issues, has been shown to distort the shape of the tree in Chapter 4. Recent work shows that such difficulties pose major problems for dating the tree as well. For example, McMahon and McMahon (2006) reconsider the study done by Forster and Toth (2003) and find that the dates calculated by these researchers for the PIE root (8100±1900 BCE) and for the Celtic split (3200±1500 BCE) deviate significantly from the dates expected from historical evidence, or obtained by other dating methods. This discrepancy is due in part to "an accumulation of minor errors due to borrowing, misclassification, or poor selection of meanings" (McMahon and McMahon 2006: 158) – that is, the same problems that distort the shape of the tree, as discussed in the previous chapter. Crucially, McMahon and McMahon conclude that undetected borrowing results in conclusions in which "the time depth of the family will have been artificially *extended*, pushing the original split of Celtic earlier than was in fact the case" (2006: 158–159, italics mine).

Going back to the Gray–Atkinson model, languages that are known to be particularly prone to borrowing are consistently erroneously dated as having diverged earlier than they actually did. Examples of this pattern are numerous; we shall limit ourselves to only two of them here. The most glaring blunder concerns Romani: not only is Romani mistakenly taken to have split off from the rest of the Indo-Aryan branch before any other language, as discussed at length in Chapter 4, the date of the Romani split is wrong as well. Bouckaert *et al.* (2012) place it around 1500 BCE (3,500 years ago); linguistic evidence, however, suggests a much later date of around 1000 CE (1,000 years ago).[3] As mentioned in Chapter 3, a number of grammatical changes that characterize the transition from Middle Indo-Aryan (MIA) to New Indo-Aryan (NIA) languages that happened circa 1000 CE, and which are shared by Romani, show that Romani could not have separated from the other Indo-Aryan languages before that time. One such change, mentioned in Chapter 3, is the loss of the neuter gender and the reassignment of the formerly neuter nouns to either masculine or feminine gender. This change encompassed Romani as well, which has only two genders, masculine and feminine (Matras 2002: 72). Crucially, almost all of the formerly neuter nouns in Romani were reassigned to the same gender as their cognates in other NIA languages, such as Hindi. For instance, the neuter *agni* 'fire' in MIA became the feminine *āga* 'fire' in Hindi and the likewise feminine *jag* in Romani. Given that there are several dozen formerly neuter nouns in Romani that had been reassigned to the same gender as in Hindi, the probability of the same change happening independently in the two languages is virtually nil. The most likely explanation of these parallel changes is that Romani was spoken in India at the turn of the second

---

[3] As mentioned earlier, the newly substituted version of the Supplementary Materials places the Romani split at 2,500 years ago (500 BCE), still a millennium and a half too early.

millennium, with the loss of the neuter gender and the reassignment of formerly neuter nouns to masculine or feminine genders occurring before the language split off from the rest of the Indo-Aryan family. Thus, the Romani exodus must be dated to around 1000 CE.

A potential problem with using the gender system to date the Roma exodus from India is the fact that not all MIA languages have lost the neuter gender. Marathi and Oriya, for example, have retained the three-way gender system. It is notable that both Marathi and Oriya are spoken at the southern edge of the Indo-Aryan realm. Further south, many of the Dravidian languages, such as Kannada and Tamil, have three-way gender systems. That the number of genders in a language may result from linguistic contact with neighboring languages is evident from the fact that Kolami, a Dravidian language spoken farther north and surrounded by Indo-Aryan languages, has a two-way gender system.

But fortunately for historical linguists, Romani exhibits a number of other phonological and morphological properties that characterize it as a NIA language (Matras 2002).[4] These include such grammatical developments as the loss of the elaborate nominal case endings present in Old and Middle Indo-Aryan and their reduction to a simple opposition between nominative and oblique. For example, the word 'boy' in Romani has only two forms: the nominative *raklo* and the oblique *rakles-*, comparable to the Hindi *laṛkā* and *laṛke-*, respectively. Other case-like meanings are expressed by former postpositions, repurposed as clitics, and attaching to the oblique form (some of these clitics have been subsequently grammaticalized into suffixes in Romani).

Another development shared by Romani with other NIA languages is the simplification of certain consonant clusters, as in MIA *sappa* 'snake' > Romani *sap*, and MIA *ratta* 'blood' > Romani *rat*. Finally, Romani shares with its NIA brethren such as Hindi the disappearance of the MIA past tense conjugation and the substitution of the past participle, still visible in some dialects of Romani. The past participle shows agreement in gender, as in *ov gelo* 'he went' vs. *oj geli* 'she went'. These forms are comparable to the Hindi *vo gayā* 'he went' vs. *vo gayī* 'she went'. These shared patterns indicate that an earlier form of Romani was part of the Indo-Aryan dialect continuum during the transition period to the NIA phase, which took place in medieval times, perhaps as early as the eighth or ninth century CE or as late as the tenth century CE (for further details, see Matras 2010: 32–33). However, it is absolutely certain from this grammatical evidence that Romani did not split off from the rest of the Indo-Aryan tree as early as 1500 BCE (3,500 years ago) or even 500 BCE (2,500 years ago).

---

[4] We thank Yaron Matras for a most helpful discussion of Romani.

Russian, another language known for its relatively high level of borrowing, is also given an erroneously early differentiation date. According to the Gray–Atkinson model, Russian split off from the rest of the East Slavic tree (which erroneously includes Polish in the Gray–Atkinson model, as discussed in Chapter 4) approximately 1,000 years ago (this date did not change in the newly substituted set of results). However, as Sussex and Cubberley (2006: 80) put it, "the East Slavs were culturally, religiously and linguistically coherent" at least "until the sacking of Kiev by the Tartars in 1240". Geopolitically, circa 1000 CE, we can differentiate East Slavic principalities, such as Polotsk Principality in what is now Belarus, Volynia Principality in today's Ukraine, and Rostov-Suzdal' Principality in what was to become northern Russia. Some of these principalities, however, span the modern Russia–Ukraine border: for example, Chernigov Principality centered around the city of Chernigov in what is now Ukraine but also included lands around Kursk, which are now Russia. The three peoples, Russians, Ukrainians, and Byelorussians, emerged as linguistically, culturally, and geopolitically distinct groupings centuries later. Linguistically, Russian emerged as a distinct language from Belarusian and Ukrainian chiefly as a result of two historical developments that postdate the timing of the Russian split in the Gray–Atkinson model by about 400 years. The first development was the gradual absorption of what is now Belarus and Ukraine into the Grand Duchy of Lithuania and later the Kingdom of Poland, a process that began in 1386. The second set of events that set Russian on a different course vis-a-vis Belarusian and Ukrainian was the incorporation into the Russian state of the Novgorod Republic, which extended from the Baltic Sea to the northern Ural Mountains, where a distinctive dialect of (Old) Russian had developed. The Russian annexation of Novgorod began in 1478 with a series of wars between the Grand Duchy of Moscow and the Novgorod Republic. In subsequent years, a large part of the republic's population was resettled elsewhere, and peasants from Moscovy were transplanted to the Novgorod lands. As a result, elements from the Novgorod dialect were incorporated into Russian (but not into the vernaculars of the Lithuanian Rus'), as discussed by Andrey Zaliznyak.[5] For example, recall from Chapter 4 (discussion surrounding Table 4.2) that the dialect of Old Novgorod did not undergo the so-called Second Slavic Palatalization, retaining the original /k, g, x/ in place of the innovative /ts, z, s/ in roots such as *kěl-* 'whole' and *xěr-* 'gray'. Nor did the Second Slavic Palatalization apply in Old Novgorod across morpheme boundaries, in locative case forms of nouns such as *rukě* 'hand', *nogě* 'leg', *snoxě* 'wife of brother or son' and in verbal forms such as *pomogi* 'help' (imperative singular), as discussed in Zaliznyak (2004).

---

[5] See Zaliznyak's lecture on the history of East Slavic at onlinetv.ru/video/1607/?autostart=1

In Old Russian, as spoken in Moscow, Kiev, Chernigov, and elsewhere, the Second Slavic Palatalization resulted in forms such as *tsѣl-* 'whole', *sѣr-* 'gray', *rutsѣ* 'hand', *nozѣ* 'leg', *snosѣ* 'wife of brother or son', and *pomozi* 'help'. Modern Russian combines palatalized roots from "southeastern" dialects of Old Russian with the forms that show no palatalization across morpheme boundaries: *tsѣl-/sѣr-*, but *rukѣ/nogѣ/snoxѣ/pomogi*. While the loss of palatalization at morpheme boundaries can be viewed alternatively as an instance of paradigmatic leveling by analogy (i.e. retaining the same root-final consonant across the forms in the paradigm), the presence of other Novgorod-dialect-derived forms in Modern Russian, such as the locative forms of feminine *a*-stem and masculine nouns (e.g. *vъ zemlѣ* 'in the ground', *na nožѣ* 'on knife'), alongside the genitive forms from "southeastern" dialects of Old Russian (e.g. *u sestry* 'to sister', *do zemli* 'to the ground'), suggests that contact between the two dialectal groups is implicated.[6] As the processes that differentiated Russian from the rest of East Slavic began in the late fourteenth and fifteenth centuries, it is hardly the case that the Russian language was already distinct nearly half a millennium earlier, as in the Gray–Atkinson model. Being a borrowing-prone language, Russian appears in their model to be substantially older than it actually is.

So how do we reconcile such examples of borrowing-prone languages appearing older than they actually are with Gray–Atkinson's claim that "borrowing [makes] languages seem [...] younger than they really are"? The effects of borrowing – whether it shortens or lengthens branches of the phylogenetic tree – depend on whether borrowing occurs between closely related languages or more distantly related ones. For example, lexical exchange between Polish on the one hand and Belarusian and Ukrainian on the other hand makes the three languages appear more closely related to each other than they actually are. According to the tree in Supplementary Materials of Bouckaert *et al.* (2012), Polish diverged from Belarusian around 1500 CE, much later than it actually did.[7] In contrast, Russian has borrowed extensively from languages outside the East Slavic grouping: Old Church Slavonic (South Slavic) and Turkic languages were particularly significant "donors". This makes Russian appear more distinctive and therefore older. The same is true

---

[6] Curiously, both Old Novgorod and "southeastern" Old Russian exhibited syncretism between genitive and locative forms of feminine *a*-stem nouns: *do zemlѣ* 'to the ground' and *vъ zemlѣ* 'in the ground' in Old Novgorod and *do zemli* 'to the ground' and *vъ zemli* 'in the ground' elsewhere in Old Russian. While most paradigm changes in Russian resulted in more rather than less syncretism, the incorporation of forms from different dialects resulted in distinct genitive and locative forms in Modern Russian: *do zemli* 'to the ground' but *v zemle* 'in the ground'.

[7] In the new version of the tree, Polish split from Belarusian and Ukrainian around 1300 CE, still too late.

in regard to Romani, which borrowed not from other Indo-Aryan languages, but from languages in other Indo-European branches: Greek, Armenian, and Iranian. Provided there is a sufficient level of undetected (or underdetected) borrowing among Indo-European branches, the age of the PIE root is unduly pushed back in time.

The second factor that contributes to erroneously long branches and old divergences involves gaps in the Swadesh lists where the translations are not known (as discussed in Holm 2012). Since the data is "coded as binary characters showing the presence or absence of a cognate set in a language" (Bouckaert *et al.* 2012, Supplementary Materials: 2), such gaps count as additional absences. Thus, gaps are essentially undistinguishable from lexical replacements, whether "internal" (i.e. neologisms) or "external" (i.e. borrowings). This problem is particularly significant for extinct, ancient languages, such as Hittite and Tocharian. According to Holm, Bouckaert *et al.*'s list for Tocharian contains eighteen gaps, which constitute 8.78 percent of the total list. For Hittite, the number is even higher – twenty-five gaps, or 11.4 percent of the total list. Furthermore, the Hittite list contains a large number of so-called "singletons" – that is, words showing no connection to (or cognation with) other languages. Counting both gaps and singletons, 50 percent of the items in the Hittite list are mistaken as substitutions by the computational algorithm. Bouckaert *et al.* (2012) date the divergence of Tocharian from Armenian at 5,100 years ago (3100 BCE) and the divergence of the Tocharo-Armenian branch from the rest of the tree at 6,900 years ago (4900 BCE). Anatolian languages, including Hittite, are estimated to have split off from the rest of the Indo-European tree 8,500 years ago (6500 BCE).[8] However, as the authors themselves concede, some uncertainty surrounds the positioning of the "basal sub-groups – Tocharian, Albanian, Greek and Armenian" (Bouckaert *et al.* 2012, Supplementary Materials: 8–9). Thus, if some of these groups can be shown to have diverged later, the highest-order split into Anatolian and non-Anatolian languages may also shift to a later date.

The third factor that creates an illusion of a slower rate of change – and consequently of an older root of the tree – concerns another bias in the data used by Bayesian phylogenetic dating studies: that concerning sweeping substitutions in descendant languages. As noted by Garrett (2006: 148), in a number of cases a word in the known common ancestor of a certain branch (Latin, Sanskrit, etc.) has been replaced by a related word in all or most descendant languages. One of Garrett's examples is Latin *ignis* 'fire', which

---

[8] In the new version of the tree, Tocharian no longer forms a common branch with Armenian, and splits off the rest of the Indo-European tree at 7,200 years ago. Anatolian languages are shown to have split off from the rest of the Indo-European tree 8,000 years ago (6000 BCE), that is 500 years later than in the original results.

has been replaced by reflexes of Latin *focus* 'hearth' throughout the Romance branch: Italian *fuoco*, Spanish *fuego*, Portuguese *fogo*, French and Walloon *feu*, Catalan *foc*, Sardinian *fogu*, Provençal *fuèlha*, Romansh *fiug*, Friulian *fûc*, and Romanian *foc*. Similarly, Latin *caput* 'head' has been supplanted in numerous descendants by a derivative of Latin *testam*, which originally meant 'shell, ceramic pot' but that had changed its meaning by the process of synecdoche sometime before the fourth century CE – that is, before Latin split into daughter languages. Hence now we have Italian *testa*, French *tête*, Walloon *tiesse*, Sardinian *testa*, Provençal *testo*, Romansh *testa*, and Friulian *teste* (although witness Spanish *cabeza*, Portuguese *cabeça*, Catalan *cap*, and Romanian *cap*, which are reflexes of the Latin *caput* 'head'). Another example, also mentioned by Garrett, is the archaic Sanskrit *hanti* 'kills', which has been replaced by reflexes of a more recent Sanskrit form *mārayati* throughout the Indo-Aryan languages. According to Garrett's calculation, if a mere 5 percent of data is of this type, it will make a 6,000-year old PIE appear 9,000 years old – exactly the gap that separates the Steppe and the Anatolian hypotheses.

Note that undetected borrowings, gaps in the data where translations of meanings in the Swadesh list are not known, and sweeping substitutions in descendant languages all bias the resulting dates *in the same direction*: they make divergences look older than they actually are. Together, these problems are clearly sufficient to add up to the 3,000-year timing difference in the emergence of PIE in the Anatolian and the Steppe hypotheses. Since undetected borrowings are a major factor in the miscalculation of the age of PIE, it is tempting to limit one's data to those lexical items that are *a priori* known for their low mutation rates, for example, by using Swadesh-100 instead of Swadesh-200 list. But as McMahon and McMahon (2006: 159) point out, this route is even more treacherous, as limiting the data in such a fashion would result in a smaller number of items, which in turn "will also increase the negative effect of individual coding errors, with each such error potentially contributing 1000 years to the dating estimates".

Problematic calibration points

Other problems are introduced into the Bayesian phylogenetic dating methods by the use of calibration points, which are supposed to be incontestably dated through historical records. That is, instead of calculating the dates of *all* divergence points on a language tree by way of some presupposed constant rate of change (e.g. 5 percent or 14 percent per millennium) from the present day back, such studies peg some of the splits to clearly dated historical events or written documents; the dates of other splits are calculated probabilistically in relation to the dates that are taken to be known *a priori*. Establishing such calibration points, however, proves to be far more complicated than it sounds. As it turns out, Bouckaert *et al.* (2012) provide erroneous dates for several key divergence points.

A prime example of such problems is the alleged separation of Romanian from the remaining Romance languages, which the authors calibrate at 270 CE, when Dacia ceased to be part of the Roman Empire (cf. the Supplementary Materials for Bouckaert *et al.* 2012, although their "consensus tree" shows this split as occurring much earlier, around 2,000 years ago). However, it is not clear whether the Romanian language directly stems from the Latin spoken in the Roman province of Dacia or from the Latin of a later group of migrants.[9] If the latter scenario is true, then the date of separation between Romanian and its Romance sisters must be later, indeed perhaps much later, than 270 CE. Because the first preserved Romanian text dates only from the sixteenth century, we do not have direct evidence of its early stages. Thus, the evidence for the later migration scenario is necessarily indirect. One possible argument in favor of the later migration scenario is that the Romans occupied Dacia for only about 170 years before abandoning it, which may not have been long enough for Latin to have firmly taken hold. In this respect, Romania can be compared to Britain, which was occupied by Rome for a much longer period but which ultimately failed to become a Romance-speaking land. However, evidence from numerous borrowed Latin words and morphemes in Celtic languages, such as Welsh, Cornish, and Breton, strongly suggests that mass bilingualism must have been present in Roman Britain, in turn implying a large community of native Latin speakers there. That Britain did not ultimately become a Romance-speaking land is a result of later events, not the lack of initial Latinization.

More solid if still indirect evidence in support of the later-arrival theory can be pieced together based on the findings of Romanian dialectology. Specifically, Romanian dialects are quite homogeneous and mutually intelligible to a high degree, which does not fit the scenario of Romanian being a direct descendant of Latin spoken in Dacia prior to 270 CE. Under such a scenario we would expect a much more strikingly differentiated set of dialects, comparable to, say, the dialectal situation in northern France until recently, where mutual intelligibility between non-adjacent dialects was low. The surprising uniformity of Romanian dialects indicates that Romanian did not descend from the Latin once spoken in Dacia, and therefore that the date when Dacia ceased to be a part of the Roman Empire is irrelevant to dating the emergence of the Eastern Romance branch. It is also significant that the Roman Province of Dacia covered less than half of the territory of present-day Romania: for

---

[9] We thank Stephane Goyette (personal communication) for an extensive discussion of the "Romanian split".

example, the Bucharest region, whose dialect is the basis of standard Romanian, never belonged to the Empire. If Romanian goes back to the Latin of Roman Dacia, as the 270 CE date of the separation presupposes, it must have spread into lands that were not part of Dacia. But if this is the case, we would expect to find a greater dialectal differentiation in the "old Romanian territories" compared to the lands that the language reached later, in parallel, for example, with a greater dialectal differentiation in the core Russian lands (European Russia) compared to the more recently acquired territories (Siberia and the Far East). This expectation, however, runs contrary to fact, as not only are Romanian dialects relatively homogeneous, they are equally homogeneous across all parts of the country. Such basic facts of Romanian dialectology, however, make perfect sense if Romanian spread over present-day Romania (and Moldova, which was never part of the Roman Empire) long after the fall of the Roman Empire from some other place. (It is also worth noting that Bouckaert et al.'s graphic representation of the Romanian split on their animated map[10] is bizarre, as it depicts the divergence event as taking place in the area of Rome, creating the impression that Romanian diverged from Latin in the center of the Empire, with speakers of (proto-)Romanian subsequently moving eastwards.)

If Romanian did not emerge in what is now Romania, where did it arise? Most scholars working on this topic think that it developed just to the north of the Jireček Line, which runs through central Bulgaria and along the modern border between Serbia and Macedonia. Under the Roman Empire, Latin prevailed to the north of this line, while Greek was dominant to the south (Hall 1974: 70). Significantly, the Latin-speaking areas found to the north of this line in antiquity, in what is now northern Bulgaria and southern Serbia, had been under Roman power long before, and long after, Dacia was part of the Roman realm. As was true elsewhere in the Empire, distinctive dialectal features began to emerge in this area as early as the second century CE, perhaps influenced by the pre-existing Thracian languages of the region. After Slavic-speaking peoples occupied the lowland parts of this area during the early Byzantine period, the Latin speakers retreated to rugged highlands, and eventually spread both to the north and the south. As this occurred, their language began to diversify, eventually giving rise to the various Eastern Romance languages, which include not only Romanian but also the several distinctive so called Vlach languages, which were, and to some extent still are, widely scattered through the Balkan Peninsula, well into what is now Greece. The presence of words of Germanic (specifically, Gothic), Thracian, and Slavic origins in Eastern Romance languages, particularly in Romanian, is often cited as another

---

[10] Available online at language.cs.auckland.ac.nz/

argument for the emergence of Eastern Romance in the Balkans and not in (former) Dacia (cf. Matley 1970: 84).

As we can thus see, a simple "270 CE" calibration point for the separation of the Eastern Romance languages from the other members of the Romance family, based on the historical event of the Roman withdrawal from Dacia, is misleading, telling us nothing about the actual history of these tongues. In terms of historical linguistics, the date is arbitrary. And as it turns out, many of the other historical dates used as calibration points in Bouckaert et al. (2012) have even less significance.

Atkinson and Gray (2006: 101) defend themselves against such charges by arguing that "the step-by-step removal of each of the 14 age constraints on the consensus tree revealed that divergence time estimates were robust to calibration errors across the tree". But if many of the fourteen calibration dates are incorrect – and especially if all these errors are *in the same direction* of making the tree appear older rather than younger – certainly such calibration mistakes will add up.

Another example of a problematic calibration point is the date for the Slavic split used by the Gray–Atkinson team, as it is also too early. They place the separation of the Slavic languages into constituent branches circa 450 CE.[11] This date is based on the following "historical information" (see Bouckaert *et al.* 2012, Supplementary Materials: 48, italics ours):

Old Church Slavonic and East Slavic texts date to *beginning of 9th century* and indicate significant divergence by this time. This split must have occurred after the Balto-Slavic divergence.

It is not clear, however, what early East Slavic texts from the "beginning of the 9th century" they refer to, as all known documents that are identifiably Old Russian (as the common East Slavic proto-language is called by Slavicists), or that merely contain elements of it, date from the eleventh century. According to Sussex and Cubberley (2006: 81), the earliest manuscript "to contain Russian elements, even if only in copyists' errors" is the Ostromir Gospel dating from 1056–1057 CE. In it, Sussex and Cubberley "find the beginnings of a Russianized Church Slavonic, which spread gradually to liturgical, ecclesiastical and chancery documents [. . .] where the use of Church Slavonic was obligatory" (2006: 81). (The Novgorod Codex, discovered only in 2000, is now generally considered the oldest East Slavic book, making the Ostromir Gospel the second oldest, but not by much, as the Novgorod Codex dates from the first quarter of the eleventh century.)

---

[11] Their calibration point is formulated as follows: "log normally distributed with mean 300.0 and 0.6 standard deviation with offset of 1200.0" (Bouckaert *et al.* 2012, Supplementary Materials: 48).

Another well-known Old Russian document, *The Primary Chronicle*, is also much younger than "the beginning of the 9th century": although it describes a history of Kievan Rus' from about 850 to 1110, it was originally compiled by a monk named Nestor working at the court of Sviatopolk II of Kiev, who ruled from 1093 to 1113 (it is believed that the *Chronicle* was composed closer to the end of Sviatopolk's rule). Moreover, as is the case with many other medieval manuscripts, the original *Chronicle* and the earliest known copies have been lost, and the two oldest extant copies date from an even later period: the Laurentian Codex was compiled in 1377 and the Hypatian Codex dates from the fifteenth century. A fourteenth-century copy of an eleventh-century chronicle describing events of the ninth century can hardly be used as hard evidence for the language of the ninth century or even of the eleventh century: copyists not infrequently changed the text of the original, introducing elements of the language as spoken in their own day. Yet another Old Russian document, known from over 110 extant copies, is *Rus'kaya Pravda*. It too must have been composed no earlier than the late eleventh century, as the oldest parts of the document refer to the rule of Yaroslav the Wise (1019–1054). Other portions were added as late as the thirteenth century; again, the numerous extant copies date from the thirteenth to the eighteenth centuries. Finally, one of the best sources of information about Old Russian is the collection of birch bark documents from Old Novgorod, which "show even more evidence of a native Russian idiom" (Sussex and Cubberley 2006: 81). But even the oldest birch bark letters uncovered so far (documents 246, 247, 591, and 915-I in the online database of the Russian birch bark documents) date from the second quarter of the eleventh century (1025–1050), placing them between the Novgorod Codex and the Ostromir Gospel.[12]

In actuality, native-language writing anywhere in the Slavic world did not even exist at "the beginning of the 9th century". Cyril and Methodius started developing a writing system for Slavic only in 862/863, and no physical copies of manuscripts remain from their time. As for the East Slavic realm, literacy arrived only with the adoption of Christianity in Kiev in 988 CE. Thus, this key piece of "historical information" in Bouckaert *et al.* (2012) is simply wrong. It does not come as a surprise then that in their earlier work Gray and Atkinson (2003) date the split at circa 700 CE. Sussex and Cubberley (2006: 20) place the Slavic split more accurately "by about the tenth century AD" and write rather vaguely about "the breakup of Slavic unity in the first millennium AD".

The use of such a vague temporal description as "in the first millennium AD" by Sussex and Cubberley (2006) underscores another important issue: how does one date a linguistic divergence "event" that spans a temporal interval

---

[12] The online database of the Russian birch bark documents is available online at http:// gramoty.ru

that can be as long as several centuries or even millennia? This is obviously a matter of interpretation. In the case of Slavic languages, research in historical linguistics shows that the earliest dialectal divergences date from the fourth century, and that the last shared innovations for the entire grouping (e.g. the rise of the neo-acute tone, discussed in detail in Schenker 1995: 98) can be dated to the ninth century. Another late common innovation is the borrowing of the word for 'king'. All three major branches of Slavic share this loanword: compare Serbo-Croatian (South Slavic) *kralj*, Czech (West Slavic) *král*, and Russian (East Slavic) *korol'*. Because languages in the three branches inherited the common form and applied their respective sound changes, such as pleophony in East Slavic, we can reconstruct the ancestral form to the Proto-Slavic **korl'ĭ* 'king'. This word was borrowed into Proto-Slavic from Germanic; more specifically, it goes back to the name of Charlemagne in Old Low German, *kar(a)l* (cf. Bernecker 1924: 572–573; Trubachev 1984: 82–89; Gluhak 1993: 342–343; Dolgopolsky 2000: 405–406). The dates of Charlemagne's rule – from 768 to 814 CE – thus provides an important clue for Slavic unity as late as the ninth century.

The consensus choice of a relatively late date for the Slavic split, somewhere between 900 and 1000 AD, is thus linked to the well-documented fact that until that time the Slavic-speaking world was a continuum of mutually comprehensible dialects. Difference among Slavic modes of speech, documented in Schenker (1995: 162–164), were not pronounced enough to justify treating them as distinct languages. Thus, according to Schenker (1995: 69), "at the time of the Moravian mission (863), and for perhaps two or three generations beyond it, one may still speak of Slavic linguistic unity". In short, Bouckaert *et al.*'s (2012) date of circa 450 CE for the Slavic split is almost certainly much too early.

The same problem, not surprisingly, applies to other linguistic divergence "events" that are firmly dated by the Gray–Atkinson approach. Consider, again, the Romance branch. Bouckaert *et al.* (2012) use two calibration points for Romance languages: the Roman presence in Dacia (112–270 CE) to date the Romance split (essentially, the splintering of the Romanian/Vlach branch) and the Strasburg Oaths (842 CE) to date the split between the Spanish/Portuguese and French/Walloon branches. As we have already seen, the former calibration point is highly problematic. Let us now turn to the Western Romance languages, focusing on French, Italian, and Spanish. As with Slavic languages, the timing of Western Romance divergence depends on how we construe the split.

The earliest evidence of Romance dialectal divergence comes from a period as early as the beginning of the first millennium CE, if not earlier.[13] Late Latin, as it was spoken by both educated and uneducated speakers during the late

---

[13] Adams (2007: 2, 684) claims that regional variation in Latin existed "not only in the late Empire but even in the Republic" and "can be traced back at least to 200 BCE".

Roman period, exhibited pronounced differences both over time and space, and began differentiating while the Empire was still powerful. While frequently mentioned by the ancients, regional and social variation, especially in the earlier period, was rarely reflected in literary Latin sources. Instead, "the extant Latin of ancient sources at first sight scarcely displays any local features but presents itself as a unitary system" (Galdi 2011: 564). One therefore has to look for different sorts of materials to bear witness to the early stages of the regional diversification of Latin. One such source is the plays by Plautus and Terence, many of whose characters were slaves; dialogues between them appear to reflect the lower register of Latin at the time. Another window into how Latin was actually spoken in the third and fourth centuries CE is a corpus of Late Latin texts, especially those that condemn linguistic "errors" in spoken Latin, such as *Appendix Probi*.

A third important line of evidence about regional variation in Latin comes from inscriptions; the ones discovered in Pompei, which were buried in volcanic ash in 79 CE – nearly 400 years before the fall of the Western Roman Empire – are particularly instructive. One conspicuous feature of these inscriptions is the lack of the Latin ending *-t*, placed on verbs in the third person singular, which is assumed to reflect how Latin was spoken in Pompei (Bonfante 1968).[14] As it happens, this change corresponds to the history of the Italian language: where Latin had *venit* for 'he/she comes', Italian today has *viene*. Yet this well-attested change did not affect all Latin dialects simultaneously. In the Iberian Peninsula, the final *-t* on third-person verbs was retained into the early ninth century, as evidenced by texts in Mozarabic, a Romance language that was spoken in the southern part of the Iberian Peninsula. Since these texts are short verses written in the Arabic script (spelling the final *-t* with the Arabic letter *dad*) by scribes proficient in writing Classical Arabic rather than Latin, we can be virtually certain that they recorded the pronunciation of the Romance vernacular in the Iberian Peninsula at the time rather than carrying on a spelling convention from Latin. Elsewhere in the Romance-speaking world, the final *-t* survived even longer. French, in some ways the most innovative Romance language, retained the final *-t* in verb forms such as *vient* for even longer, as the modern spelling indicates.[15] (Indeed, this sound is still pronounced under some circumstances – namely, when a following word begins with a vowel: for example, in *Vient-il?* 'Is he/she coming?') Sardinian was one of the first languages to diverge from the

---

[14] The exact delimitation of the geographical area where the final *-t* in verbs was lost at that time is discussed in more detail in Adams (2007: 92–93; 2013: 148–149).

[15] Scholars disagree as to when precisely the final *-t* disappeared in pronunciation in French, but it was maintained at least into the ninth century and possibly even as late as the sixteenth century. For a discussion and references, see Adams (2013: 149–150).

rest of the Romance family, yet some varieties of it still keep a final-*t* in such verbs to this day. Thus, we have good evidence that the loss of the third-person-marking-*t* that took place in the Latin of Italy (or even more locally at Pompei) had not spread to the Latin of the Iberian Peninsula (Spain and Portugal), Gaul (today's France), or Sardinia until after the fall of the Empire. Such evidence clearly indicates that the dialectal differentiation of Latin that would eventually yield the various Romance languages had begun hundreds of years *before* the fall of the Western Roman Empire.[16]

Moreover, geographical differences in how people spoke Latin throughout the Roman Empire were evident even to the Romans themselves, as noted in Wright (2011: 61), who finds evidence for geographical variation "in the tales of visitors to Rome, even those who acquired some social status (including one or two emperors), whose speech betrayed the fact that they came originally from Spain or Africa. Such geographical particularities trumped those of social class or levels of education; St Augustine of Hippo (in Africa) suffered such opprobrium in Milan." Similarly, Cicero refers to the poets of Corduba in Spain as *pingue quiddam sonantibus atque peregrinum* 'sounding rather thick and foreign' and "some years later Quintilian mentions the existence of certain sounds which allow one to recognize people of particular nations" (Galdi 2011: 567; see also Adams 2007: 123–147). Galdi attributes the existence of regional variation in Latin "to several factors, such as the influence of the substrate languages (in the form of interference or through the intrusion of loanwords), the coinage of local terms, the retention of words that fell out of use in other areas (and thus developed to be dialectal forms)" (2011: 567). Kortlandt (1990: 132) makes essentially the same point by identifying "the formation of Romance with the imperfect learning of Latin by a large number of people during the expansion of the Roman empire". One of the main forces behind the diversification of Latin was the Roman army, as conquering soldiers were generally the first ones to bring Latin to the far corners of the growing Empire. Solodow (2010: 36) recounts a story from the historian Tacitus, describing

a vivid scene during a military campaign. Two brothers belonging to a Germanic tribe stand on opposite banks of a river and spiritedly debate the proper stance to be taken towards the Romans [. . .] And when [Tacitus] mentions that the debate was conducted mostly in Latin and explains that the brothers had learned the language through military service with the Roman army, he indicates one way by which familiarity with Latin spread among native people.

The Romans encouraged Latin-based education in the provinces, especially for the children of the elites; "Britain, Gaul, Spain, and north Africa were soon

---

[16] For a further discussion of geographical variation in Latin, from the early Republic until the end of the Empire, see Galdi (2011) and Adams (2007).

producing distinguished orators and writers, teachers and scholars," writes
Solodow (2010: 37). He goes on to cite a passage from Augustine (*On the
City of God*, 19.7) that reveals that Latin was viewed by the Roman government as "cementing [the] empire together". As Latin gained ground throughout
the Empire, first in its cities and then in the countryside, many of the conquered
people became bilingual.[17] But such massive learning of Latin as a second
language resulted in non-native speakers introducing patterns and constructions from their native tongues. Children who grew up in such linguistically
mixed communities incorporated some non-Latin patterns into their otherwise
Latin speech. Such substratum influences are a well-known vehicle of
language change, although individual instances are often difficult to prove
(see McMahon 1994: 221–222 for further discussion and examples). Changes
were also happening in regional variants of Latin for other reasons as well (see
Adams 2007: 711–720), and gradually a plethora of dialects, and eventually
distinct languages, emerged.

But from what time were these varieties of Latin sufficiently different to be
characterized as distinct languages? This is once again a matter of interpretation; as Hall (1974: 102) put it: "No-one rang the church-bells and proclaimed: 'Hear ye! Hear ye! Latin is dead, and the Romance languages are
now fully differentiated from each other!'" Bouckaert *et al.* (2012) refer to the
"beginning of repetition of Latin liturgical formulas without comprehension
in sixth to eighth centuries CE" as historical evidence for the divergence of
Romance languages. Indeed, this failure of the common people to understand
the sermons delivered at Mass concerned the Church authorities and led to the
issuing of an edict in 813 CE, at the Council of Tours, requiring priests to
translate their sermons "*in rusticam romanan linguam aut theotiscam* 'into the
rustic Roman or German tongue'" (Hall 1974: 105). However, all we can
conclude from this is that the popular speech had become differentiated from
the official Latin of the Church, not that regional varieties of it ceased to be
mutually comprehensible.

The Gray–Atkinson model further takes the Strasburg Oaths, pronounced by
Louis the German and by the soldiers of Charles the Bald of France in 842 CE,
to be evidence that French and Iberian/Spanish were distinct languages by that
time.[18] Indeed, the text of the Oaths exhibits some features "that most clearly

---

[17] For a detailed discussion of societal and individual bilingualism in the Roman world, see
Mullen (2011).

[18] Charles the Bald and the soldiers of Louis the German took the corresponding oaths in
"German" (*teudisca lingua*). Thus, the two kings took their oath in the language of the other's
subjects, while their followers then took an oath in their own language. This arrangement was
done to create the most widespread confidence in the alliance of the two kings against their
brother Lothair. (See Hall 1974: 111–116 and Solodow 2010: 268–276 for the texts, transcription, glosses, and detailed discussions of the Oaths.)

[stamp] the Oaths as French, and no longer Latin, and not Italian or Spanish either" (Solodow 2010: 273). One such feature is the loss of the unstressed final vowels in the words *amur* 'love', *savir* 'to know', *quant* 'how much', and *dreit* 'right'. In Latin these words were spelled with a final vowel (*amore*, *sapere*, *quantu*, and *directu*) which was most likely pronounced as an undifferentiated "schwa" by the Late Latin period. In Italian and to some degree in Spanish, the word-final vowel has been preserved to this day (Italian: *amore*, *sapere*, *cuanto*, and *diritto*; Spanish: *quanto*, *derecho* but *amor*, *saber*), while in (modern) French it has disappeared (*amour*, *savoir*, *quant*, and *droit*). (The final vowel appears in the Oaths if it was an -*a*, as in *cosa* 'thing', or if it followed an otherwise unpronounceable consonant cluster, as in *fradra*, *Karle*, and *nostro*; French went on to lose those vowels in pronunciation as well, although they are retained in the form of *e-muet* 'silent e' in *chose*, *frere*, *Charles*, and *nôtre*.) Other features that characterize the text of the Oaths as Gallo-Romance, as opposed to Ibero-Romance and Italo-Romance, include the preservation of a two-way case distinction between nominative and oblique (e.g. *Deus* vs. *Deo* 'God') and the replacement of *dare* 'to give' by *donare*. To recap, the Oaths exhibit some innovations that had occurred in Romance on its trajectory to becoming French but not Italian or Spanish. Another text, known as *Sequence of St. Eulalia* (in French: *Cantilène de sainte Eulalie*), written just a few decades after the Strasburg Oaths, brings us even closer to Modern French. Unlike the Oaths, which were originally composed in Latin and reflect the high-brow, archaizing language of the elites, largely devoid of regional features, the *Sequence of St. Eulalia* was composed in the vernacular and reveals even more unmistakable evidence of the Romance vernacular spoken in northern France circa 880 CE (see Hall 1974: 112; Solodow 2010: 276–285 for a detailed discussion).[19]

However, the appearance of certain regional features in the linguistic varieties spoken in different parts of the Romance world does not mean that these varieties were so mutually incomprehensible as to form distinct languages. Hall (1974: 113–116) attempted to reconstruct the Oaths in vernacular varieties of several regions, as they would have been pronounced circa 842 CE, including Old North French (based on the reconstruction of the phonemics of the *Sequence of St. Eulalia*); a conservative Italo-Romance dialect of the Cassino area (based on the Cassino depositions); a more advanced, diphthongizing variety of Italo-Romance of the Tuscan area; a conservative, non-lenited Ibero-Romance and a more advanced, lenited and diphthongizing variety thereof;

---

[19] While the language of both the Strasburg Oaths and the *Sequence of St. Eulalia* can be easily categorized as belonging to the "French" branch, the more precise classification of the Oaths as northern French (*langues d'oïl*), Occitan, or Franco-Provençal and of the *Sequence of St. Eulalia* as northern French (*langues d'oïl*) or Walloon remains highly controversial.

Sardinian; and pre-Romanian. Based on these reconstructions, Hall drew an isogloss map of the Romance world in the mid-ninth century CE. Some of the isoglosses – those representing the loss of final vowels, the preservation of the case-system, and the replacement of *dare* 'to give' by *donare* – separate Gallo-Romance from both Italo-Romance and Ibero-Romance. In contrast, other isoglosses unite Gallo-Romance with Ibero-Romance, as opposed to Italo-Romance, or Sardinian. One such feature is the change from /kt/ > /jt/ in both Gallo-Romance and Ibero-Romance, as in /drejt/ 'right' and /derejtu/, respectively (in contrast to /derettu/ or /diritto/ in Italo-Romance dialects and /direttu/ in Sardinian). Another common feature of Gallo-Romance and Ibero-Romance is the replacement of /omne/ 'every' by formations with /kata/: the reconstructed Gallo-Romance form is /časkunə/ and the reconstructed Ibero-Romance form is /kata/ or /kada/, depending on the dialect. At the same time, Italo-Romance had /onne/ and Sardinian had /onnia/. Other features, however, unify Gallo-Romance with Italo-Romance, in opposition to Ibero-Romance and Sardinian: for example, the former but not the latter dialects exhibit a synthetic future tense, as in /salvərai/ 'I shall succor' in Gallo-Romance and /ssalvarao/ or /ssalvaro/ in Italo-Romance.[20] Importantly, all three varieties exhibit shared innovations, such as the replacement of /skire/ 'to know' by /sapere/. Hall's own conclusion is that "the western Romance area (including Sardinia!) still formed a single [dialectal continuum], whereas pre-Roumanian was already a separate language by any criterion" (1974: 113). Île-de-France, Castile, and Florence were only three among about a dozen linguistic centers in this dialectal continuum; their importance as the birthplaces of contemporary French, Spanish, and Italian standards derives from our modern equation of languages with nation-states (cf. Max Weinreich's famous quip that "a language is a dialect with an army and a navy"). For a medieval observer, Old Provençal and Gascon in southern France and Picard and Normand in northern France were just as important.[21] Old Provençal in particular exerted significant influence on French to its north, Spanish to its southwest and Italian to its southeast (e.g. the Spanish designation of itself, *espagnol*, is an Old Provençal word).

Crucially, even a classification of modern Romance varieties into those that belong to the Gallo Romance ("French"), Ibero Romance ("Spanish"), and Italo-Romance ("Italian") branches is not as obvious as it may seem. For example, Friulian and Ladin are variously classified as either "French" or "Italian", while Catalan is sometimes placed in the "French" category and sometimes in the "Spanish". Bouckaert *et al.* (2012) place Friulian and Ladin

---

[20] For a more detailed discussion of the development of future tense in Late Latin, see Adams (2011: 277–280).

[21] On the early form of Gascon, see Chambon and Greub (2002).

in the "Italian" branch and Catalan in the "Spanish" branch, but this view is not widely shared among historical linguists, and may reflect modern geopolitical contamination, more than anything else. The Ethnologue classifies Friulian and Ladin as "French" (more precisely, Gallo-Romance) and Catalan as "Spanish" (more precisely, Ibero-Romance), while the Orbilat.com website (based on an earlier edition of the Ethnologue, apparently) categorizes Catalan and Ladin as "French" (Gallo-Romance and its subgroup Rhaeto-Romance, respectively) and Friulian as "Italian" (Italo-Romance). Those varying modern classifications reflect the intermediate nature of those tongues, which resulted from their continuing sharing of innovations and extensive contact. Aslanov (2002) describes the situation that obtained in the Medieval Romance-speaking world by such French terms as *mélange* 'blending' and *brouillage* 'jamming'. This blending is particularly obvious from such texts as the Franco-Venetian versions of *Chanson de Roland,* the text of which exhibits the syntactic structures and lexical elements typical of the northern French varieties (*langues d'oïl*) and morphophonetic characteristics of the Venetian dialect (see Aslanov 2002: 16 and the references cited therein).

The Romance-speaking world was evidently still perceived as "dialects in the same diasystem" ("dialectes d'un même diasystème", Aslanov 2002: 14) by both Romance speakers and outsiders as late as the thirteenth century. Tellingly, the opening passage of the Strasburg Oaths refers to the language in which Charles the Bald made the declarations that Louis the German swore to observe as "Romance language" (*romana lingua*), not "French".[22] The term *lingua franca* was used throughout the Middle Ages for a pidgin combining Romance and non-Romance elements that was used in the Eastern Mediterranean basin (now called Mediterranean Lingua Franca). The Romance elements in this pidgin came from the tongues we would now distinguish as belonging to the "French", "Spanish", and "Italian" branches. The term *lingua franca* originated from common usage in the medieval non-Romance-speaking world, whereby all Romance-speaking Western Europeans were called "Franks", or *faranji* in Arabic and *phrankoi* in Byzantine Greek. (Also tellingly, there is no trace of intra-Romance translation in the early Crusader States although translation to and from non-Romance languages, such as Armenian, Greek, and Arabic, was commonplace.) Aslanov further notes that in Old High German the term *walahisk* (cognate with the English *Welsh*) originally referred to the neighboring Romance-speaking peoples of the mixed Gallo-Roman stock and their tongues: French, Franco-Provençal, Provençal, northern Italian dialects, and so on. In the Slavic languages this term was extended to their Romance-speaking neighbors who had no Celtic ("Welsh") roots, such as the Italians

---

[22] Wright (2011: 64) makes a similar point, noting that "*romanice* and *latine* seem to have been essentially synonymous terms, even in the writings of ninth-century Carolingians".

(cf. the Polish *Wloch* 'Italy') and the Romanians. (Eventually, it narrowed even further to designate only one group within Eastern Romance, the Vlach.) Similarly, Jewish scholars writing in Medieval Hebrew – many of whom were themselves speakers of a Romance tongue – used the term *la'az* indiscriminately for all Romance varieties; they also mixed forms from "French" and "Spanish" varieties, such as Franco-Provençal and Castilian Spanish, when explaining a difficult Hebrew word, as if these were dialects of the same language. This is not to say that medieval writers did not perceive any differences among the linguistic varieties in the Romance-speaking world. Indeed, as pointed out in Aslanov (2002: 14), both the famous complaint of Conon de Bethune (*Chansons*, III, 8–14), annoyed at being mocked for his Picard accent, and the parody of the Anglo-Norman in the *Roman de Renart* (*Roman de Renart*, I, 2420, 2511, 2513, 2859, 2911, 2995, 3034) show a clear awareness of the differences among the dialects of northern France (*langues d'oïl*).

To recap, the Romance-speaking world of the ninth century – when the Strasburg Oaths were written – cannot be depicted as one in which French, Italian, and Spanish have already developed into distinct and mutually incomprehensible languages. Thus, it is impossible to pinpoint precisely the date of the Romance split, which starts with the diversification of Latin as the Roman state expanded and ended hundreds of years after the fall of Western Empire in the fifth century CE.

As this chapter has shown, the new Bayesian methods of dating the emergence of linguistic branches constitute at best only a slight improvement over the older and thoroughly discredited approach of glottochronology. The computational techniques used tend to produce systematic dating distortions, while the idea of using precise calibration points to fix the resulting temporal sequences in accordance with the historical record fails to withstand scrutiny. Despite the many protestations to the contrary, the results are anything but "robust". And as we shall see in the next chapter, the phylogeographical components of the analysis turn out to be every bit as problematic as the phylogenetic analysis. Here again, the more we scrutinize the finding of "Mapping the Origins", the more errors we uncover.

6   The historical-geographical failure of the Bayesian phylogenetic model

Our key objection to the Gray–Atkinson approach to Indo-European origins and expansion is not that it merely fails, but rather that it fails repeatedly, returning incorrect results at almost every turn. As this is itself a rather spectacular claim, it must be substantiated in some detail. This chapter thus examines the accuracy of the model used in the celebrated 2012 paper, "Mapping the Origins and Expansion of the Indo-European Language Family", as reflected in both the maps that it uses as input (see Maps 3–6) and the maps that it produces. Two output maps capture our initial attention. One is a conventional map (Map 7) that shows the dates at which Indo-European languages most likely reached particular parts of Europe and western and southern Asia, within 95 percent probability parameters. More important is the authors' elaborate animated map (Maps 10–20), which portrays not just the language family's expansion but also its division into branches. Here viewers are invited to "watch the unfolding of the Indo-European languages in time and space", beginning some 6,500 years BCE and concluding precisely at 1974 CE.[1]

These maps are tremendously important, as they allow us to test the performance of the model, particularly its phylogeographical component, against the empirical record. We have a tremendous amount of information about the "unfolding" of most Indo-European branches over the past several thousand years, when written records have been periodically preserved. As it turns out, neither the authors' static map nor their animation comes close to capturing the historically documented patterns of Indo-European expansion, either of the language family as a whole or of its constituent branches. If the model fails so fully when it comes to the documented past, it is hardly reasonable to assume that it nonetheless functions well in regard to the prehistoric period, when it cannot be tested in such a manner. It thus fails with respect to the Uniformitarian Principle, discussed in Chapter 3. Numerous discrepancies between the static and animated maps provide further evidence of the model's failure.

---

[1] The quoted line is from "movie caption" found in the Supplementary Materials of Bouckaert *et al.* (2012).

Scrutinizing the output of the Gray–Atkinson model is, however, a perilous task, as these maps are not necessarily what they purport to be: straightforward visualizations of Indo-European expansion. On the surface, the animated map indicates that Indo-European languages had reached only a tiny corner of Russia by the late twentieth century and had not yet extended into far southern Spain, northern Scotland, or northern Scandinavia. The static map shows similar patterns, but not to the same extent. Yet if one reads the fine print that appears in the Supplementary Materials to "Mapping the Origins", the maps actually only indicate that it is highly probable that Indo-European languages spread into the areas so indicated *no later* than the dates provided. All that the model signifies in regard to Russia, in other words, is that Indo-European languages probably did not begin to spread into the region *after* 1974 CE (as shown on the animated map), with no stipulations about when they might have first established themselves; surely this is one of the weakest geographical points ever made in a scholarly paper. As a result of such equivocation, other features of the maps might also indicate something other than what they apparently show. Green lines that ramify across the animation as the timeline moves forward, for example, seem to indicate the diversification of Indo-European into separate subfamilies along with the subsequent movement of these novel language groups into new territories. As a result, they will be treated as such in the following discussion. But it is possible that these lines actually indicate something else, as no key or explanation of any kind is provided, in violation of the basic conventions of cartography. Other features of the animated map remain mysterious, such as the abrupt color changes that periodically appear, with large areas shifting from yellow to various shades of green as the time-bar progresses. This lack of basic explication makes it seem as if the maps are designed more to impress than to edify or inform.

How the Gray–Atkinson model undermines itself

Before we examine the failure of the maps that accompany "Mapping the Origins", it is necessary to specify more precisely how the patterns that they show test the model that produced them. A signal flaw of Gray and Atkinson's proposed solution of the Indo European question is not that it merely favors demic diffusion over migration, linguistic conversion, or other forms of language expansion, but rather that it *presupposes* it. In purporting to assess Colin Renfrew's Anatolian thesis against the near-consensus view, the authors do leave the place of origination open, but they assume that the processes of language group expansion posited by Renfrew are necessarily true – building them into their statistical model – while rejecting the countervailing claims made by Renfrew's opponents. All of this is done, moreover, without discussion, let alone justification; instead, such key presumptions precede analysis, as if the Steppe school's crucially divergent *processual* views had not even been considered. And although the authors do admit that languages occasionally spread more rapidly than the plodding pace entailed by demic diffusion, as when Latin encompassed the western half of the Roman Empire, they regard such processes to be so rare as to be ignorable. Other features of the Gray–Atkinson model further bias the outcome against the Steppe hypothesis, such as the exclusion of historically attested Indo-European languages that had been spoken in the grassland belt in ancient times, such as Scythian.[2]

As the model thus rules out the main mechanism of language expansion hypothesized by proponents of the Steppe school, it can hardly be said to fairly test that school's claims against those of the Anatolian thesis. But as it does explicitly employ the mechanism of expansion favored by the Anatolian school, it can reasonably be regarded as testing that hypothesis, at least as the authors have operationalized it. If the data are adequate for the task and if the various postulates embraced by the authors largely conform to reality, then the model should produce results for the historical period that are largely coincident with the spatial and temporal patterns known from documentary sources. If the output does not accord with this foundation of knowledge, then we can safely conclude that the model itself fails. Such failure does not, however, automatically invalidate the Anatolian hypothesis itself, but it does rule out the manner in which the hypothesis is put into formal terms by the authors of "Mapping the Origins".

Opening miscues: the Hittite fallacy

The animated map indicates that by 6500 BCE Anatolia, the Balkan Peninsula, and the northern Fertile Crescent were occupied by peoples speaking Indo-European languages (within 95 percent probability parameters), although the static map largely limits the spread of the family at this time to Anatolia, while other maps on the website indicate a smaller homeland in south-central Anatolia. Restricting our analysis to the animated map, we note that it shows no lines of linguistic divergence into subfamilies in the opening frames. One might therefore assume that the model indicates that a largely undifferentiated Indo-European-speaking population occupied all of Anatolia and the Balkans at the time. If so,[3] the depiction is almost certainly fanciful, as this region is much too

---

[2] Although the vast majority of specialists think that the Scythians spoke an Indo-European language (or languages), some doubt persists, as the surviving information is spotty and as steppe-zone confederacies were often composed of numerous subgroups. As the authors of the website *Indo-European Chronologies* put it, "Scythians could be a mess of Indo-European, Turkish, Uralic tribes synthesizing different cultures". (http://indoeuro.bizland.com/project/chron/chron3.html)

[3] Again, we must admit that it is possible that such mapping only indicates, within 95 percent probability parameters, that PIE was spoken *somewhere* in the zone so indicated, but not

large to have been dominated by such closely related Neolithic languages. Expansive zones of tightly related languages are generally encountered only in particular social environments, such as when migrational streams quickly overrun large expanses of land and then begin to differentiate. According to John Robb (1993), the territories of single or closely related languages could have been relatively broad among Paleolithic hunter–gatherers, knit together by social networks necessitated by low population density, but in sedentary Neolithic farming communities, areas of relative linguistic homogeneity would have been highly restricted, counting relatively few speakers. Robb further contends that language group size and territory would have generally increased in the late Neolithic and into the Bronze Age, due to enhanced social integration and political centralization. But in his well-theorized model, language diversity and territorial fragmentation would have been at their height in Anatolia around 6500 BCE. At that time, one would expect to find scores of languages belonging to several different families in central Anatolia alone, rather than the barely differentiated Indo-European languages spanning Anatolia and the Balkans depicted in the Gray–Atkinson model.

But even if one limits Proto-Indo-European (PIE) at this time to a much smaller central Anatolian core, serious problems are still encountered. The main issue here involves the complex mixture of languages attested in this region in the Bronze Age. Based on written records that go back as far as the seventeenth century BCE, we know that Hittite and its related languages in the Anatolian branch of Indo-European coexisted with several non-Indo-European tongues. If, as postulated by the Gray–Atkinson model, Indo-European languages had blanketed this homeland for thousands of years prior to the emergence of the Hittite Empire, the local non-Indo-European languages would have to be regarded as intrusive, having diffused into the area from elsewhere. Yet everything that we know of Anatolian history indicates that the opposite situation obtained.

From royal archives at Hattusa and other historical sources, we know that Hittite was the official language of a powerful empire that dominated central Anatolia in the middle centuries of the second millennium BCE. It was presumably the main tongue of its ruling aristocracy and merchant class, but not of the bulk of its peasantry.[4] The Hittite Empire was a multilingual polity, although as the eminent Anatolian linguist H. Craig Melchert (2003:13) notes,

---

necessarily over its entire extent. If so, however, the model could indicate Indo-European origins in the Balkans or the Caucasus, ideas that the authors explicitly reject. Other maps found on their website, moreover, definitely tie PIE to a more limited portion of Anatolia, but one that is probably still much too large for a Neolithic language group. The lack of basic explanation obviously presents a major obstacle to such analysis.

[4] Although Melchert (2003: 15) more cautiously opines that "There is no reason to doubt that Hittite was a spoken language for at least some of the ruling class". Watkins (2008: 7), on the other hand, more forcefully claims that "Hittite was clearly the language of the ruling classes".

we know little of its "true socio-linguistic situation". But it does seem clear that even in the imperial core, Luvian, another Anatolian (hence Indo-European) language, vied with Hittite and eventually largely supplanted among the elite (Yakubovitch 2010). More to the point, many if not most subjects of the Hittite state spoke Hattic, a non-Indo-European language that may have been related to the languages of the Northwest Caucasian family. A few Hattic texts have survived, largely of a ritual nature (Bryce 1998: 11). Broader Hattic cultural elements were clearly evident in the Hittite realms of art and mythology, but not in those of administration, law, or diplomacy (Bryce 1998: 16). A few Hittite political terms, however, were borrowed from Hattic, including those for "administrative district", "crown prince", and "throne" (Melchert 2003: 20). The Hurrians, another non-Indo-European-speaking people found in the Empire – and outside of it, in opposing states – also contributed to Hittite culture. As Wilhelm (2008: 103) informs us, "Hurrian played an important role in [Bronze-Age] Anatolia as a language of learning and ritual", yet it appears to have borrowed little if anything from the Indo-European tongues of the region.

In fact, the very name "Hittite" derives, by way of the Hebrew Bible, from the non-Indo-European Hattic people. The Hittites referred to themselves as the Nesa, and their own language as Nesili, often rendered Nesite, a term derived from the town of Nesa, or Kanes, located in central Anatolia roughly 150 kilometers southeast of the imperial capital of Hattusa (cf. Yakubovitch 2010). Nesa was evidently the first seat of Hittite power, and the Hittites continued to regard it as their homeland, as reflected in their own ethnonym. But they called their country as a whole "Hatti", or the land of the Hattic people, referencing not themselves but rather one of the groups they ruled over (Collins 2008: 31). Neighboring peoples such as the Assyrians also used a term derived from "Hatti" to refer to this state, and by extension its Nesa rulers as well. We, of course, do the same.

To the extent that this widely accepted understanding of the term "Hittite" is correct, the Anatolian hypothesis loses credibility, as it would require an extraordinarily unlikely chain of events. The Gray–Atkinson model tells us that the Nesili (Hittite) language can be traced back to stateless, Neolithic farmers living in central Anatolia, a people whose language family had diffused throughout Anatolia millennia before the establishment of the Hittite Empire. It would further require us to believe that thousands of years later, the Nesa people established a state ruling over a non-Indo-European-speaking Hattian peasantry that must have "diffused" into the land from elsewhere, given the hypothesized early Indo-Europeanization of the Anatolian Peninsula.[5] These

---

[5] In Renfrew's (1987: 56) account, the non-Indo-European-speaking peoples of Bronze-Age Anatolia apparently stemmed from populations that had coexisted in the same general area as the Indo-European speakers, having undergone only minor, local movements that put them in complete proximity with the Hittites proper (Nesili). This far-fetched thesis, however, requires a many-millennia-long period of complex linguistic interspersion, a pattern ruled out by the geographical model used by the Gray–Atkinson approach.

subordinated newcomers, moreover, would have referred to their new territory as their own country, and their indigenous rulers would have agreed, renaming their land in reference to this relatively powerless population. The Nesa would also have massively borrowed religious and artistic motifs from the hapless Hattians, perhaps including their own tutelary deity (Collins 2008: 175), while largely ignoring their political and legal systems.

Such a scenario defies logic, common sense, and historical precedence. But had the Nesa (or Hittites proper) been a people of foreign origin who migrated into Anatolia, intermingled with and eventually established rule over the indigenous Hattic and Hurrian speakers, then the situation would be perfectly reasonable. Similar processes, after all, have played out in many other ancient civilizations the world over. Powerful newcomers often adopted cultic elements from indigenous populations while imposing their own political and legal systems on them and spreading their own languages as well. The fact that the Hittites also borrowed terms for much of the native Anatolian flora and fauna from the non-Indo-European languages in the region (Melchert 2003: 17) is further evidence against their autochthonous origin.

As a result of these and other lines of evidence, virtually all Hittite specialists view the Hattians and the Hurrians as the indigenous elements, and the Nesa and other Anatolian speakers such as the Luvians as relative newcomers.[6] In the current consensus view, the Indo-European speakers are seen as having gradually infiltrated into the region and then amalgamated with the indigenes, rather than having massively invaded and conquered them in a single event. As Trevor Bryce (2002: 8) summarizes, "Indo-European speakers may have first entered Anatolia during the third millennium, or even earlier. After their arrival one branch of them intermingled with a central Anatolian people called the Hattians [... such that] the Hittite population and civilization were primarily an admixture of Indo-European and Hattian elements." Or as Melchert (2003: 23) starkly puts it, "We emphatically reject the claim [...] for Indo-European speakers in Anatolia since 7000 BCE [...] The virtual complete absence of evidence for linguistic contact between Proto-Indo-European [...] and the known ancient languages of the area (Hattic, Akkadian, and Sumerian) also preclude an Indo-European linguistic continuity in Anatolia of five thousand years."

The non-Indo-European Hurrian people, it must also be noted, occupy a prominent place in Indo-European studies by virtue of the fact that a number of their rulers and deities evidently had Indo-European, and more specifically Indo-Aryan, names. By the same token, words of Indo-Aryan origin, particularly

---

[6] Macqueen (1986: 33, 26) considers the Hattian question to be "open", but he also states that "evidence for the original 'homeland' of the Indo-European languages seems to be overwhelmingly against a situation in Anatolia, and this means that speakers of an Indo-European language must have entered Anatolia at some time from some other area". Yakubovitch (2008: 7), in contrast, remains "agnostic" on the question of Anatolian linguistic origins.

ones pertaining to horses, are also found in their lexicon. The best-known example of such terms comes from the Hittite horse-training manual of Kikkuli, a master horse trainer from the Hurrian kingdom of Mitanni, which is "still" in print (Nyland 2009). Despite the fact that Kikkuli wrote in Hittite (Nesite) and was from a Hurrian-speaking land, he used many Indo-Aryan terms with obvious affinities to Sanskrit. Scholars of earlier generations thus tended to attribute the formation of the Hurrian kingdom of Mitanni to Indo-European-speaking, chariot-driving invaders who established themselves as a ruling aristocracy. More recent work, however, downplays this element, stressing instead the preponderance of the indigenous Hurrian component in the Mitanni state. As Eva von Dassow (2008: 84) concludes, "The linguistic evidence suggests that speakers of an Indo-Aryan language were few, at most, even in Mittani". But even if few in numbers, they were nonetheless present, and a number of them were politically significant. More to the point, the presence of Indo-Aryan speakers in the Bronze-Age Middle East indicates long-distance migration of Indo-European speakers into the region, one that was not associated with the much earlier spread of the Hittite (Nesite) language.

Regardless of this Mitanni controversy, the peculiarity of Hittite and its related languages plays a crucial role in the Gray–Atkinson scheme. Their model generates an Anatolian heartland for the language family in part because Anatolian is the most distinctive branch of Indo-European, having branched off from the main trunk before any of the other languages did.[7] For the Indo-European family as a whole, the deepest diversity is thus encountered when one examines the Anatolian languages in relation to the family's other branches. Such deep diversity, in turn, often indicates a place of origin, both in regard to linguistic evolution and to biological evolution as well. Geneticists are thus able to trace the origins of crop species to their genetic diversity centers, places where highly distinctive cultivars as well as wild progenitors can be found. In such areas, long periods of selective breeding have ensured the emergence of numerous distinctive strains, only some of which subsequently spread out of the original zone of domestication.

The same logic does indeed work well for determining the place of origin of some language families. Austronesian, which includes most languages of

---

[7] The status of Hittite and its sister languages on the linguistic tree, however, remains uncertain. Most scholars include the Anatolian languages within the Indo-European family, while others (Sturtevant 1962; Adrados 1982) call the grouping that includes Anatolian languages "Indo-Hittite", reserving the term "Indo-European" for its non-Anatolian branch (which is referred to by the scholars who include Anatolian within Indo-European as "Nuclear Indo-European"; cf. Figure 4 in the Appendix). Followers of the Indo-Hittite hypothesis typically assume an earlier date for the Anatolian split than do other scholars. Regardless of the labels used, the essential relationship stands: Hittite and its sister Anatolian languages diverged from the other languages in the Indo-European family well before it split further.

Insular (island) Southeast Asia, Madagascar, and the islands of the Pacific Ocean, is traceable to Taiwan on this basis. Here, diversity near the root of the family is overwhelming: of the eleven primary branches of Austronesian, ten are limited to the so-called Taiwanese Aborigines, now largely restricted to the rugged eastern highlands (Blust 1999; *inter alia*). The ancestral Proto-Austronesian language split into separate families long ago on Taiwan, only one of which successfully spread outside of the island. This non-Taiwanese Malayo-Polynesian subfamily, however, expanded over a larger portion of the Earth's surface than any other language group, provided that one counts sea-space as well as land. In doing so, it diversified magnificently, but its diversity over most of its expanse is relatively superficial, limited to the smaller branches and leaves. Austronesian's *deep* diversity in Taiwan thus firmly links its origin to the island, as Russell Gray has himself concluded from a detailed study (Gray *et al.* 2009). In this case, Bayesian phylogenetic analysis accords well with traditional inquiry in historical linguistics.

According to Gray and his co-authors, the same situation is encountered in regard to Indo-European, where the deepest division separates the long-extinct Anatolian subfamily from the main stem. Yet in this case, the diversity center principle does not apply. Whereas in the Austronesian case, ten out of eleven major branches are found in Taiwan, its proposed homeland, in the Indo-European situation the ratio reversed. Here only one of ten major branches – Anatolian – was once spoken in the area postulated as the family's birthplace, and as far as we know it was never a "bushy" branch with numerous distinctive languages. Although Anatolian is indeed the oldest Indo-European subfamily, we have no reason to assume that it simply stayed put at its point of origin. It is instead quite likely that the Anatolian languages were differentiated from the so-called Nuclear Indo-European (i.e. non-Anatolian) languages by losing contact with them through the process of migration.

If anything, the diversity center principle suggests someplace other than Anatolia as the PIE homeland, as the non-Anatolian "half" of the family is the one that developed numerous distinctive branches. An even deeper problem concerns the near impossibility of non-Anatolian Indo-European languages diffusing simultaneously to the east and west of Anatolia, yet at the same time sharing a number of significant innovations that the Anatolian branch missed, as discussed in Chapter 9 below.

Further mapping miscues

Hurrian and Hattian were not the only historically attested ancient non-Indo-European languages found in the area pictured as having been occupied by Indo-European speakers in 6500 BCE on the Gray–Atkinson animated map, and by 4500 BCE on their static map. On the island of Lemnos in the Aegean, for example, an unrelated language associated with a sophisticated pre-Hellenic population persisted at least until the fifth century BCE; not coincidentally, the Bronze-Age Lemnians have been described as having built Europe's first city (Abulafia 2011: 20). The Lemnian tongue seems to have been a member of the extinct Tyrsenian family, which also encompassed Etruscan and Rhaetic, languages spoken in the Italian Peninsula and environs through the first millennium BCE (Rix 1998). The Gray–Atkinson model, however, shows Italy as having been overrun by Indo-European speakers circa 2500 BCE at the latest. The only way to make sense of such a distributional pattern within the confines of the model is to assume that the Proto-Tyrsenian speakers were Mesolithic foragers who adopted the Neolithic package from the Indo-European newcomers and then preserved their languages in small pockets within an Indo-European sea for several millennia before abruptly expanding themselves at a much later time at the expense of Indo-European speakers. But such a scenario does not fit with what little is known about the Tyrsenian languages, which seem to have been too closely related to have existed in isolation from each other for so long a period; as Rix (2008: 142) argues, "Lemnian and Rhaetic are so close to Etruscan that Etruscan can be used to understand them". It is more likely that these were simply languages of sedentary agriculturalists that withstood much later thrusts of the Indo-European Greek and Italic branches, a scenario that fits well with the Revised Steppe hypothesis. Alternatively, Tyrsenian languages could have spread westward from the Aegean through Bronze-Age seaborne migrations, owing in part to what Broodbank (2013: 464) calls the "surge of innovation in maritime technology" that occurred in the late second millennium BCE. Either scenario, however, runs against the Gray–Atkinson model. As a result of such problems, the mapping of the Indo-European realm circa 500 BCE found in Bouckaert *et al.* (2012) deviates substantially from the mapping of the same phenomenon derived from actual linguistic, historical, and archeological sources (see Maps 8 and 9).

Many other inexplicable patterns are found on the authors' static map of Indo-European expansion (Map 7). It depicts Ireland, for example, as having become Indo-European-speaking thousands of years before central and south-western France, and before Lithuania as well. Although we do not know when the Indo-European language family arrived in Ireland (Mallory 2013b), it almost certainly reached central France much earlier. Yet the map shows small parts of western France as non-Indo-European-speaking as recently as 400 years ago, along with northeastern Scotland, northern Norway, the Balearic Islands, Corsica, Crete, Cyprus, Gotland, and almost all of Russia. To be fair, all that the model actually indicates is that such areas almost certainly did not become Indo-European-speaking *after* that date. But such an excuse cannot be granted to the mapping of areas that were, as far as we know, *never* Indo-European-speaking as having been so hundreds or even thousands of years ago. Examples here include Georgia, Chechnya, most of Dagestan, and the Basque Country of Spain. Imaginary ancient Indo-European outliers are also shown as scattered across the Saharan and Arabian deserts, while fanciful medieval Indo-European outliers are strewn over Tibet and Burma. In what is now Romania, moreover, different areas are unreasonably shown as having become Indo-European-speaking in different periods of time spanning thousands of years.

Other patterns on the map oddly follow modern political boundaries that could not conceivably have had anything to do with the expansion of the Indo-European language family. Examples here include the mapping of Moldova as a non-Indo-European island within an Indo-European sea, the abrupt termination of Indo-European languages precisely at the border between Latvia and Estonia,[8] and the fact that the extent of the language family's expansion almost exactly tracks the northern border of modern Tajikistan in the vicinity of the Fergana Valley. All of these features are beyond suspicious, raising red flags with any readers familiar with the linguistic history of western Eurasia. It is well known, for example, that the modern division of the Tajik (Indo-European) and Uzbek (Turkic) languages along the Tajikistan–Uzbekistan boundary mostly reflects Soviet-era geo-ethnic machinations (Bacon 1966: 17–18) along with Uzbekistan's post-Soviet policy of forcing an Uzbek identity on local Tajiks.[9]

When we turn to the authors' animated map, or "movie" as they prefer to call it, deeper problems are encountered (Maps 10–20). As the animation unfolds, Indo-European is shown as diverging into branches in particular times and places in a manner that almost always fails to accord with what is known from both historical and linguistic sources. A branch that includes Greek and Albanian (as mentioned in Chapter 4, the existence of this branch is itself quite uncertain) is shown as having reached Greece from Anatolia circa 3000 BCE, and then finally diverging into its Greek and Albanian sub-branches in the vicinity of northern Euboea around 2000 BCE, although neither limb shows any more extension for another several thousand years. By the year 1 CE, the Albanian branch has moved into Thessaly, while the Greek branch has pushed south to the vicinity of Athens, where it stays put. The Albanian line does not reach Albania until around 1400 CE, and in the sixteenth century one of its side-branches begins to drift across the sea, eventually reaching Calabria in the mid-1800s and northern Sicily in the early 1900s. Needless to say, such

---

[8] The Uralic Livonian language was spoken in Latvia until its last speaker died in 2013. See: languagesoftheworld.info/geolinguistics/endangered-languages/obituary-last-speaker-livonian-language-died-age-103.html

[9] For a Tajik perspective on this issue, see: http://tajikam.com/index.php?option=com_content&task=view&id=68&Itemid=36

depictions are contradicted by the historical record, which is fairly complete for this part of the world since the middle of the first millennium BCE. The mapping of Slavic languages is equally off-base. Here we see the Balto-Slavic branch diverging from the main Indo-European stem circa 2500 BCE along what is now the Slovakian–Hungarian border and then expanding to the northeast. Around 200 BCE, the South Slavic languages diverge from this stem and head south, reaching what is now northern Serbia around 600 CE and central Macedonia circa 1000 CE. The East Slavic languages, on the other hand, branch off around 825 CE in far southern Poland, and do not reach Russia until the late 1500s. Needless to say, all of these scenarios contradict what is known of the development of this language group.

More amusing is the authors' depiction of an Insular North Germanic maritime creep. Not only does their model not allow migration, it permits no instances of rapid movement at all. Sailing across the sea to settle a new land, as occurred after the Norse discovered a virtually uninhabited Iceland in the ninth century, is simply not permissible. As a result, the Insular North Germanic language branch, which includes Icelandic and Faroese, is depicted as having taken several hundred years to reach the islands after it departed from the continent circa 700 CE. We are thus forced to imagine its speakers living on boats that slowly drifted northward in a constant direction, eventually reaching Iceland after many generations at sea.

Almost as absurd is the depiction of the development and spread of the Romance group. These languages are shown as having separated from Latin in central Italy in the early centuries of the first millennium, and then slowly diffusing across Western Europe and into Romania through the medieval and early modern periods; such mapping, however, contradicts the authors' use of 270 CE as a calibration point for the Romanian split (see Chapter 5). Moreover, the branch that includes Spanish and Portuguese does not reach the Iberian Peninsula until about 950 CE, whereas the one that encompasses French and Walloon is not shown as reaching central France until circa 1725 CE. Such a depiction is of course nonsensical, as Latin spread across the western half of the Roman Empire centuries earlier and then largely differentiated in place, eventually yielding the Romance languages and dialects spoken today, as discussed in Chapter 5.

Admitted errors and preservation bias

Intriguingly, the authors admit to their erroneous portrayal of the spread of the Romance languages, blandly noting that their model cannot accommodate the "rapid expansion of a single language", such as "the initial rapid expansion of Latin" (Bouckaert *et al.* 2012, Supplementary Materials: 19, 27). But history counts hundreds of such instances of rapid language spread, and if a model cannot account for them, then it simply cannot get the story right. Yet even the assumption that Latin spread "rapidly" is itself open to question, if "rapid expansion" of a language means that virtually everyone within a given territory comes to speak it as their native tongue within a few generations after it was introduced. Latin probably did not become the mother tongue of the majority of the population in what is now northern France until the late Roman period, several centuries after the area came under Roman rule, and it evidently never became the native language of the *majority* of the population in England, Wales, or the Basque Country (although evidence of extensive linguistic contact between Latin and Celtic languages of Britain, or Latin and Basque, suggests a large number of bilingual speakers; cf. Chapter 5). Reasoning out such thorny issues, however, is made difficult if not impossible by the authors' failure to define what they mean by "rapid". Does any language spread at a pace faster than that entailed by demic diffusion count? If so, most instances of language expansion cannot be handled by the authors' statistical model.

Gray and Atkinson also acknowledge that their model fails to account for the spread of Celtic languages on the European mainland, and as a result their model brings Indo-European languages to Iberia at an admittedly tardy date. This flaw also accounts for the fact that Ireland is shown as having been "Indo-Europeanized" before central France, as the Insular Celtic subfamily, unlike the vastly larger mainland branch, is included in the authors' database. The continental Celtic languages were ignored simply because they were not adequately recorded; the methodology used necessitates such a maneuver, as the basic vocabulary of inadequately recorded languages cannot be plugged into the computational model. What the authors fail to acknowledge, however, is the fact that this same problem recurs repeatedly. Scores of Indo-European languages fell into extinction without being written down. This problem is exacerbated by the fact that the distribution of extinct but recorded Indo-European languages was anything but random. As it turns out, those that are documented well enough to be included in the database were all located in the southern and western portions of the early Indo-European zone, precisely where literacy and state formation emerged first. As a result, the vast swath of the steppes disappears from view. Yet most experts are virtually certain that the various Scythian and Sarmatian languages spoken in this area several thousand years ago belonged to the Indo-European family, even if we know little of their vocabulary and grammar. Is it thus any wonder that the model fails to support a steppe origin for the family?

To understand the depth of this particular mire, imagine a more extreme situation. Picture a scenario in which a given language family is known from historical sources to have once covered a large expanse of land, but had eventually been limited to a small corner of that range, covering, say, 10 percent of the original area. Imagine as well that all of the recorded extinct languages in the same family just happened to have also been restricted to the same limited area. If one were to perform a phylogeographical analysis of this language family, what would be the chance that the model would indicate origination outside of that small zone of language survival and ancient data availability? The answer is simple: nil. Yet on the basis of the mere facts given above, the actual likelihood of the language family having originated outside of that restricted area would be in the order of 90 percent.

Such intrinsic preservation bias in "Mapping the Origins" is enough to discredit the entire approach, as it ensures the rejection of the Steppe hypothesis that is ostensibly being tested against the Anatolian theory. But in a refrain that is now getting old, this is merely an initial problem. Poor data quality is ultimately a lesser flaw than the embrace of false assumptions. Better and more complete data can theoretically be acquired – although that would be extraordinarily unlikely in the case of an extinct language such as Scythian – but fallacious postulates invalidate the analysis before it even begins. And here the morass is deep indeed.

7   Unwarranted assumptions

As the previous chapter demonstrated the historical-geographical failure of the Gray–Atkinson statistical model, this chapter takes on more foundational issues to explain why it backfires so completely in this regard. Here we argue that the approach is geographically doomed at the outset by three key unwarranted assumptions underpinning the "Mapping the Origins and Expansion of the Indo-European Language Family" article (Bouckaert *et al.* 2012). The first such assumption – that languages spread through a process of demic diffusion – has already been grappled with, but we have not yet fully outlined its ramifications, nor have we explained the ways in which languages generally do expand into new territories. The second fallacy concerns the geographical distribution of language groups, and by extension that of other human socio-cultural aggregations. The Gray–Atkinson model erroneously assumes that languages are universally patterned into spatially discrete, non-overlapping units that can be modeled and mapped as simple polygons. In actuality, languages are generally characterized by complex patterns of interspersion that defy simple mapping into territorial blocks that neatly fit together like pieces of a jigsaw puzzle. The third fallacy is the most fundamental. Here we encounter the idea that linguistic evolution is so similar to biological evolution that it can be analyzed in the same terms, using the same tools. In actuality, the proliferation of languages is only vaguely analogous to organic evolution, and must therefore be conceptualized in its own terms, through linguistically appropriate methods. Such techniques need not be fully divorced from those of the evolutionary biology, but neither can they be identical.

Gray and Atkinson readily admit that their approach requires simplifications that do not accord perfectly with reality. They defend such a tactic with the trivially true observation that all scientific endeavors require the use of simplifying assumptions. But just because some simplification is necessary does not mean that any form of simplification is therefore acceptable. Standard scientific procedure requires that one demonstrates that one's simplifying assumptions match actual conditions reasonably well. A physicist judiciously assumes, for example, that a billiard ball is a perfect sphere because the object in question does indeed approach the state of full sphericity, a quality that can be measured. But assuming that languages spread by means of demic diffusion is an entirely different kind of proposition, as it does not begin to approximate reality as we know it. As the main assumptions found in "Mapping the Origins" are not justified in any manner, they do not fulfill the basic scientific mandate. Instead, they are better regarded as debilitating meta-assumptions: unjustified and unjustifiable simplifications made for the sake of convenience.

As we have repeatedly emphasized, the Gray–Atkinson model of Indo-European origins postulates linguistic expansion through demic diffusion, a process originally formulated by the geneticist Luigi Luca Cavalli-Sforza, which Renfrew (1994: 120) defines as occurring when a language "move[s] as the [...] population slowly expands in a wave of advance". (In the Gray–Atkinson model, however, demic diffusion does not occur *solely* along a wave of advance, as it also periodically throws more distant outliers into the new lands ahead of the front.) The demic diffusion process entails movement into territories that are new to the group in question, although such lands are usually already inhabited by a pre-existing population. Nothing in the original genetic demic diffusion model stipulates the fate of such indigenes: they could be supplanted, incorporated into the advancing population, or continue to exist in enclaves within their original homeland. What it does presuppose, however, is that relations between the newcomers and the original inhabitants will have no measurable effect on the former group's rate of advance.

Although we do not deny that the mechanism of demic diffusion can play a role in the expansion of languages and linguistic branches, we think that is overshadowed by other processes of language spread. The demic diffusion thesis fails as an overarching model for three main reasons. First, as discussed previously, it precludes migration, which has been ubiquitous in the human past. Second, it portrays the advance of a given language into a new territory as an even process, if not an inexorable one. In actuality, such movements are molded by both the physical and human geography of the landscapes in question, and generally proceed in pulses, occasionally stalling out altogether and sometimes even going into reverse, processes that were clearly evident in the Germanic *Drang nach Osten* ("drive to the east") into Slavic-speaking lands in the medieval period. Third, and perhaps most important, the demic diffusion model regards the process as essentially biological, with languages spreading as their native speakers spread. In actuality, languages often expand into new areas through the social process of second-language acquisition by non-native speakers, followed by the eventual rearing of children in the new tongue by their bilingual parents. In some circumstances, moreover, population movement can actually run in the opposite direction of language movement. As Nichols (1992: 20) shows, "in the North Caucasus [...] there is a long-standing tendency for languages to move in one direction and people to move in the opposite direction: steppe and lowland languages move uphill and mountain people move downhill" (see also Nichols 2013: 43 for a more detailed discussion of this phenomenon).

The ubiquity of human migration

In the late nineteenth and early twentieth centuries, archeologists stressed migration in part because the process was so widespread in early historical times. Long-distance movements of sizable groups were especially common in Europe and environs in late antiquity, a time sometimes known as the "Migration Period" or the *Völkerwanderung*. Some population movements during this period were massive and highly organized if ethnically heterogeneous, as when a loosely estimated 80,000 Vandals and Alans under King Gaiseric crossed the Strait of Gibraltar and headed into North Africa. Others were more diffuse and less tightly organized, as when the Anglo-Saxons flowed into Britain and when Slavic speakers infiltrated southward all the way to the Peloponnesian Peninsula in the early Byzantine period (Heather 2010; Geary 2003). To be sure, scholars of earlier generations often misconstrued such movements, viewing migratory groups as distinct ethnic groups or even nations, united by a single language and sense of common identity, whereas in actuality most were diverse assemblages tied together more by politics than identity (see Heather 2010). But it is undeniable that episodes of migration during this period were common and often massive.

Peter Heather's (2010) reconstruction of Slavic expansion in the early medieval period is worthy of more extended consideration, as it sheds light on a number of key processes under consideration here. As Heather demonstrates, Slavic movements were not all of a kind, as conditions changed over time and different processes were involved in different areas. But even the more dispersed episodes, such as that taking Slavic speakers westward to the Elbe River, cannot reasonably be modeled as a "wave-of-advance" (demic diffusion), as far too much ground (900 kilometers) was covered too quickly (150 years). And instead of advancing randomly, Heather argues, these people seem to have sought out "wooded uplands rather than the more open plains", owing to their swidden ("slash-and-burn") agricultural orientation (2010: 422). Such a subsistence system, moreover, pre-adapted these early Slavic-speaking peoples to migration, a process facilitated as well by their relatively simple yet highly functional material culture. Yet as Heather continues, such an explanation still fails to account for the extraordinary scale of Slavic expansion in this period, which encompassed most of central and eastern Europe. He thus turns to processes of acculturation to round out the narrative. Most of the lands of central Europe occupied by the Slavs at this time were politically chaotic and partially depopulated, owing to the exodus of large numbers of Germanic-speaking peoples, including political leaders and the most effective military units. A similar loss of order occurred in the Balkans after the Eastern Roman Empire's abandonment of the Danube frontier in 614 CE and the transferal of the elites to coastal enclaves and the imperial core. The Slavic groups that subsequently moved into these areas were generally quite small in scale, but they were nonetheless militarily capable, owing in part to enforced tutelage under the Avar Khanate. Such groups seem to have subjugated the disorganized remnants of the pre-existing populations, but then accepted them into their own societies after "conversion" to their Slavic language and lifeways. Owing to its relatively egalitarian nature, Slavic culture at the time had its own draw. As Heather (2010: 434) summarizes:

[S]ome early Slavic groups were remarkably "open" in terms of their group identity, being willing to accept prisoners [. . .] as full and equal members of their society. This is remarkable. Many societies are willing to take in outsiders, but it is more usual for the latter to have to adopt, at least initially, relatively inferior social positions.

If true, this account goes a long way toward solving the mystery of the extraordinarily rapid nature of Slavic-language expansion during this period. It also points to both the ubiquity and complexity of the process of migration, as well as that of linguistic conversion.

Recorded movements of large numbers of people are not merely a feature of the Migration Period, but in actuality long predate it. Some of these population transfers have been framed as invasions, such as the incursions of the mysterious "Sea Peoples" that wreaked havoc at the end of the Bronze Age in the eastern Mediterranean,[1] and others as colonization, such as the spread of Greek and Phoenician settlements along the shores of the Mediterranean in the first half of the first millennium BCE, but both forms of advance entailed processes that can only be modeled as migration and not diffusion. In a few cases, we actually have demographic data, such as that pertaining to the 20,000 Celtic "Galatians" who settled in Anatolia in the third century BCE, although all such numbers remain highly uncertain.[2] Such movements, moreover, were by no means limited to western Eurasia; key events in South Asian history involved the substantial migrations of peoples of Central Asian origin into the region,

---

[1] Abulafia (2011: 52) describes the "Sea People" as composed of "fluid and unstable alliances of pirates and mercenaries, able occasionally to form large enough navies and armies to pillage [important] centers". Broodbank (2013: 464) reflects current scholarship in casting doubt on traditional interpretations of the incursions of the "Sea Peoples" as "ethnically organized discrete events", but he still insists on the "likelihood of frequent multilateral and sometime cumulative large-scale relocation, much of it by young men – the most footloose, aggressive and armed element in most populations".

[2] Darbyshire et al. (2000: 78), argue in an understated manner that the 20,000 figure, which stems from Livy, is "open to question" and that "other Galatians could have subsequently boosted the total". But they also write that "it is beyond question that the ultimate goal of these migratory movements was to acquire land for permanent settlement".

such as the Yuezhi in the first century BCE and the Hephthalites (White Huns) of the sixth century CE (Wink 2001).

Admittedly, few of these recorded migrations of the ancient period brought about lasting linguistic change, as the newcomers usually adopted the languages of the native inhabitants, even when they came as conquerors. But in some cases their languages persisted for centuries; the Celtic Galatian tongue might have been spoken in central Anatolia until the sixth century CE (Freeman 2001), while Crimean Gothic may have persisted until the late eighteenth century.[3] And in a few instances, permanent linguistic change followed, as when the Magyars stormed into the Danubian Basin. The signal lesson from ancient and early medieval history is therefore that mass migration was relatively common and could result in linguistic expansion or relocation.

But even if migration was relatively common in the ancient world, it does not necessarily follow that it was widespread in prehistoric times, before the formation of large-scale societies and before the development of writing allowed such mass movements to be recorded. Renfrew would likely counter that the migrations recounted above were rare events either propelled by the "systems collapse" of tightly organized civilizations or made possible by the emergence of complex, hierarchical societies capable of organizing them.[4] But if we turn to other sources of information from other parts of the world, the evidence is overwhelming that sizable movements of people occurred well before the development of complex societies – movements that could and did radically transform the linguistic geography of entire continents.

Perhaps the best linguistic evidence for major prehistoric migrations comes from North America. Unlike Eurasia, almost all the major language families there were characterized by profound spatial discontinuity. Most of the Na-Dené languages, for example, were found in the far northwestern portion of the continent, as would be expected considering the fact that their ancestral speakers arrived in North America well after those of the other Native American groups (with the exception of the speakers of Eskimo–Aleut languages). But some Na-Dené languages, such as Navaho and Apache, were located in the U.S. Southwest, while others were found in northwestern California and southeastern Oregon. According to the diffusion model, people speaking Na-Dené languages would have had to have slowly drifted southward, occupying all of the intermediate areas between Alaska and New Mexico; subsequent diffusions of several other languages into the southern half of this zone would have then occurred, leaving major pockets of Na-Dené speakers

---

[3] On Crimean Gothic, see Krause and Slocum, "Gothic Online" (University of Texas at Austin, Linguistics Research Center: utexas.edu/cola/centers/lrc/eieol/gotol-10-R.html)

[4] Some scholars have even argued that the "barbarian invasions" of late antiquity actually involved mere "elite transfer" rather than migration, a position thoroughly demolished by Heather (2010).

stranded among peoples speaking language belonging to other families. But not only is such a scenario extraordinarily unlikely, if not impossible, but archeological and ethnohistorical evidence strongly indicates that the ancestors of the Navahos and Apaches *migrated* into their current homeland along specific pathways roughly around 1000 CE (Seymour 2012). Renfrew (1994: 120), in contrast, attributes these features of Na-Dené distribution to "elite dominance, amplified by horse-back riding" – developments that occurred, to the extent that they occurred at all, centuries later.

Similar patterns obtained in regard to languages spoken by other peoples of pre-Columbian North America, some of whom were farmers rather than hunter–gatherers. The Siouan and Iroquoian language families had similarly disjunct distributional patterns, as did the Algic family. Some Algic-speaking groups ended up on the coast of northwestern California, thousands of kilometers from the family's northeastern core. Here they found themselves adjacent not only to Na-Dené-speaking peoples, but also to other groups speaking languages in other families. Such profound linguistic discontinuity and interspersion can easily be explained on the basis of migration, yet make no sense when regarded from the perspective of demic diffusion.

Admittedly, some of the discontiguous nature of Native American language families resulted from populations fleeing the encroachment of European settlers, but the basic patterns had been established well before colonization. In some cases, multiple long-distance migrations occurred; in that of the Tuscarora, the second movement entailed a return to the homeland. The Tuscarora are an Iroquoian-speaking group whose ancestors left the Great Lakes region and resettled in what is now North Carolina well before English settlers arrived. After suffering a major defeat at the hands of the North Carolina Militia in 1713, a large contingent of the Tuscarora returned to the Great Lakes area, where they were welcomed by their distant relatives into the Iroquois League to become the group's sixth nation, a standing that they retain to this day (Wallace 2013).

In the demic diffusion model as theorized by Colin Renfrew (1987), such geographical patterns as we find in indigenous North American linguistics would have to be regarded as mysterious, as he regarded movement over such distances as so difficult and hazardous as to be inconsequential. But if migration can be perilous, it can also be rewarding, and if many individuals have a sedentary bent, others are adventuresome and risk-taking. More specifically, instances of migration can be explained in any number of ways, as discussed by Anthony (2009). Resource-rich regions can beckon, probably one of the reasons why the salmon-endowed Northwest Coast of North America ended up with such pronounced linguistic diversity at the family level. In low-population-density environments, intergroup conflicts often lead to the ready exodus and relocation of defeated or disgruntled clans into previously unclaimed lands; according to Kopytov (1987), such processes helped generate the complex ethnic mosaics that characterize much of sub-Saharan Africa. In densely populated areas, population pressure can push groups out of a homeland core into more favorable locales situated at some remove. A prime historical example here would be the Greek colonization of the shores of the northern Mediterranean and Black seas beginning in the eighth century BCE.

As Renfrew (1987) recognizes, technological advantages, often combined with demographic pressure, can drive members of one group into the territory of another. Yet he regards such a process as highly limited, found only when agriculturalists gradually encroach upon the lands of hunter–gatherers or when complex societies capable of mounting invasions of conquest establish "elite dominance". In actuality, relatively minor differences can be highly significant, sometimes allowing less complex societies to overwhelm those at a higher level of political and cultural sophistication. Consider, for example, the process by which Thailand was transformed from a mostly Mon- and Khmer-speaking area to one dominated by languages in the Tai family. A thousand years ago, the Mon kingdom of Dvaravati was a highly cultured Hindu-Buddhist state based in the central lowlands of what is now Thailand, whereas the Tai speakers were organized in petty, illiterate chiefdoms in the uplands of what is now southern China. But as the Tai speakers mastered the art of canal-based rice agriculture, their population expanded, allowing them to push south into the more sparsely populated southern lowlands, a region that had been characterized by less productive flood-based farming (O'Connor 1995). Partly as a result, Tai political power and language prevailed, but Mon (and Khmer) cultural and intellectual forms persisted as well, leading to the social and cultural fusion that would eventually give rise to the modern Thai and Lao peoples.

Many other processes have historically given rise to mass migration. Climatic fluctuations, for example, periodically undermined subsistence systems, forcing peoples to seek new lands. A single event, such as a volcanic eruption or tsunami, could do the same, as has been hypothesized for the migration of the ancestors of the Na-Dené-speaking Apaches and Navajos to the U.S. southwest (Seymour 2012).[5] Perhaps more important has been the domino effect; if one group successfully occupies the territory of another less powerful one, then the latter group in turn may relocate into the territory of a third group, forcing them to migrate, and so on. Such a process was ubiquitous in the Eurasian steppe zone after the domestication of the horse; the Magyars, for example, entered Europe partly because of pressure from the Pechenegs, a Turkic-speaking group. An inverse process can occur when a group abandons its own territory, for whatever reason, and thereby creates an inviting vacuum.

---

[5] The event in this case would have been the White River Volcanic Ash Fall, dated at about 800 CE.

When leading elements of the Germanic peoples of east-central Europe moved into the lands of the collapsing Western Roman Empire, Slavic-speaking peoples quickly filled the resulting partially empty lands, and evidently did so without extensive political coordination.[6]

Evidence for far-ranging human migration is also found in the deepest reaches of prehistory, many millennia before the Neolithic Revolution. The rapid peopling of the Americas, for example, is difficult to account for if one insists that plodding demic diffusion was the only allowable process. More convincing is the study of Y-DNA and mitochondrial DNA haplogroups, which trace lineages of descent from one common ancestor in the male and female lines respectively. It is not a coincidence that specialists conceptualize the spread of haplogroups in terms of migrations, and map them accordingly. Most human populations, and particularly those of central Eurasia, exhibit pronounced diversity in both their Y- and mt-DNA, which means that their lines of descent can be traced back to multiple ancestors, often from widely scattered areas of origination. By the same token, most haplogroups are themselves distributed widely, crossing numerous cultural and "racial" divides. Explaining such genetic diversity on the basis of demic diffusion makes no sense, as one would have to hypothesize multiple instances of populations fully diffusing over the territories of other peoples, processes that would take too much time to accord with the dates established by genetic analysis.

Some researchers studying human haplogroups think that they can identify specific Y-DNA lineages that mark early Indo-European expansion into both Europe and southern Asia. These markers tend to indicate a steppe origin, fitting well with the scenario of expansion laid out by David Anthony and other researchers in the Revised Steppe school. Haplogroup R1a seems to be a possible candidate for the Proto-Indo-European speakers; it finds its highest modern frequency in Poland and Ukraine, and is also relatively widespread in parts of Central Asia and northern India.[7] A recent genetics paper (Lazaridis *et al.* 2014) that posits three ancestral populations for modern Europeans has also been interpreted as offering strong evidence for a substantial movement of Indo-European-speaking people from the steppes into Europe some five millennia ago. As Gregory Cochran and Henry Harpending argue on their blog, *West Hunter*:[8]

---

[6] The Avar Khanate, however, did play a role in this episode of Slavic expansion.
[7] See, for example, the discussions in *Eupedia Genetics* (www.eupedia.com/europe/Haplogroup_R1a_Y-DNA.shtml#migration_map) and in *Polishgenes* (http://polishgenes.blogspot.com/2013/04/r1a-and-r1b-as-markers-of-proto-indo.html).
[8] The blog post is entitled "Silver Blaze" and was posted on February 17, 2014. See http://westhunt.wordpress.com/2014/02/17/silver-blaze/

All this is pointing to a big wave of genetic change around 3000 BC, a wave that did not originate in the Near East (including Anatolia) [. . .] Although [Lazaridis *et al.*] mentioned such possibilities in an earlier related paper, they make no mention of the Indo-Europeans. They don't even use the word *language* anywhere in the supplement. All this while they're clearly working out the origin and scope of the Indo-European invasion!

Such research, however, is still in its early stages, and conclusions often shift rapidly. Linking language to genetics, moreover, is a perilous endeavor, as language can and often does spread independently of gene flow. We are therefore wary of wading into these waters, as are most historical linguists (as Cochran and Harpending uncharitably put it, "They're going to need strong evidence, and a baseball bat, to get linguists to pay attention").[9] Still, we find it significant that the majority of scholars working in the history of Eurasian genetics favor the Steppe theory over the Anatolian hypothesis, explain the spread of genes through processes of migration, and find human genetic admixtures to be extremely common. We also find it intriguing that the people of Sardinia, a non-Indo-European-speaking island prior to the Roman conquest, seem to be the best genetic approximation of Europe's Neolithic agriculturalists (cf. Patterson *et al.* 2012: 1085). To the extent that this assertion is true, Neolithic newcomers in Europe were almost certainly not Indo-European speakers.

Language spread and population spread

In the demic diffusion model of linguistic advance, one would expect the languages of indigenous societies to have relatively little influence on those of the newcomers slowly spreading into their territories. Expanding populations in such a scenario might pick up words for place names or previously unfamiliar plants, animals, or objects – as occurred in the case of British settlers in North America – but it would be less likely for them to acquire major portions of their vocabulary from the peoples that they were supplanting or seamlessly incorporating, much less to drastically change their grammatical structures or sound systems due to such contact. Such borrowing would be especially limited if the native peoples were hunter–gatherers, living sparsely on the ground, and the newcomers were sedentary farmers with much higher population densities, as is imagined in the Anatolian model.

In the migration–infiltration model favored by most proponents of the Steppe hypothesis, different dynamics would be expected. In this scenario, the language of the newcomers would be expected to borrow more extensively

[9] For the source of this quote, see http://westhunt.wordpress.com/2014/02/17/silver-blaze/

from those of the more numerous indigenes. As the two groups would often be living in close proximity, it would be advantageous for members of both groups to learn the language of the other. Pervasive bilingualism, especially if it persists for more than a generation, can result in extensive code-shifting, which can allow words and grammatical patterns to cross from one language to another, often without conscious intent. Migrant men, especially those of elite status, would also be expected to take wives and concubines from the native population. In such a situation, women will generally learn their husbands' language (see Forster and Renfrew 2011) yet often retain elements of their own phonology, vocabulary, and even grammar, which they can in turn pass on to their children.

Through such exchange, original languages can be heavily transformed, even to the extent that new languages can emerge from the resulting fusion. To be sure, one of the original tongues will almost always retain some degree of primacy, as fully "mixed languages" are rare, although they do exist. But the contributions from the language that eventually dies out can still be massive, resulting in a so-called stratum. The influence of a language with lower power or prestige is called as a substratum (or substrate), whereas the influence of a language with higher power or prestige is called a superstratum. (Influence from a language whose prestige is neither higher nor lower is regarded as "adstratum".) If massive second-language learning is entailed in the creation of such a partially mixed language, the process of grammatical simplification might be expected (cf. McWhorter 2011).

If Indo-European languages spread largely by pastoralists migrating into the lands of sedentary cultivators, one would expect to find linguistic traces of the pre-existing non-Indo-European tongues. As it turns out, languages in several major Indo-European branches do show evidence of substantial substrates, particularly Greek, Germanic, and Indo-Aryan. Such evidence, however, is far from watertight. Proving substrate influence is not easy, and most of the substrata discussed below have been challenged, although such challenges have also provoked their own counterarguments. All that we can conclude is that the jury is still out. We therefore do not regard such substrata as offering conclusive proof against the Anatolian model. They are like many of the other arguments forwarded in this book, indicative rather than decisive. But when one line of evidence after another all point in the same direction, as they do, eventually the case must be regarded as essentially resolved.

In Greek, the sole surviving member of its own Indo-European branch, words that may be of non-Indo-European origin number in the thousands. Robert Beekes (2010) controversially argues that most of the non-Indo-European elements in Greek derive from "one language, or a group of closely related dialects or languages" that he deems "pre-Greek", which most likely existed in the peninsula prior to the coming of Indo-European speakers. Not surprisingly, many of these words are place names, which could have been adopted even if the non-Indo-European "pre-Greeks" had been foragers. But other derivations point in the opposite direction, indicating that the autochthonous population had achieved a high level of cultural and technical sophistication, exceeding in many respects that of the newcomers. Much of the Greek vocabulary pertaining to the seas and shipping, Mediterranean agriculture, political institutions, and building and engineering is apparently of pre-Greek origin. So too are a number of theological terms and personal names, even those of great heroes like Odysseus. It is hardly likely that such terms would have been borrowed from a pre-existing hunter–gatherer population. Admittedly, some of the non-Indo-European words in Greek were almost certainly borrowed from Semitic languages, although recent research indicates that the number of such loanwords is relatively small.[10]

If the first Indo-European speakers had entered Greece along with the initial wave of Neolithic expansion, as posited by the Gray–Atkinson approach, they would not have acquired terms for basic Neolithic technologies from the pre-existing inhabitants. Yet they most likely did. As Robert Drews (1988: 178) argues in *The Coming of the Greeks*:

Linguistic evidence in fact almost requires us to assume that the first Greek speakers in the land secured their pottery from non-Greek potters. The Greek words for potter's clay (*keramos*), for a potter's kiln (*keramion*), and for a range of ceramic vessels [. . .] did not come from the proto-Indo-European vocabulary.

Although Drews's argument that the "coming of the Greeks" – and hence of Indo-European speakers – to the peninsula of Greece occurred later than the conventional date of 1900 BCE is controversial, all dates found in the specialized literature on the subject are much later than those provided by the Anatolian school. Drews's conclusion, moreover, is relatively uncontroversial: the migration of the earliest Greek (or proto-Greek) speakers "did not ethnically transform the land; instead it seems to have superimposed upon the indigenous population of Greece a small minority of PIE speakers" (1988: 199–200). Although we doubt that "Proto-Indo-European" is the correct word, as the original Indo-European tongue would have diversified much earlier, his general picture of social interaction and linguistic transformation among the Greeks and pre-Greeks seems to be largely on track.

The language (or languages) of the pre-Greeks is impossible to determine, as is the family (or families) to which they belonged. It has been suggested that they may have been related to the non-Indo-European Minoan language, or

---

[10] See Jerker Blomqvist's review of Rafał Rosół's *Frühe semitische Lehnwörter im Griechischen* (Frankfurt am Main: Peter Lang, 2013), in the online *Bryn Mawr Classical Review* (http://bmcr. brynmawr.edu/2013/2013-11-54.html).

perhaps to the Lemnian language, spoken on the Aegean island of Lemnos until at least the fifth century BCE. Lemnian, in turn, was closely related to Etruscan and Rhaetic. The evidence, however, is too fragmentary to make any conclusive statement.

Evidence of a large substratum in the Indo-Aryan languages, tracing back to Vedic Sanskrit, is relatively strong (Witzel 1999). Here we find numerous lexical items, syntactic changes, and phonological features (in particular retroflex consonants) that would be difficult to explain in any other manner. Some of these features can be tied to the extant Dravidian and Munda (Austroasiatic) families, but others apparently derive from an unknown tongue (or tongues) that Masica (1979) labels "language X". As seems to be the case in the pre-Greek and pre-Germanic substrates, non-Indo-European terms in Vedic Sanskrit are concentrated in the domains of agriculture, animals and plants, and technology. Cultural terms, including some pertaining to music, dancing, and religious observations, are found as well. Again, such evidence strongly suggests that the pre-Indo-European peoples of South Asia were settled farmers. If true, the Gray–Atkinson model of the Indo-Europeanization of South Asia is invalidated. Renfrew's Anatolian thesis, however, is not challenged in this particular instance, as he surmises that the Indo-Aryan languages could have spread via steppe pastoralists, limiting his Neolithic thesis to the Indo-Europeanization of Europe.

More intense controversies swirl around the possibility of a major non-Indo-European substratum in the Germanic languages (see Roberge 2010). It has been argued that up to one-third of the Germanic lexicon cannot be unambiguously traced back to Indo-European roots, and the language family has a number of syntactical peculiarities that are difficult to account for. Several scholars have thus contended that the Germanic family emerged from a contact language spoken by both the Indo-European newcomers and indigenous inhabitants. According to John Hawkins (1990), Germanic terms of non-Indo-European origin are concentrated in several domains: seafaring, agriculture, engineering, war, social institutions, and biology (animal names). If Hawkins is correct, the non-Indo-European speakers who eventually adopted proto-Germanic would have been agriculturalists with a relatively high degree of technological and political sophistication.[11] Such a situation fits well with the Steppe hypothesis, but would make no sense from the Anatolian perspective.

---

[11] A number of historical linguists have cast considerable doubt on the non-IE Germanic substrate hypothesis. See, for example, Roland Schuhmann (2012). A number of early loanwords into Proto-Germanic, moreover, are of Celtic origin; see, for example, "Annotated list of loan words, and possible loanwords, in Proto-Germanic", University of Pennsylvania Linguistics Department: http://www.ling.upenn.edu/~kroch/courses/lx310/handouts/handouts-09/ringe/celt-loans.pdf

In western Eurasia, substrates have also been proposed for other Indo-European subfamilies, most of which would indicate that the pre-Indo-European inhabitants had been settled cultivators. Armenian words that apparently derive from a pre-existing language in the now extinct Hurro-Urartian family, for example, include terms for 'field', 'garden', 'town', 'grain', 'apple', 'plum', and 'kettle' (Greppin and Diakonoff 1991). In some cases, a single language can have a substrate not found in other tongues of the same subfamily. Sardinian, for example, often regarded as the most conservative and aberrant Romance language (see Chapter 4), was influenced by the non-Indo-European Paleo-Sardinian language (or languages), which bequeathed to Latin-derived Sardinian plant names and toponyms, some of which may preserve indigenous grammatical suffixes. The Catalan linguist Eduardo Blasco Ferrer (2010) links this long-extinct language to Basque, but this seems far-fetched, considering the lack of surviving Paleo-Sardinian material. Paleo-Sardinian, in turn, is associated with the remarkable Bronze-Age Nuragic civilization of the island, famous for its numerous and elaborate fortress-towers.

Whatever their possible contributions to surviving Indo-European languages, the pre-Indo-European tongues of Europe were almost certainly highly diverse, belonging to a number of separate families. Such diversity, in agrarian non-state-level societies and in the absence of large-scale migration, is the global norm. With the coming of the Indo-European languages, however, diversity plummeted. In some areas, such as Europe's Celtic heartland in the Iron Age, very similar dialects/languages were spoken over a vast area, a situation all but precluded by demic diffusion, as linguistic diversification would have proceeded as the original language slowly spread. It is thus for good reason that Don Ringe, in surveying the pre-Indo-European languages of Europe in the context of Indo-European expansion, concludes that:

We cannot avoid the inference that there were substantial migrations of people speaking IE languages into Europe in the prehistoric period [...] On the other hand, it seems impossible that the populations speaking IE languages could suddenly have become large enough to overrun vast territories and crowd out the earlier inhabitants; that scenario probably violates the UP [uniformitarian principle] too. But we do not need to posit vast folk migrations to explain the spread of IE language.[12]

The role of advection in modeling population expansion

Perhaps the most damning evidence against the demic diffusion hypothesis, however, comes from studies of the initial Neolithic advance into Europe by other computational model-builders. Of particular significance is an article by

---

[12] The quotation is from the *Language Log Website*; see http://languagelog.ldc.upenn.edu/nll/?p=980

Davison *et al.* (2006) that appeared in the *Journal of Archaeological Science.* This paper shows that demic diffusion alone is too slow to account for the actual spread of farming across Europe that occurred between 7000 BCE and 2000 BCE. As a result, they argue that even in this gradual process, diffusion must have been complemented by advection, which in the physical sciences refers to the mass movement of particles propelled by some medium, and which can be translated into terms pertinent to human prehistory as "migration".

The geographical model used by Davison *et al.* (2006) is also vastly more complex than the one employed six years later in "Mapping the Origins", allowing much finer distinctions. Whereas the Gray–Atkinson approach assumes diffusion across an "isotrophic plain", or one featureless in all directions, Davison and her colleagues take geographical space to be highly anisotropic, which means that its properties vary in different directions. They are therefore able to take into account spatial variation in both human mobility and the carrying capacity of the land. Their calculations also encompass differences in altitude and latitude, which do not play any role in the Gray–Atkinson model. Second, Davison *et al.* focus on the role played by coastlines and major river paths, such as the Danube and the Rhine. Such waterways are accounted for by introducing a mathematical advection term confined to the proximity of such major rivers and coastlines. The Gray–Atkinson model, in contrast, distinguishes only "land" and "water", the latter category including open seas, island-dotted inland seas, and rivers, without noting that some forms of water tend to impede movement while others more often facilitate it. Their basic model regards land as vastly easier to cross than water, although in their alternative "sailor model" this difference disappears. (Under their basic assumption, water is so difficult to diffuse across that many Mediterranean islands are mapped as never having been reached by Indo-European speakers.) Third, the model of Davison *et al.* is validated against radiocarbon dates of archeological finds, especially those involving the Linear Pottery (LBK) and the Impressed Ware traditions along the Danube–Rhine corridor and the Mediterranean coastline, respectively. The model used in "Mapping the Origins", to the contrary, runs afoul of archeological evidence, as discussed in Chapters 8 and 9 below.

Although the Gray–Atkinson team claims to be forwarding "a feature-rich geographical model where different locations can have different migration patterns" (Bouckaert *et al.* 2012, Supplementary Materials: 11), such "features" simply do not exist in their actual mathematical model. Although the authors elsewhere claim that the geographical distinctions that they do draw (particularly, separating land from water) "could in principle be extended to incorporate other geographic features such as mountains or deserts" (2012, Supplementary Materials: 12–13), they do not incorporate anything of the sort in their calculations. As it is, they have the Indo-European diffusion front advancing along ridges well in excess of 20,000 feet (6,000 meters) in elevation in the Tian Shan Range of Central Asia.

As mentioned above, in the truly feature-rich geographical model employed by Davison *et al.* (2006), diffusion alone appears to be too slow to account for the actual advance of Neolithic societies across Europe. In their alternative diffusion-cum-advection model, the lines of population advance no longer cross the major river paths; instead, they run alongside them as population moves along such corridors. Even though they still restrict advection to the vicinity of waterways, it significantly affects the overall propagation speed of the agricultural advance. The spread of the Neolithic population along the Danube and Rhine valleys causes it to reach France, Belgium, and Denmark – and consequently the British Isles and Scandinavia – sooner than in the diffusion-only model. Although "still having suffered a 500-year delay due again to the inhibiting effects of the water barrier" (2006: 649), the population front reaches the British Isles and Norway after only 3,500 years, which is 1,500–2,000 years earlier than in the diffusion-only model. These patterns and dates are much more in accord with the radiocarbon dates of archeological finds than those of the diffusion-only model.

But as sophisticated as the Davison *et al.* (2006) model is, it still leaves out some important differences in physical geography that would have influenced the initial spread of agriculture into Europe. Soil type was particularly important in the Neolithic, when crude tools made it difficult to cultivate heavy clay soils. Fertile and friable loess soils, which have a scattered distribution, were instead preferred. Thus, instead of mindlessly diffusing across Europe in a wave-like advance, the earliest farmers were probably often searching for loess, a process that would have greatly influenced their pace of advance (see Boggard 2002).

A final problem in the geographical model used in both "Mapping the Origins" and in Davison *et al.* (2006) is that they are in some ways ahistorical, giving no account to technological or organizational change that would have greatly impacted the pace of group expansion, and essentially disallowing the possibility of historical contingency. Such a flaw is not particularly significant in the Davison *et al.* (2006) article, as it is limited to the Neolithic, when the pace of technological development was relatively slow. It is a major defect, however, in "Mapping the Origins", which takes us from the Neolithic to modern times. Consider, for example, the maritime realm. In the basic Gray–Atkinson model, sea-space is vastly more difficult to cross than land, although such differences disappear in the alternative "sailor model". Note, however, that both versions are applied trans-historically. In actuality, both the possibility and the ease of crossing long spans of water depend on maritime technology. What was at one time an impassable barrier can eventually become a convenient passageway. Once sea-worthy ships and effective navigational techniques are acquired, the seas tend to facilitate rather than retard movement. As Paine (2013: 11) describes the general dynamic in rather understated terms, "Travel by water was often faster, smoother, more efficient, and in many circumstances safer and more convenient than overland travel".

The fallacy of spatial contiguity

It is not merely the *spread* of languages that is severely misconstrued by the Gray–Atkinson approach. A more specifically geographical fallacy is also built into their statistical model, albeit one that is also found in almost all attempts to conceptualize the spatial texture of language groups. As is clear from the authors' base-map of extinct and extant Indo-European languages, they model all languages spoken at any given time as fully confined within cleanly demarcated, non-overlapping, and fully contiguous spatial units. All languages, in other words, are mapped within their own discrete polygons. Such a tactic is employed even in the case of contemporary Romani, which is scattered across Europe in often-mobile communities; in the Gray–Atkinson input map, the language of the Roma is confined to one small corner of the Balkans.

One might object that the authors do not actually view linguistic geography in such a simplistic manner, but only map it that way out of expedience, as it would be crushingly difficult to cartographically divide Romani into thousands of separate and untethered parcels. But be that as it may, such convenience is still highly distorting, as the errors that it forces only compound as the model runs through its calculations. And as if to add insult to injury, the input base-maps used in "Mapping the Origins" have a low degree of accuracy even for languages that are closely confined to specific territories (see, for example, Maps 21 and 22).

To appreciate the manner in which the shoddy base-maps used in "Mapping the Origins" distort the findings, one only has to consider the Moldovan example. One of the oddest features of the authors' output map is its depiction of Moldova as a non-Indo-European island enveloped in an Indo-European sea, which would appear to mean that this country had never been occupied by speakers of Indo-European languages.[13] The seemingly inexplicable Moldovan blank-spot on the output maps make sense when one examines the authors' input map of existing and extinct Indo-European languages, which oddly neglects the country, treating it as if it were not Indo-European-speaking even at present. In actuality, the Moldovan language is merely a variety of

---

[13] In actuality, however, the map only indicates that it is highly unlikely that Moldova was occupied by Indo-European speakers after the 1650 CE termination date of the time scale of the static map, unlike the surrounding areas, which were highly unlikely to have been occupied by Indo-European speakers after much earlier dates.

Romanian; differences between Moldovan and Standard Romanian are almost exclusively lexical rather than grammatical. But even the most ardent Moldo-venists, who promote independent Moldovan identity and culture and take the position that Moldovan is a separate language, concede that it is an Eastern Romance, and hence an Indo-European, language. In ancient and early medi-eval times, moreover, a variety of other Indo-European languages, including Gothic, had blanketed the territory of present-day Moldova.

Similarly, the animated map's bizarre tracing of the supposed Greek–Albanian branch also stems from mistakes on the input map, where ancient Greek is inexplicably restricted to Attica while modern Albanian is divided into four separate languages, one of which is shown as the only Indo-European ever to have been spoken on the island of Sicily, yet northern Albania itself is erroneously depicted as non-Indo-European-speaking. Many additional errors in the base-map further deform the output maps that form the centerpiece of the authors' supposedly decisive phylogeographical analysis.

But even if all such basic errors could be eliminated, the underlying conception of language distribution would still undermine the results. The idea that languages are necessarily contained within contiguous and cleanly demarcated territorial blocks is inappropriate for the contemporary world, and is doubly misleading for the pre-modern period before would-be nation-states began to push for linguistic homogeneity within their boundaries. One cannot even assume that a single small-scale community is necessarily united by a common language. In the tribal communities of the Vaupés region along the Brazil–Colombia border, "each person must marry someone from a different language group", as people speaking the same language are considered too closely related to wed (Dixon 1997: 24).

Empires in particular were almost always polyglot affairs, multilingualism being one of the defining characteristics of imperium. More to the point, their various tongues were usually territorially interspersed, forming complex and shifting patterns. German and French ethnographic cartographers in the late 1800s and early 1900s made magnificent efforts to capture such complexity when mapping the Austro-Hungarian Empire and the Balkan provinces of the Ottoman Empire, and some of their products are marvels of precision.[14] But when it comes to a scale as fine as that of the urban neighborhood, even their efforts failed to convey how complex the situation could be. All such maps, moreover, ignore pervasive multilingualism, assuming that one can find a single language dominating a specific territory if one moves down to an adequately localized spatial scale. This particular problem is unfortunately

---

[14] Many of these maps are available online. See, for example: lib.utexas.edu/maps/historical/balkan_ serbs_1914.jpg and http://upload.wikimedia.org/wikipedia/commons/b/bf/Ethnic_map_of_Balkans_- _russian_1867.jpg

omnipresent, plaguing even contemporary language mapping at the continental scale; how often do linguistic maps of South America, for example, show Paraguay to be fully bilingual in Spanish and Guaraní, as it essentially is?[15]

But empires and other non-national states were not the only political environments in which deep complexity of language distribution obtains. The tongues of pastoral peoples, for example, are often scattered over vast areas, interspersed with those of farming peoples. Some maps of the Fulani language, for example, show it extending over a huge swath of land extending from Senegal to Chad and beyond, yet in this same zone scores of other languages are also spoken (it should also be noted that Fulani serves as a *lingua franca* in the region).[16] Even the languages of fully sedentary peoples can be spatially dispersed, due either to their own recent migrations or to incursions by other peoples, although in the absence of integrative mechanisms such separated languages will eventually diverge. An equally intractable problem is that of the dialect continuum, which complicates the mapping of Fulani and many other contemporary languages as well. In such a continuum, dialects spoken on the opposite sides of the range can be completely non-interintelligible, thus seeming to form distinct languages, but as one traverses the gradient, no significant language border is ever crossed, as change remains gradual. Mapping such groups of related tongues as a single, coherent language falsely conveys the impression that the people who speak them compose a single linguistic community. In actuality, localized dialect clusters in such situations form the more relevant linguistic units. In the contemporary world, debates over how to map such dialect continua can be highly contentious. In Pakistan, for example, the status of a tongue such as Saraiki is hotly contested: is it a distinct language in its own right, or merely a dialect of Punjabi?[17] Yet even Punjabi itself can be viewed as part of a dialect continuum that encompasses most of the Indo-Aryan languages of northern South Asia.

All of these problems are encountered in the linguistic base-map used in "Mapping the Origins". Here a set number of discrete languages are considered, even though some of them should probably be classified as mere dialectal variants, such as the three Breton languages, whereas others ought to

---

[15] The stability of bilingualism in Paraguay, however, is uncertain, as Choi (2005) reports that urban areas are increasingly Spanish-speaking whereas Guaraní may be prevailing in many rural areas.

[16] See, for example, the maps in the "Fulfulde Language Family Report" by Annette Harrison and Irene Tucker: SIL International 2003, found at http://www-01.sil.org/silesr/2003/silesr2003-009.html

[17] Although the Ethnologue classifies Saraiki (spelled there as "Seraiki") as a separate language, Wikipedia regards it as a dialect of Punjabi, citing numerous scholarly sources that agree. See also the webpage of the Department of Saraiki at Bahauddin Zakariya University, Multan, Pakistan, which claims that it is an "ancient language": bzu.edu.pk/departmentindex.php?id=33

be subdivided into several separate languages, such as Kurdish (the Kurdish "dialects" of Kurmanji and Sorani are more linguistically distinct than are Spanish and Portuguese, and perhaps even Spanish and French [see Hassanpour 1992]). The authors' general tendency is to divide much more finely in Europe than in Asia, which not only evinces a Eurocentric attitude but also skews the model's output. More problematic is the authors' recourse to cartographic gymnastics to fit all their 103 extant and extinct Indo-European languages into single polygons. Again, Kurdish exemplifies this flaw, as the main body of the language is connected to an outlier in northeastern Iran by an absurdly narrow and entirely fictional isthmus that extends across northern Iran. Troublesome as this maneuver may be, it is not the final way in which Kurdish is misapprehended. In the northeastern Iranian outlier, Kurdish is actually interspersed with both Farsi and a local Turkic language, rather than forming a contiguous block. And in the core region of Kurdistan, moreover, the map excludes many clearly Kurdish-speaking places.

As mentioned above, the Moldovan example shows how the Gray–Atkinson language base-map is contaminated by political considerations. Such inappropriate mapping occurs elsewhere as well. Luxembourgish, for example, is counted as a distinct language unlike other Franconian dialects only because Luxembourg is currently a sovereign state. As a quick glance at the base-map (Map 3) reveals, moreover, the current-day distribution of languages in central and eastern Europe is portrayed as almost fully coincident with the territories of existing states. Romanian is thus shown as almost exactly contained within Romania, ignoring both Hungarian-speaking areas within the country as well as the Romanian-speaking areas outside of it. Polish is also shown as fitting almost perfectly into Poland, Ukrainian into Ukraine, and so on. In the case of Polish and Poland, the congruence of language and country is admittedly relatively close – but that is only because of the recent extermination of millions of Yiddish speakers followed by the expulsion of millions of German speakers. The modern language map in this part of the world is thus in large part an artifact of recent political history, and thus cannot serve as a neutral template for determining the most likely pathways of linguistic "diffusion" over the past several thousand years.

Yet the authors go so far as to misuse modern geopolitical units in mapping long-extinct ancient languages. They paint Vedic Sanskrit (Map 6), for example, as precisely bounded by the territory of Punjab as it existed under the British Raj, thus taking early Sanskrit speakers up to the crest of the Himalayas in what is now the Indian state of Himachal Pradesh. They similarly map Classical Armenian as essentially coterminous with the modern Republic of Armenia, another clear case of geopolitical contamination.

The authors specify that their linguistic base-map (Map 3) is derived from the Ethnologue, a well-respected global language database maintained by SIL, originally a Christian missionary society.[18] In most areas, however, the authors' mapping deviates substantially from that of the Ethnologue, yet they provide no explanations for such departures. Consider, for example, their depiction of the Modern Greek language (or languages). Unlike the Ethnologue, they restrict Modern Greek to the mainland, leaving Crete, (southern) Cyprus, Rhodes, and most other Greek islands blank. Yet on the island of Lesbos, they demarcate a completely separate language in the Greek branch, which they deem "Greek ML". The Ethnologue, however, regards the dialect of Lesbos as Modern Greek, as do virtually all other sources. (On the other hand, the Ethnologue does distinguish a separate Tsakonian Greek language on the mainland that Gray and Atkinson ignore.) To be sure, the Greek of Lesbos does have a number of peculiar archaic features, but that is true of many other dialects of the language (Joseph 2006). We can find no warrant for mapping Lesbian Greek as a separate modern language, and thus remain mystified by this maneuver.

But even if we consider only the Ethnologue's own maps, the problem of political corruption remains. As O. T. Ford (2013) shows in an important recent geography dissertation, Ethnologue cartographers often unduly divide single languages along political or ethnic boundaries.[19] As he writes:

Ethnologue divides speech varieties [. . .] by such conventional cues as tribal identity – and yet catalogs its elements by linguistic relationships. The established means of distinguishing between language and dialect in the field of linguistics itself is by means of mutual intelligibility, which, while quantitative (two dialects must be said to be mutually intelligible not absolutely but *to a certain degree*), is at least empirical. To support the notion that Ethnologue has abandoned the empirical criterion of mutual intelligibility for conventions of country and tribe, this study identifies hundreds of cases where at least one linguistic source describes as mutually intelligible two dialects listed as separate languages in Ethnologue; and in several cases, that source is Ethnologue itself. (2013: 5)

The root problem here is that the distribution of language defies our most basic cartographic conventions, and as a result language maps typically conceal almost as much as they reveal. To some extent, this problem is not unique to language; a truism in geography is that a perfect map can only be made at a 1:1 scale, which would also be a perfectly useless map. Maps necessarily exclude vast amounts of potentially pertinent information. Language, however, turns out to be particularly difficult to capture in cartographic form, precisely for the

---

[18] This specification is found in the caption of figure S6, the language base-map, found in the Supplementary Materials.

[19] Some of these distortions in the Ethnologue are a result of their specific goals, linking to such issues as the use of certain writing systems and languages of literacy, which are distinct from those of linguistics *per se*.

reasons sketched out above. Far from meaning that we should therefore abandon language mapping, such complications rather necessitate that we pay more attention to it. But by the same token, we do need to be wary of any attempt to use crude language maps in seemingly rigorous efforts to determine the origin and spread of language families.

We should not be surprised that most language maps are overly simplified. It is extremely easy, after all, to map a given area as neatly divided into separate linguistic regions. If such regions are viewed as coinciding with the territories of nation-states, the process becomes easier still. But if one wants to make an adequately accurate map, the cartographical challenges can quickly become overwhelming. Consider, for example, the following complexities, all of which existed over large parts of eastern and central Europe at various times prior to the mid-twentieth century: linguistic differentiation between cities and the countryside, as well as differentiation among cities and between neighborhoods within individual cities; scattered villages with languages distinct from those of other villages in the vicinity; linguistic differences between settled lowlands and more pastorally oriented uplands; complex dialect continua in which, at times, certain prestige dialects vie for more general acceptance; widely distributed learned languages used by the elite, or certain segments of the elite, but not the general populace; and languages spoken by low-status itinerant groups that move through the landscape as their speakers relocate their encampments.[20] Some of the various languages alluded to above, moreover, are closely related, some are distantly related, and others are completely unrelated to any others found in the area. Add to such complexities change over time, which is sometimes quite rapid, and cartographic depiction becomes a daunting task indeed.

At a more abstract level, such problems are not unique to language mapping, but are rather intrinsic to the entire cartographic endeavor. The ubiquitous "world political map", for example, can be a highly misleading document, as it leads one to think that the terrestrial world is completely divided into unambiguous, holistic political units that can be simultaneously conceptualized as internationally recognized sovereign states, independent countries, and nations, entities that supposedly maintain a monopoly on the legitimate use of force within their own boundaries; such a taken-for-granted vision is referred

---

[20] In the Hapsburg domains, most cities were generally German speaking, but over time significant non-German urban populations emerged outside of the German-speaking core of the empire; Yiddish-speaking communities were scattered over many mostly non-Yiddish areas; Vlach was widespread in many pastoral uplands in otherwise non-Vlach areas; the "Serbo-Croatian" dialect continuum is especially complex, and its main constituent dialects do not correspond with the modern, politically defined languages that emerged out of it; Latin was used as an administrative language of Hungary as late as the 1700s; Romani was, and is, associated with often mobile communities.

to by O. T. Ford (2013) as the "country model of the world". But despite the ubiquity of this model, the global geopolitical environment is actually a vastly more complicated matter, replete with such features as unrecognized but existing states (Somaliland), fully recognized non-states (Somalia), states recognized by only a handful of other states (Abkhazia), insurgent-held zones (parts of Syria), unrecognized annexations (Western Sahara), hotly disputed state-level boundaries (Kashmir), "national" governments that have less authority than their constituent regional governments (Belgium), nominally independent countries in "free association" with another vastly more powerful state (Marshall Islands), non-independent countries in "free association" with another more powerful state (Cook Islands), colonial remnants with varying degrees of autonomy (American Samoa, Northern Marianas), feudal remnants with some but not all aspects of full sovereignty (Andorra), non-independent but self-governing "constituent countries" that are parts of larger "kingdoms" (Greenland, Curacao), autonomous regions with some aspects of sovereignty (Aceh), large numbers of exclaves/enclaves, including 102 pieces of India located "within" Bangladesh, one of which (Dahala Khagrabari) is an enclave within an enclave within an enclave, localized militias associated with legitimate political parties that are stronger than their country's national armed forces (Hezbollah), military bases under the sovereignty of a foreign power (British-owned Akrotiri and Dhekelia on Cyprus), military bases effectively under the sovereignty of a foreign power but officially under an essentially fictitious lease (Guantanamo Bay), collections of independent states that nonetheless fall under one symbolic head of state (most of the British Commonwealth), collections of independent states that have ceded essential aspects of their sovereignty to supranational organizations (the European Union), sovereign but officially non-national federations (the United Arab Emirates, Russia), one self-declared plurinational state (Bolivia), one small territory that seasonally alternates between two different countries (Pheasant Island between France and Spain), and one sovereign military order that has morphed into an international medical society (Knights of Malta). It is for good reason that Steven Krasner (1999) refers to sovereignty – and more generally the entire realm of global diplomacy – as "organized hypocrisy". Although it might be objected that such irregularities are both insignificant and well understood, we doubt that they actually are. It would rather seem that the grotesquely abridged view of global geopolitics conveyed by the standard world political map remains highly influential. The early twenty-first-century U.S.-led invasions of Afghanistan and Iraq, for example, were predicated in large part on the idea that both polities were coherent nation-states that could easily be transformed though a quick process of "regime change". Recent events have shown that the actual geopolitical conditions of Iraq and Afghanistan are a bit more complicated.

Again, none of this is to argue that mapping, whether of language groups or of polities, is a hopeless endeavor. Quite the contrary; we rather contend that many of these complexities can be partially captured through the use of map layers, made possible by the techniques of GIS (Geographic Information Systems). It would be highly desirable, in other words, for scholars to move beyond the "coloring book" view of the world introduced in the first years of elementary education, one that entails nothing beyond marking off distinct chunks of territory separated from other equally distinct chunks by heavy lines or bright colors. More specifically, the degree of linguistic homogeneity within a given bounded polygon could theoretically be measured, just as sphericity can be reduced to a number. In such a scheme, an area in which every person is monolingual in a dialect-free language that is not found outside the area would receive a score of "1", just as a perfect sphere has a sphericity of "1". If, on the other hand, everyone in the area speaks a different unrelated language, all of which are also found elsewhere, the "linguistic homogeneity index" would be zero. Other ways to map linguistic non-homogeneity can be devised as well.

The evolutionary fallacy

The final fallacious and unexamined assumption found in "Mapping the Origins" is perhaps the most fundamental one, as it runs through the entire Gray–Atkinson approach to language history. This is the idea that linguistic evolution is so similar to biological evolution that it can be analyzed in exactly the same manner. At first glance, this proposition does not seem unreasonable. The parallels between organic and linguistic evolution are indeed pronounced, and in some ways it has been biologists who have adopted linguists' ways of thinking about evolution and change rather than vice versa (Atkinson and Gray 2005). Both processes entail replicating codes that continually change, giving rise to novel varieties that increasingly differ from their progenitors over time. As a result, "phylogenetic trees" showing descent from common ancestors are a common feature of both evolutionary biology and historical linguistics. And as Lightfoot (2002) shows, many attempts have been made over the years to explain language change on the basis of evolutionary principles, some of which, such as that of Croft (2000), are more sophisticated than others.

But despite their similarities, organic evolution and linguistic evolution are in many ways highly dissimilar processes. Encoding information for communication is not the same as encoding information that generates life: language is in many ways vastly more fluid and complex than the genetic code; individual languages are much less clearly differentiated from each other than are species; and language is a social phenomenon, given to influences largely irrelevant for biological evolution. The key differences can be summarized as follows: biological evolution is unconstrained but governed by natural selection (any mutation can happen, but which mutations remain in the pool depends in large part on natural selection), whereas linguistic variation, seen in terms of deep grammatical properties, is constrained by a system of parameters but is not subject to natural selection.[21] As Mark Baker shows, the change of a single parameter can result in systematic modifications throughout a given language, which alone tells us that "the distinct grammatical systems that we see in the world did not evolve by a gradual and unconstrained process of cultural evolution" (2001b: 116). As a result, the branching trees of linguistic descent are merely analogous to the phylogenetic diagrams of biological evolution, and do not indicate the same kind of relationships. Limited aspects of language change, such as those pertaining to vocabulary and sounds, might be partially explicable on the basis of evolutionary principles (Croft 2000), but at the deeper level of syntactic transformations, this possibility necessarily breaks down.

Although organic evolution operates through a much more restricted set of message-carrying units than does human language, it nonetheless produces diversity at a much deeper level. To be sure, the number of possible human languages, both extant and extinct, as well as those that may arise in the future, is vast, but all human languages are a "variation on a theme", guided by the same built-in parameters. Some languages put verbs before subjects and objects, while others place them at the ends of sentences, but all languages apparently have verbs, subjects, and objects (Baker 2001b). Some languages (i.e. polysynthetic languages) can build sentence-long words packed with numerous prefixes, infixes, or suffixes, while others (i.e. isolating languages) use stand-alone, stripped-down words to do the grammatical work of express-ing tense, number, and so on, but all languages make words from morphemes – and all construct sentences. As a result of this limited space of possibilities, completely unrelated languages evolving on their own often come to share fundamental grammatical traits.

By the same token, even clearly related languages may appear to have next to nothing in common with each other, because linguistic evolution, unlike that of the biological realm, moves at a rapid clip and often makes overwhelming transformations. In language, deep grammatical properties can radically change, often taking on the same forms as those encountered in wholly unrelated tongues. Related languages can therefore often be linked only through investi-gations into their ancestors. Hindi and Italian, for instance, are dissimilar in almost every respect. For example, Hindi makes a phonemic distinction between aspirated and unaspirated voiced stops, has subject–object–verb word

---

[21] See Nichols (1992: 276) for a discussion of the very limited domain in which natural selection might be said to operate on languages.

order and postpositions, and uses the ergative–absolutive alignment in the preterite and perfect tenses; Italian, in contrast, has no aspirated voiced stops, has lost the case system except with pronouns, employs a subject–verb–object word order, uses prepositions rather than postpositions, and is characterized by nominative–accusative alignment. On casual inspection, Hindi would seem to have much more in common with the non-Indo-European languages of the Indian subcontinent than it does with Italian. Indeed, exchange among the languages of the region has been so pronounced as to generate a *Sprachbund*, or linguistic convergence zone (Masica 1976). As a result, actual linguistic relationships are often anything but obvious, and can only be discerned though intensive study. A fluent speaker of the major Germanic languages, for example, might be nonplussed to learn that Frisian is more closely related to English than it is to Dutch. Yet according to some specialists, even Low German is "phylogenetically" closer to English than it is to (High) German – even though Low German is generally regarded as a mere dialect (or group of dialects) of German (cf. Goossens 1973).

As a result of these processes, relatedness at the family level and overall linguistic similarity often fail to correspond. Maps showing major language patterns thus bear little if any resemblance to maps depicting linguistic families. Even something as seemingly basic as word order correlates poorly with lines of descent. For example, Indo-European languages can be SVO (subject–verb–object), such as English, Romance, and most Slavic languages (but Sorbian, a Slavic language, is SOV); SOV, such as the Indo-Iranian languages (yet Kashmiri is SVO); or VSO, such as the Insular Celtic languages (yet Cornish is SVO). Some other families, such as Austronesian, have an even greater variability in the basic word order: Niuean is VSO, Malagasy is VOS, Rotuman is SVO, and Tuvaluan is OVS (see Dryer 2013).

Similarly, features of morphological typology (how words are formed from morphemes) often cross-cut connections established by common descent. Whereas Proto-Indo-European, like most of its daughters, was a *synthetic* language (building words from multiple non-root morphemes), English and Afrikaans are relatively *analytical* (with low ratios of morphemes to words), which gives them a certain affinity with Mandarin Chinese (a highly analytical language). Analytical languages are found in Africa (Hausa, an Afroasiatic language), Asia (Vietnamese, an Austroasiatic language), Oceania (Rapanui, an Austronesian language), and the Americas (Kipea, Kiriri). In phonology as well, similar patterns obtain, as sound inventories often fail to show systematic correspondences with language families (see Dryer and Haspelmath 2013). The Indo-European languages of South Asia, for example, are in many respects more phonologically similar to the Dravidian languages of the same region than they are to most other languages in their own family. One of the characteristic phonological markers of the region, the rich inventory of retroflex consonants, is also scattered across the rest of the world, found in about 20 percent of all languages belonging to a wide variety of families.

Again, the contrast with biological evolution is stark. The farther removed organisms are from each other on the tree of life, the fewer genes they share. As a result, anything like a "biological *Sprachbund*", in which all species in a given area come to share certain basic traits, is an obvious absurdity. Even when convergent evolution results in similarities between distantly related organisms, the parallels are relatively superficial. As a result, modern genetic inquiry can establish precise levels of biological relatedness, a process that has revolutionized taxonomy over the past few decades. In the biological realm, moreover, the farther one moves up different branches of evolutionary descent, the more distinctive the organisms found along it generally become. Chordates (the phylum that includes vertebrates) share a distant common ancestor with echinoderms (sea stars and their relatives), and some tunicates, primitive members of phylum Chordata, might be mistaken by unschooled observers for sea lilies in phylum Echinodermata. But no one would ever confuse any mammal with a sand dollar, a sea cucumber, or any other echinoderm, animals characterized by radial rather than bilateral symmetry. The two phyla have simply evolved in entirely different directions. If linguistic evolution worked in such an ever-differentiating manner, it is questionable whether translation between distant languages would even be possible.

The intense mutability of language also means that linguistic trees, unlike those of the organic realm, cannot be traced back to their initial root, as after 8,000 to 10,000 years, everything has been rearranged so completely that no traces of affiliation remain (Nichols 1992: 2, 184). When it comes to organisms, the farther back one traces the relationships, the clearer the branching patterns become. Taxonomists long debated, for example, whether the red panda was a member of the bear family, the raccoon family, or a family of its own, but no one ever doubted that it belongs to order Carnivora, class Mammalia, phylum Chordata, and kingdom Animalia.[22] But to what higher-order division does Indo-European belong? Some linguists have suggested larger groupings, such as a Eurasiatic macrofamily that also includes the Uralic, Altaic, and Eskimo-Aleut families, and a Nostratic superfamily that in most versions adds Dravidian and Afroasiatic while subtracting Eskimo–Aleut. But the evidence here is inconclusive at best, and these hypotheses have been rejected by most linguists (see Campbell 1998; Ringe 1998; Salmons and Joseph 1998; Vine 1998; *inter alia*).

As it turns out, even some seemingly well-established families apparently derived from the exchange of traits rather than descent from a common

---

[22] Recent molecular analysis places the red panda in its own family, the Ailuridae.

ancestor. The once commonplace Ural–Altaic family was proven to be a typological and areal grouping of Uralic and Altaic, as its characteristic features, such as agglutinative morphology and vowel harmony, turned out not to have been derived from common descent (Janhunen 2001, 2007). Moreover, it now seems to most experts that even Altaic is not a legitimate language family, but is instead a mere areal aggregation of the Turkic, Mongolic, and Tungusic families, which evidently borrowed intensively from each other (see Clauson 1956, 1959; Doerfer 1963, 1988; Schönig 2003; Georg 2004, 2005; Vovin 2005; Johanson 2010). Crucially, the farther one looks back in time, the more dissimilar these Altaic branches become; if the language family were genuine, one would expect more similarity in the older languages. (In the well-established Indo-European family, for example, Vedic Sanskrit is much more similar to Latin than Hindi is to Italian.) A biological analogue would be the discovery that mammals actually evolved from three distinct lineages – one perhaps in the bony fish category, another possibly a reptile, and a third maybe even an insect – that were able to exchange milk- and hair-producing genes, and thus came to superficially resemble each other. Such a scenario is of course daft, precisely because linguistic evolution is only vaguely analogous to organic evolution.

Linguistic evolution differs from organic evolution for a variety of reasons, but a crucial factor is that vastly less sharing occurs across biological lineages. We now know that genes can jump from one species to another, but the process is still relatively rare. In the organic realm, change generally occurs as a result of random mutations acted upon by natural selection, not from the borrowing of elements from other species. When it comes to languages, however, sharing is ubiquitous. Languages are almost always borrowing words, and sometimes they adopt the grammatical properties of other languages as well (see Chapter 3). At times, two completely unrelated languages essentially merge to create a hybrid tongue. To be sure, linguists are almost always able to determine which language contributed more elements and basic structures, and hence should count as the parent tongue. When it comes to creole languages, however, such determinations are not always easy. In regard to grammar, different creoles of completely different parentage are often more similar to each other than they are to any of their source languages.

In some cases, admixtures of vocabulary, grammar, and phonology run so deep that linguists abandon the quest for unambiguous classification. Cappadocian Greek, for example, is slotted by some sources into the seemingly impossible "Greek–Turkish" language family.[23] Does Indo-European therefore encompass this language? Other sources, such as Ethnologue, place this

---

[23] Wikipedia, for example: http://en.wikipedia.org/wiki/Cappadocian_Greek

language in the Greek branch of the Indo-European family, but Turkish influences on Cappadocian Greek run deep: some of its sounds have been borrowed from Turkish along with vowel harmony; it has developed agglutinative inflectional morphology and lost (some) grammatical gender distinctions; and its basic word order is SOV (Janse 1998, 1999, 2001, 2009a, 2009b, 2011). And Cappadocian Greek is by no means the only example of such a "mixed language". What kind of language, for example, is Media Lengua, or *Chaupi-shimi*, which uses a largely Spanish lexicon yet is grammatically structured like Quechua (see Muysken 2010; Winford 2010)? Or Mitchif, which combines nouns and nominal bound morphemes from French with verbs and verbal bound morphemes from Cree (an Algonquin language spoken in Canada)? An organic equivalent would be something unthinkable, on the order of a mammal–crustacean hybrid: milk-producing but equipped with a chitinous exoskeleton. Such mixtures are so absurd that they have generated their own nonsense genre, as exemplified by Sara Ball's delightful flip-book, *Crocguphant*, which allows children to construct such impossible beasts as the eponymous creature that is part **croc**odile, part ja**gua**r, and part ele**phant**.

Linguistic family trees must therefore be taken as often showing lines of *partial* descent, unlike the phylogenetic diagrams of organic evolution. To gain a more complete understanding of linguistic relatedness, it is necessary to complement families of language descent with other kinds of linguistic connections. The various languages of a *Sprachbund*, for example, derive from different families or (subfamilies), yet nonetheless come to share many features through long histories of mutual interaction (see Emeneau 1956; Campbell *et al.* 1986; Thomason 2000; Dixon 2001; Joseph 2010). Likewise, the notion of linguistic strata takes into account the influences imposed by one language on another. Another useful complement to the linguistic tree is the so-called wave model, or *Wellentheorie*, originally devised by Johannes Schmidt and Hugo Schuchardt to explain some of the characteristics of the Germanic languages that seemed to defy the phylogenetic approach. In wave theory, fluid dialect continua replace the stable, geographically bounded languages required by models predicated on direct descent from ancestral tongues. Here, innovations can occur at any given points within a dialect continuum; such changes then spread outward in a circular manner, eventually dissipating as the distance from the innovation center increases (see Labov 2007). If a bundle of innovations substantially overlap and become thoroughly entrenched, a new dialect, or even language, can be said to have emerged. But according to wave theory, such a "language" is still best viewed as an impermanent collection of features at the intersections of multiple circles.

Wave theory does recognize, however, the fact that a single language/dialect can appropriate an entire dialect continuum, subordinating more localized speech forms and eventually driving them into a moribund state if not full extinction, as indeed has been the case in regard to Standard German over most of Germany. Such a process, however, generally requires the power of the state, mercantile networks, or some other overarching institution. Such geographically expansive and culturally potent organizations, however, are a feature of the historical past; for most of humankind's prehistoric existence, the means necessary for producing linguistic standardization over broad areas were lacking. We are so used to the modern world of mass communication over vast distances and of language-standardizing governments and educational systems that we easily forget that in earlier times, and in many remote areas to this day, different linguistic environments prevailed. Overall, we suspect that for most of human history, the wave theory captures the process of language diversification as well as the standard phylogenetic model. As Nichols (1992: 23) argues, the "tree model" works best in linguistic "spread zones", areas in which single language families have expanded broadly. Dixon (1997: 3) concurs, finding the tree model appropriate for periods of rapid language change and expansion, but not for the longer periods of "equilibrium" when linguistic areas emerge and are continually reconfigured as innovations spread over numerous languages, whether related by common descent or not. As he shows, the tree schema works vastly better for some language groups (such as Indo-European, Austronesian, Semitic) than for others (such as the hypothesized language families of Australia). As a result of such complexities, the two models seem to complement each other relatively well.

Conceptualizing language differentiation in terms of biological evolution also exacerbates the problems of geographical modeling discussed earlier in this chapter. Biological speciation occurs after distinct populations of a given species no longer interbreed and therefore begin to evolve in separate directions, which, in simplified terms, can take place either because they become spatially separated (allopatric speciation), or because they move into new niches in the same area (sympatric speciation). In the linguistic realm, on the other hand, such processes do not occur; as Nichols (1992: 277) argues after an exhaustive analysis, "No evidence of anything like speciation has been found in this or any other typological work". New languages, moreover, can emerge even if the populations that speak them continue to communicate with each other, as multilingualism is relatively common. (A biological counterpart to multilingualism is of course unthinkable). As a result, the diversification of languages must be conceptualized as a broad process, not as a series of discrete events.

Yet in "Mapping the Origins", linguistic evolution is modeled precisely in terms of speciation-like *events*; as the authors' write, "we can only represent the geographic extent corresponding to language divergence events".[24] In the

---

[24] The quotation is from the caption for Figure S4 in the authors' online Supplementary Materials: sciencemag.org/content/suppl/2012/08/22/337.6097.957.DC1/Bouckaert.SM.REVISED.pdf

authors' animated map as well, new language branches are depicted as sprouting in particular places in particular times, and then as spreading outward from these points of origination by way of diffusion. We find it rather ironic that the Anatolian school, which began with an insistence on "processual" accounts of cultural change, would in the end conceptualize the development of new language branches in terms of events rather than processes.

Finally, in the Gray–Atkinson scheme, not only do new languages emerge strictly on the basis of evolutionary descent from a single common ancestor, but they also do so only on the basis of changes in words. In their model, words are to languages as genes (or precisely, proteins encoded by genes) are to organisms. But words are just one aspect of language, and can hardly be considered more fundamental than grammar or sounds. As discussed in Chapters 3 and 4, lines of linguistic descent can appear quite different if syntax and phonology are considered along with the lexicon.

Part III

Searching for Indo-European origins

As the research program of the Gray–Atkinson approach fails to withstand scrutiny, its conclusions must therefore be regarded with suspicion if not rejected outright. But even if we deny the finding of "Mapping the Origins and Expansion of the Indo-European Language Family" and other research papers that use phylogenetic and phylogeographical analysis to locate the Indo-European homeland in Neolithic Anatolia, it does not follow that the language family necessarily originated in the steppe zone several thousand years later. Although most Indo-Europeanists support the Steppe theory, a complete consensus has not been reached. Archeologists such as J. P. Mallory and David Anthony have persuasively argued in favor of a homeland in the Pontic Steppes during the Chalcolithic or early Bronze Age, but the evidence is not yet adequate to make conclusive statements. In the following three chapters, we will therefore examine the linguistic evidence about the location and timing of the emergence of Proto-Indo-European in some detail, examining as well comparative geo-historical arguments. Doing so provides further evidence against the Anatolian hypothesis, especially as operationalized by the Gray–Atkinson approach. Yet in the end we are still unable to irrefutably locate a homeland and assign a date. But such a lack of certainty need not concern us, as rock-solid certainty is a feature of mathematics, not science, much less human history. As numerous lines of evidence all indicate origination in the steppe zone roughly 4,000 to 6,000 years ago, we must at least provisionally accept the Steppe hypothesis.

The first two chapters in this part focus on linguistic analysis. Chapter 8 returns to the question of dating, showing how the traditional techniques of historical linguists allow scholars to determine relative dates and occasionally absolute dates (within a range) as well. Using these methods, especially in regard to vocabulary elements pertaining to vehicles and domesticated animals, we uncover strong evidence against the Anatolian hypothesis and in favor of the competing Steppe theory. Chapter 9 seeks more specifically to locate the original homeland, relying primarily on linguistic reconstructions of past environments, evidence of contact with other language families, and indications derived from linguistic relationships and migrational histories. Chapter 10 takes a different approach, looking to other times and places to draw out general tendencies in regard to linguistic relationships between pastoral and agricultural peoples.

8   Why linguists don't do dates? – Or do they?

In Chapter 5, we identified a number of general limitations and specific errors associated with Bayesian phylogenetic dating methods, which make it "not likely to tempt historical linguists to accept the proposed dates" (McMahon and McMahon 2006: 159). Such difficulties, however, do not mean that mainstream historical linguists have nothing to say about dating Indo-European origins and diversification. The traditional comparative method is quite good at establishing relative chronologies that place linguistic events in historical sequence, without fixing them to calendar dates, and in some cases even absolute dates (or at least date ranges) can be established by conventional historical linguistic approaches.

Relative chronologies

When it comes to individual lexical items, historical linguists look for various clues to establish the etymology and the relative chronology of the development of words. For example, Edward Sapir (1916/1949: 434–435) pointed out that "the objects [...] denoted in English by the [unanalyzable] words *bow, arrow, spear, wheel, plough* [...] belong to a far more remote past than those indicated by such [analyzable] words as *railroad, insulator, battleship, submarine, percolator, capitalist,* and *attorney-general*". Another technique, applied with remarkable success by Sapir in his study of Navajo (Sapir 1936), involves deriving historical information from cultural items whose linguistic designations have obviously changed their meaning; Sapir's example of such a phenomenon in English is the word *spinster*, which changed its meaning from 'one who spins' to 'unmarried female of somewhat advanced age'. Mallory (1976: 45) takes non-productive (i.e. irregular) morphology to likewise indicate the relative antiquity of the words (and by extension, of the associated concepts); for example, the irregularity of such plurals as *ox/oxen, sheep/sheep,* and *calf/calves* is taken as evidence of the great age of stockbreeding among speakers of English and their linguistic ancestors. This argument is problematic, however, as the retention of irregular forms such as *foot/feet* and *tooth/teeth* but not of the irregular plural of *book* (Old English *bēc*, which after

Table 8.1 *Latin and French cognates*

Latin	French	translation
causam /k/	chose /ʃ/	'thing'
corem /k/	coeur /k/	'heart'
kattum /k/	chat /ʃ/	'cat'
aurum	or	'gold'

the Great Vowel Shift would have resulted in the form *beek*) is a reflection not of the fact that feet and teeth predate books but of the higher frequency of the irregular plural forms of 'foot' and 'tooth' compared to that of 'book' in the Middle English period.

Yet another strategy used to reconstruct the relative chronology of words and associated concepts rests on the assumption that "items which are represented by terms which have cognates widely spread across the languages in the family are likely to be older than terms which lack such a wider distribution among the related languages" (Campbell 2000: 11). For example, just as the irregular plural form of *sheep* is indicative of the word's antiquity, so is the fact that the cognate set for 'sheep' across Indo-European languages is broad, including Luwian *hawi*, Sanskrit *avis*, Greek *o(w)is*, Latin *ovis*, Lithuanian *avis*, Proto-Slavic *ovьca* (cf. Russian *ovca*), Old Irish *oi*, and English *ewe*.

More important than the reconstruction of relative chronologies of words is the reconstruction of relative chronologies of sound changes that affect the entire lexicon. Our first example comes from the development of modern French from Latin, illustrated in Table 8.1 (the pronunciation of the initial consonant in the first three words is shown in transcription as well).

These words illustrate two sound changes that occurred as (a dialect of) Latin transformed into French. One change is the transformation of /k/ into /ʃ/, mentioned in Chapter 4 above. This change applied only in front of a low back vowel /a/, as can be seen from the fact that *coeur* 'heart' retained the original /k/. Another change involves the diphthong /au/ turning into /o/. Crucially, the two changes must have occurred in a particular order: palatalization of the velar first, and the vowel change second. Had the vowel change taken place before the palatalization, the original *au* in *causam* would have become *o*, and the palatalization rule would not have applied to this word at all, leaving it as /kozam/, eventually to become modern French /koz/ rather than /ʃoz/. In this case, the vowel change "bleeds" the palatalization: the application of the vowel change creates a context in which the palatalization rule can no longer apply. Thus, although we cannot tell without historical records when exactly the two changes occurred on the way from the local variety of Latin to French, we can deduce their relative chronology.

Another example concerns the development of the English word *foot* and its plural form *feet*. This word derives from the Proto-Indo-European (PIE) form **pód*, which is cognate with Latin *pēs/pedis*, Sanskrit *pad-*, and Lithuanian *pãdas* 'sole (foot)'. Consider the consonants first. The transformation from *pVd* (where *V* symbolizes some vowel) to *fVt* involves two changes: *p > f* and *d > t*. Each of the two changes was part of a larger transformation that involved a whole class of sounds: *p* was changed alongside *t* and *k* into *f*, *θ*, and *h*, respectively, whereas *d* changed alongside *b* and *g* into *t*, *p*, and *k*, respectively. The relative chronology of these two changes is easy to establish: the voiceless stops *p*, *t*, and *k* must have become fricatives first, and the devoicing of voiced stops *b*, *d*, and *g* into *p*, *t*, and *k* must have occurred later. Had the order of the two changes been reversed and the devoicing applied first, the original **d* inherited from PIE would have become **t*, and then this new *t* and the original **p* would both have changed to fricatives. Thus, the original **pVd* would have become **pVt* and then *fVθ*, leaving English with *footh* instead of *foot*. Clearly, this is not what actually happened, so we can deduce that the change from voiceless stops into fricatives happened before the devoicing, without attaching absolute dates to these changes (known as stages of Grimm's Law, or the First Germanic Consonant Shift, which happened in Proto-Germanic).

And how did the vowel alternation in *foot/feet* come about? In Proto-Germanic, as in PIE, the singular and plural forms had the same vowel **ō*, as in **fōts/*fōtiz* (the macron over the vowel means that it is pronounced long). Both the final *z* and the *i* were later lost, for reasons that need not concern us here, and the vowel in the plural form changed from *ō* to *ī*. Moreover, this latter transformation happened in several stages: first, *ō* was fronted into a long *ø* (this process is known as Germanic umlaut), then it was unrounded into *ē*, then raised to *ī* by the process known as the Great Vowel Shift. We know from written records that the latter change must have happened circa 1500 CE; likewise, we also know from textual sources that the form *fēt* was attested in the Old English period (i.e. from the sixth to late eleventh century CE). From this we can deduce that the initial fronting of *ō* must have happened earlier, in the Pre-Old English stage. Thus, while we cannot attach a precise date to this change, we can put constraints on it, on the basis of a relative chronology with respect to other changes that can be dated in absolute terms based on extra-linguistic information.

Establishing a relative chronology of sound changes can also help us understand layers of borrowing to and from a given language. This point can be illustrated with Latin words originally containing a velar stop /k/ that were borrowed into Basque at different times (cf. Trask 2000: 45–46). The Latin word *cellam* 'chamber' preserves a velar stop in the Basque form *gela* 'room'; it must have been borrowed in the early period, before Latin underwent sound changes that affected its velar stops. In contrast, Latin *caelum* 'sky', which appears in Basque as *zeru*, with the initial consonant pronounced as /s/, must have been borrowed later, after Latin velar stops have been palatalized and assibilated, turning the Latin word into */tselo/. Finally, Latin *cepullam* 'onion' must have been borrowed into Basque in the intermediate period, when the velar stops of Latin were palatalized but not yet assibilated: its Basque form *tipula* is a reflex of the Latin form containing a palatalized velar $*k^j$, which Basque turned into an alveolar stop.

More generally, an analogy can be drawn between the historical linguistic and genealogical enterprises. Linguistic evidence alone can reveal relative chronologies but not absolute dates; similarly, in genealogy "it is one thing to know who is whose mother, or grandfather, or sibling, but quite another to date earlier lives in family trees, in the absence of documentary evidence" (McMahon and McMahon 2006: 159). More precisely, generational information can be *reconstructed* (e.g. on the basis of information from names, with surnames typically reflecting male-line descent and patronymics allowing the placement of people in their respective generations), whereas specific birth and death dates for the various family members need to be *known* directly. Such dates can be *estimated* based on biological limitations that restrict the human generation interval to between 15 and 45 years in the case of maternal descent (it can be somewhat longer in the case of paternal descent). Yet such estimates are never precise or very reliable; while the general expectation is that of "stratified generations" (i.e. one's aunts and uncles being approximately the same age as one's parents, one's great-aunts and great-uncles being approximately the same age as one's grandparents, and so on), deviations from that pattern, such as an aunt who is younger than her niece, are not hard to come by. As for languages, the situation is if anything more uncertain as there is no apparent analogue for the human generation interval: there are no external (e.g. biological) limitations on how quickly or slowly a language can change to the extent that it is no longer recognized as an extension of its ancestor. Consequently, the development of a "grandmother" language into its "granddaughters" may take longer or shorter periods of time. For instance, the development of Proto-Germanic into its "granddaughter" languages, such as English and Norwegian, took considerably longer than the development of Proto-Slavic to its "granddaughters", such as Polish and Russian: Proto-Slavic was spoken approximately from the fifth to the ninth century CE, at which time Old English and Old Norse were already distinct languages.

It is clear from well-documented instances of relatively recent linguistic history that languages change not at a constant rate (see the summary of criticisms of glottochronology in Chapter 5), but in fits and starts. Ringe *et al.*'s (2002: 60) Uniformitarian Principle (see Chapter 3) forces us to assume that the same variability in the rate of linguistic change applies to early periods in human (pre-)history. However, it also forces us to assume that the amount of change – not only lexical but also phonological and grammatical – that happened during comparable time spans in prehistory and in historical times should be comparable as well. Based on this assumption, Garrett (2006) argued against the Gray–Atkinson model, indicating that the date that it assigns to PIE is several millennia too early.[1] Garrett's argument is illustrated with five numerals ('three', 'five', 'seven', 'eight', and 'nine') in PIE and three Indo-European branches: Greek, Indo-Iranian, and Italic. For each branch, he considers a modern representative (Modern Greek, Waigali, and Spanish, respectively), as well as intermediate proto-languages of approximately the same age (Proto-Greek, Proto-Indo-Iranian, and Proto-Italic). He compares the temporal distance between PNIE (i.e. Proto-Nuclear-Indo-European, the common ancestor of all Indo-European languages except those in the Anatolian branch) and the intermediate proto-languages, on the one hand, and between the intermediate proto-languages and the modern languages, on the other hand. Garrett notes that, if one assumes the Gray–Atkinson date for PNIE (i.e. 7,000–8,000 years ago) to be correct, the two temporal intervals are approximately of the same length, on the order of 3,500–4,000 years (though Proto-Italic may be somewhat younger). Yet, Garrett (2006: 144) notes that during the latter temporal interval (i.e. intermediate proto-languages to modern descendants) "significantly more phonological change has taken place than occurred" in the interval from PNIE to intermediate proto-languages. Moreover, a major restructuring of nominal and verbal inflection occurred en route from the same intermediate proto-languages to their modern descendants, while the morphosyntactic changes from PNIE to the intermediate proto-languages were much less substantial. If PNIE predates the intermediate proto-languages by approximately the same time interval as the one that separates those intermediate proto-languages from their modern descendants, what accounts for the two periods being radically different in the amount of phonological and inflectional change that characterizes them? A relatively conservative period of little change would have been necessary, followed by a period of much more rapid transformations, in contradiction to the Uniformitarian Principle. As a result, the Gray–Atkinson model requires that we make "the unscientific assumption that linguistic change in the period for which we have no direct evidence was radically different from change we can study directly" (Garrett 2006: 144). Here again, the Steppe hypothesis, which posits that PIE was spoken approximately two millennia after the date produced by the Gray–Atkinson model, is more compatible with the facts described by Garrett (2006).

---

[1] Similar argument is found in Darden (2001) and Anthony (2007).

From relative to absolute chronology: the case of Romani

Although relative chronologies of various historical linguistic changes are fascinating in their own right, absolute chronologies, whereby linguistic events are assigned calendar dates, are obviously more valuable. But establishing such absolute chronologies based solely on linguistic facts is virtually impossible, as words and grammatical structures rarely bear direct signs of when they were born. The only way to establish absolute linguistic chronologies is to correlate linguistic facts with dates fixed by other means. In the simplest case, written materials illustrating particular linguistic phenomena can be dated by radiocarbon methods – and in some cases by the text itself. For example, the Kirkdale sundial, found at St. Gregory's Minster in North Yorkshire, England, which exhibits a loss of the genitive case in Old English, can be dated by its reference to "the days of Earl Tostig" – that is, Tostig Godwinson. Brother of King Harold Godwinson, he held the title of Earl of Northumbria from 1055 to 1065 and died in the battle of Stamford Bridge in September 1066. From this and similar texts, we can conclude that the loss of distinct genitive forms happened as early as the mid-eleventh century, during the late Old English period.

Because such direct indications of when a given linguistic development occurred are not always available, historical linguists must engage in more subtle sleuthing, looking for both grammatical changes and loanword patterns that can be dated independently. Work on Romani provides a good example. The origin and migration history of the Roma must be reconstructed based on linguistic evidence, as little information can be gleaned from written records, either their own or those of other peoples (as discussed in Chapter 3). Since the late eighteenth century, it has been known that the Roma trace back to the Indian subcontinent, from where they migrated westward (Rüdiger 1782; Marsden 1783). The earliest mentions of the Roma in Europe date from the mid-1300s, by which time they must have reached the Balkans. The reasons for the Roma exodus are controversial. Most scholars now believe that the Roma originated as one of the service-providing castes in India that left the subcontinent as camp followers, making their living by providing crafts and services to military forces (Matras 2010: 39). This middle-of-the-road explanation treats the early Roma neither as aimless wanderers, as they are often depicted in the non-specialized literature, nor as a prestigious caste of warriors and priests, as portrayed by some Romani activists (cf. Kochanowski 1994).

Whatever the reasons behind the Roma migration that ultimately brought them to Europe, linguistic evidence helps us understand the timing of the differentiation of the Romani language – and consequently, the timing of their migration. An examination of the sound system and grammar of Romani reveals that an earlier form of the language was spoken in India as late as

1,000 years ago. As discussed in Chapter 5, Romani underwent a number of widespread changes that affected the northern Indo-Aryan-speaking area during the second half of the first millennium, including the restructuring of the gender system, the general reduction of the older system of nominal case inflection to an opposition between nominative and non-nominative (oblique), the simplification of some consonant clusters, and the collapse of the past participle. These changes characterize the transition from Middle Indo-Aryan (MIA) to New Indo-Aryan (NIA) languages.

However, an examination of the loan component of the Romani lexicon may suggest an earlier date for the Roma exodus from India, sometime between the sixth and ninth centuries CE (see Campbell 2000: 5–6). As mentioned in Chapter 4, the Romani lexicon has a significant Greek component, suggesting a prolonged sojourn in a Greek-speaking area characterized by intense and widespread Romani–Greek bilingualism (see Matras 2010: 35–37). The Romani vocabulary contains numerous lexical roots of Greek origin, including words from the Swadesh-200 list, such as *luludí* 'flower' (< Greek *lulúdi*), *kókalo* 'bone' (< Greek *kókkalo*), and *drom* 'road' (< Greek *drómos*). Grammatical vocabulary has also been borrowed, including *pale* 'again' (< Greek *pale*), *komi* 'still' (< Greek *akómi*), and *panda* 'more' (< Greek *pánta* 'always'), as well as the numerals *eftá* 'seven', *oxtó* 'eight', and *enjá* 'nine'. Derivational markers have also been borrowed, such as the abstract nominalizer *-imos*, the participal marker *-imen*, the adjectival markers *-itiko/-itko*, and the ordinal marker *-to*. Greek has influenced Romani syntax as well: the default word order in Romani is Verb–Object, as opposed to all other Indo-Iranian languages that obligatorily show Object–Verb order. Other grammatical features that can be attributed to Greek influence are the prenominal definite article, the postnominal relative clause introduced by a general relativizer *kaj* (as in *o manuš **kaj** giljavel* 'the man who sings'), and the contrast between a factual complementizer *kaj* and a non-factual one *te*. This massive linguistic borrowing prompts a speculation that the Roma stayed in a Greek-speaking area, most likely somewhere in the Byzantine Empire, for many generations, possibly as long as two or three centuries (Matras 2010: 39).

The second largest set of loanwords in Romani comes from Armenian; these loans include words for everyday items such as *bov* 'oven', *grast* 'horse', and *kotor* 'piece'. Different scholars have provided varying estimates as to the number of Romani lexical roots of Armenian origin, ranging from twenty (Matras 2002: 23) to fifty-one (Boretzky 1995). The different counts are partially due to the fact that it is sometimes difficult to distinguish loanwords of Armenian and Iranian origin, because of the massive Iranian influence on Armenian; distinguishing Iranian loans from shared Indo-Iranian cognates is more difficult still. Similarities among Iranian languages make it difficult to determine whether a given loan comes from Persian, Kurdish, or even

Ossetian. Nonetheless, several Persian etymologies for Romani words have been accepted, including *ambrol* 'pear' (< Persian *amrūd*), *avgin* 'honey' (< Persian *angubīn*), and *pošom* 'wool' (< Persian *pašm*); see also Hancock (1995).

The presence of significant Armenian and Iranian components in the Romani lexicon has often been interpreted as suggesting successive phases of migration, first from India to Persia (where Persian words could be borrowed), then to the northern Fertile Crescent or southern Caucasus (where Armenian words were absorbed), and finally to the Byzantine Empire.[2] Allowing at least a few generations' sojourn in each of these locations – long enough for a significant amount of borrowing to occur – would indicate an earlier date for the initial exodus from India than the one established on the basis of phonological and grammatical properties of Romani shared with other NIA languages. Paradoxically, Roma *could not* have left India before 1000 CE to allow for the changes that characterize Romani as a NIA language, and yet the Roma *must* have left before 1000 CE to allow enough time for consecutive sojourns in Persia, the northern Fertile Crescent, and Greece. The conspicuous absence of Arabic loanwords – except for isolated items such as *dzet* 'oil' from the Arabic *zēt* 'olive oil', which can be explained as indirect borrowings via Persian or Armenian – also suggests that the Roma left Iran before, or at least not long after, the Muslim conquest of 644 CE, which in turn means that they must have left India well before 1000 CE.[3]

So how can the thesis that the Roma stayed in Iran for several generations before leaving in the seventh or eighth century be reconciled with the phonological and grammatical evidence for the Roma leaving India as late as 1000 CE? One solution, originally proposed by Matras (1996; 2002: 25; 2010: 35), is to look not at the present-day location of the Persian and Armenian languages, but at their historical distribution. This theory takes the Roma in one migration phase in the eleventh century CE from India directly to eastern Anatolia, which had just come under the rule of Seljuks of Rum (1077–1307),

---

[2] Certain phonological and grammatical changes which occurred in Romani after it separated from the other Indo-Aryan languages but before the Roma's arrival in Europe could be explained as influences of languages of the Caucasus and Anatolia; however, it is difficult to prove that these changes were not independent developments (for a more detailed discussion, the interested reader is referred to Matras 2010: 34–35).

[3] An alternative explanation for the lack of Arabic loanwords takes the Roma via a northern migration route through the Pamir, south of the Caspian Sea, through the Caucasus, along the southern Black Sea coast, on toward Constantinople, and thence to Europe; this northern migration route receives further support from the few loanwords attributed to Georgian (e.g. Romani *khilav* 'plum' from Georgian *khliavi*) and Ossetian (e.g. Romani *vurdon* 'wagon' from Ossetian *wærdon*, and Romani *orde* 'here' from Ossetian *ortä*); more on alleged Georgian and Ossetian loanwords in Romani in Matras (2002: 24). However, one cannot exclude the possibility that these isolated loans were transmitted via other languages, such as Armenian.

who supplanted the Byzantine Greeks in the region after the fateful Battle of Manzikert in 1071 CE. Although the Seljuk elite were Turkic-speaking, the official language of the Sultanate of Rum was Persian. Because Byzantine Greek, Armenian, and Kurdish were all widely spoken in eastern Anatolia at the time, the various loan components of the Romani lexicon could in principle have been picked up in the same period and in the same place. Keeping in mind that the Roma had not converted to Islam and would have been in contact mostly with the non-Muslims (chiefly Christians, but also Yezidis and Jews) of eastern Anatolia, the lack of Arabic loans is not particularly surprising. Assuming that the Roma were camp followers making their living by providing crafts and services to military forces, their arrival in eastern Anatolia at roughly the same time that the Seljuks established their rule in the area makes sense as well. We do find it odd, however, that Romani has few roots of Turkic origin, as would be expected under such a scenario.

As a result of such considerations, we can reasonably settle on the date circa 1000 CE for the Roma exodus from India, and consequently of the Romani split from the rest of the Indo-Aryan family tree – a whopping 2,500 years later than the date calculated by the Gray–Atkinson model (or 1,500 years, according to their newly substituted results). This later date, supported by the historical linguistic evidence outlined above, receives further support from genetic studies, which place the "founding event" (i.e. the Roma exodus from India) "approximately 32–40 generations ago" (Morar et al. 2004). Assuming 25–30 years per generation, this figure nicely matches the 1000 CE date derived from linguistic studies.[4]

The upshot of this discussion of the Roma exodus from India and the consequent differentiation of Romani from other Indo-Aryan languages is that traditional historical linguistic methods, coupled with evidence from written sources, archeology, genetics, and other disciplines, can provide absolute dates, contrary to the claims of the Gray–Atkinson approach that "linguists don't do dates". In the following pages, we turn our attention to applying such traditional historical linguistic methods to the dating of PIE.

Linguistic paleontology and the "wheel problem"

Although in principle lexical and grammatical borrowings, as well as shared phonological and grammatical changes, can shed light on the migrational history of a language, as discussed above, the farther back one looks into the

---

[4] A more recent genetic study (Mendizabal et al. 2012) places the Roma in northwestern India "2,158±1,178 years" ago (i.e. between 1324 BCE and 32 CE); while this finding, as the authors of the study admit, is "in agreement with previous historical records that locate the Roma in Europe at least 1,000 years ago", it is not particularly informative as it makes no reference to when the Roma actually left the Indian subcontinent.

past, the less reliable such evidence becomes, due in part to the changing locations of the different language groups involved. For example, intense linguistic contact between early Indo-European languages, especially Proto-Indo-Iranian, and Proto-Uralic, has been well established (see Häkkinen 2012), yet without knowing where exactly Proto-Uralic was then spoken, we can only use this information to make conjectures about the location of the PIE *Urheimat*. (Language contact in the context of the PIE problem is discussed further in Chapter 9.)

Other varieties of linguistic information, however, can help us fill in the gaps in historical knowledge encountered in regard to non-literate, undocumented peoples, such as the original Indo-Europeans. In the absence of written records, scholars can turn to so-called *linguistic paleontology*, a field of study that examines the reconstructed vocabulary of a proto-language to find clues about the culture, social organization, and geography of its speakers. Introduced by Adolphe Pictet in 1877, linguistic paleontology remains one of the best ways to date linguistic divergence events at the requisite time depth, despite the challenges that it faces from semantic shifts and new archeological discoveries, as we shall see below. For example, the techniques of linguistic paleontology have allowed scholars to date the development of the Uralic language family, and especially of its Finno-Ugric branch, in reasonable detail. This work is based on correlating such historical linguistic information with evidence derived from other fields, such as palynology (for the prehistoric distribution of trees), and archeology (in regard to the local origins of agriculture, metallurgy, and the like) (see Campbell 1997a, Hajdú 1969, Hajdú and Domokos 1987, Joki 1973, and Anttila 1989, among others).

Linguistic paleontology is based on the assumption that the things that the reconstructed words denote actually existed at the time when these words were used to denote them.[5] For example, if a PIE word $*sneig^wh$- for 'snow' can be reconstructed, it stands to reason that the Indo-Europeans would have known snow. If they had a word $*h_2erh_3$- for 'to plow', they must have known and used some form of plowing. And if their vocabulary included words like $*ph_2tér$- 'father', $*meh_2ter$- 'mother', $*b^hráh_2ter$- 'brother', $*su̯ésor$- 'sister', $*suH$- 'son', and $*d^hugh_2tér$- 'daughter', then they must have cared about such familial relationships.[6] Reconstructing not only individual lexical items, but

---

[5] It should be noted, however, that in some cases the existence of words denoting certain concepts indicates not the actual existence of such physical entities but their existence in the mental world of the speakers. For example, the existence of words *Santa Claus* and *unicorn* in present-day English does not mean that Santa Claus and unicorns exist in the physical environment of English speakers, but that they have mental concepts denoted by these words.

[6] The exact meaning of these reconstructed PIE terms is not evident; for a detailed discussion see Kullanda (2002). Similarly, Hoffman (2010) shows that the meanings of the Biblical Hebrew roots for 'brother', 'sister', 'father', 'son', etc. were not limited to their modern familial senses.

also well-elaborated lexical fields (semantic domains) with several interrelated terms is particularly valuable for the purpose of reconstructing the culture associated with a proto-language. For example, the reconstruction of terms pertaining to maize and maize agriculture in Proto-Mayan, including words for 'maize', 'corncob', 'ear of corn', 'atole [a corn drink]', 'to sow', 'to harvest/pick corn', 'to grind', 'metate [grindstone for corn]', 'to roast [grains]', 'flour', and so on, confirms that Proto-Mayan speakers were already maize agriculturalists before the diversification of the Mayan language family (Campbell 1997b). As for the Indo-Europeans, aspects of both their material and non-material culture can be reconstructed in this fashion, though in the following pages we shall focus on material culture, whose elements in the archeological record can be reliably dated by radiocarbon methods. (For a more detailed discussion of the culture of the Indo-Europeans, see Mallory 1989, Beekes 1995, Mallory and Adams 1997, Mallory and Adams 2006, and the references therein.)

Recall that the Anatolian hypothesis, originally proposed by Renfrew (1987) and advocated by the Gray–Atkinson approach, associates PIE with the spread of agriculture in the seventh millennium BCE, whereas the Steppe hypothesis associates the Indo-Europeans with the domestication of the horse and more broadly with the so-called *secondary products complex* – plowing, carting, wool, and dairy – that arose in the late fourth and early third millennium (Sherratt 1981, 1983, 1997; Anthony 2007). In this regard, the parts of the reconstructed Indo-European vocabulary that pertain to secondary products are particularly instructive.

To begin with dairy, PIE vocabulary had a word for cow, $*g^w\acute{o}u$- (cf. Latin *bōs*, Greek *boũs*, Sanskrit *gaús*, Latvian *gùovs*, Old Church Slavonic *govę̌db*, Tocharian A *ko*, Tocharian B *kau*, Old English *cú*).[7] Also reconstructed are words $*h_2o\d{u}i$- 'sheep' (cf. Latin *ovis*) and $*h_2eg^wno$- 'lamb' (cf. Latin *agnus*), although the reconstruction of the word for 'goat' is more problematic (see Beekes 1995: 36; Wodtko *et al.* 2008: 233–235). The word for 'milk' is also difficult to reconstruct conclusively, though 'milking' in PIE was apparently $*h_2mel\acute{g}$- (cf. Greek *amélgō*, Old English *melcan*, etc.). It is important to note that dairy consumption was made possible by a genetic mutation that led to a development of lactase persistence, and hence lactose tolerance, in adults. Several such mutations occurred independently in Europe, India, and parts of Africa (cf. Ingram *et al.* 2009). Crucially, these mutations were not directly linked to the spread of agriculture some 3,000 years earlier: to this day, southern Europe has significantly lower levels of lactase persistence (and hence higher levels of lactose intolerance) than northern Europe, although

---

[7] Here and below, the forms listed in parentheses are the cognates on the basis of which the PIE roots are reconstructed.

agriculture developed much earlier in the south than in the north of the subcontinent. Moreover, the Fertile Crescent, where agriculture first appeared and the European cropping complex is thought to have originated, remains relatively lactose intolerant. Even in populations that eventually developed some degree of lactase persistence, the relevant mutations and consequently the ability to consume dairy products did not spread quickly, nor did they affect entire populations. For example, the famous Tyrolean Iceman, who lived several millennia after the arrival of agriculture in southern Europe, was genetically lactose intolerant (cf. Keller *et al.* 2012).

Besides milk, sheep must have also provided the original Indo-European speakers with **HulHn-* 'wool', which was the basic material out of which clothing was made (cf. Latin *lāna*, Gothic *wulla*; other derivatives attested also in Anatolian, Greek, Indo-Iranian, Baltic, Slavic, Celtic, and Germanic; see Garrett 2006: 145). Another useful domesticated animal was the ox, **uksen-* (cf. Tocharian *okso*, Welsh *ych*, Gothic *auhsa*, etc.).

But even more important than the ox was the horse, **h₁éḱu̯o-* (cf. Lycian *esbe*, Cuneiform Luvian *azzuwas,* Hieroglyphic Luvian *á-zú-wa-,* Tocharian A *yuk*, Tocharian B *yakwe*, Old Irish *ech*, Latin *equos*, Sanskrit *áśvas*, Avestan *aspō*, Old Persian *asa, Old* English *eoh*, Lithuanian *ašvà*, etc.).[8] If the ox made plowing and carting possible, the horse made these processes easier and faster. The reconstructed PIE vocabulary contains the words 'plowing' (reconstructed as **h₂erh₃-* based on such cognates as Lithuanian *ariù*, Greek *aróō*, Latin *arō*, Old Irish *airim*, and Gothic *arjan*) and 'carrying in a vehicle' (reconstructed as **u̯eǵʰ-* based on cognates such as Sanskrit *váhati*, Lithuanian *vežù*, Latin *vehō*, Greek *ókhos* 'wagon', and Gothic *ga-wigan* 'to move').[9]

Much ink has been spilled on the topic of whether **h₁éḱu̯o-* referred to wild or domesticated horses, and if horses were ridden by early Indo-Europeans or served to pull military chariots or peaceful plows (Renfrew 1998; Renfrew 2000: 431–434; Anthony 1986, 2007, 2011; Levine 1990; Anthony and Vinogradov 1995; Owen 1991; Gamkrelidze 1994; Mallory 1989). A related discussion (see Clackson 2000: 443–446; Anthony 2011) concerns the role of the horse in early Indo-European myth and ritual. As interesting as these debates are, they are not particularly relevant to the topic under consideration

---

[8] It is not clear whether the Greek *hippos* 'horse' is another reflex of the same Proto-Indo-European word (cf. Beekes 1995: 37; Ringe 2006: 3). Moreover, although the Latin word *equos* did not survive into any Romance languages in its masculine form, the feminine form did; compare Spanish *yegua* (cf. Wright 2011: 62) and Romanian *iapa* 'mare'. The words *equine* and *équestre* in modern French are later loanwords from Latin, as evidenced by the retention of the intervocalic velar. Regular sound changes would have changed the root into **ive-*, a form that survived dialectally until recently.

[9] Some scholars, however, doubt the validity of the latter reconstruction, suggesting that the PIE form meant 'hover, float' and that "the application to vehicular transport is a later development" (Clackson 2000: 445).

here: whatever the role of the horse in early Indo-European society, the linguistic reconstruction clearly indicates that speakers of PIE (or at least PNIE, as we shall see below) were quite familiar with horses. Since horses could have been domesticated only in an area where wild horses were common, the fact that PIE had a word for 'horse' narrows down the timing and location of the language group, regardless of whether the word referred to wild or domesticated animals.

Whether the early Indo-Europeans also had words for 'wheel' and other parts of wheeled vehicles – and were therefore familiar with wheel technology – has also provoked intense debate. The importance of these reconstructed words derives from the fact that there is no evidence for wheeled vehicles before the middle of the fourth millennium BCE (Mallory 1989; Anthony 2007). Yet, the existence of such terms in PIE and/or its immediate daughter languages strongly suggests that their speakers were familiar with wheeled vehicles.

As a result of these facts, the advocates of an early Anatolian origin of Indo-European must explain why there is no archeological evidence of wheels for several millennia after the supposed origination of the language family. They have generally responded by pointing out that "parallel semantic shifts or widespread borrowing can produce similar word forms across different languages without requiring that an ancestral term was present in the proto-language" (Atkinson and Gray 2006: 92). A particularly good example of how this phenomenon works in modern, well-documented languages is outlined in Heggarty (2006: 189): the English word *mouse* acquired a new sense in computing, then this new sense was "borrowed" (or more precisely, calqued) into other European languages; as a result, German *Maus*, Dutch *muis*, and Russian *myš* (as well as their equivalents in other languages) all acquired this new meaning more than a thousand years after the languages split. However, a closer look at the reconstructed PIE wheeled-vehicle terms, drawing heavily on the work of Don Ringe (cf. Ringe 2006), reveals that while a few of the items might be explicable as independent innovations or borrowed terms, a set of wheeled-vehicle terms *must* have been inherited from PIE or its near-descendants. To show such necessity, we need to examine the evidence of linguistic contact between Indo European branches   or the lack thereof – and of puzzling, irregular reflexes of PIE forms in its daughter languages (or, again, the lack thereof). In general terms, if a reconstructed word fits perfectly into the phonological and inflectional systems of its language, with nothing falling out of line, the default hypothesis is that it is an inherited word. Admittedly it remains conceivable that it could still be a loanword, but the odds are vanishingly low.

With such considerations in mind, let us begin our exploration of the Indo-European wheeled-vehicle vocabulary with the root of the family tree. As the

Anatolian branch is widely accepted as the first one to have split off from the trunk, any lexical item that has reflexes in at least one Anatolian language and at least one non-Anatolian language can be reconstructed for PIE. As it turns out, at least two wheeled-vehicle terms satisfy that criterion, together constituting good evidence that the early Indo-Europeans used draft animals to pull vehicles (or plows). The first such word means 'thill' (i.e. the pole that connects the yoke or harness of the draft animals to a vehicle). Ringe reconstructs this term's basic form as *$h_2éyHos$ ~ *$h_2éyHes$ or *$h_3éyHos$ ~ *$h_3éyHes$, and its collective form as *$h_2iHséh_2$ or *$h_3iHséh_2$ (see also Pokorny 1959; Melchert 1994). Its derivatives are found in Hittite (Anatolian), as well as in Proto-Slavic and Vedic Sanskrit (non-Anatolian). Ringe argues that because all these derivatives in descendant languages mean 'thill', we must reconstruct the meaning of the PIE term unambiguously as 'thill'. Moreover, this word is not derived from any known verb root, so the possibility of parallel semantic shifts must be excluded. Finally, this word could not have been borrowed into or out of Anatolian languages, as the separation of this branch from the rest of the family was "clean", as evidenced from the fact that Anatolian shares no distinctive innovations with any other subfamily of Indo-European (cf. Melchert 1994: 60–91; Ringe 2000). Thus, this single word constitutes one piece of *prima facie* evidence that speakers of PIE used draft animals to pull vehicles.

A second term that pertains to draft animals and is attested in both Anatolian and non-Anatolian languages is 'yoke'; it is reconstructed as *$iugóm$, based on Hittite *iukan*, Vedic Sanskrit *yugám*, Latin *iugum*, Welsh *iau*, Old English *ġeoc*, Old Church Slavonic *igo*, and so on. Although it is related to the verb root *$ieug$- 'join', this term does not mean just any kind of apparatus for joining. Instead, it consistently means 'yoke' in descendant languages; as a result, Ringe reconstructs that meaning for PIE. Moreover, he points out that "the formation of 'yoke' is a peculiar archaism, and that its shape – like its meaning – is a kind of linguistic fossil in Indo-European languages" (Ringe 2006: 3; see also Garrett 2006: 145).

It has been suggested that a third word, meaning 'wheel', can be reconstructed based on both Anatolian and non-Anatolian daughters of PIE: Hittite *hurkis* vs. Tocharian A *wärkänt* and Tocharian B *yerkwantai*. However, Ringe (2006) convincingly shows that the words in the two Tocharian languages reflect different reconstructed Proto-Tocharian forms, and the form that can be reconstructed on the basis of the Hittite form is different from the other two. It is possible that all three attested forms are derivatives of the verb root *h_2uerg- 'turn', but all three must have derived as independent innovations. Thus, we are left with two words indicating that speakers of PIE were harnessing draft animals by using a till and a yoke, to conveyances or plows of some sort. Whether at this point these conveyances had wheels or were more similar to sleds (in winter) or the North American travois, remains to be seen.

But in the Gray–Atkinson model the highest-order split of the Anatolian branch is not the only diversification event that long predated the appearance of the wheel in the archeological record in the middle of the fourth millennium BCE (i.e. around 5,500 years ago). The second split, whereby PNIE differentiated into the Tocharian and non-Tocharian branches, is dated at around 7,900 years before present in Gray and Atkinson (2003) and at about 6,900 years in Bouckaert *et al.* (2012).[10] These authors therefore face an additional challenge posed by words pertaining to wheeled vehicles that can be reconstructed for PNIE based on cognates in both Tocharian and non-Tocharian languages. At the level of PNIE, the word for 'wheel' is reconstructed as $*k^w ek^w lo$- (collective form $*k^w ek^w léh_2$). The cognates in descendant languages include Vedic Sanskrit *cakrám*, Avestan *čaxrō*, Homeric Greek *kúklos*, Old English *hwēol*, as well as Tocharian A *kukäl* and Tocharian B *kokale* meaning 'chariot'.

Gray, Atkinson, and their colleagues dismiss this reconstruction of 'wheel' in PNIE by arguing that the cognates in descendant languages derived independently from the verb root $*k^w elh_{1/2}$- 'turn'. Although this scenario is in general possible, linguistic analysis reveals further complications. As Ringe convincingly shows, the formation of $*k^w ek^w los$ from $*k^w el$- is unique, as it involves reduplication, a zero-grade root, and a thematic vowel. According to Ringe (2006: 4), "the probability that it could have been formed independently more than once is virtually nil".[11] Nor is it likely that descendant languages would have inherited a word with the abstract meaning of 'circle' or 'cycle' and then shifted it to the concrete meaning of 'wheel'; although semantic shifts from concrete to abstract are well attested, the reverse meaning shift, from abstract to concrete, is unusual at best (Sweetser 1990; Traugott and Dasher 2001; Garrett 2006: 145). Finally, it is not possible that the Tocharian languages borrowed this term from non-Tocharian languages or vice versa. Based on the lack of shared innovations and of other borrowings, Ringe concludes that the linguistic ancestors of Tocharians severed all contact with other Indo-European groups early and completely. Although the Tocharians subsequently came into contact with speakers of Iranian languages (Winter 1971; Ringe 1991: 105–115; Ringe 1996: 92; Kim 1999), by that time numerous regular sound changes had occurred in all the relevant languages, allowing loanwords from this later period to be easily identified by their foreign "sound signatures". However, the Tocharian word for 'chariot' shows no signs of foreign

[10] This split is dated at 7,200 years ago in the new version of the Supplementary Materials.
[11] In contrast, derivatives of the non-reduplicated $*k^w el$-, such as the Old Church Slavonic *kolo* 'wheel', can indeed be independent innovations derived by productive patterns.

phonology and is therefore not a loanword. Consequently, the word for 'wheel' must have existed in PNIE, and therefore its speakers must have been familiar with the object.

Similar considerations allow us to reconstruct another PNIE root that is indirectly related to the wheeled-vehicle vocabulary, the word for 'horse'. Based on cognates from both Tocharian and non-Tocharian languages (e.g. Tocharian A *yuk*, Tocharian B *yakwe*, Old Irish *ech*, Latin *equos*, Sanskrit *áśvas*, Avestan *aspō*, etc.), it can be reconstructed to PNIE as *$h_1 é\hat{k}uo$- (cf. also Wodtko *et al.* 2008: 230–233). Some scholars have attempted to reconstruct it even further, to PIE itself, based on forms found in Anatolian languages (Lycian *esbe*, Cuneiform Luvian *azzuwas,* Hieroglyphic Luvian *á-zú-wa-*). Although the word for 'horse' is found on numerous clay tablets in Hittite, it is unfortunately impossible to tell how it was pronounced in that language because the scribes never spelled the word out but used a logogram (word-sign) instead, one of many adopted as part of the cuneiform writing system. Could the word for 'horse' have been borrowed into or out of the Anatolian branch? The answer, however, is inconclusive as different sequences of sound changes could have produced the attested Lycian and Luwian forms, depending on whether the word was inherited from PIE or borrowed from a non-Anatolian language. Therefore, PIE reconstructions of this word remain controversial, while the PNIE reconstruction stands on firm evidential ground.

The same logic applies to later splits that also predate 3500 BCE (when wheeled vehicles are attested in the archeological record) in the Gray–Atkinson model: if a word pertaining to wheeled vehicles can be reconstructed for a common ancestral language based on cognates from the two branches found after the split, the speakers of that ancestral language must have had wheeled vehicles, meaning that the early dates advanced by the Gray–Atkinson approach are probably wrong – unless of course evidence is unearthed for wheeled vehicles from an earlier era. According to Gray and Atkinson's early study (2003), the third split in the Indo-European family tree is that of the Greco-Armenian branch, at around 5300 BCE. They also split off from the Indo-Iranian languages (plus Albanian) at around 4900 BCE and the Balto-Slavic languages at approximately 4500 BCE. Even the date assigned to the Celtic split from the Italo-Germanic branch (4100 BCE) predates the appearance of the wheel in archeological record by a good margin. According to the refined model presented in Bouckaert *et al.* (2012), the differentiation of the Greco-Albanian plus the Indo-Iranian branch (as well as the split *between* the Greco-Albanian and Indo-Iranian branches), and the separation of the Balto-Slavic languages from the rest of the tree, occurred before 3500 BCE (although the split between Italo-Celtic and Germanic languages is dated after that time).[12] All of these early dates are challenged by the reconstructions of words pertaining to wheeled vehicles based on cognates from Greek, Indo-Iranian, or Balto-Slavic languages *and* cognates from Italic, Celtic, or Germanic languages.

One prominent example is the word for 'axle', *$h_2ek\hat{s}$-, based on cognates such as Greek *áksōn*, Old Church Slavonic *osь*, Lithuanian *ašìs*, as well as Latin *axis*, Welsh *echel*, Old English *eax*, and Old High German *ahsa*. Thus, the most recent common ancestor of all these languages must have split from the Indo-European stem not circa 5300 BCE (as in Gray and Atkinson 2003) or circa 4600 BCE (as in Bouckaert *et al.* 2012), but after 3500 BCE.[13] Another reconstructed form that must have existed in the common ancestor of all non-Anatolian/non-Tocharian Indo-European (i.e. PSIE; see Figures 1, 2, and 4 in the Appendix) languages is the verb root meaning 'transport/convey in a vehicle'. Its derivatives include Vedic Sanskrit *váhati*, Avestan *vazaiti*, Lithuanian *vẽža*, Old Church Slavonic *vezetъ* (and probably Greek *ókhos* 'wagon'), as well as Latin *veh-* (cf. also Old Irish *fecht* 'trip', Gothic *ga-wigan* 'to move', and Old English *wegan* 'to move'). The probative value of this item is questionable, however, as most of the derivative words shifted meaning in one of two directions: most of the nominal derivatives refer to wheeled vehicles, while verbal derivatives in many languages, including Latin and Old Church Slavonic, widened in meaning to denote conveying in other types of transport, such as boats. However, this term can still be used as evidence for wheeled vehicles as far back as the common non-Anatolian/non-Tocharian Indo-European language (i.e. PSIE) "in the context of the whole set of reconstructable forms" (Ringe 2006: 6).

A third reconstruction concerns another root meaning 'wheel', *$(H)roth_2ó$- (collective form: *$(H)roteh_2$ 'set of wheels'). Its derivatives in descendant languages include Vedic Sanskrit *ráthas* 'wagon, chariot' and Lithuanian *rãtas* 'wheel, circle' (plural *rataĩ* 'wagon'), as well as Latin *rota* (derived from the collective form but reinterpreted as the singular), Old Irish *roth*, Welsh *rhod*, and Old High German *rad*. While this word is derived by productive PIE morphological processes from the verb root *$(H)ret$- 'run', it is unlikely that *all* the derivatives came about via independent parallel developments. Moreover, the attestation of reflexes of the collective form in Italic and

---

[12] According to the new version of Supplementary Materials, all major Indo-European branches diverged prior to the "wheel line" (3500 BCE), including the most recent major split – between Celtic and Romance – which they now place right at 3500 BCE. Thus, the presence of "horse-and-wheel" cognates in *any two major branches* presents a problem for this model.

[13] Ringe (2006: 6) points out that the reconstructed form of 'axle' appears to be "a linguistic fossil even in the reconstructable ancestor", meaning that this word possibly traces back to an even earlier form of Indo-European language. If true, this would mean that the split of the non-Anatolian/non-Tocharian Indo-European branches occurred even later than suggested in the main text.

Indo-Aryan languages suggests that a derivative meaning 'a set of wheels' is also old, inherited from a common PSIE ancestral tongue. An instructive contrast is provided by the words for 'hub': most Indo-European languages derived this term from 'navel' by using *different* morphological means (e.g. different ablaut [regular vowel variation] grades of the root, different suffixes, etc.), which strongly suggests parallel developments.

To recap, comparative reconstruction yields not just isolated words but a much larger "terminological ensemble in a coherent semantic field" (Garrett 2006: 145). First, the words for 'thill' and 'yoke', and possibly 'horse' (whether domesticated or wild), can be reconstructed to the oldest common ancestor of all Indo-European languages, PIE. Second, the word for 'wheel' can be reconstructed for the last common ancestor of the non-Anatolian languages, PNIE. (The word for 'horse' may belong to this category as well.) Finally, additional terms for 'axle', 'transport/convey in a vehicle', and another term for 'wheel' (as well as the collective form for 'set of wheels') trace back to PSIE, the common ancestor of all non-Anatolian/non-Tocharian Indo-European languages. In the Gray–Atkinson model, all these proto-languages predate 3500 BCE, a date from which archeological evidence of horse domestication and wheeled vehicles is not available.

Archeological evidence of horsemanship and wheeled vehicles

It is now time to give an equally close look at the archeological evidence, especially as it pertains to horses and wagons. Recall that a word for 'horse' can be reconstructed at least for PNIE (even if its reconstruction for PIE remains questionable). Therefore, by the logic of linguistic paleontology, speakers of PNIE knew horses, whether wild or domesticated. According to the Gray–Atkinson model, PNIE split into Tocharian and non-Tocharian branches as early as 4900 BCE (Bouckaert *et al.* 2012) or even 5900 BCE (Gray and Atkinson 2003). Moreover, according to the same model, proto-Tocharian speakers migrated eastwards via the northern Fertile Crescent and Iran. Therefore, the first question we must ask is whether horses were known in Anatolia, the Fertile Crescent, or the larger Middle East some 6,500–8,000 years ago.

Humans were certainly familiar with horses ages ago, depicting them in Paleolithic cave art as early as 25,000 BCE (the famous "Spotted Horses" in Pech Merle cave, Dordogne, France, were painted circa 18,000 BCE). These animals were wild horses that were hunted for meat. But about 10,000–14,000 years ago, wild-horse habitat contracted significantly when the favorable Ice Age steppe was replaced by dense forest over much of the Northern Hemisphere. In Eurasia, horses virtually disappeared from warmer areas such as Iran, lowland Mesopotamia, and the Fertile Crescent. Nor do horses appear in the faunal record of early Neolithic sites in Ireland, Italy, Greece, India, or, most significantly, in western Anatolia. In all these regions, the earliest horses appear to arrive from somewhere else, after 4000 BCE in western Anatolia or even later in most parts of Europe and India (Mallory and Adams 1997: 275). Large herds of wild horses survived only in the steppe zone in central Eurasia, although small populations persisted in isolated pockets of naturally open pasture in Europe, central Anatolia, and the Caucasus Mountains. However, in those areas where small populations of wild horses survived into the Holocene, they were rarely eaten by people, as they were too scarce. In central and eastern Anatolia, all equids together total less than 3 percent of the animal bones excavated from sites near human habitations. Horse bones, however, constitute only a small fraction of equid bones and total less than 0.3 percent of the total animal remains. In comparison, in archeological sites in the western steppe zone, horse bones constitute 13 percent of the total, while in the Volga–Ural burials they constitute 40 percent of the total animal bone finds (Anthony 2011). In central and eastern Anatolia, where horse bones are meager, more than 90 percent of equid remains come from onagers (*Equus hemionus*; the "Asiatic wild ass") and another donkey-like animal that went extinct circa 3000 BCE, *Equus hydruntinus* (Russell and Martin 2005; Anthony 2007: 198). Onagers were by far the most common wild equids of the ancient Near East. Curiously, no word for 'donkey' can be reconstructed for PIE (Beekes 1995: 36). While absence of evidence should not be confused with evidence of absence, this vocabulary gap still strongly suggests that speakers of PIE knew horses but not donkeys or their close relatives, indicating yet again that Anatolia is the wrong place for the PIE homeland.[14]

As for the invention of the wheel, and consequently of wheeled vehicles, the evidence points in the same direction, away from Anatolia and later than 6500 BCE. Instead, 3500 BCE does seem to be in the right time frame. The earliest, though uncertain, piece of evidence is a track that might have been made by wheels, preserved under a barrow grave at Flintbek in northern Germany and

---

[14] We cannot exclude the possibility that the reconstructed PIE form *$h_1ék\mathring{u}o$-referred to onagers rather than horses, as such meaning shifts from one species to another are not unknown (see also Chapter 9). That the Armenian reflex of this PIE word, *eš*, means 'donkey' rather than 'horse' is worthy of notice in this context. However, given that Armenian is exceptional in this respect, it is more economical to hypothesize that the PIE word meant 'horse' and Armenian underwent a meaning shift. The idea that the Armenian derivative of PIE *$h_1ék\mathring{u}o$-underwent a semantic shift is developed in Watkins (1994: 462). He notes that the Armenian word for 'horse', *ji*, is a cognate of the Sanskrit *háya-* 'steed' (i.e. a superior form of horse). Armenian, he claims, kept the "semantic hierarchy between *ji* and *eš* ... as we can observe between *háya-* and *áśva* in Vedic" (1994: 462), but downgraded both terms. Moreover, the "clean" separation of Anatolian and later Tocharian speakers from the rest of the family tree, mentioned in the main text above, precludes the possibility of a later, borrowed semantic shift from a more general meaning (e.g. 'large quadruped') to 'horse', the meaning attested in Anatolian and Tocharian languages, as elsewhere in the family.

dated as far back as 3600 BCE. However, as discussed in detail by Anthony (2007), the real explosion of evidence across the ancient world begins about 3400 BCE, with four independent lines of evidence appearing between 3400 and 3000 BCE: written and pictorial depictions, clay models, and actual wagon remains.

The oldest written evidence of a wheeled vehicle, a 'wagon' sign impressed on clay tablets, was found in Eanna temple precinct in Uruk, in what is now Iraq. Radiocarbon dates for charcoal found in the same layer as the tablets averaged about 3500–3370 BCE. These dates, however, may be too early, as the radiocarbon dates tell us not when the wood was burned, but rather when it was created by the tree that it came from. It is therefore possible that the charcoal found at the site came from the dead heartwood of a large tree, implying a later date. Also significant is the fact that the 'wagon' sign appears only three times in the tablets, whereas the sign for 'sled' – a transport device dragged on runners rather than rolled on wheels – occurs 38 times, suggesting that sleds were far more common than wagons in Uruk at that time.

The oldest pictorial evidence of a wagon is a two-dimensional image, about 3 centimeters by 6 centimeters, incised on the surface of a decorated clay mug of the Trichterbecker (TRB) culture found at the settlement of Broncice in southern Poland. The image appears to portray a four-wheeled wagon, a harness pole, and a yoke – recall that the words for 'thill' and 'yoke' are reconstructed for the common ancestor of all Indo-European languages, PIE. The mug is dated about 3500–3350 BCE, representing the earliest and latest radiocarbon dates of other finds, such as cattle bones, found in the same pit. Two other images of what appears to be draft animals pulling a two-wheeled cart, found in central Germany and in the Russian steppes near the mouth of the Volga River, date from approximately the same period: the image from Germany is placed between 3400 and 2800 BCE, and that from southern Russia dates between 3500 and 3100 BCE.

The earliest three-dimensional ceramic models of wagons, found in two graves of the Late Baden culture in Budakalász in eastern Hungary, date to about 3300–3100 BCE. Other graves in Budakalász and other Late Baden sites in Hungary, as well as graves of the partly contemporary Globular Amphorae culture (3200–2700 BCE) in central and southern Poland, also revealed paired oxen that had been sacrificed. A small circular clay object that *might* be a model wheel, perhaps from a small ceramic wagon model, found at the site of Arslantepe in eastern Turkey, also dates from the same period, 3400–3100 BCE.[15]

---

[15] Occasionally, sensationalist reports appear in the popular media claiming the discovery of archeological evidence for early horse domestication or of the invention of the wheel. For example, BBC News reported in August 2011 that "Saudi officials say archaeologists have

Remains of the oldest actual wagons and carts, some 250 in total, have been found under earthen burial mounds known as kurgans, in the steppes of southern Russia and Ukraine. These vehicles had a revolving-wheel design; their wheels were solid rather than spoked and were 50–80 centimeters in diameter. The wagons themselves were small, only about 1 meter wide and 2 meters long, presumably designed to reduce drag while keeping the vehicle adequately sturdy. The earliest radiocarbon dates on wood from these wagons average around 3300–2800 BCE. Remains of wagons, wooden wheels, and axles have also been discovered in the mountains of Switzerland and south-western Germany. These vehicles, with revolving axles, which are less efficient yet easier to make than revolving wheels, date to about 3200 BCE, suggesting that separate regional wheel-design traditions already existed by that time. Sometime after 3000 BCE, revolving axles were largely replaced by the revolving wheels, as revealed by finds in the Netherlands and Denmark.

To recap, the 3500 BCE date for the first wheels and wagons poses an insurmountable challenge for the Anatolian theory of Indo-European origins, proposed originally by Colin Renfrew and advocated more recently by the Gray–Atkinson approach. According to this theory, by 3500 BCE the Indo-European language family would have been "bushy, multi-branched, and three thousand years old" (Anthony 2007: 75). As a result, David Anthony argues that the sheer age and diversity of the family would have necessarily precluded horizontal transmission (i.e. borrowing) of vocabulary elements across multiple Indo-European subfamilies. But lexical items pertaining to technological innovation can spread quickly over vast areas; witness the rapid spread of computer terminology among – and well beyond – the languages of the same Indo-European family in the last seventy years or so. Still, the possibility that the common Indo-European vehicle vocabulary stems from borrowing alone is excluded on purely linguistic grounds, such as the phonological changes that occurred independently in the family's various descendant branches, as discussed above.

The only alternative solution available to proponents of the Anatolian theory is to contend that PIE was spoken *in essentially an unchanged form* for some 3,000 years, from the first farming era to the days of the first wagons/wheels

begun excavating a site that suggests horses were domesticated 9,000 years ago in the Arabian Peninsula" (bbc.co.uk/news/world-middle-east-14658678). However, it is not clear what evidence Saudi archeologists might have uncovered that would suggest such an early date of horse domestication in a place where no evidence of wild horses has ever been found. Similarly suspect are media reports from December 2012 that claim that Turkish archeologists "unearthed a toy cart … carved from stone, complete with two wheels and a working axis. Archaeologist Mesut Alp confirmed his suspicions that the cart dates back to the Stone Age, making it at least 7,500 years old and proving an early knowledge of the wheel" (http://finance.yahoo.com/news/lies-beneath-hidden-discoveries-turkey-090000478.html). Again, it is not clear what the basis for this early date is; moreover, other discoveries at the same site received much later dates.

(cf. Renfrew 2001; Anthony 2007: 77–81). Such a scenario would require a homogeneous and extraordinarily slow rate of change over the enormous area supposedly encompassed by the Indo-European family by 3500 BCE, which was characterized at the time by small-scale tribal groups with highly diverse material cultures. This supposition, however, directly contradicts the Uniformitarian Principle (see Chapter 3): everything that we know about language change in historical times tells us that modes of speech do not remain static over such a long period of time and over such vast expanses of territory. Moreover, several studies (see Nettle 1996, 1999, 2000a, 2000b) suggest that linguistic change proceeds at a higher speed in small-scale societies than in large, homogeneous ones. In a small-scale social order, an innovation introduced by one individual can rapidly become known to all members of the community; moreover, an innovation is more likely to survive in a small community because the number of individuals who might reject the innovation is relatively low. In regard to lexical replacement, the rate of change can be further accelerated by the effects of the common word taboo phenomena (see Comrie 2000: 37–38). It has also been established that tribal languages unaffected by outside forces tend to be more varied than tribal material cultures; therefore, one would expect that the linguistic diversity of Neolithic/Eneolithic Europe would have been more pronounced than its material-culture diversity (Mallory 1989: 145–146; Anthony 1991; Anthony 2007: 80).[16] Finally, the territory that the Indo-European family occupied during the relevant period according to the animated maps produced by the Gray–Atkinson approach is vastly too large to have been covered by a single language; there is no ethnographic or historic warrant for postulating such a large, stable language territory among tribal farmers or pastoralists. Thus, PIE could not have been spoken in Neolithic Anatolia and still have existed in largely the same form three thousand years later when wagons were invented.

We are thus brought to the inevitable conclusion that the evidence from linguistic paleontology, especially as it pertains to horses, wheels, and wheeled-vehicle vocabulary, simply cannot be brought into agreement with the Gray–Atkinson model, which dates the highest-order Indo-European split as early as 6700–6500 BCE. Thus, the evidence from the wheeled-vehicle vocabulary determines the *terminus post quem* circa 4000 BCE. In other words, PIE could not have started splitting into its daughter languages prior to that time. Can we also determine the *terminus ante quem*, a time after which PIE could not have split? The answer is positive: the time depth of PIE can be determined by the dates of the earliest attested Indo-European languages. The earliest Anatolian (Hittite) texts inscribed on clay tablets date from 1700 BCE.

[16] See also Don Ringe's post on the *Language Log* website: http://languagelog.ldc.upenn.edu/nll/?p=980

The oldest Greek texts date from circa 1400 BCE (though it is possible that Greeks were present in Greece as early as 2200 BCE). The oldest evidence of Indo-Iranian (in the form of the "Mitanni" words preserved in cuneiform texts) also dates from circa 1400 BCE. Since these three groupings have each undergone a series of changes from the reconstructed language, PIE must be dated to sometime earlier than 1700 BCE. Most scholars thus set the *terminus ante quem* circa 2500 BCE. In other words, PIE must have split into daughter branches at some point between 4000 BCE and 2500 BCE, though it is likely that the split happened in the earlier part of this range. In the following chapter, we shall look for clues from linguistic paleontology as to *where* PIE was spoken.

9   Triangulating the Indo-European homeland

In the previous chapter, we have shown that evidence from linguistic paleontology, especially as it pertains to vocabulary elements associated with wheels and wheeled vehicles, is congruent with the later date, circa 3500 BCE, for the highest-order split of the Indo-European family (which separated Anatolian languages from the rest of the family). In this chapter, we examine what linguistic (and to a lesser extent, archeological) evidence can tell us about the location of the Indo-European homeland. In particular, we will examine three types of sources: clues from linguistic paleontology, evidence of language contact with other groups, and reconstructions of the migration histories of the various groups involved.

Clues from linguistic paleontology

Although archeological evidence of a material culture contains no traces of the language or languages spoken by the people who produced the artifacts, language – documented or reconstructed – does contain traces of the speakers' material life. Linguistic paleontology searches the reconstructed vocabulary of a proto-language for clues about how and where its speakers lived. Firm conclusions about environment and culture, however, can be drawn only if the signals from linguistic paleontology are bolstered by evidence from other fields, such as archaeology and palynology (the study of fossil pollen).

As discussed in the previous chapter, which focuses on the timing of Proto-Indo-European (PIE), the logic of linguistic paleontology holds that if a proto-language had a reconstructable word for a certain concept, its speakers were therefore familiar with that concept. For example, reconstructing the terms for wheeled vehicles, which appear in the archeological record only as far back as 3500 BCE, serves to invalidate hypotheses that place PIE farther back in time, such as the Gray–Atkinson neo-Anatolian hypothesis. Linguistic paleontology can shed light not only on *when* but also on *where* a given proto-language was spoken. For example, reconstructions of Proto-Salishan vocabulary from western North America include some "two dozen [reconstructed plant and animal terms] represent[ing] species found only on the coast", including 'harbour seal', 'whale', 'cormorant', 'seagull' and the like, which "suggest[s] a coastal, rather than an interior, homeland for the Salish", a family of languages spoken not only on the Pacific coast but also as far inland as Montana and Idaho (Kinkade 1991: 143–144, cited in Campbell 2013: 427). Additional linguistic paleontology clues allowed Kinkade (1991: 147, cited in Campbell 2013: 427) to narrow down the proto-Salishan homeland even further:

> extend[ing] from the Fraser River southward at least to the Skagit River and possibly as far south as the Stillaguamish or Skykomish rivers [. . .] From west to east, their territory would have extended from the Strait of Georgia and Admiralty Inlet to the Cascade Mountains.

The locations of several other language families' respective homelands have also been reconstructed on the basis of evidence from linguistic paleontology. Siebert (1967) placed the original homeland of the Algonquian family "between Lake Huron and Georgian Bay and the middle course of the Ottawa River, bounded by Lake Nipissing and the northern shore of Lake Ontario" (Campbell 2013: 425). Fowler (1972) concluded that the homeland of the Numic family (a subgroup of the Uto-Aztecan family) was "in Southern California slightly west of Death Valley" (Campbell 2013: 427). (The homeland of the Uto-Aztecan family as a whole remains more controversial.) Much work has been done on locating the Proto-Uralic homeland (or the homeland of its largest constituent branch, Finno-Ugric), yet the answer remains elusive. (We return to the question of the Proto-Uralic homeland in the next section.)

While the logic of the linguistic paleontology method is self-evident, what exactly can be learned from specific reconstructions is often open to interpretation. For example, most scholars agree that there are no reconstructable PIE words for Mediterranean and Southwest Asian animals and plants, such as 'cypress tree', 'palm tree', 'date tree', 'olive', 'camel', or 'donkey'.[1] Although each such *argumentum e silentio* for any particular meaning is always weak, the combined absences of roots for various southern plants and animals, as well as the presence of the roots for 'snow' ($*sneig^wh$- and $*\hat{g}^he\underset{.}{i}om$-) or possibly 'winter', suggest a northerly location. However, even in Anatolia and the Levant, highland areas receive abundant snowfall. The roots for 'snow' could therefore indicate a high-altitude rather than a high-latitude location, especially in conjunction with the root $*g^werH$- for 'mountain'. Clearly, much uncertainty surrounds these kinds of arguments.

---

[1] Soviet scholars Tomaz Gamkrelidze and Vjačeslav V. Ivanov have argued that PIE had words for such southern animals as the panther, the lion, and the elephant. But, as pointed out in the subsequent section of the main text, most scholars reject these reconstructions as erroneous; see Beekes (1995: 49).

Another controversial PIE reconstruction is the root *mori, which presumably means 'sea'. If this term is indeed traceable all the way back to PIE, then by the logic of linguistic paleontology one might assume that the speakers of PIE must have lived near a large body of water of some type. Note, however, that the relevant cognates come from the northwestern Indo-European languages: Lithuanian *māres, Old Church Slavonic *morje, Latin *mare, Old Irish *muir, Gothic *marei. No relevant cognates are found in the Anatolian, Tocharian, Greek, Armenian, Albanian, or even Indo-Iranian branches of the family. The Greek word *thalassa 'sea', for example, almost certainly comes from a pre-Indo-European substrate. As a result of such absences, the root *mori cannot be reliably reconstructed all the way back to PIE. It is possible that the Indo-European branches that lack a word for 'sea' once had it but later lost it, perhaps by acquiring it from the local substratum language, as has been proposed for the Greek *thalassa (as discussed in Chapter 7). Alternatively, it is possible that the root *mori 'sea' was coined by – or borrowed into – the common ancestor of a particular branch of the Indo-European family.

As it turns out, determining whether a word that is absent in many descendant languages stems from PIE is often a difficult matter. In the case of 'sea', the issue is further complicated by the fact that even in the Germanic and Celtic languages we find other roots meaning the same thing, as evident in the English word *sea itself. Moreover, some of the roots for 'sea' can also refer to other types of water bodies. For example, the German cognate of the English *sea, *See can refer to either 'lake' or 'sea', whereas German *Meer refers to either 'sea' or 'ocean' while the Dutch word *meer generally means 'lake'. Scottish Gaelic *loch refers to either 'fresh-water lake' or 'salt-water sea inlet'. Similarly, Russian *more, just like its English counterpart *sea, can also refer to a large landlocked body of water, such as the Aral Sea, the Caspian Sea, the Dead Sea, or the Sea of Galilee. Thus, it is possible that PIE speakers were familiar not with the sea in the sense of the ocean, but rather with a large interior body of water.

An additional twist is added to the 'sea' mystery by the root *lok̂so-, putatively meaning 'salmon' (cf. Tocharian B *laks, Proto-Germanic *lahsaz, Old High German *lahs, Icelandic *lax, Lithuanian *lãšis, Russian *losos'). Unlike the root for 'sea', this word is not limited to the younger branches of the Indo-European family. Its presence in Tocharian means that it must have existed at least in Proto-Nuclear-Indo-European (PNIE), if not in PIE itself. But salmon is found only in northern seas and the rivers that flow into them, a fact that has been used by some scholars against the idea that the Indo-European family originated in the steppe zone. But it is also true that closely related species in the family Salmonidae, such as trout, are found in the rivers of southern Russia and Ukraine, as well as in the mountainous lakes of Armenia. The conclusion that PIE *loksos referred not to a specific species but to 'any large anadromous salmonid fish' is reached, for example, by Diebold (1985: 11).

It is also possible that the PIE word *lokʰso- referred not to 'salmon' or 'trout', but to 'fish' in general, eventually narrowing its meaning in descendant languages. An illustrative example of how such narrowing might have happened comes from a different language family: Athabascan. The Proto-Athabascan *łu:q'ə is reconstructed to have meant 'fish' because it is the "common denominator" of meanings in modern descendant languages. In Navajo, spoken in landlocked areas, łóó' means 'fish'. Its cognate in Hupa, spoken in Northern California, ło:q' means 'fish' or more specifically 'salmon'. In Tlingit, however, the reflex of the Proto-Athabascan root l'ook means neither 'fish' nor 'salmon', but specifically 'silver/coho salmon' (*Oncorhynchus kisutch*). Other species of salmon are referred to in Tlingit by separate words: t'á (*Oncorhynchus tshawytscha*), gaat (*Oncorhynchus nerka*), téel' (*Oncorhynchus keta*), and cháas' (*Oncorhynchus gorbuscha*). The generic term for 'fish', which by default refers to any kind of salmon, is xáat. In parallel to the Tlingit case, the PIE *lokʰso- may have simply meant 'fish', with descendant languages narrowing the meaning to 'salmon', 'trout', or some other locally available variety of fish. Admittedly, such a scenario is less likely for the Indo-European family than for languages in the Athabascan family spoken where salmon served as the staple food. However, it cannot be excluded altogether because we cannot be certain that the Tocharian B *laks* meant 'salmon' rather than 'fish' or 'trout' (or some other fish species).

Another much-discussed set of clues about the location of the Indo-European homeland comes from the names of various types of trees. German philologists in the first half of the nineteenth century were preoccupied with finding the PIE *Urheimat* through tree names, favoring – unsurprisingly – a more northern homeland. But as we shall see below, the linguistic paleontology argument based on tree names is not without flaws. First, let us consider PIE reconstructions of tree names and what can be learned from them. Upon a thorough study of the topic, Friedrich (1970: 1) claims that PIE speakers recognized and named at least eighteen categories of trees, but PIE (or "large groups of PIE dialects") contained at least thirty names of trees, "attested in varying ways and degrees in languages of the descendant stocks, but particularly in Italic, Germanic, Baltic, and Slavic, and to a lesser degree in Celtic and Greek". The discrepancy between the number of tree categories and the number of labels used to designate them stems from the fact that "a considerable number of [. . .] arboreal units have two or more alternate names or forms [. . .] specifically, the oak and the willow have three each, and five trees have two each: the yew, the apple, the maple, the elm, and the nut (tree)" (Friedrich 1970: 4). In the case of the nut (tree), the two forms are "complimentary geographically" (Friedrich 1970: 4), as one form is reconstructed based on the reflexes in eastern branches (Baltic, Slavic, Greek, and Albanian), while the other form is reconstructed based on derivatives in western branches (Italic,

Celtic, and Germanic). In other cases, the two (or more) forms must have referred to distinct species or subspecies, or perhaps distinct functions (e.g. tree in nature vs. material used in religious ritual). Moreover, Friedrich (1970: 1) maintains that the thirty or so tree names

refer to categories of trees that in the main correspond to generic groups such as the birch (*Betulus*), but are limited in other cases to single species, such as the Scotch pine (*Pinus sylvestris*); some PIE classes cross-cut the familiar ones of the English language, or of the language of Linnaean botany, as when, for example, **Ker-n-* includes both the wild cherry (*Prunus padus*), and the cornel cherry (*Cornus mas*).

The eighteen categories of trees whose names have been reconstructed for PIE, their names (in some cases more than one name per category, as discussed above), and the languages/branches that have reflexes of these PIE forms, are listed in Table 9.1 (based on Friedrich 1970: 24–25, Table 2; for the specific reflexes of these PIE roots in the various daughter branches/languages, see Friedrich 1970: 24–25). What can we deduce about the location of the Indo-European homeland from these tree names in the reconstructed PIE vocabulary, assuming for the sake of the argument that the translations in Friedrich's study are correct?

To answer this question, we turn to the map database compiled by EUFOR-GEN, a European forestry conservation program.[2] As can be seen from Map 23 in the Appendix, and as has been long noted by advocates of linguistic paleontology, common beech – known scientifically as *Fagus sylvatica* – is not found east of the line that runs from Klaipeda in western Lithuania down to the Crimea, although a related species, oriental beech, or *Fagus orientalis*, is found in northern Anatolia, Crimea, on the slopes of the Great Caucasus Mountains, and in the Alborz Range south of the Caspian Sea) (see Map 24). The limited distribution of the tree has been taken as *prima facie* evidence that the original Indo-Europeans must have lived to the west of this line, rather than in Russia or (eastern) Ukraine. Note that this "beech argument" is in direct contradiction to the "horse argument": areas where beech and horse were found in the relevant time period do not in general overlap.

The distribution of other species for which Indo-European roots have been reconstructed by Friedrich (1970) sheds new light on the problem of the PIE homeland – or throws a wrench into the works, depending on how one

---

[2] It should be noted, however, that the EUFORGEN database contains information on the modern distribution of various tree species. Their (pre)historical distributions may differ, but no equally detailed information is available on the habitat zones of various trees in earlier epochs. Some maps of earlier distributions of different types of trees are provided in Friedrich (1970), but the maps do not include Anatolia, so no information about trees growing there in the Holocene can be drawn from these maps.

Table 9.1 *Tree categories whose names are reconstructed for PIE (based on Friedrich 1970: 24–25)*

Tree categories	PIE tree names	IE branches with reflexes of the PIE form
Birch	*b^herH-ĝ-o-	Slavic, Baltic, Italic, Germanic, Indic, Iranian
Conifers	*pitu-	Greek, Italic, Indic, Albanian
	*pi/uK-	Slavic, Baltic, Greek, Italic, Celtic, Germanic
Junipers and cedars	*el-u̯-n-	Slavic, Baltic, Greek, Armenian
Populus	*osp-	Slavic, Baltic, Greek, Germanic, Indic, Iranian
Willows	*s/wVlyk	Greek, Celtic, Germanic, Anatolian
	*wyt-	Slavic, Baltic, Greek, Celtic, Germanic, Indic, Armenian
Apples	*abVl-	Slavic, Baltic, Italic, Celtic, Germanic
	*maHlo-	Greek, Albanian, Anatolian, Tocharian
Maples	*klen-	Slavic, Baltic, Greek, Celtic, Germanic
	*akVrno-	Greek, Italic, Germanic, Indic
Alder	*aliso-	Slavic, Baltic, Greek, Italic, Celtic, Germanic
Hazel	*kos(V)lo-	Slavic, Baltic, Italic, Celtic, Germanic
Nut (tree)s	*knu-	Italic, Celtic, Germanic
	*ar-	Slavic, Baltic, Greek, Albanian
Elms	*Vlmo-	Slavic, Italic, Celtic, Germanic
	*u̯-iĝ-	Slavic, Baltic, Germanic, Iranian
Linden	*lenTā-	Slavic, Baltic, Greek, Italic, Germanic, Albanian
	*lēipā-	Slavic, Baltic, Greek, Celtic
Ash	*os-	Slavic, Baltic, Greek, Italic, Celtic, Germanic, Albanian, Armenian
Hornbeam	*grōb^h-	Slavic, Baltic, Greek, Italic, Albanian
Beech	*b^hāĝo-	Slavic, Greek, Italic, Celtic, Germanic, Albanian
Cherry	*K(e)r-n-	Slavic, Baltic, Greek, Italic, Albanian
Yews	*eywo-	Slavic, Baltic, Greek, Italic, Celtic, Germanic, Armenian, Anatolian
	*tVk̂so-	Slavic, Greek, Italic, Iranian
Oaks	*g^welH-	Slavic, Baltic, Greek, Italic, Indic, Albanian, Armenian
	*ai̯g-	Greek, Italic, Germanic
	*perk^w-	Slavic, Baltic, Italic, Celtic, Germanic, Indic, Albanian, Armenian, Anatolian
	*dóru-	Slavic, Baltic, Greek, Italic, Celtic, Germanic, Indic, Iranian, Albanian, Armenian, Anatolian, Tocharian

looks at it.[3] Silver birch (*Betula pendula*) is found in an extensive zone stretching throughout Northern and Eastern Europe and across the Pontic steppe zone (see Map 25). Common ash (*Fraxinus excelsior*) grows in Western, Central, and Eastern Europe, the Caucasus, and northern Anatolia (see Map 26).

---

[3] It might be better to examine the distribution of different trees at the level of the genus rather than species, but such data are not easily available at this point.

The distribution of European white elm (*Ulmus laevis*) extends through most of Central and Eastern Europe, including the northern part of the steppe zone, but it is virtually unknown in Anatolia (see Map 27). Eurasian aspen (*Populus tremula*) is found in Europe, central Russia, western Kazakhstan, and sporadically in the steppe zone of southern Russia and Ukraine, yet is virtually unknown in Anatolia (see Map 28). The distribution of silver fir (*Abies alba*) is limited to an even smaller area; like beech, it too is not found east of the Klaipeda–Crimea line (see Map 29). Of the various other conifers on which information is available in the EUFORGEN database, only Brutia pine (*Pinus brutia*) and black pine (*Pinus nigra*) grow in the areas of interest for us, specifically in coastal Anatolia (see Maps 33 and 34; two other coniferous species, *Pinus halepensis* and *Pinus sylvestris*, grow sporadically through southern and northern Anatolia, respectively). Black alder (*Alnus glutinosa*) grows in Western and Central Europe and sporadically throughout Russia, Ukraine, the North Caucasus, and the mountainous areas of northern and eastern Anatolia (see Map 30). (A related species, Italian alder, or *Alnus cordata*, is found only in southern Italy.) Field maple (*Acer campestre*) is found extensively throughout Europe, as well as in northern Ukraine and central Russia, in the North Caucasus, and along a narrow coastal strip in northern Anatolia (see Map 31). Black poplar (*Populus nigra*) grows almost everywhere in Europe (except the most northern areas), the steppe and forest zones of Russia, Ukraine, and western Kazakhstan, the Caucasus, Anatolia, and northern Fertile Crescent (see Map 32).[4] Wild apple (*Malus sylvestris*) grows in the steppe zone, but only sporadically in Anatolia (see Map 35). Linden (*Tilia cordata*) grows in parts of the steppe zone, but not in Anatolia. Wild cherry (*Prunus avium*) is not common to either the steppe zone or Anatolia (see Map 36). As for the oaks, one species (*Quercus petraea*) grows in Anatolia but not the steppes, while another (*Quercus robur*) grows sporadically in both the steppe zone and Anatolia (see Maps 37 and 38). The distribution of the various tree species in the two areas identified as the candidate PIE locations according to the Steppe and Anatolian hypotheses in Bouckaert *et al.* (2012, Supplementary Materials: Figure S5) is summarized in Table 9.2.

Comparing the two areas – the steppe zone vs. central and southern Anatolia – it is clear that the former is a better candidate for the PIE homeland than the latter, as it includes many more tree species known to the speakers of PIE. In fact, only the sporadic distribution of some coniferous species in coastal Anatolia and the appearance of certain oak species in parts of Anatolia point towards Anatolia as the Indo-European *Urheimat*. Birch, alder, and poplar are

---

[4] The EUFORGEN database contains no information on the distribution of junipers and cedars, willows, hazel, nut trees, hornbeam, or yews.

Table 9.2 *The distribution of tree species in the two candidate PIE locations according to the Steppe and Anatolian hypotheses*

Common name	Species	Steppe zone	Southern and Central Anatolia
Beech	*Fagus sylvatica*	–	–
Birch	*Betula pendula*	Sporadically in the north, not in the south	Sporadically in central Anatolia
Ash	*Fraxinus excelsior*	In the west only	–
Elm	*Ulmus laevis*	In the north only	–
Aspen	*Populus tremula*	In the north, sporadically elsewhere	–
Conifers	*Abies alba*	–	–
	Pinus brutia, Pinus nigra		Sporadically in coastal Anatolia
Alder	*Alnus glutinosa*	Sporadically in the north	Sporadically
Maple	*Acer campestre*	In the northwest only	–
Poplar	*Populus nigra*	Yes	Yes
Apple	*Malus sylvestris*	Yes	Sporadically
Linden	*Tilia cordata*	Yes	–
Cherry	*Prunus avium*	–	–
Oak	*Quercus petraea, Quercus robur*	Sporadically	Yes

not informative, as all three grow in both areas (the former two only sporadically, however). Beech, most coniferous species, and cherry present a problem for both hypotheses at first glance, as neither grows in either one of the two areas; we shall revisit the "beech problem" below. The distributions of ash, elm, aspen, maple, wild apple, and linden, however, point to the steppe zone, as these trees are found in parts of the steppe zone but not in Anatolia.

Although the distribution of the various tree species points to the Pontic steppe zone as the prime candidate for the PIE homeland, this argument is not without flaw. First, as mentioned above, some species with reconstructed PIE roots, most notably beech, are found neither in the steppe zone nor in Anatolia. This so-called "beech argument" has been used by various scholars to limit the area in which PIE might have been spoken (see Schrader 1890; Schrader and Nehring 1923/1929; Mallory 1973; Gamkrelidze and Ivanov 1984; *inter alia*). However, tree names often provide unreliable evidence. For example, the root for 'beech' is reconstructed as *$b^h\bar{a}go$- (Friedrich 1970: 25) on the basis of such cognates as Greek *phāgós*, Latin *fāgus*, Old English *bōc*, and Russian *buzina*. However, names of plants and animals often acquire new meanings by shifting their referents from one species to another. In fact, the Greek reflex of the PIE root *$b^h\bar{a}go$-, *phāgós*, also means 'oak' (Beekes 1995: 48), while the Russian cognate *buzina* means 'elder tree, *Sambucus*' rather than 'beech'.

Several recent cases illustrate how common such name transfers can be. Before the discovery of the New World, Europeans were familiar with spice-producing plants from the *Piper* genus of the *Piperaceae* family, especially *Piper nigrum*, which gives us black pepper (cooked and dried unripe fruit), green pepper (dried unripe fruit), and white pepper (dried ripe seeds). The word *pepper* comes from *pippali,* found in several Dravidian languages of southern India, which is used for a closely related species, long pepper (*Piper longum*). Apparently, the Romans erroneously believed that black pepper and long pepper derived from the same plant, so they used the same word to refer to both. The Latin word is the source of not only the modern English *pepper* (from the Old English *pipor*) but also of German *Pfeffer*, Dutch *peper*, French *poivre*, Romanian *piper*, Italian *pepe*, and other cognate forms. When the Portuguese traveled to West Africa in the fifteenth century, they used the same term for the spicy seeds of *Aframomum melegueta*, which they deemed "Guinea pepper" or "melegueta pepper". In the sixteenth century, the English word *pepper* and its counterparts in other languages were applied as well to the unrelated New World chili pepper, the fruit of plants from the genus *Capsicum*, most of which also have a distinctively spicy taste.

Another example of species-name transfer involves *Jerusalem artichoke*, a New World plant that acquired the *artichoke* label because the taste of its edible tuber reminded Europeans of an artichoke. The *Jerusalem* tag is a folk-etymologized version of the Italian name of the plant, *girasole*, which literally means 'turns with/to the sun', which originally referred to 'sunflower', a related plant from the *Helianthus* genus.

An even more complicated story of terminological confusion and name transfer from one species to another involves the word *turkey*. Originally, the term referred to the domesticated guineafowl of West African origin that were introduced to Britain in the 1500s by "Turkey merchants" trading with the Ottoman Empire. Subsequently, the first English colonists in New England confused the large native fowl with the African bird, calling it "turkey" as well. Further name-shuffling is illustrated by the fact that the word *meleagris* (Greek for 'guineafowl') is used in the scientific names of the two species, at the species level for the West African guineafowl and at the genus level for the turkey. Note also that – in a grand example of geo-bio-linguistic confusion – many other languages call the North American fowl by a term deriving from the root for 'India', after the West Indies (itself a geographical misnomer!): compare the French *dinde* (originally, *d'Inde* 'from India'), Russian *indejka*, and Hebrew *hodu* (the same as the name of the country, India).

Returning to tree species, another reconstructed PIE root that must have changed its meaning is *b^herHĝo-*, reconstructed on the base of such cognates as Sanskrit *bhūrjá*, Ossetian *bärz*, English *birch* (Old English *berc*), Latvian *bērzs*, Lithuanian *béržas*, and Russian *berëza*, all referring to trees of the genus *Betula* (cf. Friedrich 1970: 24). However, the Latin cognate, *fraxinus*, refers to the ash tree, a completely different genus. The scientific name for its genus is also *Fraxinus*, and the two species belong to different taxonomic orders. Romance languages use the inherited Latin root to designate 'ash tree': compare French *frêne*, Italian *frassino*, Spanish *fresno*. Baltic and Slavic languages have another set of cognates for 'ash tree': Russian *jasen'*, Polish *jasien'*, Slovenian *jasen*, Latvian *osis*, Lithuanian *úosis*, Old Prussian *woasis*. Cognates of the Balto-Slavic words, also denoting 'ash tree', are found also in Old Icelandic *askr* and Latin *ornus* 'type of ash tree'. This PIE root is reconstructed in Friedrich (1970: 25) as **os* meaning 'ash tree'. Curiously, a reflex of that PIE root in Albanian, *ah*, means 'beech'. As the discussion so far makes amply clear, most of the roots reconstructed to mean a certain type of tree in PIE could easily have referred originally to a different type of tree (or perhaps to some non-species-related properties of trees: e.g. 'tall tree', 'tree with a straight trunk', or the like). Friedrich's list of reconstructed PIE tree names includes the root **dóru-*, whose reflexes in Balto-Slavic languages (e.g. *derevo* in Russian, *dervà* in Lithuanian) mean 'tree' in general. We thus agree with Diebold (1985: 11), who notes that "where linguistic paleontology frequently errs is in using the reconstructed sense and reference of such signifiers as a source for making macro- or extralinguistic inference without equally careful reconstruction of their meanings".

Besides the uncertainty about what each reconstructed PIE root referred to, there is also a problem concerning the depth of the reconstruction. Thus far, following Friedrich (1970), we assumed that each root is indeed reconstructible to PIE. However, as can be seen from Table 9.1 above, only five roots have reflexes in Anatolian languages and can be thus reconstructed all the way to PIE. Only one of the roots, **dóru-*, has a reflex in Tocharian, but it also has a reflex in Anatolian. Therefore, all but five roots can be reconstructed technically only as far as Proto-Surviving-Indo-European, or PSIE (i.e. non-Anatolian/non-Tocharian branches of Indo-European) (see Figure 4 in the Appendix). Consequently, the majority of the reconstructed tree names can only shed light on the homeland of one of the main branches descending from PIE, not of PIE itself.

To recap, the different "facts" deduced from clues provided by linguistic paleontology have resulted in different putative homelands for the Indo-European language family, ranging from Northern Europe and the Baltic area to Hungary and southern Russia. But because names for species are often reassigned, especially by peoples who move into new areas and encounter new forms of life, it is difficult, if not impossible, to determine where PIE must have been spoken on the basis of such inconsistent evidence. In the final analysis, however, reconstructed names for trees and other features of the natural world point away from Anatolia as the original PIE homeland, but not in a conclusive manner.

Clues from linguistic contact

Evidence for the location of a given proto-language can also be derived from signs of contact between languages in different families. If we observe significant borrowing from language A into language B, or vice versa, the speakers of the two tongues must have lived in close proximity, perhaps along established trade routes or in some other geographical configuration that promoted information exchange. In the case of PIE, contacts with languages in three other groupings have been documented: Uralic, Semitic, and the languages of the Caucasus. Although the latter category is geographical rather than phylogenetic in nature, grouping languages belonging to at least three distinct families (Northwest Caucasian, Northeast Caucasian, and Kartvelian), most Caucasian languages share some common features, such as ejective sounds (discussed in detail below).

Evidence of linguistic contacts between PIE and Proto-Semitic and Proto-Kartvelian, and perhaps also Hurrian (a member of the extinct Hurro-Urartian family) and Sumerian, would seemingly place PIE south of the Caucasus region, possibly in Anatolia (see Gamkrelidze 2000: 458; Illič-Svityč 1964; Dolgopolsky 1987a; Dolgopolsky 1987b: 4–12; Dolgopolsky 1988: 12–17, 24–26). Proposed examples of Semitic loanwords in PIE include PIE *septṃ 'seven' from Proto-Semitic *šabʕ-at-u-m 'seven' and PIE *h₂ster- 'star' from Proto-Semitic *ʕaθtar- 'Venus'. Note that reflexes of these roots are found in both Anatolian and non-Anatolian languages, and thus must be reconstructed all the way back to PIE. Additional examples of proposed Semitic loanwords in PIE are listed and discussed in Dolgopolsky (2000: 406). Contacts with Proto-Kartvelian are reflected in such alleged loanwords as Proto-Kartvelian *otχo- 'four' from PIE *Hok̂tō(u̯) 'tetrad' (lost in later Indo-European but traceable back by internal reconstruction); see Dolgopolsky (2000: 406).

Arguments from such evidence of linguistic contact have been used extensively to support the Armenian theory of Indo-European origins, an alternative to both the Steppe and Anatolian hypotheses, put forward by Soviet scholars Tomaz Gamkrelidze and Vjačeslav V. Ivanov. The Armenian theory places the PIE homeland just to the east of Anatolia, south of the Great Caucasus Range. Although the Armenian hypothesis has fairly close geographical affinities with the Anatolian school, its historical reconstructions are much closer to those of the Steppe school. According to the Armenian hypothesis, PIE was spoken in the fourth millennium BCE, whereas the Anatolian hypothesis places it in the seventh millennium BCE.

Gamkrelidze and Ivanov's Armenian hypothesis is based largely on presumed contacts with languages spoken to the south of the formidable Great Caucasus Mountain Range. It also relies on proposed PIE reconstructions for the names of plants and animals that suggest a southern latitude, such as 'panther', 'lion', and 'elephant' (see Gamkrelidze and Ivanov 1995: 420–431, 443–444). Most of these reconstructions, however, have been discredited since Gamkrelidze and Ivanov first put forward their theory (see Beekes 1995 for details).

Some of Gamkrelidze and Ivanov's alleged exchanges of loanwords between PIE and languages in other families are problematic as well. The key difficulty is ascertaining the direction of borrowing: which languages borrowed a given loanword from which other tongue. Consider the controversy surrounding the word for 'wine'. Since similar forms are found in Anatolian languages (Hittite *wiyana-*, Luwian *winiyant-*, Hieroglyphic Luwian *wiana-*), as well as in non-Anatolian languages (e.g. Homeric Greek *(w)oinos*, Armenian *gini*, Albanian *vēnë*, Latin *uīnum*, Gothic *wein*, Old Church Slavonic *vino*, etc.), Gamkrelidze and Ivanov (1995: 557–564) reconstruct it back to PIE as **w(e/o)ino-*.[5] Similar terms are found in a number of ancient Near Eastern languages. The Proto-Semitic form, for example, is reconstructed as **wayn-*'wine' (cf. Akkadian *īnu-*, Arabic *wayn-*, Ugaritic *yn*, Hebrew *yayin*). Similarly, the South Caucasian (Kartvelian) form **ɣwino-* 'wine' can be reconstructed on the basis of Georgian *ɣwino*, Mingrelian *ɣwin-*, Laz *ɣ(w)in-*, and Svan *ɣwinel*. Gamkrelidze and Ivanov regard this term as a *Wanderwort*, a word that spreads among numerous languages and cultures in connection with trade or cultural diffusion. This particular word for 'wine', they argue, "must have passed from one language to another at a protolanguage level, i.e. prior to the breakup of each protolanguage into separate dialects" (Gamkrelidze and Ivanov 1995: 559). But which proto-language did this word originate in? Based both on the formal phonological/morphological characteristics of their PIE reconstruction and on the importance of grapes and wine in early Indo-European traditions, Gamkrelidze and Ivanov classify the word as a PIE native that spread into Semitic and Kartvelian.[6] The idea that the word for

---

[5] Other scholars reconstruct it as **u̯iHen-~u̯iHnom ~ u̯oi̯Hno-* (Michael Weiss, personal communication), **u(e)ih₁-(o)n-* (Beekes 1995: 35), and **w(o)iH-(o)n-o(s/m)* (Gorton 2013).

[6] Gamkrelidze and Ivanov (1995: 562–563) also note a curious absence of cognate words for 'wine' and 'grape' in Proto-Indo-Iranian and Tocharian. Their explanation lies with the idea that "the place of wine as a cultic and everyday beverage was taken in the Indo-Iranian tradition by other intoxicating beverages, made from plants other than grapes". One such new cultic beverage, dedicated to the supreme deity, may have been *soma* (Sanskrit) or *haoma* (Avestan). Soma was a narcotic beverage prepared by pressing the juice out of plants with stone presses. Although the identity of *soma/haoma* remains controversial, a prime candidate is *Ephedra* (also called ma huang or Mormon tea), a plant found in desert regions of Central Asia and Afghanistan. Some scholars believe, however, that *soma/haoma* was originally made from a

'wine' is native to PIE and borrowed by Proto-Kartvelian is likewise adopted by Dolgopolsky (2000: 406). Gamkrelidze and Ivanov further derive the word for 'wine' from the verb root *$ueiH$-~ *uiH- 'weave, plait, twist', the connection being the root for 'grapevine', *uiH-ti-. Based on the work of other Soviet scholars (Vavilov 1959–1965; Kušnareva and Čubinišvili 1970), Gamkrelidze and Ivanov place the center of grape (*Vitis vinifera*) domestication in southwestern Asia, south of the Caucasus. Consequently, they locate the Indo-European homeland in that area as well.

However, this analysis is highly contentious, and the more recent research supports a different analysis. According to McGovern (2007), the Eurasian wine grape was probably domesticated in the south Caucasus (in modern-day Georgia and Armenia) some 8,000 years ago. It is therefore possible, and perhaps even likely, that Kartvelian was the ultimate source of the 'wine' root, and that PIE (as well as the Semitic languages) borrowed it, possibly at a significantly later date. Another possibility is that the forms found in various Indo-European languages are not reflexes of a shared ancestral PIE root, but are rather loanwords borrowed separately into the daughter languages (James Clackson, personal communication). This view is supported by the fact that the Latin word for 'wine' is neuter, whereas its Greek counterpart is masculine, as well as other morphological discrepancies.

The strongest argument put forward by Gamkrelidze and Ivanov in favor of the Armenian hypothesis was based on Gamkrelidze's Glottalic theory, stemming from the work of Pedersen (1951: 10–16) and Martinet (1953: 70).[7] According to this theory, PIE had glottalized (i.e. ejective) consonants $p^?$, $t^?$, and $k^?$ instead of voiced stops b, d, and g.[8] To pronounce ejective stops, in addition to creating a closure in the mouth, the space between the vocal cords, the "glottis", is closed and then sharply opened as well.[9] English speakers are familiar with this glottal closure, as it occurs in the middle of *uh-oh* (speakers of certain English dialects, particularly Cockney and Estuary English, use the "glottal stop" in place of *t* in words such as *bottle, better*, and the like).

particular variety of amanita mushroom (*Amanita miscaria*); cf. Wasson (1968), Elizarenkova (1972: 300–301), Steblin-Kamenskij (1974: 138–139). Others have suggested *Peganum harmala*, commonly called Syrian rue or harmel (Flattery and Schwarz 1989).
[7] A similar theory was simultaneously but independently published by Paul Hopper (1973).
[8] The glottalic/ejective articulation is notated here as a superscripted ʔ, the IPA symbol for glottal stop. Some sources use an apostrophe to mark glottalic/ejective articulation; however, such notation is confusing as the same symbol is often used for palatalization, a completely different process.
[9] To pronounce a plain, non-ejective *p*, the lips are pressed together (preventing the air from escaping the mouth for a short moment) and then released abruptly (which lets the air explode out of the mouth). Non-ejective *t* and *k* are pronounced with the same "close-and-release" strategy: for *t*, the tip of the tongue is pressed against, or behind, the upper teeth; for *k*, the back portion of the tongue is pressed against the soft palate (velum).

The additional closure of the glottis during the articulation of ejectives creates the dramatic burst of air that distinguishes an ejective sound from a plain one and gives it a certain "spat out" quality. Cross-linguistically, ejective sounds are fairly common, found in 92 out of 567 languages in the World Atlas of Linguistic Structures Online (WALS) sample (see Maddieson 2013).[10] But languages of the Caucasus are particularly well known for their ejective sounds. For example, Georgian (a member of the Kartvelian family) has four ejective stops and two ejective affricates: $p^?$, $t^?$, $k^?$, $q^?$, $ts^?$, and $tf^?$.

According to Gamkrelidze and Ivanov, the hypothesized presence of glottalic consonants in PIE provides a unified explanation for both Lachmann's Law for Latin (proposed by the German Latinist Karl Lachmann in the middle of the nineteenth century) and Winter's Law for Balto-Slavic (advanced by Werner Winter in 1978). Both of these laws describe a similar phenomenon in the languages under consideration: a reflex of the PIE unaspirated voiced stop b d g g^w before a consonant lengthened a preceding vowel. For example, a reflex of the PIE g in PIE *ph_2g-to- 'fortified' is responsible for lengthening the preceding vowel in the Latin $p\bar{a}ctus$ (the original short vowel is observable in Sanskrit $pajrás$). Similar process of vowel lengthening is also observed before PIE laryngeals, which are assumed to have included a glottal stop. Assuming that PIE had glottalic sounds thus allows for a unified analysis of various instances of vowel lengthening.

The Glottalic theory has also been used to rationalize the analysis under which the PIE phoneme inventory was reconstructed to have three series of stops (consonants produced by a complete closure of articulators, such as p, t, and k, and their voiced counterparts b, d, and g). Consider the labial series: prior to the Glottalic theory, it was assumed that PIE had a three-member labial series including p, b, and b^h. Such a system, however, presents a mysterious anomaly in light of the fact that typologically languages have either p^h instead of b^h (i.e. they have p, b, and p^h), or both p^h and b^h together. Under the Glottalic theory, the typologically uncommon system p, b, b^h was reformulated as a more expected one: p, $p^?$, p^h. In other words, the essence of the Glottalic theory is that the sound originally reconstructed as a voiced b was reinterpreted as a voiceless glottalized $p^?$. While glottalic/ejective articulation is phonetically different from voicing, both processes involve vocal cords and the space between them, the glottis. Moreover, it has been noted that voiced stops are equivalent to the glottalic series of other language families with respect to sound symbolism (Swadesh 1971: 219).

The Glottalic theory, however, has its own problems. Its most serious challenge concerns the typological commonality of the PIE consonant system:

---

[10] Readers who have seen the film *Avatar* will be familiar with ejective sounds from the made-up language Na'vi, created for the film.

if the system were typologically common, as proposed by the Glottalic theory, then it would be expected to be stable and, therefore, to have been preserved in at least some Indo-European daughter languages. Such preservation, however, did not occur: no Indo-European language has retained ejective sounds where the Glottalic theory postulates them. Both Ossetian (a member of the Iranian branch) and some dialects of Armenian do have glottalic sounds, but they reflect relatively recent borrowing from neighboring languages in the Caucasus. Significantly, Ossetian is the only Iranian language with such phonetic characteristics. More important is the fact that the distribution of ejectives in modern Armenian and Ossetian does not fit the Glottalic theory. If, in contrast, we assume that PIE had a typologically unusual system, as postulated by the traditional reconstruction, then it might be expected to have been replaced by more typical sound inventories, possibly with different solutions achieved in its various daughter languages, which is exactly what one does find. Because of these and other objections, the Glottalic theory has been rejected by most Indo-Europeanists, though it still has some adherents, such as Robert S. P. Beekes, Frederik Kortlandt, and A. M. Lubotsky (cf. Beekes 1995; Kortlandt 1995, 2010; Lubotsky 2007). Alan Bomhard (2008, 2011) supports the Glottalic theory in connection with the controversial Nostratic hypothesis, which posits a "mega" language family that would include the Indo-European, Uralic, Altaic, Afro-Asiatic, Kartvelian, and Dravidian families.

Gamkrelidze and Ivanov's argument for the Armenian hypothesis rests heavily on the Glottalic theory. These authors further maintain that PIE originally borrowed its ejective consonants from Proto-Kartvelian, a language that was presumably spoken south of the Caucasus Mountains. They are certainly correct in contending that sounds can be "borrowed" from one language into another.[11] Examples from the more recent history of Indo-European languages include the "borrowing" of retroflex consonants by many Indo-Aryan languages from their Dravidian neighbors and the "borrowing" of pharyngealized consonants by Domari, another Indo-Aryan language (see Chapter 3 above), from Arabic (Matras 2012: 42–43). However, even if we assume, following Gamkrelidze and Ivanov, that the Glottalic theory is correct and that PIE acquired ejective sounds from some neighboring language, Gamkrelidze and Ivanov's argument rests on two crucial yet implicit and not necessarily valid assumptions: that Proto-Kartvelian had ejective sounds as its descendants do, and that it was spoken in the same area where its descendants have been spoken in historical times. In effect, Gamkrelidze and Ivanov

---

[11] The term is used in quotes here to highlight the contrast with the more conscious nature of lexical borrowing; moreover, sound "borrowing" is dependent on lexical borrowing, much like morphological/grammatical borrowing is (see Chapters 3 and 4 above for a more detailed discussion).

project properties of modern Kartvelian languages (both phonological and geographical) onto Proto-Kartvelian, a step that needs to be at least acknowledged explicitly. But even if we make all these assumptions, the conclusion – that PIE "borrowed" glottalic/ejective sounds from Proto-Kartvelian – is not the only possible one. In addition to the Kartvelian languages spoken to the south of the Great Caucasus crest, languages found on the northern side of the mountains, and historically into the adjacent lowlands as well, also have ejective sounds, including languages in both the Northwest Caucasian family (e.g. Abkhaz) and the Northeast Caucasian family (e.g. Tsez, Avar). One must therefore consider possible connection between PIE and the ancestral forms of languages indigenous to the North Caucasus.

The existence of common typological features in PIE and Proto-Northwest Caucasian (Proto-NWC) has long been noted.[12] For instance, Matasović (2012: 283) notes that although no "certain proofs of lexical borrowing between PIE and North Caucasian" were ever found, "there are a few undeniable areal-typological parallels in phonology and grammar". Those features include "the high consonant-to-vowel ratio, tonal accent, number suppletion in personal pronouns, the presence of gender and the morphological optative and, possibly, the presence of glottalized consonants and ergativity" (2012: 283). Those features are generally attributed to PIE but are not found in the majority of languages of North and Northeastern Eurasia, yet they are common, or universally present, in the languages of the Caucasus (especially the North Caucasus). Therefore, linguists have generally analyzed such commonalities as evidence of linguistic contact between the two proto-languages (Kortlandt 1990, 1995). In addition to the above-mentioned glottalic sounds, PIE and Proto-NWC are said to have developed labiovelars (e.g. k^w) in a similar fashion: by reassigning a vowel feature to adjacent consonants. In other words, an ancestral ku may have become $k^w \partial$; Northwest Caucasian languages may have done the same thing with respect to palatalization, turning an ancestral ki into $k^j \partial$. Taken to an extreme, this sort of historical change reduces vowel inventories and generates large numbers of consonants. The ultimate example of such a process is Ubykh, a now-extinct Northwest Caucasian language, which had 81 consonant phonemes (Colarusso 1992) and a mere two vowels. Yet it is not entirely clear whether PIE and Proto-NWC acquired labiovelars via horizontal transmission (presumably, from Proto-NWC into PIE) or from parallel developments. Kortlandt (1995: 93–94) takes the former position, buttressing his argument by arguing that "the area around Majkop [. . .] was a cultural center in the formative years of the Indo-European proto-language. It is therefore easily conceivable that the Indo-European sound system originated as a result of strong Caucasian influence."

---

[12] For a discussion of lexical borrowings see Starostin (2009).

Such strong evidence of linguistic contact between the early Indo-Europeans and the linguistic ancestors of the present-day Abkhaz, Adyghe, and Kabardian peoples makes the Pontic steppes to the north of the Caucasus Mountains a more likely candidate for the Indo-European homeland than either the Armenian Highlands or central Anatolia. To begin with, the Great Caucasus Range forms a formidable physical barrier, making it likely that speakers of Proto-NWC were in much closer contact with groups to the north than with those to the south. We must also consider Nichols's (1992) contention that both Proto-NWC and Proto-NEC must have been spoken in more northerly areas of subdued topography and low altitude than their modern descendants. Later arrivals of other peoples, chiefly those speaking Turkic languages, pushed the speakers of Northwest Caucasian and Northeast Caucasian languages into their highland refuges. As a consequence, the homelands of Northwestern and Northeastern Caucasian languages were probably adjacent to the hypothesized Indo-European homeland in the Pontic steppes, which would promote considerable linguistic borrowing between the two families. All such theorizing, however, is muddled by the complex linguistic history and geography of the region. For example, it has been suggested that in remote antiquity Northwest Caucasian languages were spoken in present-day Adjara along the Black Sea Coast, where they may have left substrate traces on Kartvelian toponyms. Moreover, the position of the extinct Hurro-Urartian languages, which may have been related to the Northeast Caucasian family, is uncertain. We should therefore regard the linguistic connections between PIE and the languages found to the north of the Caucasus with some skepticism, although the existing evidence is suggestive.

Much better documented are the linkages between PIE and Uralic, which also support a more northerly PIE homeland (Ringe 1998; Dolgopolsky 2000: 407; Janhunen 2000, 2001; Kallio 2001; Koivulehto 2001; Salminen 2001; Katz 2003). Morphological and lexical resemblances between the two language families are so numerous and striking that some scholars have proposed an Indo-Uralic macro-family, which would encompass all Indo-European and Uralic languages (e.g. Kortlandt 1995). Most linguists, however, believe that such similarities resulted from extensive contact rather than common descent, attributing many resemblances, especially the lexical ones, to borrowing – usually from Indo-European into Uralic. Still, the issue remains disputed, as the border between "good evidence" of contact and evidence "too good" to substantiate mere contact, instead implying common descent, can be a fine line indeed.

In many cases, borrowings into Uralic can be identified because either their phonology or their morphology is "out of place" for the family. An often-cited example is the word *porǩo-'pig, piglet' in Proto-Finno-Ugric. The palatalization suggests that this word was borrowed from Proto-Iranian rather than PIE itself. However, crucial to our discussion is the fact that this word bears traces of Indo-European (i.e. non-Finno-Ugric) morphology. Specifically, *-os (which became *-as in Finno-Ugric due to an independent sound change) is an Indo-European masculine nominative singular ending, but it has no meaning in Uralic languages. We can therefore conclude that the whole word was borrowed as a unit and is not part of the original Uralic vocabulary, which is unsurprising, as speakers of Proto-Uralic had no domesticated animals other than dogs. In other cases, the evidence is even less clear. For example, Kortlandt (1989) argues that verbs commonly taken to be Indo-European loanwords in Uralic (e.g. Rédei 1986), including 'to give', 'to wash', 'to bring', 'to drive', 'to do', 'to lead', and 'to take', were actually inherited from an ancestral language common to both families, Indo-Uralic.

Several significant conclusions can be drawn from borrowings between Indo-European and Uralic languages. First, the contact between the two language groups must have taken place over a long period of time. In a study of the earliest contacts between the two families, Rédei (1986) divides his list of sixty-four words supposedly borrowed from Indo-European into Uralic into three groups based on their presence or absence in major subfamilies of the two groups. He finds that seven Indo-European words are attested in both Finno-Ugric and Samoyedic, eighteen Indo-European or Indo-Iranian words are attested in Finno-Ugric but not in Samoyedic, and thirty-nine Indo-Iranian words are found only in the Finnic branch. Given the history of Uralic, the first set of words must have been borrowed in the earliest period, the second set in a more recent period, and the third set in a more recent period still. Similarly, Häkkinen (2012) differentiates four layers of borrowings from Indo-European into Uralic, listed below from the oldest to the newest. Note that all these borrowings originated from the Indo-Iranian branch of the Indo-European, not from PIE. However, such layered borrowings indicate that Uralic languages must have been in contact with Indo-European languages, particularly the Indo-Iranian ones, for millennia.

1. Early Proto-Indo-Iranian *ĝuĝheu- 'to pour, libate' → Early Proto-Uralic *juxi-/jôwxi- 'to drink'
   < IE *ĝheu-
2. Middle Proto-Indo-Iranian (Pre-Iranian dialect) *dzen- → Middle Proto-Uralic *sen-ti- 'to born'
   < IE *ĝenh-
3. Late Proto-Indo-Iranian *ćatam → Late Proto-Uralic *śeta '100'
   < IE *ḱm̥tóm
4. Early Iranian zaranya → Late Proto-Uralic *serńa 'gold'
   < Late Proto-Aryan *źhar- < IE *ĝh(o)l(H)-

Wiik (2000: 469) distinguishes ten layers of Indo-European loanwords in Finnish, starting from PIE loanwords (circa 4000 BCE) and continuing to most recent borrowings from English (circa 1960). At least four of the layers date before Common Era: borrowings from PIE (e.g. *jyviä* 'grains'), Proto-Indo-Iranian (e.g. *varsalle* 'for the foal'), Pre-Baltic (e.g. *puuro-* 'porridge'), and Proto-Germanic (e.g. *ruokaa* 'food').

Importantly, similarities between Indo-European and Uralic are not limited to lexical items; elements of morphology are shared as well. Examples of shared morphemes include the pronominal roots (**m-* for first person; **t-* for second person; **i-* for third person), case markings (accusative **-m*, ablative/partitive **-ta*), interrogative pronouns (**kʷ-* 'who?, which?'), and the negative particle *ne*. Other, less obvious correspondences have been suggested, such as the Indo-European plural marker **-es* and its Uralic counterpart **-t*. This same word-final assibilation of **-t* to **-s* may also be present in Indo-European second-person singular **-s* in comparison with Uralic second-person singular **-t*. Some similarities have also been noted between the verb conjugation systems of Uralic languages (e.g. that of Finnish) and of several Indo-European languages (e.g. those of Latin, Russian, and Lithuanian). As mentioned in Chapter 3, although it is common for a language to borrow heavily from the vocabulary of another language, it is extremely unusual for a language to borrow its basic system of verb conjugation from another tongue. In fact, such deep grammatical borrowings are so rare that they are generally interpreted as either evidence for extremely intense and prolonged contact, or for common descent.

All told, such linguistic evidence suggests deep and extended contact between the Uralic and Indo-European language families, likely with a high incidence of intermarriage, which would imply close proximity in the period when the borrowings occurred. Proto-Uralic is generally accepted as having been a language of foragers living in the forests to the north of the Pontic Steppes, who, as mentioned above, had no domesticated animals other than dogs. Assuming that the early Indo-Europeans maintained contact with speakers of Proto-Uralic, they must have lived in an area bordering the forest zone. The large number of reconstructed PIE roots for various tree species, discussed in the previous section, points in the same direction.

Although Uralic undoubtedly borrowed heavily from Indo-European, it does not follow that such borrowings came directly from the ancestral proto-language itself rather than from a descendant language (or languages) of PIE. In fact, most linguists reject the idea that PIE served as the source of these transmissions, favoring instead Proto-Indo-Iranian, one of the main Indo-European branches. Here, however, the evidence is solid. We can therefore deduce that speakers of Proto-Indo-Iranian, as well as peoples speaking later forms of the languages in this subfamily, lived in close proximity to the Uralic peoples inhabiting the forest zone just to the north of the Pontic Steppes.

But even if PIE itself had no direct contact with Uralic, the demonstrated relationship between Uralic and Proto-Indo-Iranian still runs counter to the Anatolian hypothesis of Gray and Atkinson. Recall that their model posits Proto-Indo-Iranian genesis on the Iranian plateau, many hundreds of miles to the south of the likely Uralic homeland, with a subsequent eastward migration. Such a scenario maintains a significant distance between the two language groups during the crucial period of linguistic exchange, and is therefore highly unlikely if not outright impossible. It must be admitted, however, that Colin Renfrew's modified Anatolian hypothesis is not contradicted by the evidence of close contacts between the Uralic and Indo-Aryan language groups. Although Renfrew regards PIE as having been limited to the Anatolian Plateau, he speculates that the early Indo-Iranians moved north into the steppe zone, where they could have had close contact with Uralic speakers.

The evidence of contact between these two language families also sheds new light on the problem of the Uralic homeland, which is by no means completely resolved either. Some scholars place the Uralic homeland to the east of the Ural Mountains in western Siberia, others to the west, in European Russia. The Siberian hypothesis was based on two main arguments. The first one concerned the family's highest-order split, which was thought to have separated Samoyedic and Finno-Ugric; more recent analyses, however, take the highest-order split of Uralic to be between the Finno-Permic and the Ugro-Samoyedic branches (Häkkinen 2007 and his later work). The second argument was based on paleolinguistic evidence pertaining to two coniferous tree names in Proto-Uralic (*Abies sibirica* and *Pinus cembra*), but these trees have also long been present in easternmost Europe. Because of these problems, most scholars now reject the Siberian theory of Uralic origins. For example, Carpelan and Parpola (2001: 79) associate Proto-Uralic with the archeologically attested Pit-Comb Ware culture found to the west of the Urals. Thus, both the Indo-Iranian and Uralic homelands were probably located in what is now European Russia and environs. Neither the Gray–Atkinson thesis of Indo-Iranian development on the Iranian plateau nor the postulated Siberian homeland of early Uralic makes sense in light of the evidence of linguistic contact between the two language families. It remains possible, however, that PIE originated to the south of the Black Sea and that the initial homeland of Proto-Uralic was in western Siberia, with subsequent migrations generating the proximity necessary for intensive language exchange. According to this scenario, the Indo-Iranian speakers would have moved north into the southern Russian steppes while the speakers of the Finno-Ugrian branch of Uralic simultaneously spread from the east into the forest belt located to the north of the steppes. Note, however, that such large-scale migrations are precluded by the Gray–Atkinson model, as discussed in Chapter 7.

To recap, evidence of linguistic contact with other language families, though copious, does not yield firm conclusions. The etymologies of some putative borrowings remain unclear. In many cases, we cannot be sure whether the word in question is shared via borrowing or because of inheritance from a common ancestral language; in other cases, we are not certain which language family generated a shared word, or how it spread to the other languages. Conclusions about language contact often depend on the precise reconstructions of proto-languages, which have not yet been definitively established. Drawing undisputable conclusions about PIE based on evidence of contact requires certainty about the development not only of Indo-European, but also of the other language families with which it interacted. However, we are no more certain about the deep past of the Uralic, Semitic, and Caucasian languages than we are about the history of the Indo-European tongues. Thus, conclusive proof of the area of language-family origination cannot be drawn from information about the interaction of language families. But even if firm conclusions cannot be reached, the existing evidence is still strongly suggestive, pointing in the direction of the Steppe hypothesis and away from the Anatolian model of Gray and Atkinson.

Clues from the phylogenetic tree and migration history

A third line of evidence concerns the Indo-European phylogenetic tree in light of the reconstructed migration histories of the early speakers of Indo-European languages. As we shall see in the following pages, this type of evidence also leans towards the Steppe hypothesis, but again fails to offer conclusive proof.

As was shown in our discussion in Chapter 4, the exact shape of the Indo-European family tree is far from resolved. Ten major subgroupings, known as "benchmark groupings" (cf. Nichols and Warnow 2008: 777), are well established: Anatolian, Tocharian, Celtic, Italic, Greek, Armenian, Albanian, Germanic, Indo-Iranian, and Balto-Slavic. Consensus is still lacking, however, in regard to the higher levels of the taxonomic structure, as can be seen from the various trees in Figures 1–6, although virtually all scholars agree about the first two divisions. The highest-order split separated the Anatolian languages (Hittite, Luwian, and Lycian) from the rest of the family, and the next split took the ancestor of the Tocharian languages (Tocharian A and Tocharian B) on their own trajectory. Evidence from the phonological and morphological development of these languages, as well as that pertaining to the development of the wheeled-vehicle vocabulary (see Chapter 8), substantiate the consensus view that the Anatolian and Tocharian groups were the first two to separate from the main Indo-European stem.

As Don Ringe (2006 and elsewhere) conclusively demonstrates, the Anatolian and Tocharian branches split off "cleanly" from the main Indo-European stem, meaning that once the division occurred, the speakers of Proto-Anatolian and Proto-Tocharian lost contact with the other Indo-Europeans. As a result, they shared no common innovations with other Indo-European languages, nor did they borrow from or provide loanwords to them.[13] In other words, these diversification events are nicely depicted by the tree model of linguistic evolution. This kind of complete separation can be most easily effected by the migration of one subgroup, removing it from its original homeland by distance and often by geographical obstacles as well.

The prime candidates for the Indo-European homeland – the southern Russian steppes and Anatolia – are separated from each other by two profound geographical barriers: the Caucasus Mountains and the Black Sea. The east–west-oriented Great Caucasus Range presents a formidable impediment to traffic between the southern Russian steppes and the Transcaucasian region, the Middle East, and Anatolia. It is pierced by few negotiable passes, the most important of which extends along the Darial Gorge through the so-called Caucasian Gates. (It is by no means accidental that the territory of the only ethno-linguistic group historically found on both sides of the Great Caucasus Mountain Range, the Ossetians, spans the Darial Gorge.) The Black Sea was also a major barrier before the development of Bronze-Age shipping, as shown by Davison *et al.* (2006). Ancient mariners could sail only in the narrow coastal zone around the Black Sea. Similarly, easy overland movement was limited to a narrow strip along the coast, owing to the rugged mountains running parallel to it. It is therefore likely that whatever population movements occurred between the Pontic steppes and Anatolia, in either direction, did not proceed across the Black Sea or the Caucasus Mountains.

Before we can determine which of the two main competing theories of the Indo-European homeland offers a more cohesive account of the early movements that led to the clean Anatolian and Tocharian splits, another warning is in order. Any given division of a linguistic tree can result from migration or demic diffusion of either the branch that splits off from the rest of the tree, or of the branch that constitutes the main stem. (For the sake of convenience, the following discussion will use the term "migration" to refer to any process of substantial movement, whether by way of slow demic diffusion or more rapid "migration", as the term is conventionally conceptualized.) For example, the Anatolian split could have been a result of the migration of the speakers of Proto-Anatolian or of the speakers of PNIE (the "rest of the tree" at this point).

---

[13] It is possible, however, that the splits were not as "clean" as the available evidence suggests. Perhaps, Anatolian languages of which there is surviving evidence (and later Tocharian languages) were in a dialect continuum with the rest of the Indo-European realm via dialects/ languages that left no trace in the linguistic or historical record and of which no descendants survive. While such a possibility cannot be ruled out, we have no reasons to seriously entertain it either.

Similarly, the Tocharian split could have been the result of the migration of the Proto-Tocharian speakers themselves or of the remainder of the Indo-European group. Given a binary split on the tree, we cannot decide on the basis of phylogenetic evidence which of the branches relocated. Nor is the relative linguistic conservativeness of any branch helpful in this regard. While it is often assumed, implicitly or explicitly, that the group that remains *in situ* is more linguistically conservative, this assumption does not necessarily hold, as is illustrated by Icelandic, the most conservative Germanic language, the speakers of which clearly migrated over a particularly large distance in a relatively short period of time.

With such considerations in mind, let us now consider the earliest split from the Indo-European trunk, that of the Anatolian branch. The main argument for Anatolian being the initial branch derives from the fact that it lacks a significant number of grammatical features that characterize PNIE, including such verbal forms as the aorist, perfect, subjunctive, optative, and so on (Fortson 2010: 173). The links between Anatolian and PNIE were therefore probably severed before PNIE underwent these significant innovations. An alternative analysis attributes the lack of these various morphosyntactic categories in Anatolian to losses resulting from the influence of some non-Indo-European language or languages within Anatolia itself. In this scenario, Anatolian is taken to be the "innovator" instead of the more conservative branch. Regardless of whether the Anatolian or the PNIE is viewed as the innovative branch, speakers of Proto-Anatolian and those of PNIE must have fully parted ways, linguistically and geographically. How might this have happened under either the Steppe or the Anatolian hypotheses?[14]

If one assumes a Pontic-Caspian PIE homeland, the highest-order split can be envisaged as resulting from the migration of the linguistic ancestors of the Anatolian branch. Such a mass movement would most likely have passed through the Balkans (Mallory 1989: 241; Anthony 2007: 259; Anthony 2013: 8–10), entering Anatolia by the beginning of the Bronze Age, where the newcomers settled and eventually dominated indigenous non-Indo-European peoples such as the Hattians and the Hurrians (see Chapter 6). Anthony (2013) identifies the Anatolian split with the movement of steppe people into the lower Danube Valley in the wake of the collapse of agricultural tell settlements in that area. Based on archeological evidence, the breakdown of the tell culture is dated circa 4400–4200 BCE; "the archeologically undocumented shepherds who grazed their sheep on the abandoned tells in the Balkan uplands between 4200–3500 BCE could have been the distant antecedents of the Anatolian branch", Anthony writes (2013: 9). Under this scenario, PNIE

---

[14] Our discussion in the remainder of this section draws heavily on Anthony (2007, 2013) and Mallory (2013a).

would have remained in the Pontic-Caspian steppes, where its characteristic shared innovations developed. Whatever its archeological merit, this hypothesis nicely accounts for the split between Anatolian and PNIE.

The Anatolian hypothesis, however, encounters massive challenges in accounting for the Anatolian split, as it would require chains of highly unlikely events. One possible solution, proposed by Grigoriev (2002: 354–357, 412–415), is to assume that the ancestors of the Anatolian languages migrated away from the Anatolian homeland, leaving speakers of what was to become "the rest of the Indo-European family" in (eastern) Anatolia, and then subsequently returned to the region. In Grigoriev's model, the group ancestral to the Anatolians moved from Asia Minor into the Balkans, and then moved back into Anatolia during the Bronze Age under pressure from the Greeks, who had themselves made their way through the Caucasus, around the Black Sea, and then into the Balkan Peninsula. As discussed above, such migration would involve crossing formidable geographical obstacles, in the form of high, rugged mountains and deep seas, making it highly unlikely. From the linguistic perspective, while this imaginative thesis meets the minimal requirement of accounting for the separation of the Anatolian branch from the rest of the Indo-European tree, it is unduly complicated and it fits poorly with the archeological record.

The second scenario possible under the Anatolian hypothesis involves the Anatolian group remaining within the homeland while the speakers of PNIE relocated elsewhere. If they had ended up in southern European Russia, further developments would essentially be the same as those postulated under the Steppe hypothesis. This scenario is explored in Colin Renfrew's later work (Renfrew 1999), which Mallory (2013a) refers to as "Anatolian Neolithic Plan B". While accounting for the geography of the Anatolian split, this model runs into serious problems with respect to chronology. Just as the earlier model developed by Renfrew (1987) requires one to assume that PIE was spoken in an unchanged form for 3,000 years, the revised model requires a similarly untenable assumption with respect to PNIE (see Chapter 8).

But the problems confronted by the Gray–Atkinson diffusion-based model are deeper still. Recall that their model does not allow for large-scale, rapid migration, effectively ruling out the movement of PNIE speakers to the steppes under Renfrew's Neolithic Plan B, as well as the relocations of both the Anatolian speakers and the predecessors of the Greeks in the Grigoriev thesis. The Gray–Atkinson scheme is instead more akin to Renfrew's earlier proposals (i.e. what Mallory calls Anatolian Neolithic Plan A), which would have speakers of what was to become the European branches of the family slowly diffusing westward and speakers of eastern branches gradually moving eastward, while the future Anatolians (in the linguistic sense) stayed put. Under this scenario, the ancestors of Greek would be situated in Greece to the west of

Proto-Anatolian and the ancestors of Indo-Iranians would be located to the east of Anatolian. But if that were the case, how could the various non-Anatolian branches maintain the unity that characterizes PNIE? Or in the words of James P. Mallory (2013a: 148),

> How is one to explain parallel linguistic innovations both to the east and west of the region assigned to proto-Anatolian? The statisticians who devised this model seem to require some form of mutual contact at a distance, one of the stranger aspects of quantum theory that Einstein once dismissed as *"Spukhaftige Fernwirkung"* [or "spooky action at a distance"].

Barring any spooky, telepathic action, the model presented in "Mapping the Origins and Expansion of the Indo-European Language Family" (Bouckaert *et al.* 2012) and illustrated by their animated map "movie" fails to provide anything approaching a reasonable explanation for the shared development of all non-Anatolian languages, "the only feature of Indo-European phylogeny that has near universal support" (Mallory 2013a: 148).

Now let us consider the second split, that of the Tocharian languages. Under the Steppe hypothesis, the Tocharian division can be identified with the second archeologically documented movement of people from the Pontic-Caspian steppes, the one that gave rise to the intrusive Afanasievo culture in the western Altai Mountains (Anthony 2011). This migration, supported by evidence from grave inventories and genetic data, proceeded eastward across an astonishingly long distance of approximately 1,200 miles circa 3300–3000 BCE. According to Anthony (2013: 10),

> the Afanasievo migrants seem to have introduced a pastoral economy, wheeled vehicles, horses, and an accompanying new social order into mountain meadows formerly occupied by ceramic-making mountain foragers, some (many?) of whom probably were absorbed into the Afanasievo culture.

The Afanasievo material culture, moreover, exhibits traits characteristic of the Yamnaya culture (also known as "Pit Grave Culture" or "Ochre Grave Culture"), which appears to coincide in time and space with PNIE. Yamnaya kurgan grave types, a typical Yamnaya burial pose, Yamnaya-Repin ceramic types and decoration, and sleeved axes and daggers of specific Yamnaya types are all found in Afanasievo sites in the western Altai (Kubarev 1988; Chernykh *et al.* 2004). The link between the linguistic ancestors of the Tocharians and the Afanasievo culture is further explored in Mallory and Mair (2000).

Although plausible at first glance, the linking of the Tocharians to eastward steppe expansions associated with the Afanasievo or similar cultures of the Altai region and southern Siberia faces one daunting problem: the Tocharian languages retained inherited Indo-European agricultural vocabulary, but there is no evidence of arable farming east of the Urals before 2000 BCE. This is not unlike the "wheel problem", discussed in Chapter 8: if Proto-Tocharians did not practice agriculture, why did they retain vocabulary pertaining to it? It is well known that the steppe populations ate the seeds of wild plants such as *Chenopodium* and *Amaranthus*, but the semantic variance among cognates pertaining to cereal types indicates that the reconstructed roots referred to either 'wheat', 'barley', or 'millet', not some type of wild grain or pseudograin (Mallory 2013a: 151). One possibility here is that they retained some forms of cropping, but practiced it so sparingly as to leave no traces that have yet been discovered, an archeologically unsatisfying scenario.

While the fact that the Tocharian languages retained agricultural vocabulary despite the absence of evidence for agriculture in presumed Proto-Tocharian-speaking sites poses a problem for the Steppe hypothesis, the Anatolian hypothesis as advocated by the Gray–Atkinson approach faces its own obstacles in this regard. According to the Gray–Atkinson model, the Tocharian split is dated at either circa 5900 BCE (Gray and Atkinson 2003) or 4900 BCE (Bouckaert *et al.* 2012), long before the arrival of agriculture in the more easterly lands that the ancestors of the Tocharians would have had to have passed through. In other words, if the Tocharians are presumed to have engaged in some farming based on their retention of the agricultural vocabulary of their linguistic ancestors, there is no more archeological warrant for postulating movement across the Iranian plateau than there is for migration via the western Altai.

Moreover, the diffusion-based model illustrated by the animated map showcased by the Gray–Atkinson approach runs into a further problem, as it postulates that the ancestors of the Tocharians (and later the ancestors of the Indo-Iranians) moved through the northern Fertile Crescent and hence across the Iranian plateau, areas relatively densely populated by agriculturalist groups speaking non-Indo-European languages – Hurrian, Semitic, Sumerian, and Elamite – and yet remained "unscathed" by any of these languages. It is certainly more plausible that the Tocharian migration occurred through the steppe zone, sparsely populated by nomadic or semi-nomadic groups. To make matters worse, after they have survived diffusion through non-Indo-European-speaking groups, the Tocharians are depicted in the animated map as moving through impassibly high altitudes, passing along the crest of the Tian Shan Mountains at elevations in excess of 20,000 feet (6,000 meters) (see also Chapter 7).

To summarize, evidence from migration history, like clues from linguistic paleontology and language contact, generates "facts" that are open to interpretation. As a result, the Indo-European homeland controversy can only be addressed by weighing different pieces of evidence against each other, and even then the conclusions remain tentative. Yet all in all, such data show that although the Steppe hypothesis is not without flaws, much more evidence weighs on its side, as compared to the Anatolian hypothesis, especially if the latter is coupled with the diffusion-based model of the Gray–Atkinson approach.

10   The non-mystery of Indo-European expansion

If anything characterized the history of Indo-European studies from the initiation of sustained inquiry in the late eighteenth century to the emergence of the Anatolian model in the late twentieth century, it was the idea that the expansion of this language family was an extraordinary development not easily explained through ordinary processes. How could one individual language have dispersed so widely and diversified so magnificently, spreading from Western Europe to northern India in ancient times and eventually to most of the world and half of humanity? Surely, many concluded, there had to have been something exceptional going on. Figuring out what these special qualities were, they in turn concluded, might even provide a key for understanding the larger patterns of human history. While the earlier Aryan and Kurgan theories located this central dynamic in the supposedly unique qualities of the people in question, the Anatolian thesis, particularly as fleshed out by Renfrew, avoids such exceptionalism by framing Indo-European expansion in the same terms as those used to account for the spread of several other language families, such as Bantu into the southern half of Africa. But to do so successfully, it must associate Indo-European success with the principal technical breakthrough of the pre-industrial past: the development of agriculture, which was itself an extraordinary development.

All such extraordinary occurrences, however, are more apparent than real. All languages families, after all, stem from a common ancestral tongue, and a number of them count their current speakers in the hundreds of millions. Much of the expansion of the Indo-European languages, moreover, came in the modern period of global imperialism, and is thus unrelated to the processes that originally propelled the growth of the family. But more important is the fact that even the original enlargement probably involved very ordinary processes. As Mallory, Anthony, and the other proponents of the Revised Steppe school demonstrate, there is nothing unusual in the expansion of languages spoken by primarily pastoral peoples into the lands of neighboring sedentary, agricultural peoples. Indeed, that is precisely what one would expect, due both to basic demographic considerations and to the varieties of social organization that typically characterize these two forms of adaptation.

In conceptualizing the disparities between pastoral and agricultural peoples it is first necessary to note that these two terms often indicate different places along a continuum of subsistence activities rather than precise slots. Most farming peoples also herd animals, and it is not uncommon for subgroups among them to devote more attention to their flocks than to their fields. By the same token, many primarily pastoral peoples occasionally plant crops, and it is not uncommon for groups to periodically switch back and forth between primarily pastoral and primarily agricultural orientations, depending on climatic fluctuations, changing relations with neighbors, and so on. Even fully nomadic pastoralists, moreover, almost always interact with some intensity with neighboring farmers, exchanging animal products for grain and other agricultural goods in addition to craft products, as Renfrew himself (1987) emphasizes. Such interdependence, in turn, can help push the languages of the herders into the lands of the farmers, initiating long-term processes of language change.

In the typical dynamic between (mostly) agricultural and (mostly) pastoral peoples, certain advantages are generally held by the latter groups, which enhance the ability of their languages to expand. Such advantages are not limited to equestrian nomads, and as a result the Steppe theory of Indo-European origins is not contingent on the domestication of the horse, although horses certainly amplify all such benefits. Even pedestrian pastoralists often gain an upper hand on their farming neighbors, enhancing the ability of their languages to spread, as in the Luo example from eastern Africa highlighted by Anthony (2007: 118).

In some cases, an initial advantage commonly gained by pastoralists is demographic. At first glance, the edge here seems to be found on the other side; farmers can occupy the landscape at much higher population densities than herders, and agricultural peoples often have higher fertility levels than pastoralists. But fertility levels among contemporary pastoral peoples in Africa vary widely from society to society, and in some cases they are similar to those of neighboring farming groups (Mulder 1992; Hill 1985). More importantly, mortality and morbidity rates can be lower in pastoral populations than in farming communities. Partly this is a matter of nutrition, as herders usually enjoy a more protein-rich diet than their agricultural neighbors, but also important is the fact that they can more easily relocate to favorable areas when weather-related famines strike. Perhaps more significant is their reduced susceptibility to water-borne diseases. Sedentary peoples often pollute their own water supplies and thus spread various illnesses, both debilitating and deadly. Nomadic pastoralists, on the other hand, reduce such hazards by their periodic relocation to new areas with clean water. Lower mortality rates can generate higher rates of population growth, pushing pastoral peoples into new lands, including those of nearby farmers.

Such dynamics are in turn magnified by different opportunities for the intensification of food production. When the populations of farming folk expand to reach the local carrying capacity, the most common response is to intensify production by applying additional increments of labor, thereby increasing the number of people who can feed themselves on the same area of land, a process documented by the Danish agricultural economist Ester Boserup in the 1960s (Boserup 1965). As she showed, as population density increases, long-term fallow systems give way to short-term fallow and then to annual cropping and eventually, if climatic conditions allow, to multiple annual crop cycles. In traditional pastoral economies, on the other hand, opportunities for such intensification are much more limited. As a result, the usual expedient undertaken when population pressure mounts is movement into new lands, a process facilitated by the already nomadic (or semi-nomadic) lifestyles of the people in question.

Intriguingly, similar relationships sometimes even exist between agricultural peoples and hunter–gatherers. Although farmers are expected to demographically overwhelm foragers, they can only do so in lands that are climatically suitable for agriculture. Where arid areas adjoin more humid lands, a semipermanent boundary between the two modes of life can become established. One such division separated the densely populated plateau zone of central Mexico from the much more lightly inhabited deserts of the northern Grand Chichimeca during the pre-colonial period. In such a situation, hard-pressed and hardscrabble semi-nomadic foragers sometimes push aggressively into the beckoning lands of their sedentary neighbors. One of the constants of Meso-American history was the hostility between the agriculturally based civilizations of the south and the Chichimecs – a derogatory term sometimes said to mean "dog people" in Nahua – of the north. Chichimec incursions and indeed migrations periodically penetrated deeply into the Meso-American heartland. In such instances, the newcomers would eventually be acculturated into the civilization of the core, but this process did not preclude the spread of their languages. Indeed, the Aztecs themselves traced their history and their language precisely to such a series of events, and some modern experts concur (Smith 1984).

In any conflict between sedentary and (semi)-nomadic peoples, the latter will enjoy certain benefits of asymmetrical struggle. The main assets of farming peoples, such as their crops and dwellings, are highly vulnerable to hit-and-run raids from more mobile peoples. Reprisals are much more difficult to conduct, however, due to the ability of nomadic peoples to withdraw into inaccessible areas. The existence of livestock, essentially unknown in pre-Columbian Meso-America but omnipresent in Eurasia, would intensify such dynamics. Pastoral societies are often obsessed with stock raiding, as herd animals can be extraordinarily easy to steal; with proper guidance, they literally walk away with their captors. As herders have to contend with constant raiding by other pastoralists, they typically hone their skills in both livestock protection and theft. So important is such looting in pastoral and semi-pastoral societies that it has inspired epic literature, the early Irish *Cattle Raid of Cooley* (*Táin Bó Cúailnge*) being a prime example. Nearby farming folk without such a background will typically have livestock of their own, depending on them for meat and sometimes for dairy products and traction power as well. Habitual raiding by pastoralists from nearby steppe lands would thus weaken the power of the farmers while enhancing that of the herders. Such a process may have been an important component of the initial spread of Indo-European languages into Europe.

Such dynamics were of course absent from pre-Columbian North America, but they would be established after the reintroduction[1] of the horse and other large grazing animals by the Spaniards in the early modern period. Many Native American groups of the Great Plains took up an equestrian way of life that verged on – but never quite achieved – full-fledged pastoralism, as they hunted rather than herded their main source of subsistence, the bison. But they certainly bred horses, and if their way of life had persisted more than a mere two centuries, they may have eventually made the full transition. In the southern plains, the powerful Comanche federation turned livestock raiding into something of an art, periodically stripping the horses, donkeys, and mules out of the village communities of New Mexico, Texas, and northern Mexico, eventually penetrating into core mining districts of central Mexico as well, a process that proved devastating to the local economies. Not coincidentally, as Pekka Hämäläinen (2009: 171) shows in his fascinating if misleadingly titled book *Comanche Empire*, the Comanche language, which was extremely useful for trade, was itself spreading among the sedentary people of New Mexico in the mid-1800s; had the expansion of the United States not put a quick stop to the process, it is possible that a large swath of territory would have ended up Comanche-speaking. (Intriguingly, Comanche is a Uto-Aztecan language, related to the Nahua tongue of the Aztecs.)

Although the early twentieth-century American expositors of the Aryan thesis viewed the spread of the Indo-European languages in Eurasia in terms analogous to that of English in North America by pioneering "Nordics" (see Chapter 1), the spread of the Comanche tongue in early nineteenth-century New Mexico actually makes a better analogue. Joseph Pomeroy Widney and Madison Grant would have no doubt been horrified by such a suggestion.

The relationship between neighboring pastoral and agricultural peoples typically involves not merely predation and antagonism, but also a measure

---

[1] Horses evolved in North America, but perished on the continent at the end of the last glacial period some 12,000 years ago.

of mutualism. Trade is encouraged by their differing modes of subsistence, which tend to produce different forms of surplus. It can also be advantageous for farmers to allow herders to move their flocks onto their fields after the crops have been harvested; while grazing the stubble, the animals fertilize the fields and can even improve soil permeability and aeration through the action of their hooves. Such mutualistic connections are especially well attested among the intermingled farming and herding societies in the Sahel belt to the south of the Sahara. Khazanov (1983: 36), however, maintains that in most such cases the pastoralists retain the advantage and effectively exploit the cultivators. And even if the relationship is reciprocally beneficial, relations can break down if the demographic balance changes or in the event of climate shifts. Indeed, the current conflict between the pastoral Abbala Arabs and the agricultural Fur and Zaghawa of Sudan's Darfur region is sometimes explained in such terms (Hastrup 2013: 95), as is the growing strife between the nomadic Fulani and a number of sedentary peoples in interior West Africa (Folami 2010).

Whenever herders seasonally move through the lands of farming peoples, a certain degree of linguistic inter-digitization necessarily results. More permanent zones of language mixture can also be established on the same basis. Historically speaking, few agricultural landscapes are characterized by uniform cropland, as the featureless isotropic plain found in the Gray–Atkinson scenario exists only in the minds of computational modelers. Croplands are typically interspersed with rougher areas unsuitable for agriculture but well fitted for low-intensity grazing. In Bronze-Age Europe, most of these uncultivated lands were forested, which might seem to make them worthless for nomadic herders. But many forms of livestock, particularly cattle, goats, and especially swine, thrive in woodlands; it is not an accident that the wild bovine of Europe, the auroch, maintained its last holdout in the Jaktorów Forest of what is now east-central Poland.[2]

As herders move into the interstices of fragmented agricultural landscapes, complex linguistic mosaics can result. The language geography of pastoral groups is often characterized by discontinuity, broken up into numerous, often-shifting segments. Due to their relatively mobile way of life, moreover, herding peoples are often able to maintain language cohesion over relatively large areas. This feature alone gives such languages an advantage, as it facilitates travel for those who speak them. As a result, farming people not uncommonly acquire the language of a local pastoral group as a second tongue. In interior West Africa, for example, Fulani is widely spoken by agricultural groups with different native

---

[2] See the "Auroch" pages on the website *The Sixth Extinction*: petermaas.nl/extinct/speciesinfo/aurochs.htm

languages, even though it has few of the linguistic characteristics of a *lingua franca*.[3]

Additional factors also encourage the spread of languages associated with pastoral people. As David Anthony (2007) argues, systems of economic clientage and networks of religious practice can link cultivators to more powerful pastoralists, leading some members of the former group to simply switch their language and ethnicity. This process of ethnic conversion, however, can work in both directions: an old adage in Kirghizstan states that, "A bad Kirghiz becomes a Sart, while a bad Sart becomes a Kirghiz" (the Kirghiz traditionally being herders, and the Sarts farmers) (Morrison 2008: 45). Yet for reasons explained above, the advantage is usually held by the pastoralists. Sexual dynamics can also give an edge to the languages of herders. Infiltrating – or invading – men often take local wives, concubines, and female slaves, imposing their language on them. This well-attested phenomenon is often linked to the greater military clout and social prestige of the pastoralists, and to the fact that their migratory streams are often male-biased to begin with. All of these processes will tend to generate pervasive bilingualism. Over time, couples may opt to rear their children in the more widespread and prestigious intrusive language rather than in what had originally been the native tongue of the area. As a result, the language of the pastoralists may spread broadly even without invasion, direct subjugation, or the establishment of coherent political entities.

But despite all of these pastoralist advantages, in one respect farming societies maintain a definite edge: that of absolute numbers. As a result, herders entering the lands of farmers not uncommonly adopt their languages, abandoning their own. Such language change can even occur when the newcomers establish organized rule over the indigenes. Thus the Turkic-speaking Bulgars who established the Kingdom of Bulgaria in the seventh century switched to the Slavic tongue of the majority of their subjects. In East Africa, the Tutsi aristocrats who established several kingdoms in the Rwanda–Burundi area seem to have originally been a Nilotic-speaking people who eventually adopted the Bantu language of the peasants who they ruled over and intermarried with. Significantly, the distinction between the two groups was diminishing over time before it was magnified and encouraged by Belgian colonialists.

How then do we account for the fact that sometimes the language of newcomer pastoralists prevails and in other instances the language of the pre-existing farmers does so? Sheer weight of numbers is not necessarily the determining factor: the Hungarian language successfully ensconced itself in

---

[3] Tatou-Metangmo (2005), however, differentiates "conservative Fulani" from the somewhat simplified *lingua franca* version of the language that he deems "vehicular Fulani".

the Danubian Basin even though the Magyar immigrants were relatively few in number and evidently made no major genetic impact on the local population (cf. Cavalli-Sforza and Cavalli-Sforza 1995; Cavalli-Sforza 2000). Renfrew (1994: 120) attributes this kind of language change to "elite dominance", a process that he limits to relatively recent periods that contained "highly ranked societies" characterized by "central organization". As a result, he credits the medieval and early modern spread of Turkic languages to such dynamics, yet he denies the possibility in regard to the much earlier spread of Indo-European languages into Europe. But a comparative overview indicates that things are not so simple. The languages of pastoralists can spread across agricultural areas in the absence of organized states, as the Luo example highlighted by Anthony (2007: 118) indicates, just as dominating elites in full-fledged kingdoms often fail to do the same, as the Bulgarian example shows. Perhaps the quest to find a determining factor is doomed to fail by the existence of random elements. A degree of chance could be enough to tip the balance in the direction of one language or another.

Ancient Mesopotamia is an interesting place to examine the linguistic consequences of interactions between agricultural and pastoral peoples (see Ostler 2005). The original language of the world's first urbanized society, Sumerian, is a linguistic isolate, not proven conclusively to be related to any other known language. Over the first millennia of Mesopotamian civilization, however, Sumerian gradually yielded to the Semitic language Akkadian. This process was marked by a significant amount of linguistic convergence, resulting in an ancient Mesopotamian *Sprachbund*. The homeland of Akkadian is unclear, and it may have been spoken in parts of the central Tigris-Euphrates Valley at the dawn of recorded history. Many scholars, however, associate Akkadian, like other Semitic languages, with the largely pastoral tribes that periodically moved from the western and southern deserts into the fertile land between the rivers.

Akkadian enjoyed a long period of linguistic hegemony in Mesopotamia, successfully rebuffing the tongues of other nomadic tribes that periodically encroached upon the region, even those of conquerors who established their own local dynasties, such as the Amorites and the Kassites (Ostler 2005). But eventually, starting circa 1000 BCE, Akkadian would yield to Aramaic, which was almost certainly introduced through the infiltrations/invasions of arid-land pastoralists. Aramaic enjoyed a long period of primacy throughout the larger region, again withstanding numerous migrations and invasions of diverse peoples speaking a variety of languages. But it too would eventually fall to another language associated with a pastorally oriented people stemming from the desert lands: Arabic. The spread of Arabic is of course a much more complicated story, as it was linked with a powerful new religion and an accompanying imperial ideology that helped build a strong state. But one can still see the old herder/farmer dynamic at play in the expansion of this language, especially in such episodes as the conversion of the lowlands of the Maghreb from Berber tongues to Arabic. The area that is now Tunisia and the lowlands of Algeria had remained Berber-speaking long after the initial Arab conquest and conversion to Islam in the late seventh century CE. Here the linguistic transition occurred after the migration/invasion of the Banu Hilal and other nomadic Bedouin tribes from the Arabian Peninsula, an event that did not occur until the eleventh century (Abun-Nasr 1987: 69).

Such friction between cultivators and pastoralists is deeply familiar to many from the early chapters of the Bible, which recount the movement of a nomadic group into an agricultural area, followed by its own transition to a more sedentary mode of life. In this account, the relationship between the Hebrews and the autochthonous Canaanites is marked by pronounced hostility, although over time a certain degree of mutual accommodation would be reached, which in turn provoked a reaction that contributed to the development of the Jewish faith and ethnicity. Within the transitioning Hebrew society itself, a significant degree of tension is evident between those more inclined to herding and those who favored instead the cultivation of the soil. And as the story of Cain and Abel makes clear, it was long the pastoralist orientation that received general favor.

Invoking processes from ancient history to explain those in the prehistoric past is admittedly a problematic strategy. The ancient Fertile Crescent was a land of states, kings, scribes, and cities, quite unlike the farming communities of "Old Europe" that seem to have lost their original languages after the incursions of pastoral Indo-European speakers into their lands. But it is equally perilous to exaggerate the difference between ancient and the late-prehistoric times. Even in state-level polities of the Bronze Age, the world of kings and courts was far removed from that of the village communities where most people lived. As a result, the movements of pastoral peoples into the Fertile Crescent could have been experienced in a relatively similar way to what happened when Indo-European languages began to push into the stateless societies of eastern and central Europe.

11 Whither historical linguistics?

Throughout this book, we have examined novel computational methods of establishing family relationships among languages developed by the Gray–Atkinson approach, showing that they fail to provide an alternative to the traditional techniques, such as the comparative method, linguistic paleontology, and so on. It is for good reason that Kiparsky (2014: 65) calls the comparative approach "the gold standard" in historical linguistics and that Longobardi and Guardiano (2009: 1681) consider it to be "undoubtedly one of the greatest achievements of the human sciences". Still, despite their significant triumphs, none of these time-tested methods can yet provide conclusive answers to a number of the key questions of linguistic prehistory. Although multiple lines of linguistic evidence, for example, point to an Indo-European homeland in or near the Pontic steppes (as discussed in the preceding chapters), the issue remains open. Continued uncertainty, however, does not mean that the outlook for more decisive studies is gloomy, much less that we should jettison our accumulated knowledge and well-honed methods so that we can reinvent historical linguistics as a quasi-biological science. In this concluding chapter, we consider the future outlook of historical linguistics in general and of Indo-European studies in particular.

In our view, the best opportunities – as well as the biggest challenges – for historical linguistics lie with its connections to other fields, both within and outside the broad discipline of linguistics. Cultural and physical anthropology, history, and philology all have something to contribute to our understanding of the differentiation and spread of languages. Recent advances in such fields as archeology (Heggarty 2014), geochemical fingerprinting (Kamber 2009), and human genetics (Underhill *et al.* 2010; Myres *et al.* 2011; Rootsi *et al.* 2012; Patterson *et al.* 2012; *inter alia*) shed new light on prehistoric population movements, which have far-reaching effects on the structure of language groups. As for the wider discipline of linguistics, we agree with Kiparsky (2014: 88) that historical linguistics

is situated at a crossroads where almost all branches of the field meet. A historical study might draw on processing and pragmatics, morphology and corpus linguistics, sociolinguistics and syntax, phonetics and formal language theory.

As a result of such developments, studies of language contact now put the analysis of language change on a firmer footing, making substratum and superstratum hypotheses, long considered with suspicion, empirically falsifiable and therefore advanced more confidently (Matras and Sakel 2007). In particular, it has been argued that contacts both within the Indo-European family and between Indo-European and other families have had profound effects on language change (see Stilo 2004; Aikio 2006; Schrijver 2009, 2011; Kiparsky 2012; Filppula 2013; and others). In another promising development, the enhanced documentation of understudied languages, in conjunction with advances in theoretical linguistics and language typology, allows for more detailed and encompassing comparative work. Experience gained in studying one particular language family has also been successfully applied in examining other families. Sociolinguistic studies of ongoing sound changes (e.g. Labov *et al.* 2013) allow for a better understanding of similar changes in the past. Corpus linguistics permits a more fine-grained analysis of phenomena involving variation – and ultimately, historical change – conditioned by frequency (cf. the study of English vowel syncope by Bybee 2007). Needless to say, such enhanced understanding of language change clarifies language relatedness.

But perhaps the most important change in historical linguistics derives from what Kiparsky (2014: 88) calls "breaching [. . .] the Saussurian firewall between synchrony [i.e. theoretical linguistics] and diachrony [i.e. historical linguistics]". Ironically, the parallels here to biology are much stronger than Gray and Atkinson would admit. In their essay on "curious parallels and curious connections" between biology and historical linguistics, Atkinson and Gray (2005: 521–524) note a number of methodological challenges shared by the two fields, such as "developing algorithms to determine the probability that lexical characters are cognate", "model fitting and comparison", "developing methods to investigate reticulate evolution", and the like. Curiously, what they fail to note is the more general point: just as the biological classification of species, originally based on externally accessible characteristics, underwent a revolution on the grounds of progress in *theoretical* biology (i.e. the rise of molecular genetics) so too progress in the phylogenetic classification of languages must be based on progress in *theoretical* linguistics. Thus, only linguists – not biologists – can push the research frontier forward by identifying the basic building blocks of language – its "atoms", in Mark Baker's memorable metaphor (Baker 2001b) – and by examining carefully how they play out in linguistic evolution.

The most important paradigmatic change in linguistics, one continuously alluded to in this book (see especially Chapters 3 and 4), is the realization that *language is not merely words*. Thus if the main problem with the Gray–Atkinson method lies in its exclusive use of lexical material, could some of the same procedures and algorithms that they use be applied to phonological or grammatical characteristics? The remainder of this chapter considers this very question.

The "atoms" of sound: distinctive features

One possible approach, pioneered by Heggarty (2000), is to quantify *linguistic distance* (i.e. the degree of similarity/difference between any two language varieties: e.g. Italian and French) and the magnitude of *change over time* (i.e. linguistic difference between stages of a given language: e.g. Latin and Italian) in phonetic terms. Heggarty's starting point is an observation pertaining to words cognate with the Latin *castellum* 'castle'. As he argues, "it scarcely takes a linguist to tell that Italian *castello* /kas'tɛllo/, while indeed different from Spanish *castillo* /kas'tiʎo/, is far less different from it than is French *château* /ʃato/" (2000: 533). But how can one capture such an intuition in an objective manner? Heggarty's answer is to apply our knowledge of phonetics and cross-linguistic typology. After aligning correspondent phonemes (a methodological step that is itself more complicated than it seems; see Heggarty 2000: 544–547), one can look for phoneme differentiation. For example, by aligning the phonetic representations of Italian *castello* and French *château*, one notes that the Italian /k/ corresponds to the French /ʃ/ (as a result of the sound change in French, discussed in detail in Chapters 4 and 8), the /s/ is missing from the French but not the Italian word, and so on.

However, it quickly becomes clear that the number of different phonemes (as well as deleted or inserted phonemes), known as the Levenshtein distance, is still an inadequate measure of language distance. For instance, the English word *man* differs from *bad* by two phonemes, the same number that characterizes the difference between *man* and *bin*. However, the correspondences between /m/ and /b/ and between /n/ and /d/ are surface realizations of the same pattern: the loss of nasality (as can be easily ascertained by pronouncing the word *man* with a severe cold or by pinching one's nose shut). In contrast, the two phonemic differences between *man* and *bin* involve different patterns: the loss of nasality on the consonant and the change in vowel quality. Moreover, phonemes may not be the best units in which to measure change, as the examination of *distinctive features* offers a number of advantages. For example, the phonemic difference between *tap* and *tab* and between *tap* and *tan* amounts to one phoneme in each case. However, /p/ and /b/ share two features and differ in one: in the place of articulation both are bilabial, and in the manner of articulation both are stops, the only difference being that of voicing: /p/ is voiceless and /b/ is voiced. In contrast, /p/ and /n/ differ in three features: place of articulation (bilabial vs. dento-alveolar), manner of articulation (or nasality, depending on analysis of the oral/nasal distinction), and voicing (voiceless vs. voiced). Thus, the difference between /p/ and /n/ is significantly greater than that between /p/ and /b/; consequently, the latter correspondence is much more frequently attested, both in synchronic patterns (e.g. word-final devoicing in Russian: *grib* 'mushroom' and *grip* 'flu' are pronounced the same, [grip]) and in historical change. A change from /p/ to /n/, or vice versa, on the other hand, is virtually unattested. Assuming that all features are assigned equal weight, the "overall similarity rating" for /p/ and /b/ would be 2/3, or 67 percent. Heggarty further maintains, however, that different features should be assigned different weight; for example, on the grounds that the place of articulation and the manner of articulation "are standardly used to bear more phonemic distinctions than is [voicing], the similarity rating for [p] and [b] [...] actually emerges from the calculations not at 2/3, but nearer 4/5, or 80 per cent" (2000: 543).

The overall results of Heggarty's calculations accord well with common intuitions about language similarities as well as with the accepted phylogenetic classification of the languages that he examines. For example, Russian is more similar to other Slavic languages (with an average similarity rating based on forty cognates of 72.5, where 100 means full identity) than it is to modern Romance (37.6) or modern Germanic languages (39.3). In contrast, Norwegian is more similar to other modern Germanic languages (57) than to either modern Romance (40.8) or modern Slavic languages (39.3). In the comparison of modern Romance languages, Italian is the closest to Latin (63) and French is the most distinct (36). (Curiously, these results even confirm our impressionistic personal intuition that Portuguese bears more resemblance to Polish than to any other Slavic language.)

While these results are certainly interesting, they are not without problems. The first difficulty is evident if we compare the similarity ratings presented by Heggarty (2000: 539, 551) in the three charts; the relevant data are summarized in Table 11.1.

These data make it clear that the similarity ratings depend heavily on the cognate set employed – that is, the list of words on the basis on which the similarity is calculated. Going back to the original observation about the cognates of the Latin *castellum* 'castle', the calculations performed here

Table 11.1 *Similarity ratings based on different cognate sets*

Language pair	Cognates of Latin *castellum*	Cognates of the numerals 1–10	Forty selected cognates
Italian–French (Paris)	40	43	43
Italian–Spanish (Madrid)	90	68	72
French (Paris)–Spanish (Madrid)	43	54	48

confirm the common intuition that Italian and Spanish are more like each other – in fact, more than twice more like each other – than either is like French. However, the difference is much less conspicuous if we compare cognates of numerals from 'one' to 'ten': here the similarity between Italian and Spanish is only 1.5 times greater than that between Italian and French. Based on the first cognate set, Italian and Spanish are 90 percent similar, whereas based on the numerals they are merely 68 percent similar; based on the more expansive set of forty cognates, Italian and Spanish are 72 percent similar. These results confirm the point we stressed in Chapter 4: the choice of the data set can predetermine, or at least bias, the results. In this respect, Heggarty's approach shares many of the flaws of the Gray–Atkinson approach.

Two additional problems emerge when Heggarty's method is used to quantify change over time or the time depth of a particular extinct language (or an earlier stage of an extant language). First, to use his methods effectively one would need to know the precise pronunciation of the given words in the given extinct language. For such languages as Latin or Anglo-Saxon (Old English), pronunciation is fairly well understood, but for Proto-Indo-European (PIE), the manner in which reconstructed words were pronounced is notoriously controversial. We have no indisputable PIE pronunciation table to compare with those of its extant or intermediate descendants. The second problem is that rates of change (calculated as "retained phonetic similarity" between ancestral language and its descendant subtracted from 100 percent) vary from language pair to language pair. As can be deduced from Table 11.1, Latin changed vastly more in becoming modern French than in turning into any other Romance language. This observation is further confirmed by "retained phonetic similarity" ratings, in which Latin to French is rated at 36 percent, whereas Latin to Italian is 63 percent, Latin to Spanish or to Romanian 57 percent, and Latin to Portuguese 54 percent. Since all of these modern languages developed from Latin over the same amount of time, the resulting rates of change in different Romance branches vary from 20.2 percent (for Italian) to 39.2 percent (for French). The rate of change in the development from Anglo-Saxon to modern English, which took much less time, is comparable to the rate of change from Latin to French, 37.4 percent. Note, however, that the rate of change for English and French is nearly four times greater than that for Modern Greek emerging out of classical Greek (10.1 percent). It is distinctly possible, moreover, that some languages changed faster than French or more slowly than Greek. Thus, the average rate of change in phonetics is about as meaningful as the average temperature of patients in a hospital. Heggarty (2000: 554) admits as much: "rates of change in phonetics seem quite unable to give us a dating tool of any precision at all".

To summarize, neither phonemes themselves nor distinctive phonemic features appear to be good elements for quantifying the *linguistic distance* between languages and for deducing from such a measurement their related-ness. As a result, a different type of comparanda must be identified.

Phonological/morphological rules and typological features as the "atoms" of change

A promising alternative approach has been taken by Ringe *et al.* (2002) who compare and quantify phonological and morphological *changes* rather than phonological and morphological elements. While this approach is theoretically attractive, as it avoids most problems identified for both the Gray–Atkinson model and that of Heggarty, the approach of Ringe *et al.* suffers from another flaw: there are few if any such characters that can be applied meaningfully to the classification of Indo-European languages on all levels. Ringe and his colleagues identify twenty-two phonological characters and fifteen morpho-logical characters usable for high-order groupings within the Indo-European family. However, these phonological and morphological changes are not appropriate for identifying many lower-level subgroupings. Conversely, phonological and grammatical changes that are useful for identifying such lower-level subgroupings are not necessarily helpful for high-order groupings.

A good example of such complexities is the presence or absence of pleoph-ony, discussed in Chapters 4 and 5, in connection with the proper placement of Polish within the Slavic tree. Pleophony is useful for subgrouping Slavic languages, but has no value for the rest of the Indo-European tree. Similarly, the lenition of intervocalic consonants, which can be reflected in voicing, spirantization, or even deletion, helps identify Western Romance languages (those spoken north and west of the so-called La Spezia–Rimini Line) from those in the South Romance (or Italo-Romance) and Eastern (or Balkan) Romance groupings. Another innovation, which correlates with intervocalic voicing, is the use of -*s* to mark plurals of nouns regardless of gender or declension in Western Romance languages, rather than the change of the final vowel, as in Eastern and South Romance languages. Both of these innovations are illustrated in Table 11.2. Yet, these developments are of no use for classifying languages outside the Romance family.

Yet, selecting phonological and grammatical changes as comparanda also depends crucially on one's theoretical assumptions. As McMahon and McMahon (2008: 277) remind us,

the features used will depend on the depth of linguistic analysis, and often on the theoretical model being used, as different constructions may be recognized in different theories. Our historical knowledge of structural features is also less certain, and, for example, it is not currently clear whether some morphosyntactic characteristics might be more prone to borrowing than others, or might arise spontaneously from a number of different sources, and hence be erroneously thought to indicate relatedness.

Table 11.2 *Intervocalic lenition (voicing, spirantization, or deletion) and plural -s in Romance languages, illustrated with the singular and plural forms of the words for 'life' and 'wolf'*

Eastern Romance	Romanian	viață, vieți	lup, lupi
South Romance	Italian	vita, vite	lupo, lupi
Western Romance	Spanish	vida, vidas [ð]	lobo, lobos
	Portuguese	vida, vidas	lobo, lobos
	Catalan	vida, vides	llop, llops
	French	vie, vies	loup, loups

In fact, attempts have been made by the Gray–Atkinson team to construct phylogenetic language trees based on typological rather than lexical information. For instance, Greenhill, Atkinson, *et al.* (2010) analyzed a global dataset based on 99 languages and 138 typological features compiled in the World Atlas of Linguistic Structures (WALS; Dryer and Haspelmath 2013). The NeighborNet analysis of the data by Greenhill, Atkinson, *et al.* correctly grouped some of the languages in this database into known language families, such as Indo-European, Altaic, and Nakh-Dagestanian (Northeast Caucasian). However, other well-established families, including Sino-Tibetan, Uralic, Austronesian, and Trans-New Guinea, were not recovered. These authors also point out a substantial number of conflicting signals (represented in Neighbor-Net diagrams by box-like structures), leading to an inaccurate recovery of many well-attested phylogenetic relationships within major language families. For instance, the network links German to French rather than to English, a much more closely related language. When applied to a lexical rather than grammatical dataset, the same method recovered a much more tree-like signal, leading the authors to conclude that "the lexical data were a significantly better fit to the expected family trees than the typological data" (Greenhill, Atkinson, *et al.* 2010: 2446).

The problem, however, is not that typological features are inappropriate for phylogenetic work in general, but rather that we still lack an accurate and comprehensive list of all typological attributes that define cross-linguistic variation. As good a database as WALS (Dryer and Haspelmath 2013) is, with its catalog of over 140 typological features across 2,561 languages, many if not most of the features that it lists are epiphenomenal, questionable, or contain information duplicating that of other features. For instance, the Order of Genitive and Noun (Feature 86A) is epiphenomenal, as several unrelated types of both Genitive–Noun and Noun–Genitive constructions should be distinguished, as discussed by Longobardi (2001) and Crisma (in press). Another problem can be illustrated by the order of subject, object, and verb (Feature 81A), which is a composite of two related features: the order of subject and verb (Feature 82A) and the order of object and verb (Feature 83A). Even if only the order of subject, object, and verb is considered, the validity of this feature is dubious for at least three types of languages. First, in languages with Philippine-style topic marking, such as Tagalog and Malagasy, one of two elements may be considered the subject: the semantic subject (i.e. whoever did the action) or the grammatical subject, which is reflected on the verb in the form of topic marking morphology (Guilfoyle *et al.* 1992). Second, in many syntactically ergative languages the word order is determined not by whether a given element is a subject or an object, but by its case marking: ergative vs. absolutive. Third, in non-configurational languages, such as Walpiri, the predominant word order of subject, object, and verb cannot be determined at all. Moreover, many of the features listed in the WALS database describe superficial patterns rather than the deep design properties responsible for these patterns. For instance, the order of object and verb and the order of adposition and noun phrase (Feature 85A) may be determined by one and the same factor – the head-directionality parameter, which determines the relative ordering of the head (e.g. verb or preposition) and its complement (Travis 1984; Baker 2001b). As a result, most Verb–Object languages (92 percent) have prepositions, whereas an even greater majority of Object–Verb languages (97 percent) have postpositions.

The "atoms of language": parameters

As can be seen from the brief discussion above, identifying deep-design typological features that truly underpin cross-linguistic variation and change – called "parameters" – is a matter of hot theoretical debates. Even the number of parameters has been contested, with some scholars suggesting a figure between ten and twenty, and others claiming that the number of parameters must be "at least in the hundreds" (Longobardi and Guardiano 2009; this issue is discussed in greater detail in Baker 2001b). But even if a comprehensive list has not yet been compiled, pioneering work is ongoing to use parameters (or rather parameter values, to which we return below) as comparanda in determining phylogenetic relationships, most notably by the LanGeLin (Language and Gene Lineages) project headed by Giuseppe Longobardi at the University of York (Longobardi 2003, 2005; Guardiano and Longobardi 2005; Longobardi and Guardiano 2009; Longobardi *et al.* 2013).

Taking as their point of departure the groundbreaking work of Nichols (1992) and Dunn *et al.* (2005), who applied phylogenetic concerns and methods to "language structure", Longobardi and his team "explore the historical significance not of surface generalizations [like those found in the WALS database], but of syntactic parameters, which should encode the rich implicational relations supposedly connecting distinct observable phenomena at the level of abstract cognitive structures" (Longobardi and Guardiano 2009: 1683). Longobardi's project is couched in the Principles-and-Parameters framework, developed since the publication of Chomsky's (1981) *Lectures on Government and Binding*. According to this theory, the invariant human language faculty, or Universal Grammar (UG), predefines

a set of open choices between presumably binary values [...] closed by each language learner on the basis of his/her environmental linguistic evidence [...] grammar acquisition should reduce, for a substantial part, to parameter setting, and the core grammar of every natural language can in principle be represented by a string of binary symbols [...] each coding the value of a parameter in UG. (Longobardi and Guardiano 2009: 1684)

To illustrate how such parameters work, consider the so-called *wh-parameter*, which pertains to the placement of question-words (*who? what? where?* and the like). Its binary options are: (a) question-words must appear sentence-initially, or (b) they do not have to do so. In English, Spanish, and Russian, the former option is instantiated (the parameter is set as "yes", or "fronting"), whereas in Chinese and Japanese, the latter option is chosen (the parameter is set as "no", or "no fronting"). For example, in Japanese 'Who did John kick?' is rendered as *John-ga dare-o butta ka?* (literally, 'John who kicked?'). Crucially, the question word *dare-o* does not appear sentence-initially. (The placement of the object *dare-o* before the verb *butta*, in contrast to English, is controlled by a separate Head directionality parameter, discussed immediately below.)

The list of widely discussed parameters (see Baker 2001b) includes the *Polysynthesis parameter*, which determines whether a verb must include some expression for each event participant (subject, object, indirect object), either via agreement morphemes or via incorporation (set as "yes" in Mohawk, "no" in English); *Head directionality parameter*, which determines whether heads (verbs, adpositions, auxiliaries) precede their complements (set "yes" for English, "no" for Japanese); *Subject side parameter*, which determines whether the subject is placed sentence-initially (set "yes" for English, "no" for Malagasy); *Verb attraction parameter*, which determines whether the verb precedes certain adverbs such as *often* and its counterparts in other languages (set "yes" for Welsh, "no" for English); *Subject placement parameter*, which determines whether the subject precedes the verb (set "yes" for French, "no" for Welsh); and *Pro-drop parameter*, which determines whether the subject can be omitted if its reference is understood from context (set "yes" for Spanish, "no" for French). With only these six parameters in mind (in that order), French can be described as: "no", "yes", "yes", "yes", "yes", and "no". Because a particular value of one parameter can entail the irrelevance of another parameter, only four of the six parameters can be set for English: "no", "yes", "yes", "no", and the latter two parameters are undefined for English.

According to Longobardi and Guardiano (2009), the parametric framework represents, *mutatis mutandis*, theoretical progress in linguistics parallel to that of the rise of molecular genetics in biology. The key similarity between parameters and genetic markers is that both "form a *universal* list of *discrete* options" (2009: 1684). As such, the parametric approach is applicable to any set of languages, no matter how different, unlike the classical comparative method based on lexical cognates, which cannot apply to languages so distinct that no reliable sound correspondences can be identified. Another similarity between the parametric approach and the use of genetic markers in biology is that in both cases, like is compared with like: the value of a parameter in one language is compared to the value of exactly the same parameter in other languages. Also like many genetic polymorphisms, parameters are "virtually immune from natural selection and, in general, from environmental factors [and] largely unaffected by deliberate individual choice" (2009: 1686). Therefore, parameters and their values in individual languages can serve as ideal comparanda for a phylogenetic study.

For practical reasons, Longobardi and Guardiano (2009) limit themselves to parameters pertaining to the structure of noun phrases, examining sixty-three binary parameters as set in twenty-eight languages (twenty-three extant and five extinct languages). Twenty-two of these languages are from the Indo-European family; the non-Indo-European languages in the sample are Hebrew, Arabic, Wolof, Hungarian, Finnish, and Basque. The tree generated from the syntactic differences (see Figure 6 in the Appendix) "meets most of [the authors'] expectations" (2009: 1693). Basque, usually treated as an isolate, is the first outlier. Wolof, a West Atlantic language that has never been connected to any European or Mediterranean language, comes second. Both Basque and Wolof are clearly recognized as external to a node coinciding with the so-called Nostratic grouping (cf. Pedersen 1931, 1951; Illič-Svityč 1971/1984; Dolgopolsky 1988; Bomhard 2008, 2011).[1] The next outmost bifurcation singles out the (West) Semitic subgroup, containing Arabic and Hebrew. The Uralic (Finno-Ugric) family (Finnish and Hungarian in the sample) emerges correctly as well.

The branching within the remaining Indo-European family is overwhelmingly the expected one, although a few surprises are found. Among these unexpected patterns is the grouping of Slavic with Hindi, possibly explainable as reflecting the deep unity of *satem* languages (see Chapter 4). Since no other Indic or Indo-Iranian languages were included in the study, it is hard to

[1] In a more recent study, for which Longobardi and his colleagues used more refined parametric data, Wolof came out as the outlier, with Basque slightly more internal, a configuration that reflects the geographical distinction between African and non-African languages (Giuseppe Longobardi, personal communication).

evaluate how severe this problem is. The three Slavic languages used in the study – Russian, Serbo-Croatian, and Bulgarian – are connected into a Slavic group, and Hindi emerges as an outlier of this group. One could say, however, that the grouping of Hindi with the three Slavic languages reflects the so-called "Core IE languages", a branch of the IE family consisting of Balto-Slavic and Indo-Iranian languages (see Figure 4 in the Appendix and Ringe *et al.* 2002). A second problem concerns the extinct Germanic languages: while modern Germanic languages – Norwegian, English, and German – form one cluster within Germanic, the two extinct languages in the sample – Gothic and Old English – are shown as forming another distinct cluster. This tree fails, in other words, to reflect the connection between Old English and Modern English. Longobardi and Guardiano (2009: 1693) account for this configuration as an effect of time: "the two ancient varieties, chronologically closer to the common source, will naturally attract each other, and indirectly affect the position of German" as an outlier among the three modern Germanic languages. This seems to be more of an issue with the Bayesian phylogenetic method than with the use of grammatical rather than lexical data. An alternative explanation for the odd grouping of English and Norwegian is that it is a reflection of the Scandinavian influence on English (see Chapter 4). Another surprising placement is that of Grico, a Greek variety spoken in Italy, which is grouped with Eastern Romance (Romanian) as an outlier branch within the Romance subfamily. This mistake is likely explainable by factors of areal influence. Curiously, if only modern languages are considered (Longobardi and Guardiano 2009: 1701, their Figure 5), Grico is grouped with Greek and not with Romance languages. We have no explanation for this shift in grouping. It is hard to tell from the available data if the method indeed works better if only modern languages are considered (the only improvement being the correct treatment of Grico), but if this in fact turns out to be the case, it would be an additional advantage to Longobardi and Guardiano's method over previous computational phylogeny techniques that seem to work better if ancient languages are included as well.

Perhaps the clearest departure from the traditional family tree in this approach concerns Slavic languages: of the three languages considered, Russian and Serbo-Croatian are grouped together, with Bulgarian as the outlier among the three. The traditional classification, in contrast, places Bulgarian with Serbo-Croatian in the South Slavic grouping, whereas Russian falls into the East Slavic branch. However, the classification produced by Longobardi and Guardiano may not be all that surprising: it has long been noted that Bulgarian differs significantly from Serbo-Croatian because of influences from the Balkan *Sprachbund*. The most notable difference between Bulgarian and Serbo-Croatian is the presence of post-posed articles in Bulgarian (for Longobardi and Guardiano this characteristic of the nominal system is associated with parameter 12: the "+" value is assigned to the three languages in the sample with post-posed articles: Romanian, Bulgarian, and Norwegian). As a result of such distinctive features, some Slavic scholars (cf. Sussex and Cubberley 2006: 42) had proposed a four-way division of Slavic languages into (North-)West, (North-)East, South-West (Serbo-Croatian and Slovenian), and South-East (Bulgarian and Macedonian). Longobardi and Guardiano (2009: 1693) further note that Bulgarian and Romanian "continue to be well-behaved Slavic and Romance languages, respectively, with opposite values for parameter 45". One possible approach is "to argue that this persist-ence in 45 makes the two languages very different in other subtler surface properties, which go beyond the simplest noun-article phrases" (2009: 1693). While at this stage of analysis there is no conclusive list of parameters that may be more susceptible to areal interference, it is a promising avenue of research to look for ways "to single out genetic from areal sources of similarities" (2009: 1693). At any rate, it must be stressed that horizontal transmission (i.e. borrowing) of grammatical patterns is much less common than lexical borrowing (see Chapter 4). Grammatical borrowing requires prolonged and intense contact between linguistic groups, while lexical borrowing is much more ubiquitous. Therefore, interference effects in gram-mar are bound to be both less pervasive and more easily identifiable on geographical grounds. For example, Russian has borrowed a significant por-tion of its vocabulary from English and French, but not its grammatical patterns. Bortolussi *et al.* (2011) argue that the findings resulting from the application of the Parametric Comparison Method (PCM) are significantly beyond chance. The reliability of the PCM has been further tested in Longobardi *et al.* (2013), which applies the method – in order to verify and validate it – to the domains whose phylogeny is already known. This study consisted of "some experiments performed on a selection of 26 contemporary Indo-European varieties belonging to the Romance, Greek, Germanic, Celtic, Slavic, Indic and Iranian families" (2013: 123). Nine additional contemporary Indo-European languages have been analyzed: Sicilian, (Northern) Calabrese, Bovese Greek, Danish, Icelandic, Slovenian, Polish, Farsi, and Marathi. The PCM identified the main subfamilies of Indo-European "strikingly well" (2013: 124); importantly, horizontal transmission does not seem to limit the effectiveness of this method seriously enough to undermine the correct repre-sentation of the vertical (i.e. phylogenetic) relations. Importantly, the PCM is shown to be able "to reconstruct chronologically deep phylogenies using exclusively modern language data, often the only available data outside Eurasia" (2013: 123).

While it is clear that the Parametric Comparison Method (PCM) needs much fine-tuning and extension, the overall conclusion that has emerged from the LanGeLin project is that generative syntax, "and more generally the bio-cognitive framework of which it is a salient part [. . .] can [. . .] become a true historical science, capable of gaining insights into the actual (pre)history of human populations, no less than the successful historical-comparative enterprise of the 19th century" (Longobardi *et al.* 2013: 124). We find such conclusions largely convincing.

Conclusion: what is at stake in the Indo-European debate

Epistemological issues are central to the Indo-European controversy. How we acquire – or fail to acquire – knowledge about the world is, in turn, one of the abiding issues of philosophy. At the risk of gross simplification, most claims to knowledge are based either on reason and evidence or on deference to accepted authorities. The latter foundation is often religious in nature ("it must be true because it is in the Bible/Quran/Vedas/etc."), but can also be secular ("it must be true because Aristotle/Marx/etc. said so"). But as such authority-based beliefs are not open to question, they have little bearing on genuine intellectual debates. By the same token, mere appeals to intuition or mystical experiences carry no weight in scholarly discourse. In this realm, reason and evidence must reign supreme.

In the history of philosophy, two epistemological tendencies long vied for supremacy: rationalism, which contends that reason alone gives us solid knowledge, and empiricism, which stresses instead the acquisition of knowledge through the senses. To a significant degree, the struggle between these two approaches was amicably settled long ago, as both are obviously necessary. Reason alone can generate extraordinarily complex certainties through mathematics, but by itself tells us little about the world.[1] Purely empirical data, by the same token, can provide rich descriptions but gives us nothing in the way of explanation. In complex fields, such as linguistics, even adequate empirical descriptions require a certain amount of prior theory and reasoning. Science – and scholarship more generally – thus progresses through an intricate dance of reason and evidence, the one always working with the other.

But if this central epistemological issue was resolved long ago, "rationalism" and "empiricism" remain rooted as psychological inclinations. Some scholars seek grand theories and elegant solutions to seemingly intractable

---

[1] Unassailable truth, it is essential to recognize, is a property of mathematics, but not of science; science rests on verification, but verification is never absolute. This point was emphasized by the late mathematician Norman Levitt during work on the volume entitled *The Flight from Reason and Science* (Gross *et al.* 1997). "'Proof' is a math term," he would always say, "not a science term."

puzzles, based heavily on deduction and inference and ideally expressed through mathematics; others remain suspicious of such schemes and instead stress complexity, contingency, and uncertainty. Within linguistics, supporters of Chomsky often embrace the former approach, while many anti-Chomsky-minded scholars fall into the latter category. In the long run, this division is mostly productive, as the two approaches provide correctives for each other. But for such accommodation to work, partisans of both sides must play by the same rules. "Empiricists", for their part, need to accept the provisional truth of abstract models that are shown to correspond closely to reality. "Rationalists", in turn, must relinquish, or at least reformulate, their theories and models when they are contradicted by solid evidence.

Such "good-faith rationalism" is encapsulated by one of the more amusing quotations in intellectual history, reportedly uttered by T. H. Huxley ("Darwin's Bulldog") in reference to the social theorist Herbert Spencer: "His idea of a tragedy is a deduction killed by a fact" (Offer 1994: xx). The accumulation of facts has not been kind to Spencer's sociology, and his social Darwinism, based on the "survival of the fittest" (his coinage, not Darwin's), is now generally rejected. Yet as the quotation shows, Spencer was open to contradictory evidence and hence remained within the domain of productive scholarship, despite his harsh social views and his obsession with grand sociological schemes.

But when inconvenient facts cease to matter and when models lose all mooring to reality, rationalism becomes pathological. Unfortunately, we must conclude that the Boukaert *et al.* (2012) *Science* article, and much of the work in the same framework, exemplifies such an intellectual disorder. Here, as we have shown throughout this book, fact after fact contravenes almost everything that the model produces, yet all such facts are brushed aside as mere trivialities. Little if any effort is made to support the case on empirical grounds, and as a result the model assumes a reality of its own. Such a casual dismissal of all pertinent information, moreover, evidently extends to the editors of *Science*. Based on our own experience and that of other linguists we have spoken to, efforts to refute pseudo-linguistics articles in the journal have been rejected on the grounds that they did not address the underlying mathematics, which is evidently regarded as all that matters. As such, the endeavor becomes empirically non-falsifiable, hence non-scientific, despite the intention of its authors and despite the name of the august journal in question.

As certainty is not a feature of science, the determination to achieve it can paradoxically thwart the scientific quest for knowledge. Such a dynamic underlies the entire Gray–Atkinson approach to historical linguistics. To be sure, findings here are framed in the scientific language of probability, just as the phylogenetic diagrams employed include error bars – a number of which are disconcertingly long – that directly acknowledge uncertainty. But the language used undercuts such admissions. The abstract of the Boukaert *et al.* (2012) *Science* article, for example, trumpets its *"decisive* support for an Anatolian origin", boasting about the "critical role that phylogenetic inference can play in *resolving* debates about human prehistory" (italics ours). Thus, according to the authors, the case must be regarded as settled, regardless of any arguments leveled against their methods and regardless of the vast accumulation of knowledge patiently assembled by generations of historical linguists and archeologists. With the debate now supposedly settled against their interpretations, Indo-Europeanists might as well abandon their tools and toss away their libraries, as they are not even worthy of consideration, let alone refutation. When confronted with such an extraordinarily complex computational edifice, facts are accounted as mere noise.

As Robert Proctor and Londa Schiebinger (2008) argue in their path-breaking edited collection *Agnotology*, "ignorance" results not merely from the absence of knowledge, but is rather a phenomenon that can be actively created by interested parties. One of Proctor and Schiebinger's categories of induced ignorance is one resulting when realms of pre-existing knowledge are lost, which often occurs through concerted suppression. One perfect example of such Orwellian suppression of knowledge is found in Soviet-era historiography. Fortunately, we have not reached such a state of active repression in regard to Indo-European studies, but the potential for a gradual erosion of the field's ability to generate new knowledge is real and troubling. Academic positions in historical linguistics are diminishing as lavishly funded evolutionary biologists step into the breach and as ever more resources are diverted to computational and other supposedly cutting-edge approaches. As we must reiterate, such objections are not meant to disparage computational *linguistics* or to malign evolutionary *biology*. Our point is rather to defend the precious legacy of genuine historical linguistics and to refute the methods of biologically inspired pseudo-linguistics. To the extent that historical linguistics languishes in a brave new world of uncritical computational phylogenetic and phylogeographical analysis based on demonstrably false assumptions and impervious to falsification, ignorance of the human past will be bolstered just as the further acquisition of knowledge will be constrained.

Such warnings about the dangers of extreme rationalism to the field of historical linguistics may seem exaggerated, but we would argue that they have already been largely borne out in regard to a different discipline: geography. In the nineteenth-century world of Alexander von Humboldt, geography was a secure and highly respected field of study, one that provided a unified view of the world and of humankind's place within it. Today, geography is a relatively weak and threatened discipline over much of the world, and is completely absent in most of the leading universities in the United States. The reasons for geography's decline are varied, but a few signal developments stand out.[2] In the early twentieth century, environmental determinism gave the field seemingly scientific credentials. When the intellectual foundations of such determinism were demolished in the 1920s and 1930s, most geographers abandoned the field's global vision, retreating to a more local scale where they could focus on areal differentiation (in other words, mappable features that make one place differ from another). When the area studies movement of the post-WWII period began to reinvigorate the investigation of the world as a whole, geographers wanted almost nothing to do with it, in part because it seemed inadequately rigorous. By the 1950s and early 1960s, the quest for rigor led geography into a self-proclaimed "quantitative revolution" that promised to turn the field into a truly scientific undertaking. In actuality, it did nothing of the kind, as most of the work of the young revolutionaries was based on excessive rationalism divorced from real-world considerations.

A prime example of geography losing its way was Central Place Theory, initially developed in Germany in the 1930s and then elaborated by Anglo-American geographers as a supposed conceptual breakthrough in the 1960s. Central Place Theory maintains that the distribution of cities and towns of various sizes follows regular hexagonal patterns generated automatically by retail marketing behavior. The theory is entirely deductive, beginning with a set of assumptions and then working out their logical consequences. The assumptions, however, do not hold, and as a result the theory never worked as promised.[3] It is true that in some relatively flat areas urban patterns approximate the expected form, but in such cases imposed administrative hierarchies have played a much larger role than retail marketing. In regard to the United States, moreover, geographer James Vance (1971) showed that wholesaling was far more important than retailing in determining the location and relative standing of major cities. Vance was attacked at the time not so much for being incorrect as for challenging the new theoretical underpinnings of a discipline in the desperate thrall of "physics envy".

It is difficult to exaggerate the damage done to geography by the quantitative revolution. Cultural and historical geography were deemed trivial, as were any empirical studies that distracted attention from supposedly invariant spatial

---

[2] On the general history of geographical thought, see Livingstone (1992). On the relationship between geography and area studies, see Lewis and Wigen (1997).

[3] The Wikipedia article (http://en.wikipedia.org/wiki/Central_place_theory) on the subject nicely lays out these assumptions: "an unbounded isotropic (all flat), homogeneous, limitless surface (abstract space); an evenly distributed population; all settlements are equidistant and exist in a triangular lattice pattern; evenly distributed resources; distance decay mechanism; perfect competition and all sellers are economic people maximizing their profits; consumers are of the same income level and same shopping behavior; all consumers have a similar purchasing power and demand for goods and services; consumers visit the nearest central places that provide the function which they demand. They minimize the distance to be travelled. No provider of goods or services is able to earn excess profit (each supplier has a monopoly over a hinterland)."

laws. Exploring the complex interactions found in any given place now seemed quaint if not pathetic, a mere descriptive exercise that was insignificant when contrasted with mathematically rigorous studies. The prominent geographer Peter Gould (1979) went so far as to describe the rationalist movement as "Augean", implying that the quantifiers, like Hercules, were tasked with cleaning out the manure (knowledge, in this case) that had accumulated for centuries. For Gould and his fellow travelers, factual material was useful only for cherry picking in order to bolster favored theories and hence enhance one's own sense of intellectual superiority:

Today's and yesterday's facts are the last priority, at the bottom of the pyramid, to be dipped into once in a while to illustrate ... well, to illustrate what? Surely a body of theory and conceptual insight that may help a person reach, after suitably demanding mental sweat and discipline, a higher state of awareness and insight about human existence in the two dimensions of geographical space. (Gould 1973: 260–261)

For the same reasons, global geography – the core of the field as conceptualized since antiquity – vanished from the curriculum in most leading geography departments. Knowledge about the world was now seen as the mere cataloging of facts, failing to provide the conceptual purchase necessary for genuine understanding. Field study, especially in distant lands, was for the same reason actively discouraged by many; why go to Africa and suffer the inconveniences and indignities of travel in a poor land when the same universal spatial laws could be discovered in Iowa in the comfort of one's own lab? Armed with scientific-seeming techniques, geographers could now reach the height of their profession without knowing much of anything about the world.

Needless to say, the "laws" discovered by the quantitative revolutionaries of the early 1960s seldom proved very powerful, just as the explanations that they offered seldom had much explanatory power. As a result, the discipline turned against the movement almost as quickly as it had embraced it, a development further propelled by the social and intellectual upheavals of the late 1960s. The doyen of the quantitative revolution, David Harvey, abandoned the entire effort soon after publishing the movement's central text, *Explanation in Geography* (1969). In the early 1970s, Harvey – recently listed as the world's eighteenth most-cited author in the humanities – abruptly converted to Marxism, a transition followed by many other geographers at the time.[4] Within a decade, radical leftist social theory, of both Marxian and postmodernist flavor, had displaced quantitative positivism as the discipline's avant-garde. Despite the huge intellectual shift that this entailed, including the general rejection of mathematical methods, the insistence on high theory – and the

---

[4] The ranking is according to the *Times Literary Supplement*, "Most cited authors of books in the humanities, 2007", available online at: timeshighereducation.co.uk/405956.article

corresponding denigration of empirical study – remained entrenched. By the 1990s, celebrated works in "poststructuralist geography" reached the point of unintentional self-parody, yet according to their authors somehow remained within the confines of science. The concluding paragraph of Marcus Doel's *Poststructuralist Geographies: The Diabolical Art of Spatial Science* (1999: 198–199) perfectly encapsulates this tendency:

> The chaosmos that we call a world can be folded, unfolded, and refolded in many ways. It remains for a geographer, for an origamist-cum-spatial-scientist, to take up some folds and experiment with their rhythm and consistency, their intensity and affects. Our duty as geographers is simply to make space for the deforming force of alterity and to open up space to the differential currents of dissimulation, disjointure, and dissemination. Letting space take place. This is the ethic specific to poststructuralist geography. It is the diabolical art of a perverse, carcinogenic, and solicitous spatial science. It is the affirmation of everything that declines integration and swerves us away from stabilization. Derrida put it exquisitely: "Let us space."

In this view, facts play virtually no role, and a self-satisfied sense of intellectual preeminence is joined by one of moral superiority. Throughout this period of destabilizing swerves, unsurprisingly, geography departments continued to be shuttered by budget-conscious university administrations. Although excellent scholarship continues to be produced in departments of geography across the world, the discipline has become a thin shadow of its rightful self.

The decline of academic geography is more than a cautionary tale, as it also has direct bearing on the issues at hand. "Mapping the Origins and Expansion of the Indo-European Language Family" of Boukaert *et al.* is, after all, an explicitly geographical contribution, purporting to undermine the Steppe hypothesis of Indo-European origins in part through geographical modeling and cartographic explication. Yet the article itself completely ignores pertinent geographical scholarship, while geographical scholars have in turn ignored it. That such an anti-empirical work of geographical fantasy would be accepted for publication by one of the world's leading journals and then actively celebrated by the global media says a lot about the intellectual void that exists where geography should rightly be situated.

A genuine renaissance of geographical scholarship would go a long way to rectifying the intellectual imbalances analyzed in this book. As we have emphasized, examining the origins and spread of the Indo-European language family, or of any other linguistic grouping, is by necessity an interdisciplinary matter. Although historical linguists and archeologists rightly occupy center stage, geographers as well as historians, cultural anthropologists, and members of many other disciplines have crucial roles to play as well.

Geneticists in particular are able to shed light on a number of heretofore shadowy recesses of the distant past. Most linguists remain skeptical of genetic inquiry, noting correctly that the spread of language and the spread of genes often have nothing to do with each other. But genetic research does illuminate past processes of human movement and population admixture, processes that have powerful if often indirect bearing on language spread and differentiation. The techniques of evolutionary biology thus have some promise for the investigation of language history, provided that they are used to examine the biological aspects of human history and are not inappropriately employed for the study of purely linguistic phenomena.

For such promises to be fulfilled, collaborative, multidisciplinary efforts will continue to be necessary. Given the mutual distrust of geneticists and historically oriented scholars, however, such collaboration will prove challenging. As Nicholas Wade reported in the *New York Times* in February 2014, some historical geneticists refuse even to acknowledge the historians' craft: "In some sense we don't want to talk to historians [...] There's a great virtue in being objective: You put the data in and get the history out. We do think this is a way of reconstructing history by just using DNA".[5] Such an arrogant and blinkered way of "reconstructing history", however, can provide information only on a very narrow slice of the human past.

But for all of its potential, even a thoroughly collaborative, multidisciplinary approach to deep language history will not answer all questions and resolve all mysteries. Too much information has been irretrievably lost to allow such omniscience. As a result, we are nonplussed when we are asked to provide a definitive answer to the quandary of Indo-European origins, as we occasionally are. It is not enough merely to criticize the works of others, we are often told, and as a result we have been urged to advance our own theory. In actuality, something of a surfeit of such theories already exists, and we see no need to devise a new one unless, and until, the discovery of new evidence demands such reconsideration. Currently, we think that the "Revised Steppe school" provides the best explanations, those that accord most fully with the existing body of evidence, and we see no reason to try to supplant it or even to adjust it in any significant manner. But at the same time, we doubt that it provides the last word on this historically freighted subject, and we welcome all alternative theories and explanations, so long as they make good-faith efforts to argue on the basis of actual evidence and reject demonstrably false assumptions. As a result, we do not view the debate as having been "resolved", and we doubt that it ever will be. But such ultimate uncertainty only makes the issue of Indo-European origins all the more compelling. At some point, the wise course, in the words of singer–song writer Iris DeMent, is simply to "let the mystery be".

5 See Nicholas Wade, "Tracing Ancestry, Researchers Produce a Genetic Atlas of Human Mixing Events", *New York Times*, February 13, 2014. Available online at: http://www.nytimes.com/2014/02/14/science/tracing-ancestry-team-produces-genetic-atlas-of-human-mixing-events.html

Appendix

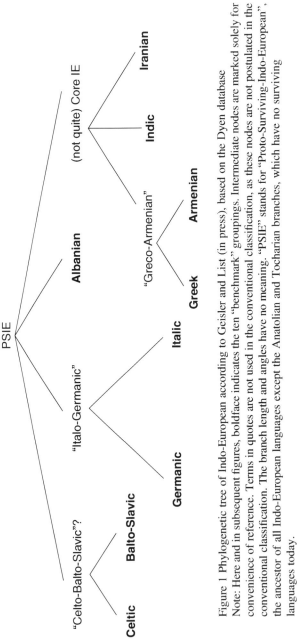

Figure 1 Phylogenetic tree of Indo-European according to Geisler and List (in press), based on the Dyen database
Note: Here and in subsequent figures, boldface indicates the ten "benchmark" groupings. Intermediate nodes are marked solely for convenience of reference. Terms in quotes are not used in the conventional classification, as these nodes are not postulated in the conventional classification. The branch length and angles have no meaning. "PSIE" stands for "Proto-Surviving-Indo-European", the ancestor of all Indo-European languages except the Anatolian and Tocharian branches, which have no surviving languages today.

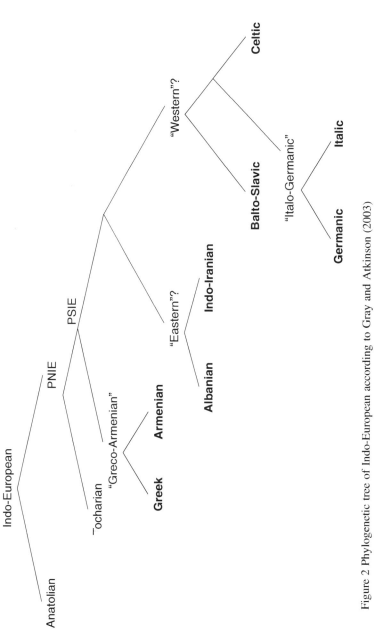

Figure 2 Phylogenetic tree of Indo-European according to Gray and Atkinson (2003)
Note: "PNIE" stands for "Proto-Nuclear-Indo-European", the ancestor of all Indo-European languages except the Anatolian branch.

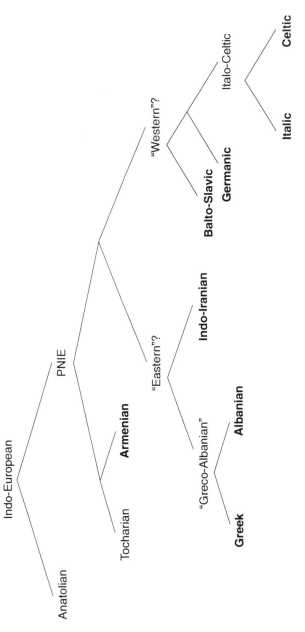

Figure 3 Phylogenetic tree of Indo-European according to Bouckaert *et al.* (2012)

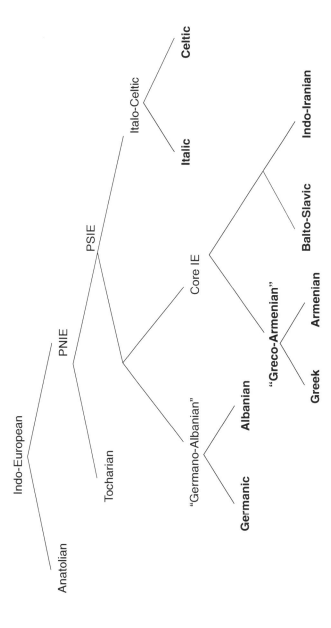

Figure 4 Phylogenetic tree of Indo-European according to Ringe *et al.* (2002)

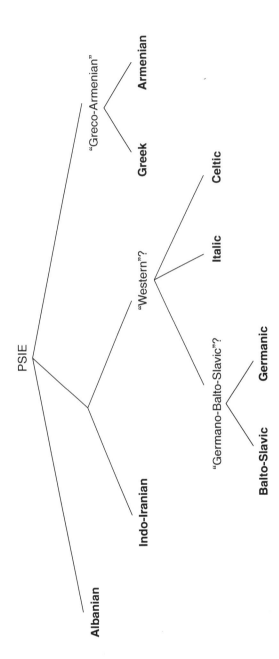

Figure 5 Phylogenetic tree of Indo-European according to Geisler and List (in press), based on the Tower of Babel database

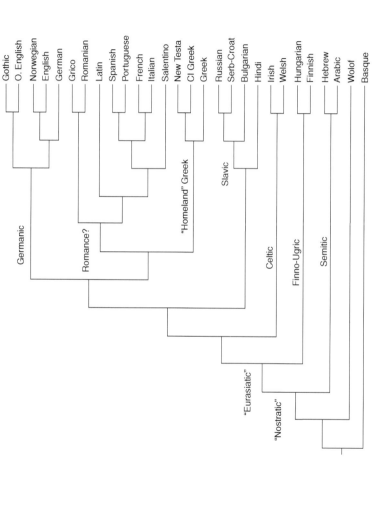

Figure 6 Phylogenetic tree of twenty-eight languages, adapted from Longobardi and Guardiano (2009)

Map 1 Approximate distribution of Indo-European languages circa 1950. The map indicates areas in which a majority of people spoke an Indo-European language as their mother tongue in the middle of the twentieth century. In such lightly populated areas as northern North America, northern and central Australia, northern Siberia, and central South America, Indo-European languages (English, Russian, Spanish, and Portuguese) were spreading rapidly at the time.

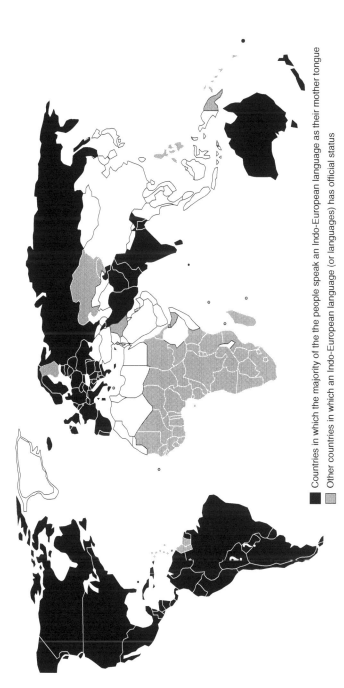

Map 2 The political status of modern Indo-European languages. In countries shown in black, the majority of the people speak an Indo-European language (or languages) as their mother tongue

□ Other countries in which an Indo-European language (or languages) has official status

Map 2 The political status of modern Indo-European languages. In countries shown in black, the majority of the population speak an Indo-European language (or languages) as their mother tongue. Some sources indicate that Bolivia and Paraguay (marked with question marks) should not be in this category, as roughly half of their people speak non-Indo-European indigenous languages as mother tongues. Fiji is also a questionable case, but the combination of native Fijians who speak English as their first language and Indo-Fijians who speak north Indian languages probably puts it in this category. The light gray countries use one or more Indo-European tongues as official languages, even though most of their people speak non-Indo-European languages at home.

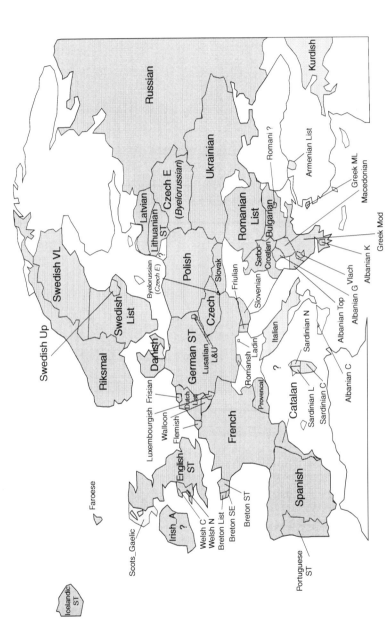

Map 3 Modern Indo-European languages of Europe, according to Bouckaert *et al.* (2012). This map is derived from the input map of modern and ancient Indo-European languages found in the Supplementary Materials of Bouckaert *et al.* (2012). The names of the languages are taken directly from Bouckaert *et al.* (2012). Some language boundaries had to be estimated, as they were obscured on the original map by language labels or by the mapping of ancient languages. Prominent examples of such obscured areas include the Kaliningrad exclave of Russia, Corsica, Ireland, and the supposed Romani-speaking area located in Bulgaria (all these examples are marked on the map with question marks). The original map also contains an obvious error, the mislabeling of "Byelorussian" as "Czech E" and vice versa. The correct labels in these cases are supplied in parentheses.

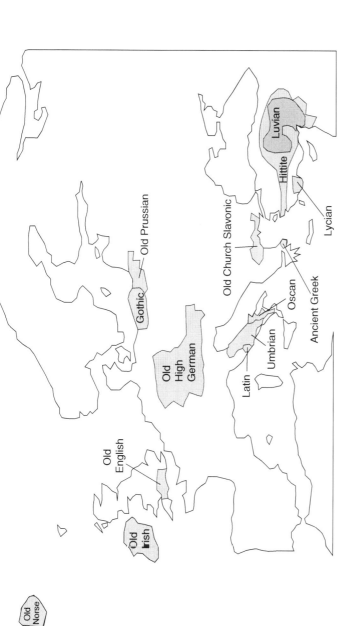

Map 4 "Ancient' Indo-European languages of Europe, according to Bouckaert *et al.* (2012). This map is derived from the input map of modern and ancient Indo-European languages found in the Supplementary Materials of Bouckaert *et al.* The names of the languages are taken directly from Bouckaert *et al.* (2012). Some language boundaries had to be estimated, as they were obscured on the original by language labels or by the mapping of modern languages. The term "ancient" is placed in quotation marks because it is not appropriate in all circumstances, yet was nonetheless used by the authors in the original. (As employed by historians of Europe and the Mediterranean, the term "ancient" conventionally refers to the period before the fall of the Western Roman Empire in the fifth century CE. Such languages as Old English, Old Norse, and Old Church Slavonic are therefore not "ancient" by such criteria. The appropriate term would therefore rather be "extinct languages". Note, however, that Bouckaert *et al.* classify Cornish as a modern language, even though its last native speaker died in the 1700s.)

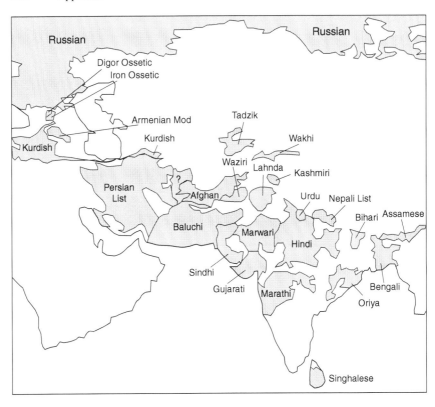

Map 5 Modern Indo-European languages of Asia, according to Bouckaert *et al.* (2012). This map is derived from the input map of modern and ancient Indo-European languages found in the Supplementary Materials of Bouckaert *et al.* The names of the languages are taken directly from Bouckaert *et al.* (2012); a number of them contravene conventional usage (such as "Afghan" instead of "Pashto"). Some language boundaries had to be estimated, as they were obscured on the original either by language labels or by the mapping of ancient languages. Along the border of eastern Iran, Bouckaert *et al.* have apparently indicated a separate language that they do not label; this area is marked on this map with a question mark.

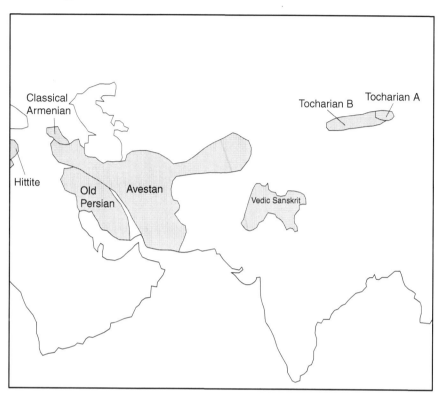

Map 6 Ancient Indo-European languages of Asia, according to Bouckaert
et al. (2012). This map is derived from the input map of modern and ancient
Indo-European languages found in the Supplementary Materials of Bouckaert
et al. The names of the languages are taken directly from Bouckaert *et al.*
(2012).

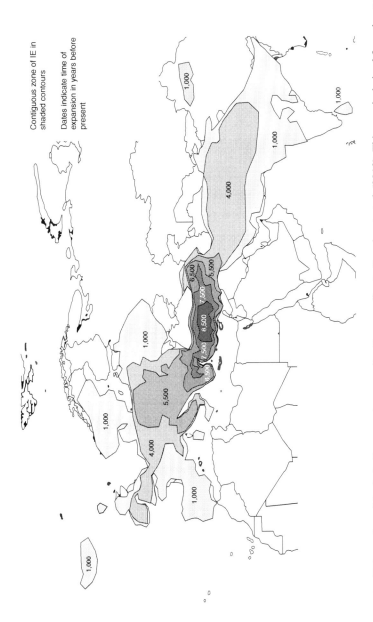

Contiguous zone of IE in
shaded contours

Dates indicate time of
expansion in years before
present

Map 7 Expansion of the Indo-European language family, according to Bouckaert *et al.* (2012). This map is derived from the static map of Indo-European languages expansion found in the Supplementary Materials of Bouckaert *et al.* As the original map is composed of colored splotches with no clear boundaries, a certain amount of approximation was necessary in order to convert it to a gray-scale map.

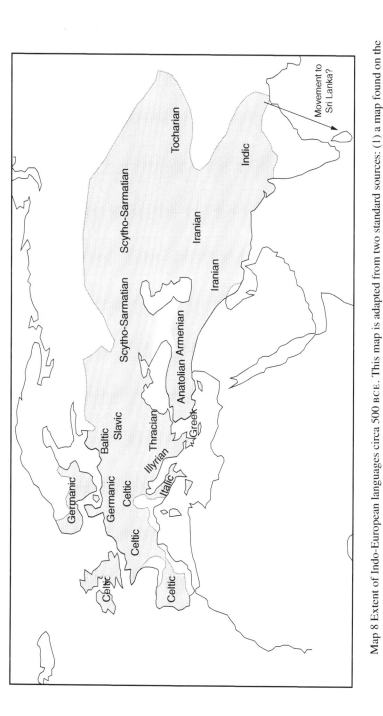

Map 8 Extent of Indo-European languages circa 500 BCE. This map is adapted from two standard sources: (1) a map found on the website *Indo-European Linguistics: A Grammar of Modern Indo-European, Dictionary and Etymology* (http://indo-european. info/indoeuropean/early-proto-indo-european-dialects-evolution/) entitled "Evolution 500 BC", and (2) a Wikipedia map entitled "Indo-European languages ca. 500 BC" (http://en.wikipedia.org/wiki/File:IE2500BP.png). An arrow was added that points to Sri Lanka, as legends claim that the first (pre)Sinhalese people arrived at the island in 543 BCE, and as many scholars think that the spread of the Indo-European language family to the island did occur in this general period. Map 8 is designed to be compared with the Map 9.

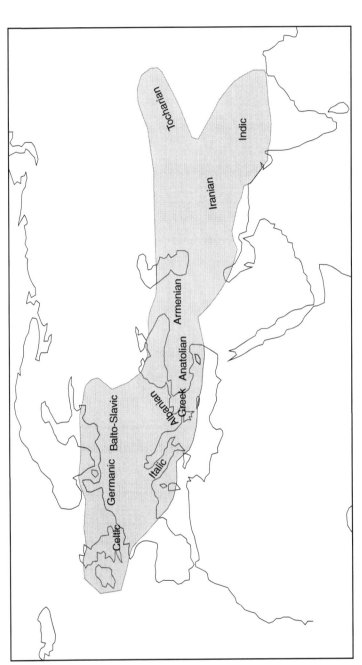

Map 9 Extent of Indo-European languages circa 500 BCE, according to Bouckaert *et al.* (2012). This map is adapted from the 500 BCE map frame from the animated map ("movie") found in the Supplementary Materials of Bouckaert *et al.* Some of the patterns found on this map fit relatively well with those found on Map 8, but the exceptions are notable: (1) Bouckaert *et al.* do not show Indo-European languages in the steppe zone at this time; (2) the authors do not show Indo-European languages in Sicily or in central and western Iberia; (3) the authors do show Indo-European languages in northwestern Italy, Sardinia, and environs; and (4) the authors do show Indo-European languages throughout the Caucasus Mountains.

Maps 10–20 are derived from frames extracted from the animated map ("movie") found in the Supplementary Materials of Bouckaert *et al.* (2012). The shaded areas show the region mapped as covered by Indo-European languages no later than the date indicated, within 95 percent probability parameters. The lines indicate the differentiation and spread of specific Indo-European subfamilies, and, eventually, individual languages. As these lines are not labeled in the original, the labels provided here were inferred. Some of the labels use language terms found in Bouckaert *et al.* ("Afghan", "Tadzik"), whereas in others more conventional labels are used ("Insular North Germanic"). Some of these labels are anachronistic, as the prefix "pre" or "proto" should be appended; these were left out in the interest of design clarity. Labels appear on the specific map that first indicates the emergence of a new branch or individual language, and are then dropped from subsequent maps. Not all minor branches and individual languages are labeled, as some are too difficult to determine, often because the lines that indicate them are covered by other lines or are more indistinguishably crowded into small areas. Note, for example, that only one line is provided for Brythonic Celtic, although the authors eventually split this branch into six separate languages (two Welsh languages, Cornish, and three Breton Languages). In Map 18, the designations "Armenian Mod" and "Armenian List" are taken directly from Bouckaert *et al.* and presumably refer to modern Armenian dialects. The same applies to "Swedish VL" and "Swedish Up" in Map 20. Finally, we were mystified by a few features on the animated map, such as the Iranian line that begins to separate from the main stem around 1500 CE and then terminates in the Caspian Sea circa 1974 CE.

Note that Map 10 also shows a smaller area of "inferred geographic origin of the Indo-European language family" derived from Figure S5 in the Supplementary Materials of Bouckaert *et al.* (2012).

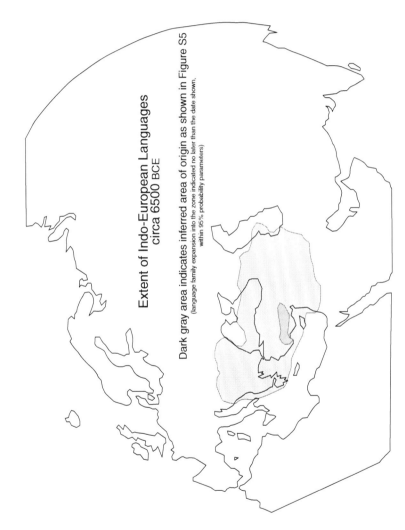

Extent of Indo-European Languages
circa 6500 BCE

Dark gray area indicates inferred area of origin as shown in Figure S5
(language family expansion into the zone indicated no later than the date shown,
within 95% probability parameters)

Map 10

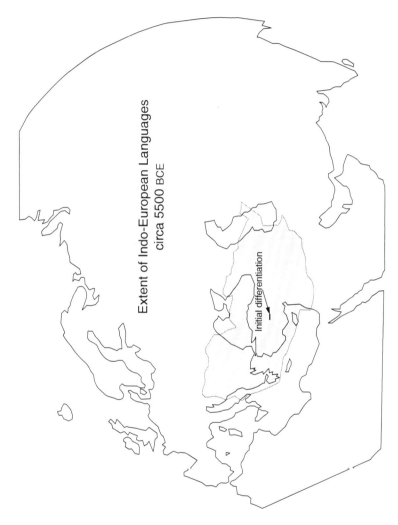

Extent of Indo-European Languages
circa 5500 BCE

Initial differentiation

Map 11

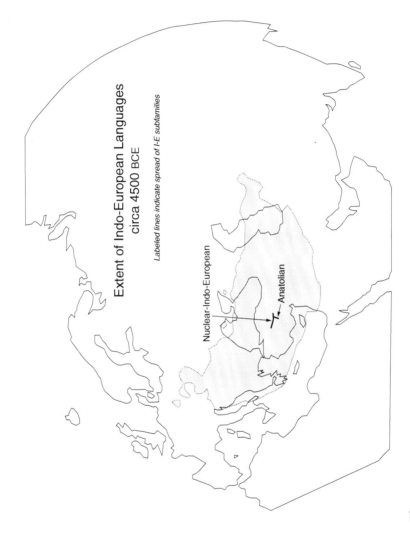

Extent of Indo-European Languages
circa 4500 BCE

Labeled lines indicate spread of I-E subfamilies

Nuclear-Indo-European

Anatolian

Map 12

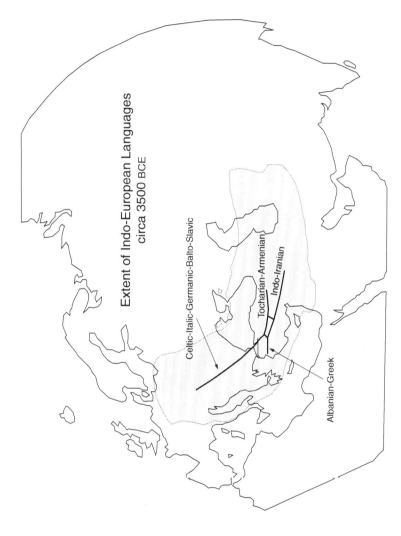

Extent of Indo-European Languages
circa 3500 BCE

Celtic-Italic-Germanic-Balto-Slavic

Tocharian-Armenian

Indo-Iranian

Albanian-Greek

Map 13

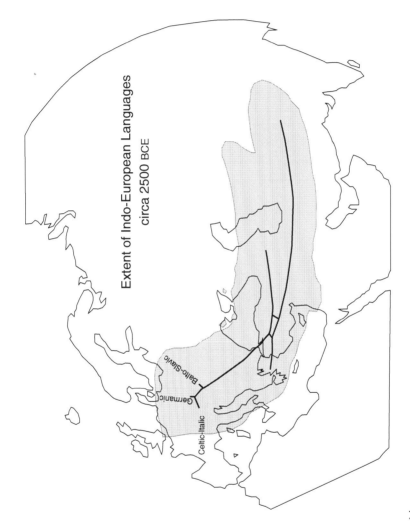

Extent of Indo-European Languages
circa 2500 BCE

Celtic-Italic

Germanic

Balto-Slavic

Map 14

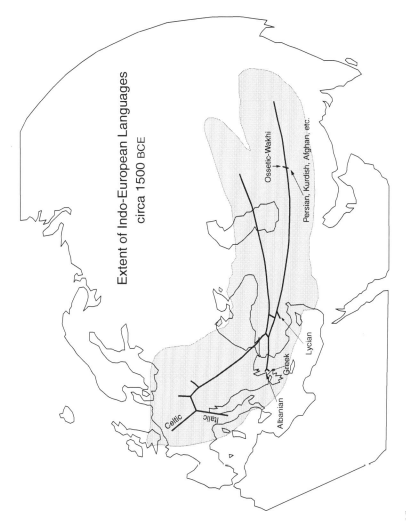

Extent of Indo-European Languages
circa 1500 BCE

Celtic

Italic

Albanian

Greek

Lycian

Ossetic-Wakhi

Persian, Kurdish, Afghan, etc.

Map 15

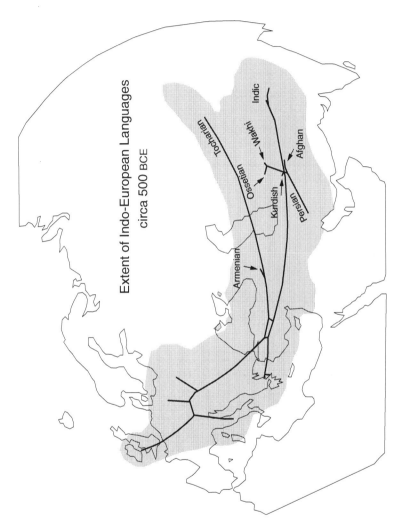

Extent of Indo-European Languages
circa 500 BCE

Tocharian
Wakhi
Indic
Ossetian
Afghan
Kurdish
Persian
Armenian

Map 16

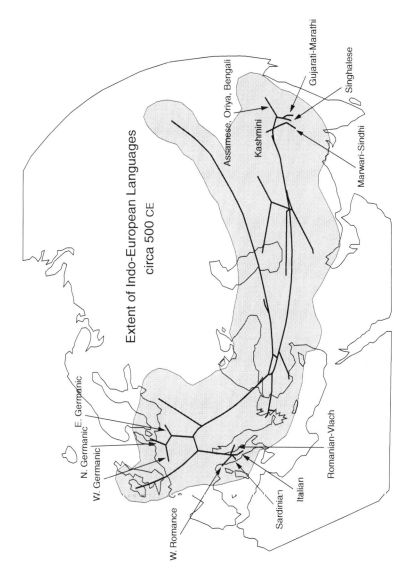

Extent of Indo-European Languages
circa 500 CE

N. Germanic
E. Germanic
W. Germanic

W. Romance

Sardinian

Italian

Romanian-Vlach

Marwari-Sindhi

Singhalese

Gujarati-Marathi

Kashmini

Assamese, Oriya, Bengali

Map 17

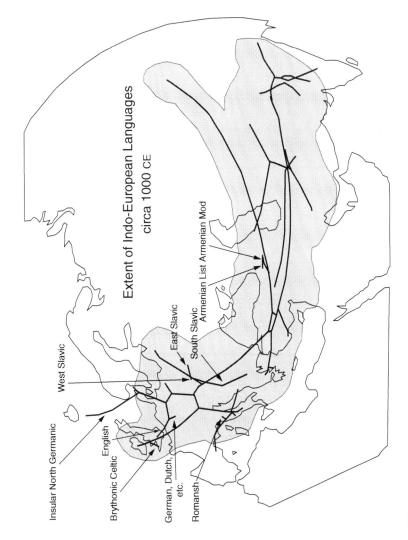

Extent of Indo-European Languages
circa 1000 CE

Insular North Germanic

West Slavic

English

Brythonic Celtic

German, Dutch, etc.

Romansh

East Slavic

South Slavic

Armenian List Armenian Mod

Map 18

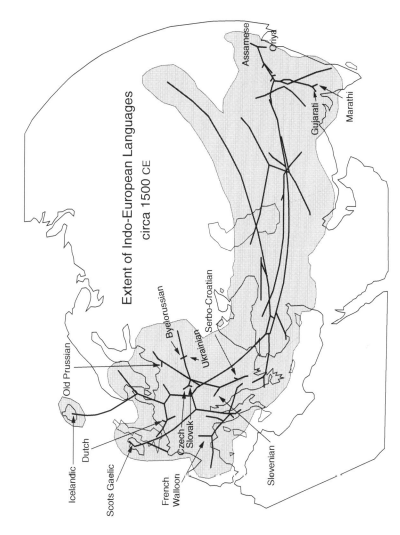

Extent of Indo-European Languages
circa 1500 CE

Icelandic

Old Prussian

Dutch

Scots Gaelic

French
Walloon

Czech
Slovak

Byelorussian

Ukrainian

Serbo-Croatian

Slovenian

Assamese

Oriya

Gujarati

Marathi

Map 19

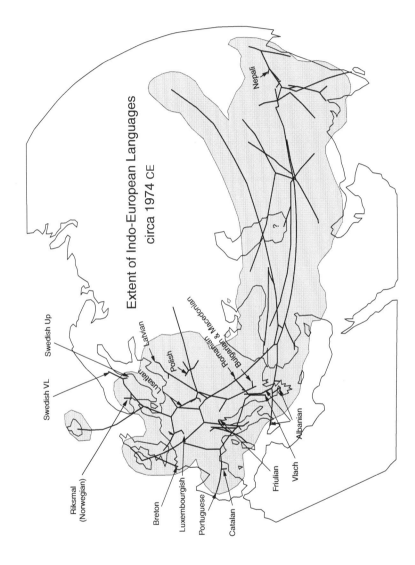

Extent of Indo-European Languages
circa 1974 CE

Swedish Up

Swedish VL

Riksmal
(Norwegian)

Breton

Luxembourgish

Portuguese

Catalan

Latvian

Polish

Lusatian

Romanian & Macedonian

Bulgarian & Macedonian

Friulian

Vlach

Albanian

Nepali

Map 20

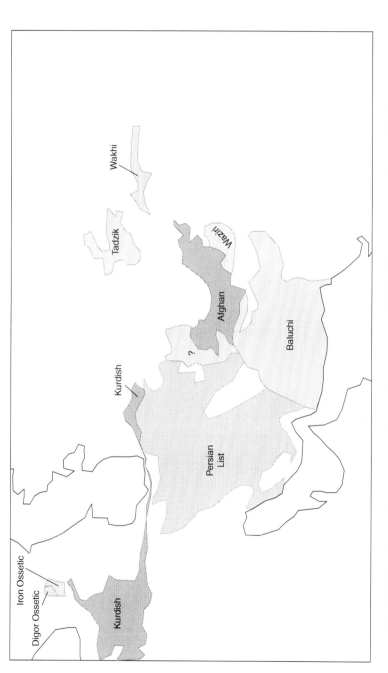

Map 21 Modern Iranian languages, according to Bouckaert *et al.* (2012). This map, together with the following one, allow a comparison of the manner in which modern Iranian languages are mapped in Bouckaert *et al.* (Map 22) and in standard linguistic cartography (Map 23). Note that the mapping and labeling system employed here is idiosyncratic. The most extreme divergence from the norm is its omission of Dari, the Persian dialect of northern Afghanistan. Most sources view Farsi ("Persian List" here), Dari, and Tajik ("Tadzik" here) as regional variants of a single Persian language.

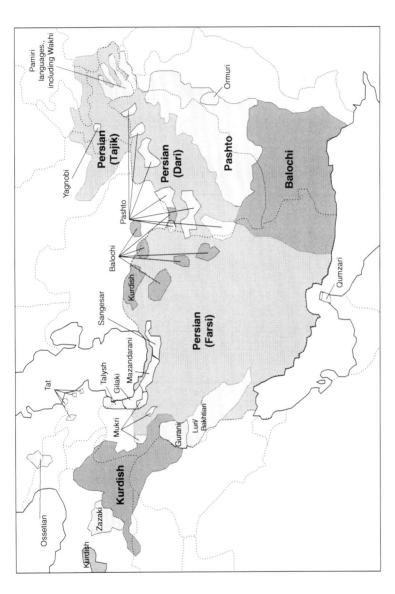

Map 22 Simplified map of Iranian languages. This map, which shows the conventional view of modern Iranian languages, was derived from a combination of a map found at *Thesaurus Indogermanischer Text und Sprachmaterialien* and a similar Wikipedia map. Both of these source maps present simplified depictions that exclude a number of small language groups. (See: http://upload. wikimedia.org/wikipedia/commons/thumb/4/4b/Iranian_tongues.svg/800px-Iranian_tongues.svg.png) and http://titus.fkidg1.uni-frankfurt.de/didact/karteng/iran/irann.htm)

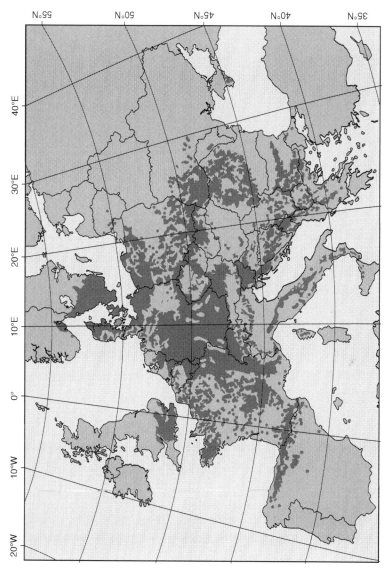

Map 23 Distribution map of beech (*Fagus sylvatica*). EUFORGEN 2009, www.euforgen.org (Published with permission.)

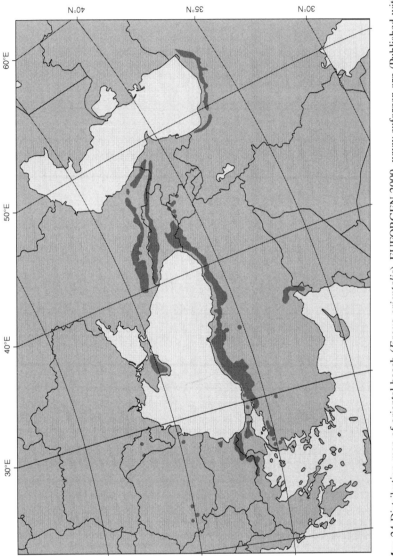

Map 24 Distribution map of oriental beech (*Fagus orientalis*). EUFORGEN 2009, www.euforgen.org (Published with permission.)

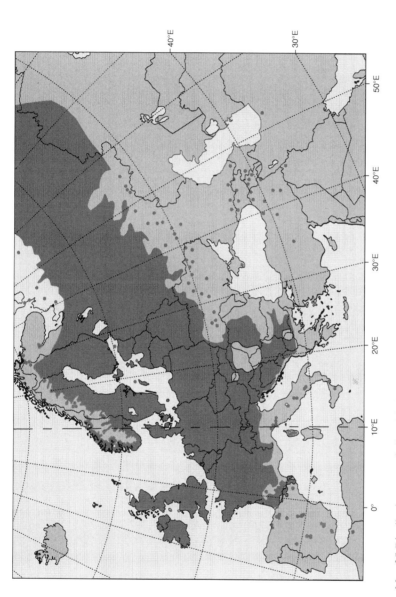

Map 25 Distribution map of silver birch (*Betula pendula*). EUFORGEN 2009, www.euforgen.org (Published with permission.)

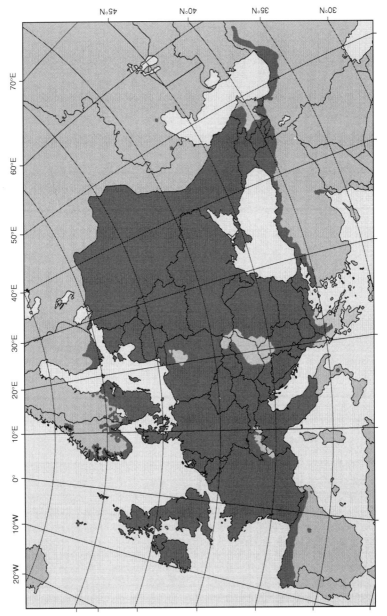

Map 26 Distribution map of common ash (*Fraxinus excelsion*). EUFORGEN 2009, www.euforgen.org (Published with permission.)

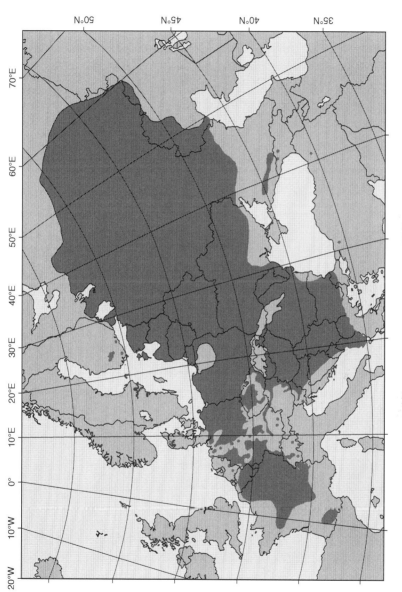

Map 27 Distribution map of European white elm (*Ulmus leavis*). EUFORGEN 2009, www.euforgen.org (Published with permission.)

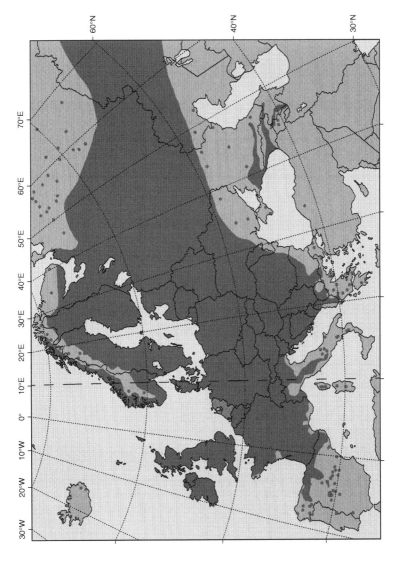

Map 28 Distribution map of aspen (*Populus tremula*). EUFORGEN 2009, www.euforgen.org (Published with permission.)

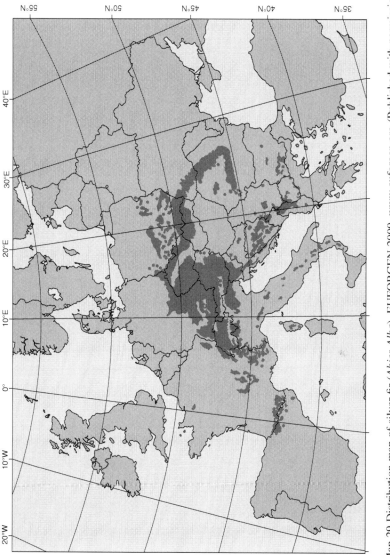

Map 29 Distribution map of silver fir (*Abies Alba*). EUFORGEN 2009, www.euforgen.org (Published with permission.)

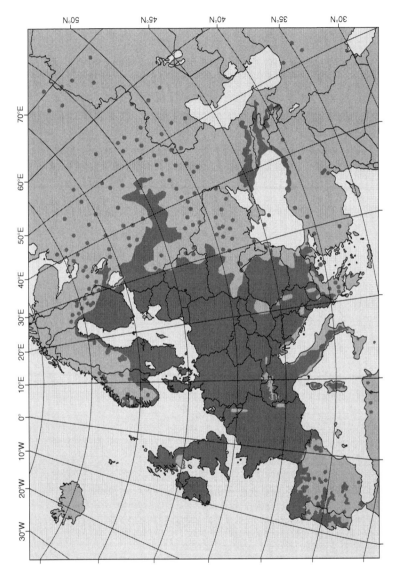

Map 30 Distribution map of black alder (*Alnus glutinosa*). EUFORGEN 2009, www.euforgen.org (Published with permission.)

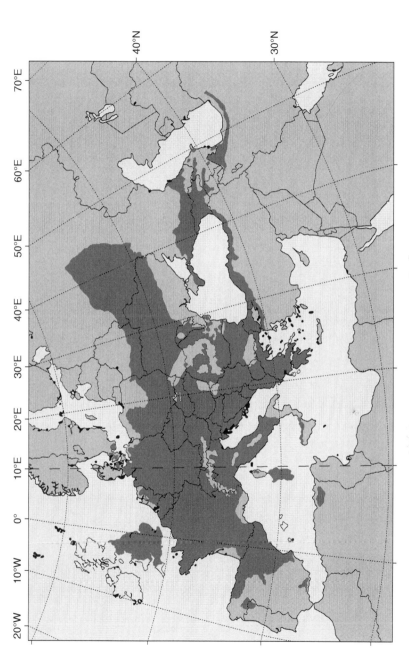

Map 31 Distribution map of field maple (*Acer campestre*). EUFORGEN 2009, www.euforgen.org (Published with permission.)

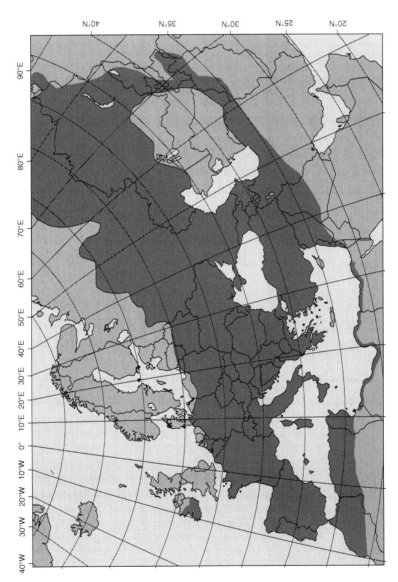

Map 32 Distribution map of black poplar (*Populus nigra*). EUFORGEN 2009, www.euforgen.org (Published with permission.)

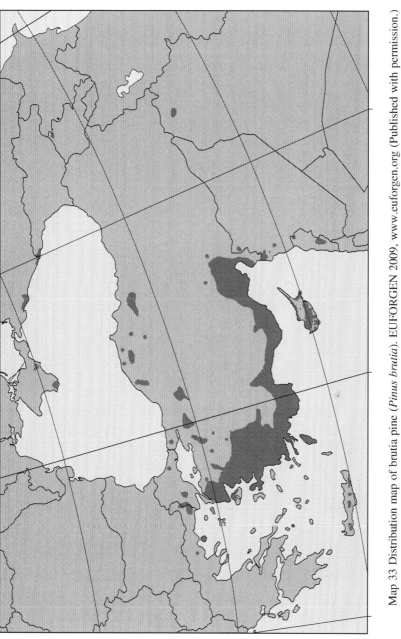

Map 33 Distribution map of brutia pine (*Pinus brutia*). EUFORGEN 2009, www.euforgen.org (Published with permission.)

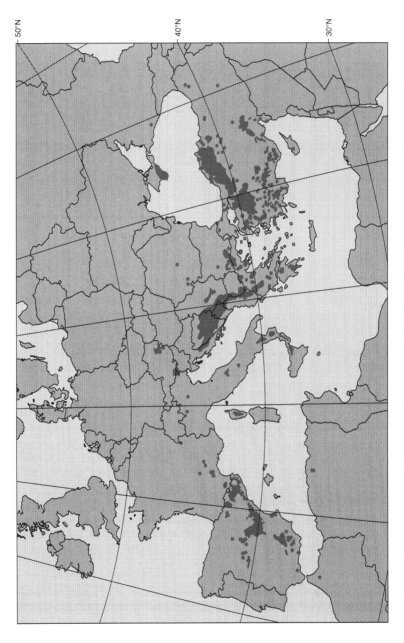

Map 34 Distribution map of black pine (*Pinus nigra*). EUFORGEN 2009, www.euforgen.org (Published with permission.)

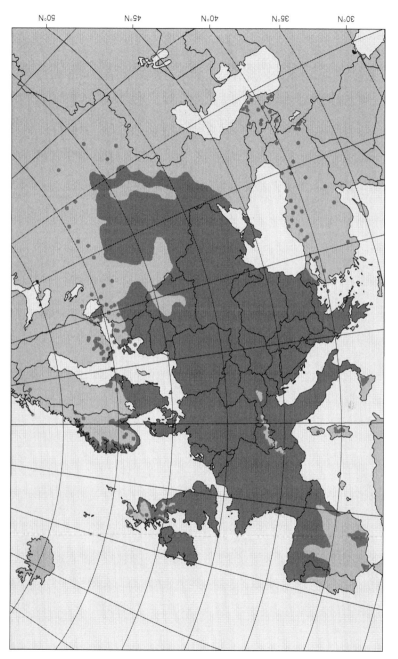

Map 35 Distribution map of wild apple (*Malus sylvestris*). EUFORGEN 2009, www.euforgen.org (Published with permission.)

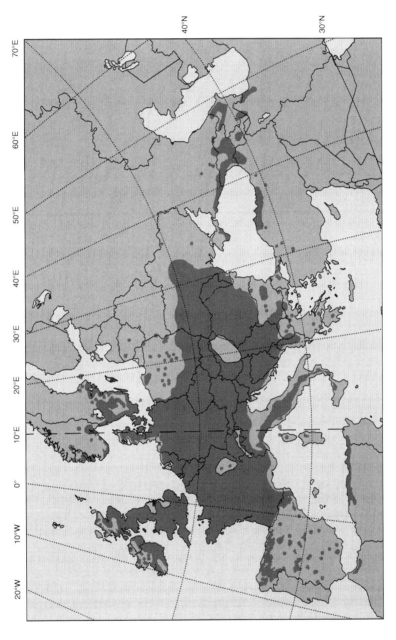

Map 36 Distribution map of wild cherry (*Prunus avium*). EUFORGEN 2009, www.euforgen.org (Published with permission.)

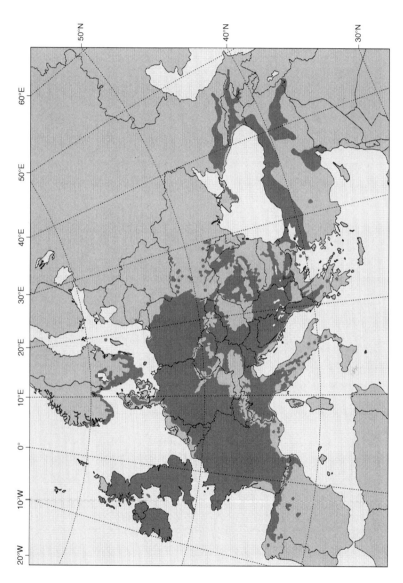

Map 37 Distribution map of sessile oak (*Quercus petraea*). EUFORGEN 2009, www.euforgen.org (Published with permission.)

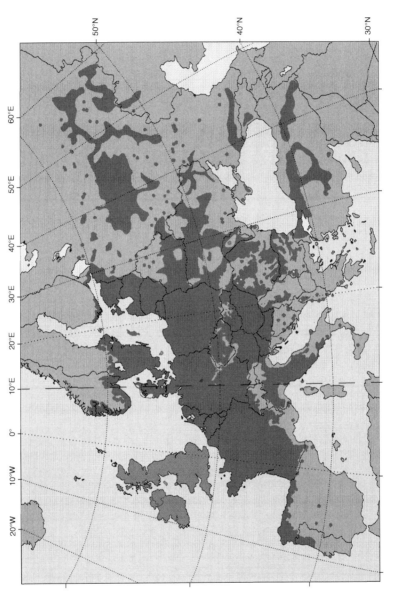

Map 38 Distribution map of pedunculate oak (*Quercus robur*). EUFORGEN 2009, www.euforgen.org (Published with permission.)

Glossary

accusative case case typically assigned to the grammatical object of a transitive verb.

adstratum influence the mutual influence of two equally dominant languages on each other (e.g. the influence of English and French on each other in Montreal).

affricate a single consonant sound that consists of a complete closure (stop) followed by a slow release (fricative); for example, the first and last sounds of *church* and *judge*.

agglutinative language a language in which words typically contain several morphemes attaching to the root, each of which typically encodes a single grammatical contrast. There is little or no interaction between morphemes in an agglutinative language.

alveolar consonant a consonant produced with a constriction or blockage between the tip of the tongue and the alveolar ridge; for example, the first sounds of *tip*, *sip*, *nip*, *lip*.

alveolar ridge the bone protrusion located just behind the upper teeth.

bilingual a person or community with a mastery of two languages.

borrowing a source of language change that involves adopting aspects of one language into another.

case a set of affixes or word forms that is used to distinguish the different roles of the participants in some event or state, or different grammatical functions (e.g. subject, object, indirect object, and the objects of various kinds of prepositions). In English, only pronouns have case forms: *he* vs. *him* vs. *his*.

cognates words of (usually different) languages that have descended from a common source, as shown by systematic sound correspondences (e.g. English *father* and French *père*)

comparative reconstruction the reconstruction of properties of a parent language through comparison of its descendant languages.

complement a phrase that appears together with a verb, a preposition or a noun, completing its meaning: *He ate the pizza. He is under the tree. He is a scholar of languages*.

conservative language a language whose forms have stayed relatively close to those of the proto-language.

consonant a sound produced by a partial or total obstruction somewhere in the vocal tract.

creole a language that originated as a pidgin and has become established as a first language in a speech community. A creole typically has a more expanded vocabulary and a more complex grammatical structure than a pidgin.

dative case the case typically assigned to indirect objects.

devoicing a change in which a voiced sound becomes voiceless. Devoicing typically occurs with sounds that are adjacent to voiceless sounds or word-finally.

dialect one of several distinguishable varieties of a language that has a unique vocabulary, sound system, and grammar. Dialects of a single language are generally (but not always; cf. dialect continuum) mutually intelligible.

dialect continuum a phenomenon whereby a range of dialects is spoken across some geographical area, with the dialects of neighboring areas differing from each other only slightly, and the dialects from the opposite ends of the continuum being much less similar to each other and possibly not mutually intelligible at all.

diglossia a situation in which two dialects or languages are used by a single language community.

distinctive feature a feature that is able to signal a difference in meaning. For example, voicing signals the difference in meaning between *pin* and *bin*.

ejective consonant a consonant pronounced with a simultaneous closure of the glottis.

ergative-absolutive language a language that marks both the direct object of a transitive verb and the subject of an intransitive verb with the same case (absolutive), while the subject of a transitive verb is marked with a different case (ergative).

fortition a change in which a speech sound becomes "stronger": for example, the change from a fricative to a stop.

fricative consonant a consonant produced with the airflow channeled through a narrow opening in the vocal tract, producing turbulence; for example, the first sounds of *fill* and *sill*.

fusional (or synthetic) language a language in which morphemes have more than one meaning fused into a single affix. For example, in Russian the same morpheme at the end of a noun encodes number, case, and declension class of the noun.

genetically related languages languages that have descended from a common ancestral language (e.g. English and Russian both descended from a common proto-language, Proto-Indo-European).

glottal stop the sound made by closing the vocal cords, stopping the airflow at the larynx.

glottis the space between the two vocal cords.

grammar the mental system of rules and categories that allows humans to form and interpret the words and sentences of their language.

grammatical gender a set of mutually exclusive kinds into which a language categorizes its nouns and pronouns. Typically, the genders of pronouns correspond to the sexes (*he* vs. *she*), and the genders of nouns are determined by their sounds (words ending in *a* are one gender, words ending in *o* are another gender, etc.) or are simply put into two or three arbitrary lists.

grammatical object the constituent of the sentence that denotes the thing that is created, moved, or otherwise affected by the action of the verb. For example, in the sentence *John kicked **the ball**, the ball* is the object.

grammatical subject has certain special properties; for example, in English the grammatical subject controls the form of the tensed verb (in the present tense): ***I** play* vs. ***He** plays*. In some other languages, only the grammatical subject may control reflexives or only the grammatical subject may be questioned.

grammaticalization a process by which nouns and verbs become grammatical markers, such as affixes, prepositions, etc.

Great Vowel Shift a set of regular sound changes affecting the long vowels of English that took place in the fourteenth and fifteenth centuries. These changes account for many of the discrepancies between the pronunciation and the spelling of English words since the spelling was established before the pronunciation changes took place.

Grimm's Law the consonant shifts that took place between Proto-Indo-European and Proto-Germanic; named after Jacob Grimm, who provided the first systematic description.

head (of a phrase) the single word in a phrase that determines the meaning and properties of the whole phrase, such as a verb in a verb phrase, a noun in a noun phrase, a preposition in a prepositional phrase: ***eat** the tomatoes, the **president** of the club, **under** the chair*.

internal reconstruction the reconstruction of a proto-language that relies on the analysis of forms within a single language.

intransitive verb a verb that does not take a direct object: *He left. He lives in Paris.*

isogloss a geographical boundary of a certain linguistic feature, such as a pronunciation of a sound, a certain lexical choice or the use of some syntactic feature.

isolate an "orphan" language with no (living) relatives; such a language belongs to a language family of its own (e.g. Basque).

isolating language a language in which grammatical concepts like tense, number or grammatical relations (e.g. subject, object, indirect object) are expressed primarily by word order and the use of free-standing words rather than by inflectional morphemes attached to words.

labial consonant a consonant produced by bringing together or closing of the lips.

language contact a source of language change that involves the speakers of one language frequently interacting with the speakers of another language.

language family a group of languages evolved from a common ancestral language.

larynx the structure of muscle and cartilage at the upper end of the windpipe that contains the vocal cords.

lenition a change of a consonant considered "stronger" into one considered "weaker". Common examples include voicing; turning into an affricate or a fricative; and other similar processes.

lingua franca a trade language; a language used as a means of communication among speakers of different languages.

loanword a word borrowed into a language from another language.

manner of articulation the type of constriction that is made for a speech sound: stop, fricative, affricate, etc.

morphemes the smallest meaningful pieces into which words can be divided: *un-touch-abil-ity*.

morphology the component of grammar that builds words out of constituent pieces (morphemes).

nasal a sound produced with the velum lowered, enabling air flow through the nasal cavity; for example, the first sound of *moon* and *noon*.

nominative case the case of the subject (in a certain type of) language: *He* loves you. (not: **Him* loves you.)

noun one of the major syntactic categories, comprising words that typically refer to a thing or person: *cat, apple, Mary, river, day*.

noun incorporation a phenomenon by which a word (usually a verb) forms a kind of compound with its direct object or adverbial modifier, while retaining its original syntactic function.

noun phrase a phrase whose head is a noun or a pronoun.

Null Subjects (Pro-Drop parameter) if a language allows Null Subjects, a subject noun phrase may be omitted without rendering the sentence ungrammatical.

palatal consonant a consonant produced with a constriction between the body of the tongue and the (hard) palate; for example, the first sounds of *you* and *university*.

palatalization (a) the effect that front vowels typically have on velar and alveolar stops, making their place of articulation more palatal (e.g. the first sound of *keep* is palatalized; (b) a change that involves a velar sound becoming a palatal, palato-alveolar, alveolar, or interdental sound (e.g. a *k* becoming a *ch*-sound).

palate the highest part of the roof of the mouth.

palato-alveolar a sound pronounced with some sort of obstruction just behind the alveolar ridge – that is, the area where the roof of the mouth rises sharply.

parameter a set of alternatives for a particular phenomenon made available by Universal Grammar to individual languages. For example, *wh*-fronting parameter defines two alternatives for placement of question words such as *who, where, why*: sentence-initially or in the same place where the answer would appear.

pharyngeal sound a sound made through the modification of airflow in the area of the throat behind the mouth and above the larynx.

phoneme a sound of language that is used to discriminate meaning.

phonology the component of grammar that determines the sound pattern of a language, including its inventory of phonemes, how they may be combined to form natural-sounding words, how the phonemes must be adjusted depending on their neighbors, and patterns of intonation, timing, and stress.

pidgin an ad hoc intermediary language used as a *lingua franca*. A pidgin typically has a very limited vocabulary and simplified grammatical structure.

place of articulation the part of the mouth, throat, or larynx where the airflow meets the greatest degree of constriction in the production of a speech sound.

polysynthetic language a language in which a word may be composed of a long string of prefixes, roots, and suffixes, often expressing the meaning of an entire sentence in English.

postposition a preposition-like part of speech that follows (rather than precedes) its complement.

preposition one of the major syntactic categories, comprising words that typically refer to a spatial or temporal relationship: *in, on, at, near, by, under, after*.

proto-language a (typically reconstructed) language that is hypothesized to be the ancestor of some group of related languages.

related languages (cf. genetically related languages.)

retroflex consonant a consonant produced by curling the tip of the tongue upward and backward; for example, the first sound of *retroflex* (for some speakers of English).

root (of a word) the most basic morpheme in a word or family of related words, consisting of an irreducible, arbitrary sound-meaning pairing: *electricity, electrical, electric, electrify, electrician, electron*.

schwa the shortest vowel pronounced with the tongue in a neutral, middle-of-the-mouth position (e.g. the initial sound of *about* and the first and last vowels of *banana*). Schwa is always unstressed.

semantic shift the process in which a word loses its former meaning, taking on a new, often related, meaning.

sound shift the systematic modification of a series of phonemes (e.g. Great Vowel Shift).

speech community a group whose members share both a particular language or variety of language and the norms for its appropriate use in social context.

stop consonant a consonant pronounced so that the airflow is completely blocked for a moment: *p, t, k, b, d, g.*

substratum influence the influence of a politically or culturally non-dominant language on a dominant language in the area (e.g. the borrowing of words into English from languages indigenous to North America).

suffix an affix which is placed after the stem of a word.

superstratum influence the influence of a politically or culturally dominant language on another language in the area (e.g. the influence of Norman French on English during the Middle English period).

syntax the component of grammar that arranges words into phrases and sentences.

synthetic language (cf. fusional language.)

transitive verb a verb that requires a direct object: *John ate the pizza.*

Universal Grammar (UG) the basic design underlying the grammars of all human languages, consisting of principles and parameters that enable the child to deduce a grammar from the primary linguistic data.

velar consonant a consonant articulated with the back of the tongue against the soft palate (i.e. the back part of the roof of the mouth, known also as the velum).

velum the soft area towards the rear of the roof of the mouth.

verb one of the major syntactic categories, comprising words that typically refer to an action or state: *break, run, love, appear.*

verb phrase a phrase whose head is a verb.

vocal cords the two muscular bands of tissue that stretch from front to back within the larynx. The vocal cords vibrate periodically to produce voiced sounds.

voiced a sound pronounced with the vocal cords brought close together, but not tightly closed, causing them to vibrate as air passes between them (e.g. /a/, /d/, and /m/ are voiced).

voiceless a sound pronounced with the vocal cords pulled apart, allowing the air to pass directly through the glottis (e.g. /t/, /s/, and /f/ are voiceless).

vowel a sound produced with little or no obstruction in the vocal tract. Vowels are generally voiced.

vowel harmony a long-distance assimilatory process by which vowels become more similar to each other in some way(s) across intervening consonants.

Bibliography

Abulafia, David (2011) *The Great Sea: A Human History of the Mediterranean.*
Oxford: Oxford University Press.

Abun-Nasr, Jamil (1987) *A History of the Maghrib in the Islamic Period.* Cambridge,
UK: Cambridge University Press.

Adams, James Noel (2007) *The Regional Diversification of Latin 200 BC–AD 600.*
Cambridge, UK: Cambridge University Press.

   (2011) Late Latin. In: James Clackson (ed.) *A Companion to the Latin Language.*
Oxford: Wiley-Blackwell. Pp. 255–283.

   (2013) *Social Variation and the Latin Language.* Cambridge, UK: Cambridge
University Press.

Adrados, F. Rodríguez (1982) The archaic structure of Hittite: the crux of the problem.
Journal of Indo-European Studies 10: 1–35.

Aikhenvald, Alexandra (2006) Grammars in contact: a cross-linguistic perspective.
In: Alexandra Aikhenvald and Robert M. W. Dixon (eds.) *Areal Grammars in
Contact: A Crosslinguistic Typology.* Oxford: Oxford University Press. Pp. 1–66.

Aikio, Ante (2006) On Germanic-Saami contacts and Saami prehistory. *Journal de la
Société Finno-Ougrienne* 91: 9–55.

Alpher, Barry and David Nash (1999) Lexical replacement and cognate equilibrium in
Australia. *Australian Journal of Linguistics.* 19: 5–56.

Anthony, David W. (1986) The 'Kurgan Culture', Indo-European origins and the
domestication of the horse. *Current Anthropology* 24: 291–313.

   (1991) The archaeology of Indo-European origins. *Journal of Indo-European Studies*
19(3–4): 193–222.

   (2007) *The Horse, the Wheel, and Language: How Bronze-Age Riders from the Eurasian
Steppes Shaped the Modern World.* Princeton, NJ: Princeton University Press.

   (2009) Migration in archeology: the baby and the bathwater. *American
Anthropologist* 92(4): 895–914.

   (2011) Horseback Riding and Bronze Age Pastoralism in the Eurasian Steppes.
Lecture delivered at Secrets of the Silk Road Symposium at University of
Pennsylvania Museum of Archeology and Anthropology, March 2011.

   (2013) Two IE phylogenies, three PIE migrations, and four kinds of steppe
pastoralism. *Journal of Language Relationship* 9: 1–21.

Anthony, David and Nikolai B. Vinogradov (1995) Birth of the chariot. *Archaeology*
48(2): 36–41.

Anttila, Raimo (1989) *Historical and Comparative Linguistics.* Second edition.
Amsterdam: John Benjamins.

Aslanov, Cyril (2002) Quand les langues romanes se confondent ... *Langage et société* 99(1): 9–52.

Atkinson, Quentin D. and Claire Bowern (2012) Computational phylogenetics and the internal structure of Pama-Nyungan. *Language* 88: 817–845.

Atkinson, Quentin D. and Russell D. Gray (2005) Curious parallels and curious connections – phylogenetic thinking in biology and historical linguistics. *Systematic Biology* 54(4): 513–526.

  (2006) Chapter 8: How old is the Indo-European language family? Illumination or more moths to the flame? In: Peter Forster and Colin Renfrew (eds.) *Phylogenetic Methods and the Prehistory of Languages*. Cambridge, UK : McDonald Institute for Archaeological Research, University of Cambridge. Pp. 91–109.

Atkinson, Quentin D., Geoff Nicholls, David Welch, and Russell Gray (2005) From words to dates: water into wine, mathemagic or phylogenetic inference? *Transactions of the Philological Society* 103(2): 193–219.

Bacon, Elizabeth E. (1966) *Central Asians under Russian Rule: A Study in Culture Change*. Ithaca, NY: Cornell University Press.

Baker, Mark (1996) *The Polysynthesis Parameter*. Oxford: Oxford University Press
  (2001a) Phrase structure as representation of "primitive" grammatical relations. In: William Davies and Stan Dubinsky (eds.) *Objects and Other Subjects: Grammatical Functions, Functional Categories, and Configurationality*. Dordrecht: Kluwer. Pp. 21–51.

  (2001b) *The Atoms of Language: The Mind's Hidden Rules of Grammar*. New York: Basic Books.

Barbançon, François, Steven N. Evans, Luay Nakhleh, Don Ringe, and Tandy Warnow (2013) An experimental study comparing linguistic phylogenetic reconstruction methods. *Diachronica* 30(2): 143–170.

Barber, Elizabeth Wayland (1992) *Prehistoric Textiles: The Development of Cloth in the Neolithic and Bronze Ages with Special Reference to the Aegean*. Princeton, NJ: Princeton University Press.

Barkan, Elazar (1992) *The Retreat of Scientific Racism*. Cambridge, UK: Cambridge University Press.

Bartholomew, John (1962) *Bartholomew's Advanced Atlas of Modern Geography*. New York: McGraw Hill.

Beekes, Robert S. P. (1995) *Comparative Indo-European Linguistics. An Introduction*. Amsterdam/Philadelphia, PA: John Benjamins.
  (2010) The Pre-Greek loanwords in Greek. *Etymological Dictionary of Greek*. Leiden/Boston, MA: Brill.

Bergsland, Knut and Hans Vogt (1962) On the validity of glottochronology. *Current Anthropology* 3: 115–153.

Bernal, Martin (1987) *Black Athena: The Afroasiatic Roots of Classical Civilization. Volume I: The Fabrication of Ancient Greece, 1785–1985*. New Brunswick, NJ: Rutgers University Press.

  (1991) *Black Athena: The Afroasiatic Roots of Classical Civilization. Volume II: The Archaeological and Documentary Evidence*. New Brunswick, NJ: Rutgers University Press.

  (2006) *Black Athena: The Afroasiatic Roots of Classical Civilization. Volume III: The Linguistic Evidence*. New Brunswick, NJ: Rutgers University Press.

Bernecker, Erich Karl (1924) *Slavisches etymologisches Wörterbuch*. Heidelberg: Winter.

Blaut, James (1999) Environmentalism and eurocentrism. *Geographical Review* 89(3): 391–408.

Blech, Rabbi Benjamin (2000) *A Complete Idiot's Guide to Learning Yiddish*. Indianapolis, IN: Alpha Books.

Blust, Robert (1999) Subgrouping, circularity and extinction: some issues in Austronesian comparative. In: Elizabeth Zeitoun and Rengui Li (eds.) *Selected Papers from the Eighth International Conference on Austronesian Linguistics*. Taipei: Academia Sinica. Pp. 31–94.

(2000) Why lexicostatistics doesn't work: the 'universal constant' hypothesis and the Austronesian languages. In: Colin Renfrew, April McMahon, and Larry Trask (eds.) *Time Depth in Historical Linguistics*. Volume II. Cambridge, UK: The McDonald Institute for Archaeological Research. Pp. 311–332.

Boggard, Amy (2002) Questioning the relevance of shifting cultivation to Neolithic farming in the loess belt of Europe: evidence from the Hambach Forest experiment. *Vegetation History and Archeobotany* 11(1–2): 155–168.

Bomhard, Allan R. (2008) *Reconstructing Proto-Nostratic: Comparative Phonology, Morphology, and Vocabulary*. Leiden: Brill.

(2011) *The Nostratic Hypothesis in 2011: Trends and Issues*. Washington, DC: Institute for the Study of Man.

Bonfante, Giuliano (1068) Quando si è cominciato a parlare italiano? In: Kurt Baldinger (ed.) *Festschrift Walther von Wartburg zum 80.Geburtstag*. Tübingen: Max Niemeyer Verlag. Pp. 21–46.

Boretzky, Norbert (1992) Zum Erbwortschatz des Romani. *Zeitschrift für Phonetik, Sprachwissenschaft und Kommunikationsforschung* 45: 227–251.

(1995) Armenisches im Zigeunerischen (Romani und Lomavren). *Indogermanische Forschungen* 100: 137–155.

Boroditsky, Lera, Lauren A. Schmidt, and Webb Phillips (2003) Sex, syntax, and semantics. In: Dedre Gentner and Susan Goldin-Meadow (eds.) *Language in Mind: Advances in the Study of Language and Thought*. Cambridge, MA: The MIT Press. Pp. 61–79.

Bortolussi, Luca, Giuseppe Longobardi, Cristina Guardiano, and Andrea Sgarro (2011) How many possible languages are there? In: Gemma Bel-Enguix, Verónica Dahl, and Maria Dolores Jiménez-López (eds.) *Biology, Computation and Linguistics*. Amsterdam: IOS Press. Pp. 168–179.

Boserup, Ester (1965) *The Conditions of Agricultural Growth: The Economics of Agrarian Change under Population Pressure*. Chicago: Aldine.

Bouchard-Côté, Alexandre, David Hall, Thomas L. Griffiths, and Dan Klein (2013) Automated reconstruction of ancient languages using probabilistic models of sound change. *Proceedings of the National Academy of Sciences* 110(11): 4224–4229.

Bouckaert, Remco, Philippe Lemey, Michael Dunn, Simon J. Greenhill, Alexander V. Alekseyenko, Alexei J. Drummond, Russell D. Gray, Marc A. Suchard, and Quentin D. Atkinson (2012) Mapping the origins and expansion of the Indo-European language family. *Science* 337: 957–960.

Bowern, Claire (2010) Correlates of language change in hunter-gatherer and other 'small' languages. *Language and Linguistics Compass* 4(8): 665–679.

Bradford, Phillips Verner and Harvey Blume (1992) *Ota Benga: The Pygmy in the Zoo*. New York: St. Martin's Press.

Broodbank, Cyprian (2013) *The Making of the Middle Sea*. London: Thames & Hudson.

Brugmann, Karl (1884) Zur Frage nach den Verwandtschaftsverhältnissen der indogermanischen Sprachen. *Internationale Zeitschrift für allgemeine Sprachwissenschaft* 1: 226–256.

Bryant, Edwin F. (2005) Concluding remarks. In: Edwin F. Bryant and Laurie L. Patton (eds.) *The Indo-Aryan Controversy: Evidence and Inference in Indian History*. London: Routledge. Pp. 468–506.

Bryce, Trevor (1998) *The Kingdom of the Hittites*. Oxford: Clarendon Press.

(2002) *Life and Society in the Hittite World*. Oxford: Oxford University Press.

Bybee, Joan (2007) *Frequency of Use and the Organization of Language*. Oxford: Oxford University Press.

Campbell, Lyle (1997a) On the linguistic prehistory of Finno-Ugric. In: Raymond Hickey and Stanislaw Puppel (eds.) *Language History and Linguistic Modelling: A Festschrift for Jacek Fisiak on His 60th Birthday*. Trends in Linguistics. Berlin: Mouton de Gruyter. Pp. 829–861.

(1997b) Linguistic contributions to Guatemalan prehistory. In: Jane H. Hill, P. J. Mistry, and Lyle Campbell (eds.) *The Life of Language: Papers in Linguistics in Honor of William Bright*. Berlin: Mouton de Gruyter. Pp. 183–192.

(1998) Nostratic: a personal assessment. In: Joseph C. Salmons and Brian D. Joseph (eds.) *Nostratic: Sifting the Evidence*. Current Issues in Linguistic Theory 142. Amsterdam: John Benjamins. Pp. 107–152.

(2000) Time perspective in linguistics. In: Colin Renfrew, April McMahon, and Larry Trask (eds.) *Time Depth in Historical Linguistics*. Cambridge, UK: McDonald Institute for Archeological Research. Pp. 3–31.

(2013) *Historical Linguistics. An Introduction*. Cambridge, MA: The MIT Press.

Campbell, Lyle, Terrence Kaufman, and Thomas C. Smith-Stark (1986) Meso-America as a linguistic area. *Language* 62(3): 530–570.

Campbell, Lyle and William J. Poser (2008) *Language Classification: History and Method*. Cambridge, UK: Cambridge University Press.

Carpelan, Christian and Asko Parpola (2001) Proto-Indo-European, Proto-Uralic and Proto-Aryan. In: Christian Carpelan, Asko Parpola, and Petteri Koskikallio (eds.) *The Earliest Contacts between Uralic and Indo-European: Linguistic and Archeological Considerations*. Mémoires de la Société finno-ougrienne 242. Helsinki: Suomalais-Ugrilainen Seura.

Cavalli-Sforza, Luigi Luca (2000) *Genes, Peoples, and Languages*. New York: North Point Press.

Cavalli-Sforza, Luigi Luca and Francesco Cavalli-Sforza (1995) *The Great Human Diasporas: The History of Diversity and Evolution*. New York: Addison-Wesley.

Cavalli-Sforza, Luigi Luca, Paolo Menozzi, and Alberto Piazza (1994) *The History and Geography of Human Genes*. Princeton, NJ: Princeton University Press.

Chamberlain, Houston Stewart (1912 [original publication in German, 1899]) *The Foundations of the Nineteenth Century*. Second edition. London: John Lane/The Bodley Head.

Chambon, Jean-Pierre and Yan Greub (2002) Note sur l'âge du (proto)gascon. *Revue de Linguistique Romane* 264: 473–495.

Chen, Keith (2013) The effect of language on economic behavior: evidence from savings rates, health behaviors, and retirement assets. *American Economic Review* 103(2): 690–731.

Chernykh, Evgenii, Evgenii V. Kuz'minykh, and L. B. Orlovskaya (2004) Ancient metallurgy in northeast Asia: from the Urals to the Saiano-Altai. In: Katheryn M. Linduff (ed.) *Metallurgy in Ancient Eastern Eurasia from the Urals to the Yellow River.* Chinese Studies 31. Lewiston: Edwin Mellen Press. Pp. 15–36.

Childe, V. Gordon (1926) *The Aryans: A Study of Indo-European Origins.* New York: Alfred A. Knopf.

Choi, Jinny K. (2005) Bilingualism in Paraguay: forty years after Rubin's study. *Journal of Multilingual and Multicultural Development* 26(3): 233–248.

Chomsky, Noam (1959) A Review of B. F. Skinner's *Verbal Behavior.* In: Leon A. Jakobovits and Murray S. Miron (eds.) *Readings in the Psychology of Language.* Englewood, NJ: Prentice-Hall. 1967. Pp. 142–143.

(1981) *Lectures on Government and Binding.* Dordrecht: Foris.

Clackson, James (1994) *The Linguistic Relationship Between Armenian and Greek.* Oxford: Blackwell.

(2000) Time depth in Indo-European. In: Colin Renfrew, April McMahon, and Larry Trask (eds.) *Time Depth in Historical Linguistics.* Cambridge, UK: McDonald Institute for Archeological Research. Pp. 441–454.

(2013) The origins of the Indic languages: the Indo-European model. In: Angela Marcantonio and Girish Nath Jha (eds.) *Perspectives on the Origin of Indian Civilization.* Dartmouth, MA: Center for India Studies, University of Massachusetts, Dartmouth. Pp. 260–288.

Clarke, Robert and Mark Merlin (2013) *Cannabis Evolution and Ethnobotany.* Berkeley, CA: University of California Press.

Clauson, Gerard (1956) The case against the Altaic theory. *Central Asiatic Journal* 2, 181–187.

(1959) The case for the Altaic theory examined. In: H. Franke (ed.) *Akten des vierundzwanzigsten internationalen Orientalisten-Kongresses.* Wiesbaden: Deutsche Morgenländische Gesellschaft. Pp. 599–601.

Colarusso, John (1992) How many consonants does Ubykh have? In: B. George Hewitt (ed.) *Caucasian Perspectives.* Munich: Lincom Europa. Pp. 145–156.

Collins, Billie Jean (2008) *The Hittites and Their World.* Leiden/Boston, MA: Brill.

Comrie, Bernard (2000) Is there a single time depth cut-off point in historical linguistics? In: Colin Renfrew, April McMahon, and Larry Trask (eds.) *Time Depth in Historical Linguistics.* Cambridge, UK: McDonald Institute for Archeological Research. Pp. 33–43.

Conklin, Harold (1949) Bamboo literacy on Mindoro. *Pacific Discovery* 3: 4–11.

Coon, Carleton S. (1963) *The Origin of Races.* New York: Alfred A. Knopf.

Crisma, Paola (in press) Triggering syntactic change: the history of English genitives. In: Diane Jonas, John Whitman, and Andrew Garrett (eds.) *Grammatical Change: Origin, Nature, Outcomes.* Oxford: Oxford University Press.

Croft, William (2000) *Explaining Language Change: An Evolutionary Approach.* London: Longman.

Curnow, T. J. (2001) What can be 'borrowed'? In: Alexandra Aikhenvald and R. M. W. Dixon (eds.) *Areal Diffusion and Genetic Inheritance: Problems in Comparative Linguistics.* Oxford: Oxford University Press. Pp. 412–436.

Currie, Thomas E., Andrew Meade, Myrtille Guillon, and Ruth Mace (2013) Cultural phylogeography of the Bantu languages of sub-Saharan Africa. *Proceedings of the Royal Society B: Biological Sciences* 280(1762): 1471–2954.

Darbyshire, Gareth, Stephen Mitchell, and Levent Vardar (2000) The Galatian settlement in Asia Minor. *Anatolian Studies* 50: 75–97.

Darden, Bill (2001) On the question of the Anatolian origin of Indo-Hittite. In: Robert Drews (ed.) *Greater Anatolia and the Indo-Hittite Language Family.* Washington, DC: Journal of Indo-European Studies. Pp. 184–228.

Daval-Markussen, Aymeric and Peter Bakker (2011) A phylogenetic networks approach to the classification of English-based Atlantic creoles. *English World-Wide* 32(2): 115–146.

(2012) Explorations in creole research with phylogenetic tools. *Proceedings of the EACL 2012 Joint Workshop of LINGVIS and UNCLH.* Avignon, France. Pp. 89–97.

Davison, Kate, Pavel Dolukhanov, Graeme R. Sarson, and Anvar Shukurov (2006) The role of waterways in the spread of the Neolithic. *Journal of Archaeological Science* 33: 641–652.

Diakonoff, Igor M. (1985) On the original home of the speakers of Indo-European. *Journal of Indo-European Studies* 13: 92–282.

Diamond, Jared (1997) *Guns, Germs, Steel: The Fates of Human Societies.* New York: W. W. Norton.

Diebold, A. Richard, Jr. (1985) *The Evolution of Indo-European Nomenclature for Salmonid Fish: The Case of 'Huchen' (Hucho Spp.).* Journal of Indo-European Studies Monograph Series, No. 5. Washington, DC: The Institute for the Study of Man.

Dixon, R. M. W. (1997) *The Rise and Fall of Languages.* Cambridge, UK: Cambridge University Press.

(2001) The Australian linguistic area. In: R. M. W. Dixon and Alexandra Aikhenvald (eds.) *Areal Diffusion and Genetic Inheritance: Problems in Comparative Linguistics.* Oxford: Oxford University Press. Pp. 64–104.

Doel, Marcus (1999) *Poststructuralist Geographies: The Diabolical Art of Spatial Science.* Lanham, MA: Rowman and Littlefield.

Doerfer, Gerhard (1963) Bemerkungen zur Verwandtschaft der sog. altaische Sprachen [Remarks on the relationship of the so-called Altaic languages]. In: Gerhard Doerfer (ed.) *Türkische und mongolische Elemente im Neupersischen, Bd. I: Mongolische Elemente im Neupersischen.* Wiesbaden: Franz Steiner Verlag. Pp. 51–105.

(1988) *Grundwort und Sprachmischung: Eine Untersuchung an Hand von Körperteilbezeichnungen.* Wiesbaden: Franz Steiner Verlag.

Dolgopolsky, Aharon B. (1987a) The Indo-European homeland and lexical contacts of Proto-Indo-European with other languages. *Mediterranean Archaeological Review* 3: 7–31.

(1987b) Cultural contacts of Proto-Indo-European and Proto-Indo-Iranian with neighboring languages. *Folia Linguistica Historica* 8(1–2): 1–36.

(1988) *The Nostratic Macrofamily and Linguistic Paleontology.* Cambridge, UK: McDonald Institute for Archaeological Research.

(2000) Sources of linguistic chronology. In: Colin Renfrew, April McMahon, and Larry Trask (eds.) *Time Depth in Historical Linguistics.* Cambridge, UK: McDonald Institute for Archeological Research. Pp. 401–409.

Donohue, Mark, Tim Denham, and Stephen Oppenheimer (2012a) New methodologies for historical linguistics? Calibrating a lexicon-based methodology for diffusion vs. subgrouping. *Diachronica* 29(4): 505–522.

(2012b) Consensus and the lexicon in historical linguistics. Rejoinder to "Basic vocabulary and Bayesian phylolinguistics". *Diachronica* 29(4): 538–546.

Drews, Robert (1988) *The Coming of the Greeks: Indo-European Conquests in the Aegean and the Near East*. Princeton, NJ: Princeton University Press.

Drummond, Alexei J., Simon Y. W. Ho, Matthew J. Phillips and Andrew Rambaut (2006) Relaxed phylogenies and dating with confidence. *PLoS Biology* 4(5): e88: 699–710.

Dryer, Matthew S. (2013) Order of subject, object and verb. In: Matthew S. Dryer and Martin Haspelmath (eds.) *The World Atlas of Language Structures Online*. Leipzig: Max Planck Institute for Evolutionary Anthropology. (Available online at http://wals.info/chapter/81; accessed on January 6, 2014.)

Dryer, Matthew S. and Martin Haspelmath (eds.) (2013) *The World Atlas of Language Structures Online*. Leipzig: Max Planck Institute for Evolutionary Anthropology. (Available online at http://wals.info/)

Dunn, Michael, Nielas Burenhult, Nicole Kruspe, Sylvia Tufvesson, and Neele Becker (2011a) Aslian linguistic prehistory: a case study in computational phylogenetics. *Diachronica* 28(3): 291–323.

Dunn, Michael, R. A. Foley, Stephen C. Levinson, Ger Reesink, and Angela Terrill (2007) Statistical reasoning in the evaluation of typological diversity in Island Melanesia. *Oceanic Linguistics* 46: 388–403.

Dunn, Michael, Simon J. Greenhill, Stephen C. Levinson, and Russell D. Gray (2011b) Evolved structure of language shows lineage-specific trends in word-order universals. *Nature* 473: 79–82.

Dunn, Michael, Stephen C. Levinson, Eva Lindström, Ger Reesink, and Angela Terrill (2008) Structural phylogeny in historical linguistics: methodological explorations applied in Island Melanesia. *Language* 84: 710–759.

Dunn, Michael, Angela Terril, Ger Reesink, R. A. Foley, and Stephen C. Levinson (2005) Structural phylogenetics and the reconstruction of ancient language history. *Science* 309 (5743): 2072–2075.

Dyen, Isidore, Joseph B. Kruskal, and Paul Black (1992) An Indoeuropean classification: a lexicostatistical experiment. *Transactions of the American Philosophical Society* 82, Part 5. Data available online at http://www.wordgumbo.com/ie/cmp/iedata.txt

(1997) Comparative Indoeuropean Database collected by Isidore Dyen; File IE-Data1.

Ehrenreich, Eric (2007) *The Nazi Ancestral Proof: Genealogy, Racial Science, and the Final Solution*. Bloomington, IN: Indiana University Press.

Eisler, Riane (1987) *The Chalice and the Blade: Our History, Our Future*. New York: Harper and Row.

Elizarenkova, T. Ja. (1972) *Rigveda. Izbrannye gimny* [= *The Rigveda. Selected Hymns*]. Moscow: Nauka.

Embleton, Sheila (1986) *Statistics in Historical Linguistics*. Bochum: Studienverlag Dr. N. Brockmeyer.

Emeneau, Murray (1956) India as a linguistic area. *Language* 32(1): 3–16.

Everett, Daniel L. (2005) Cultural constraints on grammar and cognition in Pirahã. *Current Anthropology* 46(4): 621–646.

Falk, Harry (1989) Soma I and II. *Bulletin of the School of Oriental and African Studies* 52/1(1): 77–90.

Ferrer, Eduardo Blasco (ed.) (2010) *Paleosardo: Le radici linguistiche della Sardegna neolitica*. Berlin/New York: Mouton de Gruyter.

Filppula, Markku (2013) Contact and the early history of English. In: Raymond Hickey (ed.) *The Handbook of Language Contact*. Chichester: Wiley-Blackwell. Pp. 453–452.

Flattery, David Stophlet and Martin Schwarz (1989) *Haoma and Harmaline: The Botanical Identity of the Indo-Iranian Sacred Hallucinogen "Soma" and Its Legacy in Religion, Language, and Middle-Eastern Folklore*. Berkeley, CA: University of California Press.

Folami, Olakunli Michael (2010) Climate change and inter-ethnic conflict between Fulani herdsmen and host communities in Nigeria. Paper presented at the Conference on Climate Change and Security, Norwegian Academy of Sciences, Trondheim, Norway. (Available online at http://climsec.prio.no/papers/Final_daft_climate_change_paper_kunle2%5B2%5D.pdf)

Ford, O. T. (2013) Parallel Worlds: Empirical Region and Place. Unpublished Ph.D. Dissertation, Department of Geography, University of California at Los Angeles.

Forster, Peter, Tobias Polzin, and Arne Röhl (2006) Evolution of English basic vocabulary within the network of Germanic languages. In: Peter Forster and Colin Renfrew (eds.) *Phylogenetic Methods and the Prehistory of Languages*. Cambridge, UK: McDonald Institute Monographs. Pp. 131–137.

Forster, Peter and Colin Renfrew (2011) Mother tongue and Y chromosomes. *Science* 333(6048): 1390–1391.

Forster, Peter and Alfred Toth (2003) Toward a phylogenetic chronology of ancient Gaulish, Celtic, and Indo-European. *Proceedings of the National Academy of Sciences of the USA* 100(15): 9079–9084.

Fortson, Benjamin W. (2010) *Indo-European Language and Culture: An Introduction*. Blackwell Textbooks in Linguistics. Second edition. Oxford: Wiley-Blackwell.

Fowler, Catherine S. (1972) Some ecological clues to Proto-Numic homelands. In: D. D. Fowler (ed.) *Great Basic Cultural Ecology: A Symposium*. Desert Research Institute Publications in the Social Sciences, No. 8. Reno, NV: University of Nevada. Pp. 105–121.

Fraser, Angus (1992) Looking into the seeds of time. *Tsiganologische Studien* 1: 135–166.

Freeman, Philip (2001) *The Galatian Language – A Comprehensive Survey of The Language of the Ancient Celts in Greco-Roman Asia Minor*. Lewiston, NY: Mellen Press.

Friedrich, Paul (1970) *Proto-Indo-European Trees. The Arboreal System of a Prehistoric People*. Chicago: University of Chicago Press.

Galdi, Giovanbattista (2011) Latin inside and outside of Rome. In: James Clackson (ed.) *A Companion to the Latin Language*. Oxford: Wiley-Blackwell. Pp. 564–581.

Gamkrelidze, Tomaz V. (1994) PIE 'horse' and 'cart' in the light of the hypothesis of Asiatic homeland of the Indo-Europeans. In: Bernhard Hänsel, Bernfried Schlerath, and Stefan Zimmer (eds.) *Die Indogermanen und das Pferd*. Budapest: Archaeolingua. Pp. 37–42.

(2000) On linguistic palaeontology of culture. In: Colin Renfrew, April McMahon, and Larry Trask (eds.) *Time Depth in Historical Linguistics.* Cambridge, UK: McDonald Institute for Archeological Research. Pp. 455–461.

Gamkrelidze, Tomaz V. and Vjačeslav V. Ivanov (1984) *Indoevropeysky Yazyk i Indoevropeytsy.* Tbilisi, Georgia: Izdatel'stvo Tbilisskogo universiteta.

(1995) *Indo-European and the Indo-Europeans. A Reconstruction and Historical Analysis of a Proto-Language and a Proto-Culture.* Berlin/New York: Mouton de Gruyter.

Gardani, Francesco (2008) *Borrowing of Inflectional Morphemes in Language Contact.* Frankfurt am Main: Peter Lang.

Garrett, Andrew (2006) Convergence in the formation of Indo-European subgroups: phylogeny and chronology. In: Peter Forster and Colin Renfrew (eds.) *Phylogenetic Methods and the Prehistory of Languages.* Cambridge, UK: McDonald Institute Monographs. Pp. 139–151.

Gay, Victor, Estefania Santacreu-Vasut, and Amir Shoham (2013) The grammatical origins of gender roles. BEHL Working Paper Series.

Geary, Patrick (2003) *Myth of Nations. The Medieval Origins of Europe.* Princeton, NJ: Princeton University Press.

Geisler, Hans and Johann-Mattis List (in press) Beautiful trees on unstable ground. Notes on the data problem in lexicostatistics. In Heinrich Hettrich (ed.) *Die Ausbreitung des Indogermanischen. Thesen aus Sprachwissenschaft, Archäologie und Genetik.* Wiesbaden: Reichert.

Georg, Stefan (2004) Review of etymological dictionary of the Altaic languages. *Diachronica* 21(2): 445–450.

(2005) Reply [to Starostin 2005]. *Diachronica* 22(2): 455–457.

Gimbutas, Marija (1974) *The Gods and Goddesses of Old Europe: 7000 to 3500 BC: Myths, Legends and Cult Images.* Berkeley, CA: University of California Press.

Gimbutas, Marija and Joan Marler (1991) *The Civilization of the Goddess: The World of Old Europe.* New York: HarperCollins.

Gimbutas, Marija, Miriam Robbins Dexter, Karlene Jones-Bley (1997) *The Kurgan Culture and the Indo-Europeanization of Europe: Selected Articles from 1952 to 1993.* Washington, DC: Institute for the Study of Man.

Gluhak, Alemko (1993) *Hrvatski etimološki rječnik.* Zagreb: August Cesarec.

Gobineau, Joseph Arthur Comte de (1855) *Essai sur l'Inégalité des Races Humaines.* Paris: Librairie de Firmin Didot Frères.

Goossens, Jan (ed.) (1973) *Niederdeutsch. Sprache und Literatur. Eine Einführung. Band 1: Sprache.* Neumünster: Wachholtz Verlag.

Gorton, Luke (2013) Wine and the early Indo-Europeans. Paper presented at the OSU Martin Luther King Day Linguistics Symposium. Columbus, OH.

Gould, Peter (1973) The open geographical curriculum. In: Richard Chorley (ed.) *Directions in Geography.* London: Methuen and Co. Pp. 253–284.

(1979) Geography 1957–1977: the Augean period. *Annals of the Association of American Geographers* 69(1): 139–155.

Grant, Madison (1916) *The Passing of The Great Race; or, The Racial Basis of European History.* New York: Charles Scribner's Sons.

Gravlee, Clarence C., H. Russell Bernard, and William R. Leonard (2003) Heredity, environment, and cranial form: a reanalysis of Boas's immigrant data. *American Anthropologist* 105(1): 125–138.

Gray, Russell D. and Quentin D. Atkinson (2003) Language-tree divergence times support the Anatolian theory of Indo-European origin. *Nature* 426: 435–439.

Gray, Russell D., Quentin D. Atkinson, and Simon J. Greenhill (2011) Language evolution and human history: what a difference a date makes. *Philosophical Transactions of the Royal Society B* 366: 1090–1100.

Gray, Russell D., Alexei J. Drummond, and Simon J. Greenhill (2009) Language phylogenies reveal expansion pulses and pauses in Pacific settlement. *Science* 323: 479–483.

Gray, Russell D. and Fiona M. Jordan (2000) Language trees support the express-train sequence of Austronesian expansion. *Nature* 405: 1052–1055.

Greenhill, Simon J., Quentin D. Atkinson, Andrew Meade, and Russell D. Gray (2010) The shape and tempo of language evolution. *Proceedings of Royal Society B* 277 (1693): 2443–2450.

Greenhill, Simon J., Robert Blust, and Russell D. Gray (2008) The Austronesian Basic Vocabulary Database: from bioinformatics to lexomics. *Evolutionary Bioinformatics* 4: 271–283.

Greenhill, Simon J., Thomas E. Currie, and Russell D. Gray (2009) Does horizontal transmission invalidate cultural phylogenies? *Proceedings of Royal Society B* 276: 2299–2306.

Greenhill, Simon J., Alexei J. Drummond, and Russell D. Gray (2010) How accurate and robust are the phylogenetic estimates of Austronesian language relationships? *PLoS ONE* 5. e9573.

Greenhill, Simon J. and Russell D. Gray (2009) Austronesian language phylogenies: myths and misconceptions about Bayesian computational methods. In: K. Alexander Adelaar and Andrew Pawley (eds.) *Austronesian Historical Linguistics and Culture History: A Festschrift for Robert Blust*. Canberra: Pacific Linguistics. Pp. 375–397.

(2012) Basic vocabulary and Bayesian phylolinguistics. *Diachronica* 29(4): 523–537.

Greppin, John and Igor M. Diakonoff (1991) Some effects of the Hurro-Urartian people and their languages upon the earliest Armenians. *Journal of the American Oriental Society* 111(4): 720–730.

Griffith, Gareth (1993) *Socialism and Superior Brains: The Political Thought of George Bernard Shaw*. London: Routledge.

Grigoriev, Stanislav A. (2002) *Ancient Indo-Europeans*. Chelyabinsk: Rifei.

Grollemund, Rebecca (2012) Nouvelles Approches en Classification: Application aux Langues Bantu du Nord-Ouest. Ph.D. Dissertation, Université Lumière Lyon 2. Lyon, France.

Gross, Paul R., Norman Levitt, and Martin W. Lewis (1997) *The Flight from Science and Reason*. Baltimore, MD: Johns Hopkins University Press.

Guardiano, Cristina and Giuseppe Longobardi (2005) Parametric comparison and language taxonomy. In: M. Batllori, M. L. Hernanz, C. Picallo, and F. Roca (eds.) *Grammaticalization and Parametric Variation*. Oxford: Oxford University Press. Pp. 149–174.

Gudschinsky, Sarah C. (1956) The ABC's of lexicostatistics (glottochronology). *Word* 12: 175–210.

Guilfoyle, Eithne, Henrietta Hung, and Lisa Travis (1992) SPEC of IP and SPEC of VP: two subjects in Austronesian languages. *Natural Language and Linguistic Theory* 10(3): 375–414.

Guliaev, Valeri I. (2003) Amazons in the Scythia: new finds at the Middle Don, Southern Russia. *World Archeology* 35(1): 112–125.

Hajdú, Péter (1969) Finnougrische Urheimatforschung. *Ural-Altaische Jahrbücher* 41: 252–264.

Hajdú, Péter and Péter Domokos (1987) *Die uralischen Sprachen und Literaturen.* Hamburg: Buske.

Häkkinen, Jaakko (2007) *Kantauralin murteutuminen vokaalivastaavuuksien valossa.* Master's thesis, University of Helsinki.

   (2012) Problems in the method and interpretations of the computational phylogenetics based on linguistic data. An example of wishful thinking: Bouckaert et al. 2012. Unpublished Ms., University of Helsinki.

Hall, Robert A., Jr. (1974) *External History of the Romance Languages.* New York: American Elsevier Publishing Company, Inc.

Hämäläinen, Pekka (2009) *The Comanche Empire.* New Haven, CT: Yale University Press.

Hancock, Ian (1995) On the migration and affiliation of the Domba: Iranian words in Rom, Lom and Dom Gypsy. In: Yaron Matras (ed.) *Romani in Contact. The History, Structure and Sociology of a Language.* Amsterdam: John Benjamins. Pp. 25–52.

Harvey, David (1969) *Explanation in Geography.* London: Edward Arnold.

Hasko, Victoria and Renee Perelmutter (eds.) (2010) *New Approaches to Slavic Verbs of Motion.* Language Companion Series. Amsterdam: John Benjamins.

Haspelmath, Martin and Uri Tadmor (2009) *Loanwords in the World's Languages: A Comparative Handbook.* Berlin: de Gruyter.

Hassanpour, Amir (1992) *Nationalism and Language in Kurdistan.* San Francisco: Mellon Press.

Hastrup, Anders (2013) *The War in Darfur: Reclaiming Sudanese History.* New York: Routledge.

Hawkins, John A. (1990) *Germanic Languages.* In Bernard Comrie (ed.) *The Major Languages of Western Europe.* London: Routledge. Pp. 58–66.

Heather, Peter (2010) *Empires and Barbarians: The Fall of Rome and the Birth of Europe.* Oxford: Oxford University Press.

Heggarty, Paul (2000) Quantifying change over time in phonetics. In: Colin Renfrew, April McMahon, and Larry Trask (eds.) *Time Depth in Historical Linguistics.* Cambridge, UK: McDonald Institute for Archeological Research. Pp. 531–562.

   (2006) Interdisciplinary indiscipline? Can phylogenetic methods meaningfully be applied to language data – and to dating language? In: Peter Forster and Colin Renfrew (eds.) *Phylogenetic Methods and the Prehistory of Languages.* Cambridge, UK: McDonald Institute Monographs. Pp. 183–194.

   (2014) Prehistory through language and archaeology. In: Claire Bowern and Bethwyn Evans (eds.) *Routledge Handbook of Historical Linguistics.* London: Routledge. Pp. 598–626.

Helbling, Jurg and Volker Schult (2004) *Mangyan Survival Strategies*. Quezon City: New Day.

Hill, Allan G. (1985) *The Fertility of Farmers and Pastoralists of the West African Sahel*. Fertility Determinants Research Notes No. 6. New York: Population Council.

Hoad, Terry (2006) Preliminaries: before English. In: Lynda Mugglestone (ed.) *The Oxford History of English*. Oxford: Oxford University Press. Pp. 7–31.

Hoffman, Joel M. (2010) *And God Said. How Translations Conceal the Bible's Original Meaning*. New York: St. Martin's Press.

Hoijer, Harry (1954) *Language in Culture: Conference on the Interrelations of Language and Other Aspects of Culture*. Chicago: University of Chicago Press.

Holden, Claire J. (2002) Bantu language trees reflect the spread of farming across Sub-Saharan Africa: a maximum-parsimony analysis. *Proceedings of the Royal Society of London, B* 269: 793–799.

Holden, Claire J. and Russell D. Gray (2006) Rapid radiation, borrowing and dialect continua in the Bantu languages. In: Peter Forster and Colin Renfrew (eds.) *Phylogenetic Methods and the Prehistory of Languages*. Cambridge, UK: McDonald Institute Monographs. Pp. 43–55.

Holm, Hans J. J. (2011) "Swadesh lists" of Albanian revisited and consequences for its position in the Indo-European languages. *The Journal of Indo-European Studies* 39(1/2): 45–99.

(2012) Remarks upon "Mapping the origins and expansion of the Indo-European language family" (Bouckeart et al. in *Science* 2012). Unpublished Ms., Hanover.

Hopper, Paul J. (1973) Glottalized and murmured occlusives in Indo-European. *Glossa* 7(2): 141–166.

Humboldt, Wilhelm von (1988) *On Language: The Diversity of Human Language-Structure and Its Influence on the Mental Development of Mankind*. (Originally published in 1836; translated by Peter Heath; with an introduction by Hans Aarsleff). Cambridge, UK: Cambridge University Press.

Hymes, Dell H. (1960) Lexicostatistics so far. *Current Anthropology* 1: 3–44.

Illič-Svityč, Vladislav M. (1964) Drevnie indoevropejsko-semitskie jazykovye kontakty [= Ancient Indo-European-Semitic language contacts]. In: Vladimir N. Toporov (ed.) *Problemy indoevropejskogo jazykoznanija* [= *Issues in Indo-European Philology*]. Moscow: Nauka. Pp. 3–12.

(1971/1984) *Opyt sravnenija nostraticheskix jazykov* [= *Attempt at Comparing Nostratic Languages*]. Volumes I–III. Moscow: Nauka.

Ingram, Catherine J. E., Charlotte A. Mulcare, Yuval Itan, Mark G. Thomas, and Dallas M. Swallow (2009) Lactose digestion and the evolutionary genetics of lactase persistence. *Human Genetics* 124(6): 579–591.

Irwin, Robert (2006) *Dangerous Knowledge: Orientalism and Its Discontents*. New York: The Overlook Press.

Jakobs, Neil G. (2005) *Yiddish. A Linguistic Introduction*. Cambridge, UK: Cambridge University Press.

Janhunen, Juha (2000) Reconstructing Pre-Proto-Uralic typology: spanning the millennia of linguistic evolution. In: Anu Nurk, Triinu Palo, and Tõnu Seilenthal (eds.) *Congressus Nonus Internationalis Fenno-Ugristarum, Pars 1: Orationes plenariae & Orationes publicae*. Tartu: CIFU. Pp. 59–76.

(2001) Indo-Uralic and Ural-Altaic: on the diachronic implications of areal typology. In: Christian Carpelan, Asko Parpola, and Petteri Koskikallio (eds.) *Early Contacts Between Uralic and Indo-European: Linguistic and Archaeological Considerations*. Mémoires de la Société Finno-Ugrienne 242. Helsinki: Suomalais-Ugrilainen Seura. Pp. 55–150.

(2007) Typological expansion in the Ural-Altaic belt. *Incontri Linguistici 30*. Pisa and Rome: Fabrizio Serra Editore. Pp. 71–83.

Janse, Mark (1998) Le grec au contact du turc. Relativisation, topicalisation, extraction et calquage en cappadocien. In: Bernard Caron (ed.) *Proceedings of the XVIth International Congress of Linguists*. Paper 393 [CD-ROM]. Oxford: Pergamon.

(1999) Greek, Turkish, and Cappadocian relatives revis(it)ed. In: Amalia Mozer (ed.) *Greek Linguistics '97. Proceedings of the 3rd International Conference on Greek Linguistics*. Athens: Ellinika Grammata. Pp. 453–462.

(2001) Morphological borrowing in Asia Minor. In: Yoryia Aggouraki, Amalia Arvaniti, J. I. M. Davy, Dionysis Goutsos, Marilena Karyolaimou, Anna Panagiotou, Andreas Papapavlou, Pavlos Pavlou, and Anna Roussou (eds.) *Proceedings of the 4th International Conference on Greek Linguistics (Nicosia, 17–19 September 1999)*. Thessaloniki: University Studio Press. Pp. 473–479.

(2009a) Watkins' Law and the development of agglutinative inflections in Asia Minor Greek. *Journal of Greek Linguistics* 7: 32–48. Leiden: Brill.

(2009b) Greek-Turkish language contacts in Asia Minor. *Études Helléniques /Hellenic Studies* 17: 37–54.

(2011) Agglutination and the psychology of double inflections in Cappadocian. In: Mark Janse, Brian D. Joseph, Pavlos Pavlou, Angela Ralli, and Spyros Armosti (eds.) *Studies in Modern Greek Dialects and Linguistic Theory*. Nicosia: Research Centre of the Holy Monastery of Kykkos. Pp. 135–145.

Johanson, Lars (2010) Turkic language contacts. In: Raymond Hickey (ed.) *The Handbook of Language Contact*. Oxford: Wiley-Blackwell. Pp. 652–672.

Johanson, Lars and Martine Robbeets (eds.) (2012) *Copies Versus Cognates in Bound Morphology*. Leiden: Brill.

Joki, Aulis Johannes (1973) *Uralier und Indogermanen*. Helsinki: Suomalais-Ugrilaisen Seura.

Jolly, Margaret, Christine Stewart, and Carolyn Brewer (eds.) (2012) *Engendering Violence in Papua New Guinea*. Canberra: ANU Press.

Jonas, Raymond (2011) *The Battle of Adwa African Victory in the Age of Empire*. Cambridge, MA: Harvard University Press.

Jones, William (1824) *Discourses Delivered before the Asiatic Society: and Miscellaneous Papers, on the Religion, Poetry, Literature, etc., of the Nations of India*. London: C. S. Arnold.

Joseph, Brian D. (2006) On continuity and change in the dialects of Lesbos and related areas – multilingualism and polydialectalism over the millennia. In: Angela Ralli, Brian D. Joseph, and Mark Janse (eds.) *Proceedings of the Second International Conference of Modern Greek Dialects and Linguistic Theory*, Mitilini: University of the Aegean Press. Pp. 130–141.

(2010) Language contact in the Balkans. In: Raymond Hickey (ed.) *The Handbook of Language Contact*. Oxford: Wiley-Blackwell. Pp. 618–633.

Kagan, Olga (2010) Aspects of motion: on the semantics and pragmatics of indeterminate aspect. In: Victoria Hasko and Renee Perelmutter (eds.) *New Approaches to Slavic Verbs of Motion*. Language Companion Series. Amsterdam: John Benjamins. Pp. 141–162.

Kallio, Petri (2001) Phonetic uralisms in Indo-European? In: Christian Carpelan, Asko Parpola, and Petteri Koskikallio (eds.) *Early Contacts Between Uralic and Indo-European: Linguistic and Archaeological Considerations*. Mémoires de la Société Finno-Ugrienne 242. Helsinki: Suomalais-Ugrilainen Seura. Pp. 221–234.

Kamber, Balz Samuel (2009) Geochemical fingerprinting: 40 years of analytical development and real world applications. *Applied Geochemistry* 24(6): 1074–1086.

Kassian, Alexei S. (2014) K formal'noj genealogicheskoj klassifikatsii lezginskikh yazykov (Severnyj Kavkaz) [= Towards a formal genealogical classification of Lezgian languages of the North Caucasus]. *Journal of Language Relationship* 11: 63–80.

Kassian, Alexei S., George Starostin, Anna Dybo, and Vasiliy Chernov (2010) The Swadesh wordlist. An attempt at semantic specification. *Journal of Language Relationship* 4: 46–89.

Katz, Hartmut (2003) *Studien zu den älteren indoiranischen Lehnwörtern in den uralischen Sprachen*. Heidelberg: Winter.

Kaufman, Dorit (1998) Children's assimilatory patterns and L1 attrition. In Annabel Greenhill, Mary Hughes, Heather Littlefield, and Hugh Walsh (eds.) *Proceedings of the 22nd Annual Boston University Conference on Language Development*. Somerville, MA: Cascadilla Press. Pp. 409–420.

Keller, Andreas, Angela Graefen, Markus Ball, Mark Matzas, Valesca Boisguerin, Frank Maixner, Petra Leidinger, Christina Backes, Rabab Khairat, Michael Forster, Björn Stade, Andre Franke, Jens Mayer, Jessica Spangler, Stephen McLaughlin, Minita Shah, Clarence Lee, Timothy T. Harkins, Alexander Sartori, Andres Moreno-Estrada, Brenna Henn, Martin Sikora, Ornella Semino, Jacques Chiaroni, Siiri Rootsi, Natalie M. Myres, Vicente M. Cabrera, Peter A. Underhill, Carlos D. Bustamante, Eduard Egarter Vigl, Marco Samadelli, Giovanna Cipollini, Jan Haas, Hugo Katus, Brian D. O'Connor, Marc R. J. Carlson, Benjamin Meder, Nikolaus Blin, Eckart Meese, Carsten M. Pusch, and Albert Zink (2012) New insights into the Tyrolean Iceman's origin and phenotype as inferred by whole-genome sequencing. *Nature Communications* 3: 698.

Kessler, Brett (2001) *The Significance of Word Lists*. Stanford, CA: Center for the Study of Language and Information.

Khazanov, Anatoly M. (1983) *Nomads and the Outside World*. Second edition. Madison, WI: University of Wisconsin Press.

Kim, Ronald (1999) Observations on the absolute and relative chronology of Tocharian loanwords and sound changes. *Tocharian and Indo-European Studies* 8: 111–138.

King, Ruth (2000) *The Lexical Basis of Grammatical Borrowing*. Amsterdam: John Benjamins.

Kinkade, M. Dale (1991) Prehistory of the native languages of the Northwest Coast. In: *The North Pacific to 1600*. Volume I. Portland: The Oregon Historical Society Press. Pp. 137–158.

Kiparsky, Paul (2012) Two-stress accent systems in Swedish. Paper presented at TIE 5, Oxford, September 6–8, 2012.

(2014) New perspectives in historical linguistics. In: Claire Bowern and Bethwyn Evans (eds.) *Handbook of Historical Linguistics*. New York: Routledge. Pp. 64–102.

Kitchen, Andrew, Christopher Ehret, Shiferaw Assefa, and Connie J. Mulligan (2009) Bayesian phylogenetic analysis of Semitic languages identifies an Early Bronze Age origin of Semitic in the Near East. *Proceedings of the Royal Society of London, B* 276: 2703–2710.

Kochanowski, Vania de Gila (1994) *Parlons tsigane: histoire, culture et langue du peuple tsigane*. Paris: L'Harmattan.

Koivulehto, Jorma (2001) The earliest contacts between Indo-European and Uralic speakers in the light of lexical loans. In: Christian Carpelan, Asko Parpola, and Petteri Koskikallio (eds.) *Early Contacts Between Uralic and Indo-European: Linguistic and Archaeological Considerations*. Mémoires de la Société Finno-Ugrienne 242. Helsinki: Suomalais-Ugrilainen Seura. Pp. 235–263.

Kopytov, Igor (1987) The internal African frontier: the making of African political culture. In: Igor Kopytov (ed.) *The African Frontier: Reproduction of Traditional African Societies*. Bloomington, IN: Indiana University Press. Pp. 3–84.

Kortlandt, Frederik H. H. (1989) Eight Indo-Uralic verbs? *Münchener Studien zur Sprachwissenschaft* 50: 79–85.

(1990) The spread of the Indo-Europeans. *Journal of Indo-European Studies* 18: 131–140.

(1995) General linguistics and Indo-European reconstruction. *Rask* 2: 91–109.

(2010) *Studies in Germanic, Indo-European and Indo-Uralic*. Amsterdam/New York: Rodopi.

Krasner, Stephen (1999) *Sovereignty: Organized Hypocrisy*. Princeton, NJ: Princeton University Press.

Kubarev, Vladimir D. (1988) *Drevnie Rospisi Karakola*. Novosibirsk: Nauka.

Kullanda, Sergey (2002) Indo-European "kinship terms" revisited. *Current Anthropology* 43(1): 89–111.

Kušnareva, Kariné K. and Tariel Čubinišvili (1970) *Drevnie kul'tury Južnogo Kavkaza* [= *The Ancient Cultures of the Southern Caucasus*]. Leningrad: Nauka.

Labov, William (2007) Transmission and diffusion. *Language* 83(2): 344–387.

Labov, William, Ingrid Rosenfelder, and Josef Fruehwald (2013) One hundred years of sound change in Philadelphia: linear incrementation, reversal, and reanalysis. *Language* 89: 30–65.

Lazaridis, Iosif, Nick Patterson, Alissa Mittnik, Gabriel Renaud, Swapan Mallick, Peter H. Sudmant, Joshua G. Schraiber, Sergi Castellano, Karola Kirsanow, Christos Economou, Ruth Bollongino, Qiaomei Fu, Kirsten Bos, Susanne Nordenfelt, Cesare de Filippo, Kay Prüfer, Susanna Sawyer, Cosimo Posth, Wolfgang Haak, Fredrik Hallgren, Elin Fornander, George Ayodo, Hamza A. Babiker, Elena Balanovska, Oleg Balanovsky, Haim Ben-Ami, Judit Bene, Fouad Berrada, Francesca Brisighelli, George B. J. Busby, Francesco Cali, Mikhail Churnosov, David E. C. Cole, Larissa Damba, Dominique Delsate, George van Driem, Stanislav Dryomov, Sardana A. Fedorova, Michael Francken, Irene Gallego Romero, Marina Gubina, Jean-Michel Guinet, Michael Hammer, Brenna Henn, Tor Helvig, Ugur Hodoglugil, Aashish R. Jha, Rick Kittles, Elza Khusnutdinova, Toomas Kivisild, Vaidutis Kučinskas, Rita Khusainova, Alena Kushniarevich,

Leila Laredj, Sergey Litvinov, Robert W. Mahley, Béla Melegh, Ene Metspalu, Joanna Mountain, Thomas Nyambo, Ludmila Osipova, Jüri Parik, Fedor Platonov, Olga L. Posukh, Valentino Romano, Igor Rudan, Ruslan Ruizbakiev, Hovhannes Sahakyan, Antonio Salas, Elena B. Starikovskaya, Ayele Tarekegn, Draga Toncheva, Shahlo Turdikulova, Ingrida Uktveryte, Olga Utevska, Mikhail Voevoda, Joachim Wahl, Pierre Zalloua, Levon Yepiskoposyan, Tatijana Zemunik, Alan Cooper, Cristian Capelli, Mark G. Thomas, Sarah A. Tishkoff, Lalji Singh, Kumarasamy Thangaraj, Richard Villems, David Comas, Rem Sukernik, Mait Metspalu, Matthias Meyer, Evan E. Eichler, Joachim Burger, Montgomery Slatkin, Svante Pääbo, Janet Kelso, David Reich, and Johannes Krause (2014) Ancient human genomes suggest three ancestral populations for present-day Europeans. *Nature* 513: 409–413.
Lee, Sean and Toshikazu Hasegawa (2011) Bayesian phylogenetic analysis supports an agricultural origin of Japonic languages. *Proceedings of the Royal Society, B* 278: 3662–3669.
Lees, Robert (1953) The basis of glottochronology. *Language* 29(2): 113–127.
Lefkowitz, Mary (1996) *Not Out of Africa: How Afrocentrism Became an Excuse to Teach Myth as History*. New York: Basic Books.
Lehmann, Winfred P. (1993) *Theoretical Bases of Indo-European Linguistics*. London/ New York: Routledge.
Levine, Marsha (1990) Dereivka and the problem of horse domestication. *Antiquity* 64: 627–640.
Lewis, Martin W. and Karen E. Wigen (1997) *The Myth of Continents: A Critique of Metageography*. Berkeley, CA: University of California Press.
Lightfoot, David W. (2002) Review of *Explaining Language Change: An Evolutionary Approach*, by William Croft (London: Longman, 2000). *Journal of Linguistics* 38: 410–414.
Lindholm, Charles (1982) *Generosity and Jealousy: The Swat Pukhtun of Northern Pakistan*. New York: Columbia University Press.
Livingstone, David N. (1992) *The Geographical Tradition*. Oxford: Blackwell.
Longobardi, Giuseppe (2001) The structure of DPs: some principles, parameters and problems. In: Mark Baltin and Chris Collins (eds.) *The Handbook of Contemporary Syntactic Theory*. Oxford: Blackwell. Pp. 562–603.
    (2003) Methods in parametric linguistics and cognitive history. *Linguistic Variation Yearbook* 3: 101–138.
    (2005) A minimalist program for parametric linguistics? In: H. Broekhuis, N. Corver, M. Huybregts, U. Kleinhenz, and J. Koster (eds.) *Organizing Grammar: Linguistic Studies for Henk van Riemsdijk*. Berlin: Mouton de Gruyter. Pp. 407–414.
Longobardi, Giuseppe and Cristina Guardiano (2009) Evidence for syntax as a signal of historical relatedness. *Lingua* 119: 1679–1706.
Longobardi, Giuseppe, Cristina Guardiano, Giuseppina Silvestri, Alessio Boattini, and Andrea Ceolin (2013) Toward a syntactic phylogeny of modern Indo-European languages. *Journal of Historical Linguistics* 3(1): 122–152.
Lopez, Violetta (1976) *The Mangyans of Mindoro*. Quezon City: University of the Philippines Press.
Lubotsky A. M. (2007) Sanskrit na-participles and the glottalic theory. In: Alan J. Nussbaum (ed.) *Verba Docenti. Studies in Historical and Indo-European*

Linguistics Presented to Jay H. Jasanoff by Students, Colleagues, and Friends. Ann Arbor/New York: Beech Stave Press. Pp. 231–235.

Macqueen, James G. (1986) *The Hittites and Their Contemporaries in Asia Minor.* Revised and enlarged edition. London: Thames & Hudson.

Maddieson, Ian (2013) Glottalized consonants. In: Matthew S. Dryer and Martin Haspelmath (eds.) *The World Atlas of Language Structures Online.* Leipzig: Max Planck Institute for Evolutionary Anthropology. (Available online at http://wals. info/chapter/7; accessed on January 6, 2014)

Mallory, James P. (1973) A short history of the Indo-European problem. *Journal of Indo-European Studies* 1: 21–65.

   (1976) Time perspective and proto-Indo-European culture. *World Archaeology* 8: 44–56.

   (1989) *In Search of the Indo-Europeans: Languages, Archaeology and Myth.* London: Thames & Hudson.

   (2013a) Twenty-first century clouds over Indo-European homelands. *Journal of Language Relationship* 9: 145–154.

   (2013b) *The Origins of the Irish.* London: Thames & Hudson.

Mallory, James P. and Douglas Q. Adams (1997) *Encyclopedia of Indo-European Culture.* Chicago: Fitzroy Dearborn Publishers.

   (2006) *The Oxford Introduction to Proto-Indo-European and the Proto-Indo-European World.* Oxford Linguistics. Oxford: Oxford University Press.

Mallory, James P. and Victor H. Mair (2000) *The Tarim Mummies: Ancient China and the Mystery of the Earliest Peoples from the West.* London: Thames & Hudson.

Marcantonio, Angela and Girish Nath Jha (eds.) (2013) *Perspectives on the Origin of Indian Civilization.* Dartmouth, MA: Center for India Studies, University of Massachusetts, Dartmouth.

Marsden, William (1783) Observations on the language of the people commonly called Gypsies: in a letter to Sir Joseph Banks. *Archaeologia* 7: 382–386.

Martinet, André (1953) Remarques sur le consonantisme sémitique. *Bulletin de la Société de Linguistique de Paris* 49: 67–78.

Masica, Colin P. (1976) *Defining a Linguistic Area: South Asia.* Chicago: University of Chicago Press.

   (1979) Aryan and non-Aryan elements in North Indian agriculture. In: Madhav M. Deshpande and Peter Edwin Hook (eds.) *Aryan and Non-Aryan in India.* Ann Arbor, MI: University of Michigan, Center for South and Southeast Asian Studies. Pp. 55–152.

   (1991) *The Indo-Aryan Languages.* Cambridge, UK: Cambridge University Press.

Matasović, Ranko (2012) Areal typology of Proto-Indo-European: the case for Caucasian connections. *Transactions of the Philological Society* 110(2): 283–310.

Matisoff, James (2000) On the uselessness of glottochronology for the subgrouping of Tibeto-Burman. In: Colin Renfrew, April McMahon, and Larry Trask (eds.) *Time Depth in Historical Linguistics.* Cambridge, UK: McDonald Institute for Archeological Research. Pp. 333–372.

Matley, Ian M. (1970) *Romania: A Profile.* New York: Prager.

Matras, Yaron (1996) Review of Boretzky and Igla (1994) *Wörterbuch Romani-Deutsch-Englisch für den südosteuropäischen Raum: mit einer Grammatik der Dialektvarianten.* Wiesbaden: Harrassowitz. *Zeitschrift für Balkanologie* 32: 214–224.

(2000) How predictable is contact-induced change in grammar? In: Colin Renfrew, April McMahon, and Larry Trask (eds.) *Time Depth in Historical Linguistics.* Cambridge, UK: McDonald Institute for Archeological Research. Pp. 563–583.

(2002) *Romani. A Linguistic Introduction.* Cambridge, UK: Cambridge University Press.

(2009) *Language Contact.* Cambridge, UK: Cambridge University Press.

(2010) *Romani in Britain. The Afterlife of a Language.* Edinburgh: Edinburgh University Press.

(2012) *A Grammar of Domari.* Berlin: Mouton de Gruyter.

Matras, Yaron and Jeanette Sakel (2007) *Grammatical Borrowing in Cross-Linguistic Perspective.* Berlin: Mouton de Gruyter.

McFadden, Clifford H., Henry M. Kendall, and George F. Deasy (1946) *Atlas of World Affairs.* New York: Thomas Y. Crowell.

McGovern, Patrick (2007) *Ancient Wine: The Search for the Origins of Viniculture.* Princeton, NJ: Princeton University Press.

McMahon, April (1994) *Understanding Language Change.* Cambridge, UK: Cambridge University Press.

(2005) Introduction. *Transactions of the Philological Society* 103(2): 113–119.

(2010) Computational models and language contact. In: Raymond Hickey (ed.) *The Handbook of Language Contact.* Oxford: Wiley-Blackwell. Pp. 128–147.

McMahon, April and Robert McMahon (2005) *Language Classification by Numbers.* Oxford: Oxford University Press.

(2006) Why linguists don't do dates: evidence from Indo-European and Australian languages. In: Peter Forster and Colin Renfrew (eds.) *Phylogenetic Methods and the Prehistory of Languages.* Cambridge, UK: McDonald Institute Monographs. Pp. 153–160.

(2008) Genetics, historical linguistics and language variation. *Language and Linguistics Compass* 2(2): 264–288.

McMahon, April, Paul Heggarty, Robert McMahon, and Natalia Slaska (2005) Swadesh sublists and the benefits of borrowing: an Andean case study. *Transactions of the Philological Society* 103(2): 147–170.

McWhorter, John (2011) *What Language Is (And What It Isn't and What It Could Be).* New York: Gotham Publishing.

(2014) *The Language Hoax: Why the World Looks the Same in Any Language.* Oxford: Oxford University Press.

Meillet, Antoine (1908) *Les Dialectes Indo-Européens.* Paris: Librairie Ancienne Honoré Champion.

(1925) *La Méthode Comparative en Linguistique Historique.* Oslo: Aschehoug.

Melchert, H. Craig (1994) *Proto-Anatolian Phonology.* Amsterdam: Rodopi.

(2003) Prehistory. In: H. Craig Melchert (ed.) *Luvians.* Leiden: Brill. Pp. 8–26.

Mendizabal, Isabel, Oscar Lao, Urko M. Marigorta, Andreas Wollstein, Leonor Gusmão, Vladimir Ferak, Mihai Ioana, Albena Jordanova, Radka Kaneva, Anastasia Kouvatsi, Vaidutis Kučinskas, Halyna Makukh, Andres Metspalu, Mihai G. Netea, Rosario de Pablo, Horolma Pamjav, Dragica Radojkovic, Sarah J. H. Rolleston, Jadranka Sertic, Milan Macek, David Comassend, and Manfred

Kayser (2012) Reconstructing the Indian origin and dispersal of the European Roma: a maternal genetic perspective. *Current Biology* 22(24): 2342–2349.

Milroy, James and Lesley Milroy (1985) Linguistic change, social network and speaker innovation. *Journal of Linguistics* 21(2): 339–84.

(1992) Social network and social class: toward an integrated sociolinguistic model. *Language in Society* 21(1): 1–26.

Minett, James W. and William S-Y. Wang (2003) On detecting borrowing: distance-based and character-based approaches. *Diachronica* 20(2): 289–330.

Montagu, Ashley (1964) *The Concept of Race*. Westport, CT: Greenwood Press.

Morar, Bharti, David Gresham, Dora Angelicheva, Ivailo Tournev, Rebecca Gooding, Velina Guergueltcheva, Carolin Schmidt, Angela Abicht, Hanns Lochmuller, Attila Tordai, Lajos Kalmar, Melinda Nagy, Veronika Karcagi, Marc Jeanpierre, Agnes Herczegfalvi, David Beeson, Viswanathan Venkataraman, Kim Warwick Carter, Jeff Reeve, Rosario de Pablo, Vaidutis Kucinskas and Luba Kalaydjieva (2004) Mutation history of the roma/gypsies. *American Journal of Human Genetics* 75(4): 596–609.

Moravcsik, Edith (1978) Universals of language contact. In: Joseph H. Greenberg (ed.) *Universals of Human Language*. Stanford, CA: Stanford University Press. Pp. 94–122.

Morris, Charles (1888) *The Aryan Race: Its Origins and Its Achievements*. Chicago: S. C. Griggs and Company.

Morrison, Alexander (2008) *Russian Rule in Samarkand 1868–1910: A Comparison with British India*. Oxford: Oxford University Press.

Mugglestone, Lynda (ed.) (2006) *The Oxford History of English*. Oxford: Oxford University Press.

Mulder, Monique Borgerhof (1992) Demography of pastoralists: preliminary data on the Datoga of Tanzania. *Human Ecology* 20(4): 383–405.

Mullen, Alex (2011) Latin and other languages: societal and individual bilingualism. In: James Clackson (ed.) *A Companion to the Latin Language*. Oxford: Wiley-Blackwell. Pp. 527–548.

Müller, Friedrich Max (1887) *Biographies of Words and the Home of the Aryas*. Reprinted in the *Collected Edition of Max Müller's Works*. 1912. Oxford: Oxford University Press.

Muysken, Pieter (2010) Scenarios for language contact. In: Raymond Hickey (ed.) *The Handbook of Language Contact*. Oxford: Wiley-Blackwell. Pp. 265–281.

Myres, Natalie M., Siiri Rootsi, Alice A. Lin, Mari Järve, Roy J. King, Ildus Kutuev, Vicente M. Cabrera, Elza K. Khusnutdinova, Andrey Pschenichnov, Bayazit Yunusbayev, Oleg Balanovsky, Elena Balanovska, Pavao Rudan, Marian Baldovic, Rene J. Herrera, Jacques Chiaroni, Julie Di Cristofaro, Richard Villems, Toomas Kivisild, and Peter A. Underhill (2011) A major Y-chromosome haplogroup R1b Holocene era founder effect in Central and Western Europe. *European Journal of Human Genetics* 19: 95–101.

Nakhleh, Luay, Tandy Warnow, Don Ringe, and Steven N. Evans (2005) A comparison of phylogenetic reconstruction methods on an Indo-European dataset. *Transactions of the Philological Society* 103(2): 171–192.

Nardelli, J.-F. (2013) Review of *Black Athena. The Afroasiatic Roots of Classical Civilization. Volume III: The Linguistic Evidence. The Classical Review (New Series)* 63: 142–144.

Nettle, Daniel (1996) Language diversity in West Africa: an ecological approach. *Journal of Anthropological Archaeology* 15: 403–438.

(1999) *Linguistic Diversity.* New York: Oxford University Press.

(2000a) Linguistic diversity, population spread and time depth. In: April McMahon, Larry Trask, and Colin Renfrew (eds.) *Time Depth in Historical Linguistics.* Volume II. Cambridge, UK: McDonald Institute for Archaeological Research. Pp. 665–677.

(2000b) Linguistic fragmentation and the wealth of nations: the fishman-pool hypothesis reexamined. *Economic Development and Cultural Change* 48(2): 335–348.

Nichols, Johanna (1992) *Language Diversity in Space and Time.* Chicago: University of Chicago Press.

(1997) The epicenter of the Indo-European linguistic spread. In: Roger Blench and Matthew Spriggs (eds.) *Archaeology and Language I: Theoretical and Methodological Orientations.* London: Routledge. Pp. 122–148.

(1999) The Eurasian spread zone and the Indo-European dispersal. In: Roger Blench and Matthew Spriggs (eds.) *Archaeology and Language II: Correlating Archaeological and Linguistic Hypotheses.* London: Routledge. Pp. 220–266.

(2013) The vertical archipelago: adding the third dimension to linguistic geography. In: Peter Auer, Martin Hilpert, Anja Stukenbrock, and Benedikt Szmrecsanyi (eds.) *Space in Language and Linguistics. Geographical, Interactional, and Cognitive Perspectives.* Berlin: Mouton de Gruyter. Pp. 38–60.

Nichols, Johanna and Tandy Warnow (2008) Tutorial on computational linguistic phylogeny. *Language and Linguistics Compass* 2(5): 760–820.

Nielsen, Hans Frede (1981) *Old English and the Continental Germanic Languages: A Survey of Morphological and Phonological Interrelations.* Innsbruck: Universität Innsbruck, Institut für Sprachwissenschaft.

Nyland, Ann (2009) *The Kikkuli Method of Horse Training: 2009 Revised Edition.* Sydney: Maryannu Press.

O'Connor, Richard (1995) Agricultural change and ethnic succession in Southeast Asian states: a case for regional anthropology. *Journal of Asian Studies* 54(4): 968–996.

Offer, John (ed.) (1994) *Spencer: Political Writings.* Cambridge, UK: Cambridge University Press.

Ogura, Mieko and William S-Y. Wang (1996) Lexical diffusion and evolution theory. In: Raymond Hickey and Stanislaw Puppel (eds.) *Trends in Linguistics: Studies and Monographs 101. Language History and Linguistic Modelling: A Frestschrift for Jacek Fisiak on his 60th Birthday.* Volume I. Berlin: Mouton de Gruyter. Pp. 1083–1098.

Ostler, Nicholas (2005) *Empires of the Word: A Language History of the World.* New York: HarperCollins.

Owen, David I. (1991) The 'first' equestrian: an Ur III glyptic scene. *Acta Sumerologica* 13: 259–273.

Pagel, Mark, Quentin D. Atkinson, Andreea S. Calude, and Andrew Meade (2013) Ultraconserved words point to deep language ancestry across Eurasia. *PNAS* 110(21): 8471–8476.

Paine, Charles (2013) *The Sea and Civilization: A Maritime History of the World.*
New York: Alfred A. Knopf.

Patterson, Nick, Priya Moorjani, Yontao Luo, Swapan Mallick, Nadin Rohland, Yiping
Zhan, Teri Genschorick, Teresa Webster, and David Reich (2012) Ancient
admixture in human history. *Genetics* 192: 1065–1093.

Pedersen, Holger (1931) *Linguistic Science in the Nineteenth Century: Methods
and Results.* Translated from the Danish by John Webster Spargo. Cambridge,
MA: Harvard University Press. (English translation of Pedersen 1924.
Reprinted in 1959 as *The Discovery of Language: Linguistic Science in the
Nineteenth Century*, Bloomington, IN: Indiana University Press; paperback
edition 1962).

Pedersen, Holger (1951) *Die gemeinindoeuropäischen und die vorindoeuropäischen
Verschlusslaute.* Historisk-filologiske Meddelelser 32/5. København:
Munksgaard.

Pereltsvaig, Asya (2004) Immigrant Russian: factors in the restructuring of the
aspectual system under attrition. *The Proceedings of BLS* 29S.

(2008) Aspect in Russian as grammatical rather than lexical notion: evidence from
Heritage Russian. *Russian Linguistics* 32(1): 27–4.

Pesetsky, David (2013) What is to be done? Plenary lecture at the 2013 Annual Meeting
of Linguistic Society of America. Boston, MA.

Pictet, Adolphe (1877) *Les Origines Indo-Européenes: Ou, Les Aryas Primitifs: Essai
de Paléontologie Linguistique.* Paris: Librarie Sandoz et Fischbacher.

Pinker, Steven (2007) *The Stuff of Thought: Language as a Window into Human
Nature.* Viking Publishers.

(2011) *The Better Angels of Our Nature: Why Violence Has Declined.* New York:
Vintage.

Pokorny, Julius (1959) *Indogermanisches etymologisches Wörterbuch.* Bern:
Francke.

Proctor, Robert N. and Londa Schiebinger (2008) *Agnotology: The Making and
Unmaking of Ignorance.* Stanford, CA: Stanford University Press.

Ramaswamy, Sumathi (1997) *Passions of the Tongue: Language Devotion in Tamil
India, 1891–1970.* Berkeley, CA: University of California Press.

Rea, John A. (1973) The Romance data of the pilot studies for glottochronology. In:
Thomas A. Sebeok (ed.) *Diachronic, Areal and Typological Linguistics.* Current
Trends in Linguistics 11. The Hague: Mouton de Gruyter. Pp. 355–367.

Rédei, Károly (1986) *Zu den indogermanisch-uralischen Sprachkontakten.* Wien:
Verlag der Österreichischen Akademie der Wissenschaften.

Renfrew, Colin (1987) *Archaeology and Language: The Puzzle of Indo-European
Origins.* London: Cape.

(1994) World linguistic diversity. *Scientific American* 270(1): 116–123.

(1998) All the king's horses: assessing cognitive maps in later prehistoric Europe.
In: Steven Mithen (ed.) *Creativity in Human Evolution and Prehistory.* London:
Routledge. Pp. 260–284.

(1999) Time depth, convergence theory, and innovation in Proto-Indo-European:
'Old Europe' as a PIE linguistic area. *Journal of Indo-European Studies* 27:
257–293.

(2000) 10,000 or 5000 years ago? – Questions of time depth. In: Colin Renfrew, April McMahon, and Larry Trask (eds.) *Time Depth in Historical Linguistics.* Cambridge, UK: McDonald Institute for Archeological Research. Pp. 413–439.

(2001) The Anatolian origins of Proto-Indo-European and the autochthony of the Hittites. In: Robert Drews (ed.) *Greater Anatolia and the Indo-Hittite Language Family.* Washington, DC: Institute for the Study of Man. Pp. 36–63.

Rexová, Kateřina, Y. Bastin, and Daniel Frynta (2006) Cladistic analysis of Bantu languages: a new tree based on combined lexical and grammatical data. *Naturwissenschaften* 93(4): 189–94.

Rexová, Kateřina, Daniel Frynta, and Jan Zrzavy (2003) Cladistic analysis of languages: Indo-European classification based on lexicostatistical data. *Cladistics* 19: 120–127.

Ringe, Don (1991) Evidence for the position of Tocharian in the Indo-European family? *Die Sprache* 34: 59–123.

(1992) On calculating the factor of chance in language comparison. *Transactions of the American Philological Society* 82(1): 1–110.

(1996) *On the Chronology of Sound Changes in Tocharian.* Volume I. New Haven, CT: American Oriental Society.

(1998) A probabilistic evaluation of Indo-Uralic. In: Joseph C. Salmons and Brian D. Joseph (eds.) *Nostratic: Sifting the Evidence.* Amsterdam: John Benjamins. Pp. 153–198.

(2000) Tocharian class II presents and subjunctives and the reconstruction of the Indo-European verb. *Tocharian and Indo-European Studies* 9: 121–142.

(2006) Proto-Indo-European wheeled vehicle terminology. Unpublished Ms., University of Pennsylvania.

Ringe, Don, Tandy Warnow, and Ann Taylor (2002) Indo-European and computational cladististics. *Transactions of the Philological Society* 100(1): 59–129.

Rix, Helmut (1998) *Rätisch und Etruskisch.* Innsbruck: Universität Innsbruck, Institut für Sprachwissenschaft.

(2008) Etruscan. In: Roger D. Woodward (ed). *The Ancient Languages of Europe.* Cambridge, UK: Cambridge University Press. Pp. 141–164.

Robb, John (1993) A social prehistory of European languages. *Antiquity* 67: 747–760.

Roberge, Paul (2010) Contact and the history of Germanic languages. In: Raymond Hickey (ed.) *The Handbook of Language Contact.* Oxford: Wiley-Blackwell. Pp. 406–431.

Robinson, Laura C. and Gary Holton (2012) Reassessing the wider genealogical affiliations of the Timor-Alor-Pantar languages. In: Harald Hammerström and Wilco van den Huevel (eds.) *History, Contact, and Classification of Papuan Languages: Language and Linguistics in Melanesia.* Special Issue, Part I. Pp. 59–87.

Robinson, Orrin W. (1992) *Old English and Its Closest Relatives: A Survey of the Earliest Germanic Languages.* Stanford, CA: Stanford University Press.

Rootsi, Siiri, Natalie M. Myres, Alice A. Lin, Mari Järve, Roy J. King, Ildus Kutuev, Vicente M. Cabrera, Elza K. Khusnutdinova, Kärt Varendi, Hovhannes Sahakyan, Doron M. Behar, Rita Khusainova, Oleg Balanovsky, Elena Balanovska, Pavao Rudan, Levon Yepiskoposyan, Ardeshir Bahmanimehr, Shirin Farjadian, Alena

Kushniarevich, Rene J. Herrera, Viola Grugni, Vincenza Battaglia, Carmela Nici, Francesca Crobu, Sena Karachanak, Baharak Hooshiar Kashani, Massoud Koushmand, Mohammad H. Sanati, Draga Toncheva, Antonella Lisa, Ornella Semino, Jacques Chiaroni, Julie Di Cristofaro, Richard Villems, Toomas Kivisild, and Peter A. Underhill (2012) Distinguishing the co-ancestries of haplogroup G Y-chromosomes in the populations of Europe and the Caucasus. *European Journal of Human Genetics* 20: 1–8.

Rüdiger, Johan Christian Christoph (1782) [reprinted in 1990]. Von der Sprache und Herkunft der Zigeuner aus Indien. In: *Neuester Zuwachs der teutschen, fremden und allgemeinen Sprachkunde in eigenen Aufsätzen.* Hamburg: Buske. Pp. 37–84.

Russell, Nerissa and Louise Martin (2005) Çatalhöyük mammal remains. In: Ian Hodder (ed.) *Inhabiting Çatalhöyük: Reports from the 1995–1999 Seasons.* Volume IV. Cambridge, UK: McDonald Institute for Archaeological Research. Pp. 33–98.

Ryan, Christopher and Cacilda Jethá (2010) *Sex at Dawn: The Prehistoric Origins of Modern Sexuality.* New York: Harper.

Said, Edward W. (1978) *Orientalism.* New York: Vintage.

Salminen, Tapani (2001) The rise of the Finno-Ugric language family. In: Christian Carpelan, Asko Parpola, and Petteri Koskikallio (eds.) *Early Contacts Between Uralic and Indo-European: Linguistic and Archaeological Considerations.* Mémoires de la Société Finno-Ugrienne 242. Helsinki: Suomalais-Ugrilainen Seura. Pp. 385–395.

Salmons, Joseph C. and Brian D. Joseph (1998) Introduction. In: Joseph C. Salmons and Brian D. Joseph (eds.) *Nostratic: Sifting the Evidence.* Amsterdam: John Benjamins. Pp. 1–12.

Sanderson, Michael J. (2002) Estimating absolute rates of molecular evolution and divergence times: a penalized likelihood approach. *Molecular Biology and Evolution* 19(1): 101–109.

Sapir, Edward (1916/1949) Time perspective in aboriginal American culture: a study in method. In: D. G. Mandelbaum (ed.) *Selected Writings of Edward Sapir.* Berkeley, CA: University of California Press. Pp. 389–462.

(1936) Internal evidence suggestive of the Northern origin of the Navajo. *American Anthropologist* 38: 224–225.

Schenker, Alexander M. (1995) *The Dawn of Slavic.* New Haven, CT: Yale University Press.

Schmid, Monika S., Barbara Köpke, Merel Keijzer, and Lina Weilemar (eds.) (2004) *First Language Attrition. Interdisciplinary Perspectives on Methodological Issues.* Amsterdam: John Benjamins.

Schönig, Claus (2003) Turko-Mongolic relations. In: Juha Janhunen (ed.) *The Mongolic Languages.* London: Routledge. Pp. 403–419.

Schrader, Otto (1890) *Prehistoric Antiquities of the Aryan People.* Translated by F. B. Jevons. London: Griffin.

Schrader, Otto and Alfons Nehring (1923/1929) *Reallexikon der indogermanischen Altertumskunde.* Volume II. Berlin: de Gruyeter.

Schrijver, Peter C. H. (2009) Celtic influence on Old English: phonological and phonetic evidence. *English Language and Linguistics* 13: 193–211.

(2011) The High German consonant shift and language contact. In: Cornelius Hasselblatt, H. Peter Houtzagers, and Remco van Pareren (eds.) *Language Contact in Times of Globalization*. Amsterdam/New York: Rodopi. Pp. 217–250.

Schuhmann, Roland (2012) Where is the substrate in the Germanic lexicon?. Paper presented at Etymology and the European Lexicon, 14th Conference of the Indo-European Society. University of Copenhagen. (Available online at academia. edu/1928440/Where_is_the_Substrate_in_the_Germanic_Lexicon)

Seliger, Herbert W. and Robert M. Vago (eds.) (1991) *First Language Attrition*. Cambridge, UK: Cambridge University Press.

Seligman, Charles G. (1930) *The Races of Africa*. Oxford: Oxford University Press.

Semple, Ellen Churchill (1911) *The Influences of Geographic Environment on the Basis of Ratzel's System of Anthropo-Geography*. New York: H. Holt and Co.

Seymour, Deni J. (2012) Gateways for Athabascan migration to the American Southwest. *Plains Anthropologist* 57(222): 149–161.

Sharoff, Serge (2002) The frequency dictionary for Russian. (Available online at www.artint.ru/projects/frqlist/frqlist-en.asp)

Shastri, Ajay Mitra (2005) Indo-European original home and language are myths. In: Daya Nath Tripathi (ed.) *A Discourse on Indo European Languages and Culture*. New Delhi: Indian Council on Historical Research. Pp. 97–109.

Sherratt, Andrew (1981) Plough and pastoralism: aspects of the secondary products revolution. In: Ian Hodder, Glynn Isaac, and Norman Hammond (eds.) *Patterns of the Past: Studies in Honour of David Clarke*. Cambridge, UK: Cambridge University Press. Pp. 261–305.

(1983) The secondary exploitation of animals in the Old World. *World Archaeology* 15: 90–104.

(1995) Alcohol and its alternatives: symbol and substance in pre-industrial societies. In: Jordan Goodman, Paul E. Lovejoy, and Andrew Sherratt (eds.) *Consuming Habits: Drugs in History and Anthropology*. London and New York: Routledge. Pp. 11–46.

(1997) *Economy and Society in Prehistoric Europe: Changing Perspectives*. Princeton, NJ: Princeton University Press.

Shryock, Andrew and Daniel Lord Smail (2012) *Deep History: The Architecture of Past and Present*. Berkeley, CA: University of California Press.

Sidky, Muhammad Humayun (1990) Malang, Sufis, and mystics: an ethnographic and historical study of Shamanism in Afghanistan. *Asian Folklore Studies* 4(2): 275–301. (Available online at www.khyber.org/publications/041-045/afghanshaman.shtml)

Siebert, Frank T., Jr. (1967) The original home of the Proto-Algonquian people. Contributions to Anthropology: Linguistics 1. *National Museum of Canada Bulletin* 214: 13–47.

Silver, Nate (2012) *The Signal and the Noise: Why So Many Predictions Fail – But Some Don't*. New York: Penguin.

Skinner, B. F. (1957) *Verbal Behavior*. Acton, MA: Copley Publishing.

Slaska, Natalia (2005) Lexicostatistics away from the armchair: handling people, props and problems. *Transactions of the Philological Society* 103(2): 221–242.

Smith, Michael E. (1984) The Aztlan migrations of the Nahuatl chronicles: myth or history? *Ethnohistory* 31(3):153–186.

Solodow, Joseph B. (2010) *Latin Alive. The Survival of Latin in English and the Romance Languages*. Cambridge, UK: Cambridge University Press.

Starostin, George (2008) Tower of Babel: an etymological database project. Moscow. (Available online at http://starling.rinet.ru)

(2010) Preliminary lexicostatistics as a basis for language classification: a new approach. *Journal of Language Relationship* 3: 79–116.

Starostin, Sergei A. (2007) Opredelenie ustojchivosti bazisnoj leksiki [= Defining the stability of basic lexicon]. In: Sergei Starostin (ed.) *Trudy po yazykoznaniyu [Proceedings in Linguistics]*. Moscow.

(2009) Indo-European – North Caucasian isoglosses. *Mother Tongue* 14: 77–135.

Steblin-Kamenskij, Ivan M. (1974) Flora iranskoj prarodiny. Ètimologičeskie zametki [= The flora of the Iranian homeland. Etymological observations]. *Ètimologija* 1972: 138–140.

Stilo, Donald (2004) Iranian as buffer zone between the universal typologies of Turkic and Semitic. In: Éva Ágnes Csató, Bo Isaksson, and Carina Jahani (eds.) *Linguistic Convergence and Areal Diffusion: Case Studies from Iranian, Semitic and Turkic*. London: Routledge Curzon. Pp. 35–63.

Sturtevant, Edgar Howard (1962) The Indo-Hittite hypothesis. *Language* 38(2): 105–110.

Sussex, Roland and Paul Cubberley (2006) *The Slavic Languages*. Cambridge, UK: Cambridge University Press.

Swadesh, Morris (1950) Salish internal relationships. *International Journal of American Linguistics* 16: 157–167.

(1952) Lexico-statistic dating of prehistoric ethnic contacts with special reference to North American Indians and Eskimos. *Proceedings of the American Philosophical Society* 96: 452–463.

(1955) Towards greater accuracy in lexicostatistic dating. *International Journal of American Linguistics* 21: 121–137.

(1971) *The Origin and Diversification of Language*. Chicago: Aldine-Atherton.

Sweetser, Eve (1990) *From Etymology to Pragmatics: Metaphorical and Cultural Aspects of Semantic Structure*. Cambridge, UK: Cambridge University Press.

Tatou-Metangmo, Leonie (2005) Situated knowledges and varying standpoints about language, "mother-tongues" and power in Africa. In: Ericka Engelstad and Siri Gerrard (eds.) *Challenging Situatedness: Gender, Culture and the Production of Knowledges*. Delft: Eburon Publishers. Pp. 125–147.

Taylor, Isaac (1898) *The Origins of the Aryans. An Account of the Prehistoric Ethnology and Civilization of Europe*. London: Kessinger Publishing.

Tharpar, Romila (2002) *Early India: From the Origins to AD 1300*. Berkeley, CA: University of California Press.

Thomason, Sarah (2000) Linguistic areas and language history. In: Dicky Gilbers, John Nerbonne, and Jos Schaeken (eds.) *Languages in Contact*. Amsterdam: Rodopi. Pp. 311–327.

Thomason, Sarah G. and Terrence Kaufman (1988) *Language Contact, Creolization and Genetic Linguistics*. Berkeley, CA: University of California Press.

Trask, Larry (2000) Some issues in relative chronology. In: Colin Renfrew, April McMahon, and Larry Trask (eds.) *Time Depth in Historical Linguistics*. Cambridge, UK: McDonald Institute for Archeological Research. Pp. 45–58.

Traugott, Elizabeth Closs and Richard B. Dasher (2001) *Regularity in Semantic Change*. Cambridge, UK: Cambridge University Press.

Trautmann, Thomas R. (1997) *Aryans and British India*. Berkeley, CA: University of California Press.

Travis, Lisa deMena (1984) Parameters and Effects of Word Order Variation. Unpublished Ph.D. Dissertation, MIT.

Tripathi, Daya Nath (ed.) (2005) *A Discourse on Indo European Languages and Culture*. New Delhi: Indian Council on Historical Research.

Trubachev, Oleg N. (ed.) (1984) *Etimologicheskij slovar' slavjanskix jazykov* [= *Etymological Dictionary of Slavic Languages*]. Moscow: Nauka.

Turner, Ralph L. (1926) The position of Romani in Indo-Aryan. *Journal of the Gypsy Lore Society, Third Series* 5: 145–189.

Underhill, Peter A., Natalie M. Myres, Siiri Rootsi, Mait Metspalu, Lev A. Zhivotovsky, Roy J. King, Alice A. Lin, Cheryl-Emiliane T. Chow, Ornella Semino, Vincenza Battaglia, Ildus Kutuev, Mari Järve, Gyaneshwer Chaubey, Qasim Ayub, Aisha Mohyuddin, S. Qasim Mehdi, Sanghamitra Sengupta, Evgeny I. Rogaev, Elza K. Khusnutdinova, Andrey Pschenichnov, Oleg Balanovsky, Elena Balanovska, Nina Jeran, Dubravka Havas Augustin, Marian Baldovic, Rene J. Herrera, Kumarasamy Thangaraj, Vijay Singh, Lalji Singh, Partha Majumder, Pavao Rudan, Dragan Primorac, Richard Villems, and Toomas Kivisild (2010) Separating the post-Glacial coancestry of European and Asian Y chromosomes within haplogroup R1a. *European Journal of Human Genetics* 18: 479–484.

Vance, James (1971) *The Merchants' World: The Geography of Wholesaling*. Englewood Cliff, NJ: Prentice Hall.

Vavilov, Nikolai Ivanovich (1959–1965) *Izbrannye trudy* [= Selected Works]. Volumes I–V. Moscow/Leningrad: Akademija Nauk SSSR.

Verma, T.P. (2005) Vedic language: the real Indo-European. In Daya Nath Tripathi (ed.) *A Discourse on Indo-European Languages and Culture*. New Delhi: Indian Council on Historical Research. Pp. 110–118.

Vine, Brent (1998) Indo-European and Nostratic: some further comments. In: Joseph C. Salmons and Brian D. Joseph (eds.) *Nostratic: Sifting the Evidence*. Amsterdam: John Benjamins. Pp. 85–106.

von Bradke, Peter (1890) *Über Methode und Ergebnisse der arischen (indogermanischen) Alterthumswissenshaft*. Giessen: J. Ricker'che Buchhandlung.

Von Dassow, Eva (2008) *State and Society in the Late Bronze Age Alalah under the Mittani Empire*. Studies on the Civilization and Culture of Nuzi and the Hurrians. Volume 17. Bethesda, MA: CDL Press.

Vovin, Alexander (2005) The end of the Altaic controversy (review of Starostin et al. 2003). *Central Asiatic Journal* 49(1): 71–132.

Wade, Nicholas (2014) *A Troublesome Inheritance: Genes, Race and Human History*. New York: Penguin.

Walker, Robert S. and Lincoln A. Ribeiro (2011) Bayesian phylogeography of the Arawak expansion in lowland South America. *Proceedings of the Royal Society London, Series B: Biological Sciences* 278(1718): 2562–2567.

Wallace, Anthony (2013) *Tuscarora: A History*. Albany, NY: State University of New York Press.

Wang, William S-Y. and James W. Minett (2005) Vertical and horizontal transmission in language evolution. *Transactions of the Philological Society* 103(2): 121–146.

Warnow, Tandy, Steven N. Evans, Donald Ringe, and Luay Nakhleh (2006) A stochastic model of language evolution that incorporates homoplasy and borrowing. In: Peter Forster and Colin Renfrew (eds.) *Phylogenetic Methods and the Prehistory of Languages*. Cambridge, UK: McDonald Institute Monographs. Pp. 75–87.

Warnow, Tandy, Donald Ringe, and Ann Taylor (1995) Reconstructing the evolutionary history of natural languages. Paper presented at the Workshop on Historical Linguistics. Philadelphia, PA: University of Pennsylvania.

Wasson, R. Gordon (1968) *Soma: Divine Mushroom of Immortality*. New York: Harcourt, Brace & World.

Watkins, Calvert (1994) *Selected Writings. Volume II: Culture and Poetics*. Innsbruck: Innsbrucker Beiträge Zur Sprachwissenschaft.

    (2008) Hittite. In: Roger D. Woodard (ed.) *The Ancient Languages of Asia Minor*. Cambridge, UK: Cambridge University Press. Pp. 6–30.

Weatherford, Jack (2011) *The Secret History of the Mongol Queens: How the Daughters of Genghis Khan Rescued His Empire*. New York: Broadway Books.

Whittaker, Gordon (2008) The case for Euphratic. *Bulletin of the Georgian National Academy of Sciences* 2(3): 156–168.

Widney, Joseph Pomeroy (1907) *The Race Life of the Aryan People*. New York: Funk & Wagnalls.

Wiik, Kalevi (2000) Some ancient and modern linguistic processes in northern Europe. In: Colin Renfrew, April McMahon, and Larry Trask (eds.) *Time Depth in Historical Linguistics*. Cambridge, UK: McDonald Institute for Archeological Research. Pp. 463–479.

Wilde, Lyn Webster (2000) *On the Trail of the Women Warriors: The Amazons in Myth and History*. New York: Thomas Dunne Books.

Wilde, Sandra, Adrian Timpson, Karola Kirsanow, Elke Kaiser, Manfred Kayser, Martina Unterlander, Nina Hollfelder, Inna Potekhina, Wolfram Schier, Mark Thomas, and Joachim Burger (2014) Direct evidence for positive selection of skin, hair, and eye pigmentation in Europeans during the last 5,000 y. *PNAS*. (Available online at http://www.pnas.org/content/early/2014/03/05/1316513111.abstract)

Wilhelm, Gernot (2008) Hurrian. In: Roger D. Woodward (ed.) *The Ancient Languages · of Asia Minor*. Cambridge, UK: Cambridge University Press. Pp. 81–104.

Winford, Donald (2010) Contact and borrowing. In: Raymond Hickey (ed.) *The Handbook of Language Contact*. Oxford: Wiley-Blackwell. Pp. 170–187.

Wink, André (2001) India and the Turco-Mongol frontier. In: Anatoly Khazanov and André Wink (eds.) *Nomads in the Sedentary World*. London: Routledge.

Winter, Werner (1971) Baktrische Lehnwörter im Tocharischen. In Robert Schmitt-Brandt (ed.) *Donum indogermanicum*. Heidelberg: Winter. Pp. 217–223.

Wittman, Henri Gontran, (1973) The lexicostatistical classification of the French based creole languages. In: Isidore Dyen (ed.) *Lexicostatistics in Genetic Linguistics: Proceedings of the Yale Conference*. Yale University, April 3–4, 1971. The Hague: Mouton. Pp. 89–99.

Witzel, Michael (1999) Substrate languages in Old Indo-Aryan (Rgvedic, Middle and Late Vedic). *Electronic Journal of Vedic Studies (EJVS)* 5(1): 1–67.

    (2005) Indocentrism: autochthonous visions of ancient India. In: Edwin F. Bryant and Laurie L. Patton (eds.) *The Indo-Aryan Controversy: Evidence and Inference in Indian History*. London: Routledge. Pp. 341–404.

Wodtko, Dagmar S., Britta Irslinger, and Carolin Schneider (2008) *Nomina im Indogermanischen Lexikon*. Heidelberg: Universitätsverlag Winter.

World Book Atlas (1966) Chicago: Field Enterprises Educational Corporation.

Wright, Roger (2011) Romance languages as a source for spoken Latin. In: James Clackson (ed.) *A Companion to the Latin Language*. Oxford: Wiley-Blackwell. Pp. 59–80.

Yakubovitch, Ilya S. (2008) Sociolinguistics of the Luvian Language. Ph.D. Dissertation, University of Chicago, Department of Near Eastern Languages and Civilizations and Department of Linguistics.

    (2010) *Sociolinguistics of the Luvian Language*. Leiden: Brill.

    (2011) Luwian and the Luwians. In: Sharon R. Steadman and Gregory McMahon (eds.) *The Oxford Handbook of Ancient Anatolia*. Oxford: Oxford University Press. Pp. 534–547.

Zaliznyak, Andrey Anatolyevich (2004). *Drevnenovgorodskij dialekt* [=Old Novgorod Dialect]. Second edition. Moscow: Jazyki slavjanskoj kul'tury.

Zuckerkandl, Emile and Linus Pauling (1962) Molecular disease, evolution, and genetic heterogeneity. In: Michael Kasha and Bernard Pullman (eds.) *Horizons in Biochemistry*. New York: Academic Press. Pp. 189–225.

Index

Abyssinia, 29
    see also Ethiopia
acquisition, language, 7, 58, 128, 224
adstratum influence, 136, 281
advection, xii, 140–141
    see also diffusion
Aegean Sea, 122, 138
Afanasievo culture, 206
    and Tocharian languages, 206
Afghanistan, 21, 38, 51, 148, 193, 263
Afrikaans, 77, 151
Afroasiatic languages, 20, 35–36, 151–152, 196
agglutinative morphology, 153–154, 281
agriculture, 40, 133, 137–138, 141, 168–170,
    207–208, 210, 212
    compared with pastoralism, 209
    intensification, 210
    and spread of languages, 41
    see also farming; swidden
Akkadian, 119, 193, 214
Alans, 129
    see also Ossetians
Albanian, 65–66, 81, 83, 85–86, 88–89, 100,
    123, 143, 174, 184–185, 187, 191, 202
Algic languages, 132
Altaic languages, 152–153, 196, 222
Amanita muscaria, 50
Amazons, 34
analytical languages, 151
    see also isolating languages
Anatolian hypothesis, 11, 14–15, 40, 43, 45–46,
    116, 118, 135, 169, 182, 192, 201, 205, 207
Anatolian languages, 66, 100, 120–121, 172,
    174, 182, 191, 193, 202–203, 205–206
    in the Hittite empire, 117–118
Anglo-Saxon. *See* English: Old English
animated, 103, 114, 116, 121, 123, 143, 156,
    180, 206–207, 250
Anthony, David, xi, 11, 43–46, 49, 132, 134,
    157, 163, 169–171, 177–180, 204, 206,
    208–209, 213–214

Apache, 131–133
Arabic language and script, 30, 62, 107, 112,
    166–167, 193, 196, 214, 225
    expansion of, 214–215
Aramaic, 214
archeology, 43, 58, 167–168, 216
    processual archeology, 41–42
area studies, 232
areal differentiation, 232
Armenian, 60, 65–66, 71, 85–86, 100, 112,
    139, 165–166, 177, 184, 187, 196, 202
    Classical Armenian, 145
    Modern Armenian, 196
Armenian Theory of Indo-European Origins,
    45, 192–195
Aryans, 20, 23, 26–27, 31–32, 36, 38, 44
    47
    The Aryans (book by V. Gordon Childe), 27
    in India and Iran, 38
    in "racial science", 23–24
Assyrians, 118
Atkinson, Quentin, 2–4, 7, 9, 11, 13–14, 32,
    45–47, 53, 55–56, 58–60, 63–64, 66,
    69–71, 75–77, 80–90, 92–93, 95–96,
    98–99, 104–106, 109, 114–118, 120–122,
    125, 127, 137–138, 140–142, 145–146,
    149, 156–157, 163, 165, 167, 169, 171,
    173–174, 176, 179–180, 182, 201–202,
    205, 207, 212, 216–217, 220–222, 230,
    237
Austro-Hungarian Empire, 143
Austronesian languages, 55–56, 66, 83, 87, 92,
    94, 120–121, 151, 155, 222
Avar Khanate, 130, 134
Avestan, 65, 170, 173–174, 193
Aztecs, 210–211

Babel, Tower of, 14, 19, 89–90, 240
Baker, Mark, xi, 19, 58, 150, 217
    223–224
Balkan Theory of Indo-European Origins, 45

318   Index

16580222R00181

Printed in Great Britain
by Amazon